ESTHER IN MEDIEVAL GARB

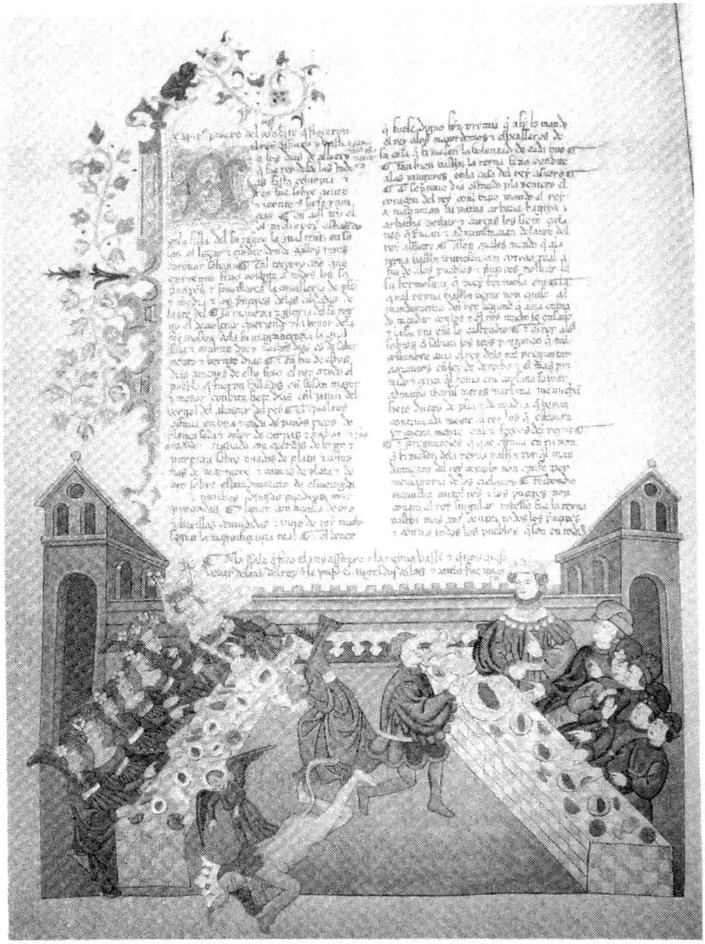

An illustration from the Duke of Alba's Castilian Bible (1422–33) depicting the banquet scene in Est 1. Note the naked Vashti in the foreground lying in disgrace with the horn and tail provided for her by the angel Gabriel (cf. B.T. Megillah 12b).

ESTHER IN MEDIEVAL GARB

Jewish Interpretation of the Book of Esther in the Middle Ages

Barry Dov Walfish

State University of New York Press

SUNY Series in Judaica: Hermeneutics, Mysticism, and Religion
Michael Fishbane, Robert Goldenberg, and Arthur Green, editors

Cover illustration is adapted from a miniature in the
British Library Miscellany, Add. 11639, fol. 260v.

Figures 1 and 3 are printed courtesy of the
British Library, London, England.

Figure 7 is reprinted from Titus Burckhardt, *Die Maurische Kultur in Spanien*, courtesy of Callwey, © 1970.

Figure 8 is reprinted from Robert Delort, *Life in the Middle Ages*, courtesy of Editions Edita.

Published by
State University of New York Press, Albany

Printed in the United States of America

For information, address State University of New York
Press, State University Plaza, Albany, N.Y., 12246

Production by Dana Foote
Marketing by Dana E. Yanulavich

Library of Congress Cataloging in Publication Data

Walfish, Barry.
Esther in medieval garb: Jewish interpretation of the book of
Esther in the Middle Ages/Barry Dov Walfish.
p. cm.—(Suny series in Judaica)
Revision of thesis (Ph. D.)—University of Toronto, 1983.
Includes bibliographical references and index.
ISBN 0-7914-1039-0 (alk. paper).—ISBN 0-7914-1040-4 (pbk.: alk. paper)
1. Bible. O.T. Esther—Criticism, interpretation, etc.—History—-Middle Ages, 600-1500. 2. Bible. O.T. Esther—Criticism, interpretation, etc., Jewish—History. I. Title. II. Series.
BS1375.2.W356 1993
222'.906'0902—dc20 91-21426
CIP

10 9 8 7 6 5 4 3 2 1

In memory of
Frank Ephraim Talmage
scholar, teacher, and friend

CONTENTS

ACKNOWLEDGMENTS

This study is based on my doctoral dissertation, presented to the University of Toronto in 1983. I am indebted to many scholars for their assistance and advice at various stages in this project. Pride of place must go to my mentor, the late lamented Frank Talmage, who saw me through the writing of the thesis. Unfortunately, I was not able to benefit from his sage counsel in preparing this revised version. It is to his memory that I dedicate this book. I would like to thank Herbert Basser, Alan Cooper, Ed Greenstein, Arthur Lesley, Binyamin Richler, Joseph Shatzmiller, Ernest Weinrib, Elliot Wolfson, and the anonymous readers from SUNY Press for their helpful comments and suggestions. I would also like to express my gratitude to Dana Foote and the editors of SUNY Press for their careful reading of the manuscript and many helpful suggestions.

My spouse Adele Reinhartz read through the entire manuscript and offered many helpful editorial suggestions. But my debt to her is much greater, for without her constant support and encouragement, the completion of this task would have been all the more difficult, if not impossible. She has been a constant source of inspiration and strength to me and my admiration for her knows no bounds. My children, Miriam-Simma, Mordecai, Shoshana, and Simcha helped keep me in touch with reality throughout the course of this seemingly interminable task. My apologies go to them for family time lost while working on this book.

The staff of the Institute of Microfilmed Hebrew Manuscripts at the Jewish National and University Library in Jerusalem and the library's circulation and reading room staff were always courteous and helpful. Daniel Frank consulted a manuscript for me at the Bodleian Library in Oxford which I would otherwise not have been able to include in my bibliography. I would also like to thank the Social Sciences and Humanities Research Council of Canada for their financial support at various stages of this project.

ABBREVIATIONS

The following abbreviations have been used in the text and notes when referring to some of the Esther commentaries used in this study.

"A"	Anonymous Northern French exegete, Commentary printed in *'Oṣar ṭov* (1878):26–32
Arama	Isaac Arama, [Commentary in] MS. JTSA (New York) L462, fols. 142v–164r.
Astruc	Solomon Astruc, *Midreshei ha-Torah*, ed. Simon Eppenstein (Berlin, 1898–99), 215–24.
EKE	Abraham Saba, *'Eshkol ha-kofer 'al Megillat 'Ester*, ed. Eliezer Segal (Drohobycz, 1903).
Gersonides	Gersonides, *Peirush Ralbag 'al Ḥamesh Megillot* (Königsberg, 1860)
GK	Joseph ibn Kaspi, *Gelilei kesef*, in *'Asarah kelei kesef*, ed. Isaac Last (Pressburg, 1902), 29–39.
Ḥadidah	Abraham Ḥadidah, [Commentary in] MS. Biblioteca Palatina (Parma) 2211, fols. 41r–49v.
Ḥalayo	Moses ben Isaac Ḥalayo, [Commentary in] MS. Österreichische Nationalbibliothek (Vienna) Heb. 178, fols. 1v–36r.
Ḥayyun	Joseph Ḥayyun, [Commentary in] MS. Russian State Library (Moscow) Guenzburg 168, fols. 60r–97v.

IbJ	Isaac ben Joseph ha-Kohen, [Commentary in] MS. JTSA (New York) L1052, fols. 51v–76v.
Immanuel	Immanuel ben Solomon, [Commentary in] MS. Biblioteca Palatina (Parma) 2844, fols. 184r–217v.
Kara	Joseph Kara, [Commentary in] Joseph Bekhor Shor, *Peirush 'al ha-Torah*, ed. J. Gad, 3 vols. (Jerusalem, 1959), 3:88–97.
Naḥmias	Joseph Naḥmias, *Commentar des R. Josef Nachmias zum Buche Esther* (Frankfurt am Main, 1891).
"Ramah"	"Ramah" [Commentary in] MS. Bibliothèque Nationale (Paris) héb. 261, fols. 1–15.
SB	Eleazar ben Judah, of Worms. *Sha'arei binah: Peirush Megillat 'Ester*, ed. Manfred R. Lehmann. New York, 1980.
Shemariah	Shemariah ben Elijah [Commentary in] MS. Cambridge University Library Mm. 6.26.2, fols. 1v–8r. *'Elef ha-magen* [on B. T. Megillah] ibid., fols. 8v–111v.
VA	Abraham Ibn Ezra, *Va-yosef 'Avraham*, ed. Joseph Zedner (London, 1850). This is Ibn Ezra's second commentary.
Zechariah	Zechariah ben Saruḳ, *Perush Megillat 'Aḥashverosh* (Venice, 1564–65).

KEY TO DEPOSITORY LIBRARIES OF MANUSCRIPTS CITED

BA (Milan)	Biblioteca Ambrosiana, Milan, Italy
BA (Rome)	Biblioteca Angelica, Rome, Italy
BA (Vatican)	Biblioteca Apostolica, Vatican City

BC (Verona)	Biblioteca Comunale, Verona, Italy
BL (London)	British Library, London, England
BL (Oxford)	Bodleian Library, Oxford, England
BM (Rouen)	Bibliothèque Municipale, Rouen, France
BML (Florence)	Biblioteca Medicea Laurenziana, Florence, Italy
BN (Paris)	Bibliothèque Nationale, Paris, France
BNU (Strasbourg)	Bibliothèque Nationale et Universitaire, Strasbourg, France
BP (Parma)	Biblioteca Palatina, Parma, Italy
BR (Leiden)	Bibliotheek Rijksuniversiteit, Leiden, Netherlands
BS (Munich)	Bayerische Staatsbibliothek, Munich, Germany
CUL (Cambridge)	Cambridge University Library, Cambridge, England
HUC-JIR (Cincinnati)	Hebrew Union College–Jewish Institute of Religion, Cincinnati, Ohio
IK (Vienna)	Israelitische Kultusgemeinde, Vienna, Austria
IŻH (Warsaw)	Institut Żydowski Historyczny, Warsaw, Poland
JC (London)	Jews' College, London, England
JNUL (Jerusalem)	Jewish National and University Library, Jerusalem
JRL (Manchester)	John Rylands Library, Manchester, England
JTS (Breslau)	Jüdisch-Theologisches Seminar, Breslau, Germany (no longer exists)
JTSA (New York)	Jewish Theological Seminary of America, New York
Kafiḥ	Private Collection of Joseph Kafiḥ, Jerusalem
Lichaa	Private Collection of Lichaa family (Karaite), Lausanne, Switzerland
MK (Jerusalem)	Mosad ha-Rav Kuk, Jerusalem
Montefiore (London)	Collection of Judith Montefiore College, Ramsgate, now housed in Jews' College, London
ÖN (Vienna)	Österreichische Nationalbibliothek, Vienna, Austria
RSL (Moscow)	Russian State Library, Moscow
SBB (Berlin)	Staatsbibliothek zu Berlin—Preussischer Kulturbesitz
SUB (Frankfurt a.M.)	Staats- und Universitätsbibliothek, Frankfurt am Main, Germany
SUB (Hamburg)	Staats- und Universitätsbibliothek, Hamburg, Germany

Sassoon	Private Collection of Solomon David Sassoon (partly sold)
TC (Cambridge)	Trinity College, Cambridge, England
UB (Erlangen)	Universitätsbibliothek, Erlangen, Germany
UB (Leipzig)	Universitätsbibliothek, Leipzig, Germany

OTHER ABBREVIATIONS

B.T.	Babylonian Talmud
J.T.	Jerusalem Talmud
R.M.	Raʿaya' mehemna'
Sarei ha-'elef	Kasher, M. M. and J. B. Mandelbaum. *Sarei ha-'elef.* 2nd ed. 2 vols. Jerusalem, 1978.
T-S	Taylor-Schechter Genizah Collection

INTRODUCTION

To medieval Jews living in the Diaspora, the Book of Esther had many attractions. Set in the Persian exile of the fifth to fourth centuries B.C.E., it tells the story of a Jewish community whose very existence was imperiled by the machinations of a wicked courtier, Haman. Thanks to the intervention and wise action of the brave and beautiful Jewish queen Esther and her clever and resourceful uncle Mordecai, the Jews of Persia were saved from total destruction. The book's vivid portrayal of court life and of the vital role of the Jewish courtier in saving the Jewish people from impending doom struck many a responsive chord in the hearts of medieval Jews. The latter too were often prey to persecutions and expulsions in the various countries of their exile and often found the good offices of a well-connected courtier to be indispensable for the welfare of their communities. In many ways, the Book of Esther was a model for Diaspora Jewry, a success story that served as a source of comfort and inspiration for them through the ages. As the centerpiece of the liturgy of the holiday of Purim, the book loomed large in the popular imagination. It is not surprising, therefore, that the Book of Esther received much scholarly attention as well. In the course of the Middle Ages, it was commented upon numerous times by scholars of almost every generation.[1] It is the purpose of this work to describe and analyze this body of exegetical literature.

Jewish biblical exegesis is relatively uncharted territory in the world of Judaica scholarship. A comprehensive history of Jewish biblical exegesis from earliest times to the present has yet to be written,[2] and studies of specific periods are also scarce. While a few treatments of individual exegetes exist,[3] studies of the exegesis of particular books are few and far between.[4] The present work traces the history of the exegesis of the Book of Esther in the Middle Ages, discussing the major exegetes of the eleventh to fifteenth centuries and their commentaries, their exegetical techniques and concerns, the Jewish and secular sources they drew upon, and the theological issues raised in their commentaries. One distinguishing feature of this study is its comprehensiveness: it deals with virtually every identified medieval Hebrew commentary on the Book of Esther as well as with several anonymous ones.[5] Many of the exegetes discussed here have never been treated at all in scholarly literature and virtually nothing is known about them. It is hoped that this study will stimulate further research in this area and thereby make a contribution toward the eventual writing of a comprehensive history of Jewish biblical exegesis. In addition, this work attempts to place the exegesis of the Book of Esther squarely in its medieval setting and to show the role played by the book in the life of medieval Jewry. In the course of this analysis, it will be demonstrated how the culture and society of the Middle Ages and the exegetes' own experiences influenced their exegesis and their portrayal and understanding of the actions of the major characters in the story. In other words, this study will demonstrate that by examining exegesis within its cultural milieu our understanding of both the text and its interpretations is sharpened and deepened. Furthermore, it will also show how biblical exegesis was often used as a medium of cultural self-expression.

The exegetes of Esther came from a variety of backgrounds, representing all of the significant schools of medieval exegesis. Table 1 lists the exegetes who will be treated in this study and provides some basic information about them and their commentaries which will help orient the reader.[6]

For various reasons, it seemed appropriate to restrict the scope of this study to Hebrew commentaries written in the Middle Ages in Western Europe.[7] Although the first Jewish exegete to produce full-length commentaries on biblical books was Saadiah Gaon, only fragments of his commentary on Esther, written in Judeo-Arabic, survive. The earliest complete Hebrew commentary to Esther we possess is that of Rashi (1040–1105). This commentary, like his other biblical commentaries, is noteworthy for its conciseness, clarity, felicitous style, and

Table 1.

EXEGETE	DATES	PLACE
Rashi	1040–1105	Northern France
Joseph Kara	b. ca. 1060	Northern France
Anonymous ("A")	12th or 13th century	Northern France
Samuel ben Meir (called Rashbam)	ca. 1080–1174	Northern France
Judah ben Samuel, he-Ḥasid	ca. 1150–1217	Germany
Eleazar ben Judah, of Worms	ca. 1165–ca. 1230	Germany
Eleazar ben Moses, the Preacher	13th century	Würzburg
Avigdor ben Elijah, ha-Kohen (Kohen Ṣedeq)	ca. 1200–1275	Germany
Tobias ben Eliezer	11th century	Byzantium
Abraham Ibn Ezra	ca. 1089–ca. 1164	Spain, Italy, and France
Jacob ben Reuben (Karaite)	12th century	Constantinople
Isaiah ben Mali, of Trani	ca. 1200–ca. 1260	Italy
Moses ben Isaac Ḥalayo (Ḥalayu?)	13th century	Italy or Byzantium [?]
Baḥya ben Asher	13th century (second half)	Saragossa
Immanuel ben Solomon, of Rome	ca. 1261–after 1328	Italy
Shemariah ben Elijah	1275–1355	Crete, Italy, and Spain
Joseph ibn Kaspi	1280–1340	Provence
Levi ben Gershom (Gersonides)	1288–1344	Provence
Joseph ben Joseph Naḥmias	14th century (first half)	Toledo
Solomon Astruc	14th century (second half)	Barcelona
Isaac ben Joseph, ha-Kohen	late 14th–early 15th century	Spain
Abraham ben Judah Ḥadidah	late 14th–early 15th century [?]	Spain
Ramah	late 14th–early 15th century	Spain
Abraham Shalom	15th century	Catalonia
Isaac Arama	1420–1494	Spain
Joseph ben Abraham Ḥayyun	15th century	Portugal
Abraham Saba	mid-15th–early 16th century	Spain and Morocco
Zechariah ben Joshua ben Saruḳ	15th century	Spain and Morocco

its skillful incorporation of midrashic material which he adapted to suit his exegetical needs.[8]

The other northern French exegetes who wrote commentaries on Esther—Samuel ben Meir, Joseph Kara, and an anonymous exegete (henceforth called "A")—all postdate Rashi. True to the methodology of the northern French school, they sought to understand the biblical text in its context (according to the method of *peshaṭ*)* without recourse to traditional midrashic interpretation that often took liberties with the text and taxed the credulity of many a medieval reader.[9]

The *peshaṭ* school of exegesis enjoyed its heyday in the mid-twelfth century. By the end of this century, the face of biblical exegesis in northern France was changing. Fewer new commentaries were being produced, and many of these were simply compilations of exegetical material by various authors whose identities were often not acknowledged.

The thirteenth century saw the return to more traditional commentary incorporating a great deal of midrashic material.[10] Most of the commentaries produced by the Tosafist schools at this time were anonymous compilations containing a mixture of philological and homiletical as well as halakhic material. Some anonymous commentaries to Esther of Ashkenazic provenance may date from this period.[11] Of special interest are the commentaries of the German Pietists (*Ḥasidei 'Ashkenaz*), written in Germany in the twelfth and thirteenth centuries, and noted for their creative and extensive use of *gemaṭria* and acrostics.

The cultural and intellectual environment of the Jews of Spain was entirely different from that of the Jews in France and Germany. Living in a milieu that was culturally and intellectually sophisticated and favorably disposed to secular studies, Spanish Jews distinguished themselves as poets, physicians, philosophers, and astronomers. This scientific awareness and cultural sophistication are reflected in the exegesis of the Spanish school which culminated in the work of Abraham Ibn Ezra whose commentaries on Esther are the only representatives of early Spanish exegesis in our corpus.

Ibn Ezra's Esther commentaries, like his other biblical commentaries, are distinguished by their concern not only for grammar and philology but also for realia. In addition, he displays great fascination with the monarchy and the workings of the royal court. His commentaries were widely read and quoted extensively by later exegetes.[12] Many of the issues he raised remained topics of discussion throughout the Middle Ages. Though, as we shall see, many of his successors disagreed with him on various points of interpretation, very few ignored him.

The thirteenth and fourteenth centuries saw commentaries pro-

---

* See below, chapter 2, for further discussion of this term.

duced in Italy, Provence, and Spain. Many of these commentaries showed the influence of the philosophy of Aristotle, especially his *Nicomachean Ethics*. In general, interest in grammar and philology waned during this period, but these matters were not ignored completely. The late fifteenth century saw the proliferation of Esther commentaries as well as their tendency toward increasing length. This phenomenon was linked to the increasing popularity of preachers and preaching during this period.[13] As the books most frequently read in the synagogue, the Pentateuch and the Scrolls were the works most commented on by homilist exegetes. This tendency continued into the sixteenth century which witnessed a veritable explosion of commentaries on the Scrolls, including Esther.[14] It is therefore convenient for the purposes of this study to set 1500 as the cutoff point for the commentaries to be included.

Many of the commentators begin their commentaries with introductions. These provide valuable insights into the exegetes' own understanding of their enterprise and the uniqueness of their approaches. Many commentators observed that the Scroll of Esther was a popular subject of exegesis and, some felt compelled to offer justification for embarking on yet another commentary. In the first paragraph of his commentary called *Gelilei kesef*, Joseph Ibn Kaspi makes a general statement of purpose and explains how his approach differs from that of his predecessors:

> Many before me have commented on this scroll and I have no intention of repeating their words. It is my custom to write books with one of two purposes in mind: either to contradict the interpretations of my predecessors or to offer new interpretations which have not been mentioned at all. Even though I do have original comments on this book, I did not see fit to write them here because this would make my commentary too long. Rather, I intend to deal with only one matter in this book and in this regard I will contradict what my predecessor said and explain my own view.[15]

R. Isaac ben Joseph, in the introduction to his Esther commentary, similarly tries to justify writing a new commentary after so many have preceded him. Such apologies become very common in the later Middle Ages as the number of commentaries increased.[16] Isaac declares that:

> There is no better method for an exegete . . . to follow, in order to come closest to the true meaning and opinion, than to gather all the understandings and opinions that he finds and that he can invent himself and to apply them to the words of the book, all the while keeping in mind that he should have greater regard for the truth than for his colleague's opinion no matter who he is. With true deliberation he should choose from all of those opinions that opinion and explanation which makes the most sense (*'asher tityasher yoter 'el ha-lev*) and which best fits in with the context of the book. This method should prove successful in the majority of cases. (IbJ, 52r–v)

He continues with a statement of purpose which justifies his undertaking:

> Inasmuch as I have seen what others have written on this book I will deal with matters which to my understanding they did not delve into deeply enough. I have decided to explain it in the aforementioned way and to offer a new understanding even of passages which seem clear and straightforward, because even in these cases the *peshaṭ* has not been sufficiently clarified, even though other exegetes have made their best efforts to explain it. And even if they were far wiser than I, they did not exhaust the subject. (Ibid., 52v)

Although Isaac's commentary does not quite live up to the expectations it raises, it is nevertheless of historical interest because of the contemporary allusions to be found in it at several points and the use it makes of recently introduced secular knowledge.[17]

In contrast, Abraham Ḥadidah gave his commentary a rather lukewarm introduction, stating that the Scroll of Esther does not require much exegesis, since it is almost self-explanatory. Nevertheless, Ḥadidah too feels that he has something to add to all that has already been written.

Most interesting in terms of structure and content is the introduction to Joseph Ḥayyun's Esther commentary, which reads almost like the introduction to a modern biblical commentary. In orderly fashion, it deals with issues such as the authorship of the book, its name, its rank among the holy books, its place among the Writings (*Ketuvim*), its uniqueness in not mentioning the name of God, the divisions of the story, the lessons (*to'alot*) to be learned from it, the time of its composition, and the method of exegesis to be followed in the commentary. Ḥayyun, in a flight of hyperbole, claims to introduce new interpretations for every verse, different from those given by other exegetes and to delve in depth into sources of difficulty, removing from them all doubt (fol. 62v).[18]

A final example is Zechariah ben Saruḳ who supplies detailed justification for writing yet another commentary on the basis of two principles: (1) that the book is divinely inspired and therefore limitless in scope; (2) that man, being composed of matter and spirit, is limited in his capacities; therefore, a human being can never totally comprehend the divine, and there is always something to be added to what has already been said about a divinely inspired book (p. 6b).

The introduction to Zechariah's commentary is quite extensive (eight pages out of a total of thirty-two) and touches on a variety of topics including the divine inspiration of the book, its miraculous nature, and the dangers of allegorizing scripture.

At the beginning of his commentary, Zechariah, who fled from Spain to Algiers at the time of the expulsion from Spain in 1492, adds a poignant personal note of explanation that gives full vent to his sorrow and frustration at the loss of his home and property and the tremendous disruption in his life that the expulsion has caused. In typical Scholastic fashion, he begins by naming three conditions that an author needs in order to be able to write: wisdom, books, and peace of mind. Because of the explusion Zechariah claims he has forgotten what he learnt, and has aged a great deal; he has lost his books (like his contemporary Abraham Saba, he was forced to bury them); and since being forced to leave his home for a new, hostile place, he has no peace of mind. Still, he feels grateful to the Jewish community of Algiers, which "is a holy community and includes wise men and men of understanding crowned with all good qualities and every perfection." By means of this commentary, he hopes to repay them for the kindness they have shown him.

Whether or not they attempt to justify themselves, most of the commentaries offer a combination of new and derived insights in a verse-by-verse exegesis of the Book of Esther. There are, however, some noteworthy exceptions to this rule. One is Joseph Ibn Kaspi's Esther commentary which deals only with selected issues. Besides the matter of the second set of letters (already mentioned above) the author deals with such questions as the position of the Jews vis-à-vis their enemies, the course of events during the eleven months preceding the fourteenth of Adar, and God's role in directing events behind the scenes.

A second exception is the commentary of Gersonides. Here, as in his other exegetical writings, Gersonides adopted a format unprecedented in Jewish exegesis. He divided the text into sections and in each section divided his commentary into three parts: (1) an explanation of difficult words, (2) an explanation of the general intent of the passage, and (3) a list of the practical lessons to be derived from the passage. These latter are divided into philosophical and moral lessons, of which fifty-one,* according to Gersonides, are to be found in the Book of Esther. Gersonides' inspiration for this emphasis on moral lessons seems to have been Maimonides who, in his *Guide of the Perplexed*,[19] lists as the two aims of the law: (1) the welfare of the soul which can be assured through the acquisition of correct opinions, and (2) the welfare of the body which is ensured by the acquisition of moral qualities useful for life in society.[20]

A third instance is the Esther commentary of Baḥya ben Asher. A distinctive feature of Baḥya's commentary to the Torah is its fourfold division. In the course of his commentary he used the methods of *peshaṭ*, *midrash*, *sekhel*, and *qabbalah*, applying each where it seemed appropriate.[21] Baḥya's commentary on Esther also draws on these methods. But rather than commenting on each verse using the various methods, he divided his commentary into three sections. In the first he commented on the entire book according to *peshaṭ*, in the second according to *midrash*, and the third according to *sekhel*.[22]

Also distinctive is Isaac Arama's commentary on Esther, which like his commentaries on the other Scrolls, is philosophical and homiletical in nature and focuses on a specific religious theme—in this case, divine providence. The commentary is divided into two sections; the first section covered 1:1–2:20, and the second, which he considered the heart of his work, discussed 2:20 to the end of the book. His method was to introduce each section with a number of questions or difficulties which he proceeded to address in the course of his commentary.[23] Arama also offers a unique interpretation of the story-line which distinguishes his commentary from all the rest.[24]

---

*In his Torah commentary, Gersonides also lists the *miṣvot* to be derived from each passage he comments on.

While it may be a commonplace to say that an exegete (or author, for that matter) is a product of his or her times, it is significant to note the degree to which an exegete's personal background and experiences are reflected in his exegesis. We will find a great variation in this regard among our exegetes. For some, such as Rashi or Isaiah of Trani, their use of the occasional vernacular word to explain a difficult Hebrew term, is the only local influence readily perceptible.* Others reveal a great deal about themselves and their cultural milieu. Abraham Ibn Ezra, demonstrates the scientific awareness and cultural sophistication that characterized the Spanish Jewish community, which lived in a milieu more favorably disposed to secular studies than other parts of Europe. Throughout the corpus of medieval commentaries, references abound to medieval courts and royalty, the role of Jewish courtiers, and Jewish-Gentile relations. Especially prominent and poignant is the impact of the Spanish expulsion on those exegetes who lived through it, such as Abraham Saba and Zecharaiah ben Saruḳ.[25] But, whether sparse or abundant, such information is a precious legacy that enables us to look at medieval exegesis from a new perspective. For medieval exegesis is valuable not only for the light it sheds on the biblical text, but also for the insight it gives us into the mind and cultural background of the exegetes. Indeed, as we shall see, in many cases it is the latter that is the most illuminating and significant.

In keeping with its two-fold purpose mentioned earlier, this book is divided into two main sections. The first part of the book deals with exegesis as an intellectual endeavor. Chapters 1 and 2 discuss the various sources, Jewish and non-Jewish, on which the exegetes drew in writing their commentaries. Chapter 3 deals with literary concerns displayed and Chapter 4 with theological issues raised in their commentaries. The final five chapters deal specifically with historical background: Chapter 5 with medieval realia, customs, and institutions that figure in the commentaries; Chapter 6 with Jewish-Gentile relations and Jewish attitudes to Gentiles; Chapter 7 with perceptions of antisemitism; Chapter 8 with the royal court; and Chapter 9 with medieval Jewish views of the monarchy. The conclusion provides a summary and overview and considers the implications of this study for future research in medieval biblical exegesis.

---

* This statement applies only to their commentaries on Esther. Much information has been gleaned from Rashi's other biblical commentaries.

In a recent survey of trends in the study of the northern French school of medieval Jewish biblical exegesis, Sara Japhet points out the hidden agenda of the scholars of the *Wissenschaft des Judentums* school in nineteenth- and early twentieth-century Europe as well as that of some modern Israeli scholars in their approach to the study of medieval biblical commentaries. She stressed the need to free the study of Jewish biblical exegesis from tendentious concerns and subordination to pressures of contemporary historical circumstances and concludes:

> It seems to me that since the "Study of the Bible" has been established as a legitimate subject in and of itself with its own special methodology, the "History of Jewish Biblical Exegesis," deserves no less. It should be approached using the appropriate historical tools and treated as a unique spiritual phenomenon which receives its literary expression in a unique area of creativity which has its own legitimacy and dynamic. Like any spiritual creation, it too can only be properly explained in accordance with its literary and spiritual presuppositions and against the full historical background out of which it grew.[26]

It is in this spirit that I have approached the study of the exegesis of the Book of Esther.

PART I

THE WORK OF THE EXEGETE

The way an exegete went about his task of interpretation depended very much on the education he received. While all were grounded in rabbinic literature, not all were masters of grammar and philology and even fewer had training in the secular sciences. In the following chapters we will examine in detail the various Jewish and non-Jewish sources that the exegetes drew on and the insights into the text that the use of these sources provided. We will also take note of their sensitivity to literary questions such as structural parallelism and plot-line and conclude with an examination of the theological issues that they addressed in their commentaries.

1

JEWISH SOURCES FOR EXEGESIS

A variety of Jewish sources were available to the medieval exegete. These included grammar and lexicography, rabbinic literature (in the case of Esther, primarily *midreshei 'aggadah), kabbalah* and the tenth-century *Book of Josippon*.

GRAMMAR AND LEXICOGRAPHY: THE TOOLS OF THE *PASHṬAN*

A major concern of exegesis is the study of the meanings of difficult words in the text and the clarification of the grammatical forms of unusual words. Such study forms the foundation upon which further clarification of the meaning and significance of the text must be based. A great deal of attention is placed on these matters in the earlier commentaries of our corpus, especially those of the northern French school and of Abraham Ibn Ezra. This interest is sustained up to the fourteenth century. The commentaries of both Joseph ibn Kaspi and Shemariah ben Elijah stress the importance of the study of grammar and logic as a propaedeutic to the thorough knowledge and understanding of the biblical text.[1] In subsequent generations, however, interest in grammar and lexicography waned.[2]

The Book of Esther, as one of the latest books of the Bible and as a book written under Persian influence, contains many difficult and unusual words that puzzled its readers and demanded clarification. Thanks to the newly developed tools of grammar and lexicography (both Hebrew and comparative Semitic) much headway was made in the Middle Ages toward a proper understanding of the meaning of the biblical text in its context. This type of exegesis is called *peshaṭ* and marked a significant break with the midrashic methods of interpretation characteristic of rabbinic literature. *Peshaṭ* exegesis first developed in Spain and North Africa in conjunction with the study of Hebrew grammar which reached an advanced level in these communities. But the concern with the contextual meaning became the hallmark of a school of exegetes in northern France in the twelfth century, and it is to this fascinating group of scholars that we now turn.

The Northern French School

Among the northern French exegetes several methods are used to elucidate the meaning of these difficult words:

1. The most common is to give a synonym for a word, either alone or in the context of a longer comment.[3]
2. A word may be compared to another word of the same root but of a more familiar form.[4]
3. A word may be elucidated by focusing on its grammatical form and comparing it with other words of the same form.[5]
4. A word's connotation may be given, usually preceded by the word *'inyan* or *lashon*.[6]
5. A difficult word may be defined briefly, or at great length.[7]
6. A word may be compared with a similar form in another biblical verse. Usually, this is done in addition to giving a meaning for the word,[8] but sometimes this is the only comment given.[9]
7. For certain words, a translation may be given in the vernacular. For Rashi and his school, this was Old French.[10]

In Table 2, the word comments of the four northern French commentaries are categorized. This table is also referred to during the

Table 2.

TYPE OF COMMENT	RASHI	KARA	"A"	RASHBAM
1. Synonyms	18	18	9	16
2. Comparison with another form of same root	3	2	2	1
3. Grammatical form	1	—	—	12
4. Connotation	—	1	5	2
5. Definitions	7	2	11	—
6. Use of biblical verses	4	4	11	9
7. Vernacular	3–5	1	—	—
8. Aramaic translation	1	—	2	1
Total	29	21	28	31

discussion of the individual exegetes. The total number of words dealt with is less than the sum of the individual comments because for some words more than one type of comment was given.

Rashi

Rashi is a very careful reader of the text and often depends on the context in which a difficult word appears to aid him in elucidating its meaning. For example, he explains the problematic word *'aḥuz* (1:6) as embroidered, apparently on the basis of its context alone.[11] He provides three different meanings for the word *davar* depending on the context of each occurrence:

1. *ki khen devar ha-melekh* (1:13). For this was the king's custom in every case to put the *matter* before all those versed in law and judgment.
2. *ki yeṣe' devar ha-malkah* (1:17). Her *act* of scorning the king.
3. *devar ha-malkhut* (1:18). A royal *decree* of revenge. [emphasis added]

Rashi's treatment of the word *shoveh*, which is the participial form of the root *ShVH* and appears three times in the Book of Esther (3:8, 5:13, 7:4), is somewhat problematic. In each case Rashi explains *shoveh* by a form of the root *ḤShSh* ("to worry or be concerned about"):

1. *ve-la-melekh 'ein shoveh le-hanniḥam* (3:8). There is no *concern*, that is, there is no gain (*'ein ḥashash, ke-lomar, 'ein beṣa'*).
2. *ve-khol zeh 'einenu shoveh li* (5:13). I am not *concerned* (*ḥash*) about all the honor that I have.
3. *ki 'ein ha-ṣar shoveh be-nezeq ha-melekh* (7:4). He is not *concerned* (*ḥoshesh*) about the damage to the king. [emphasis added]

Esther is the only book in the Bible in which the root *ShVH* appears in this form. Although the root appears elsewhere in the Bible, Rashi quotes no relevant parallels.[12] He seems to have taken 7:4 as his starting point, explaining *shoveh* according to its context and then explained the other two occurrences of the word in a similar fashion. At 3:8 he does not seem satisfied with the meaning *ḥashash* and adds a more suitable word, *besa'* ("gain"), although the connection between the two words is difficult to discern.[13]

In explaining the word *ginnat* (1:5) as a vegetable garden (*meqom zer'onei yeraqot*) Rashi may have been influenced by Mishnah Shabbat 9:7 where the term *zer'onei ginnah* appears. Aside from its three occurrences in Esther (1:5, 7:7, 7:8), where it is always associated with the word *bitan*, the word appears only in Song of Songs 6:11, *'el ginnat 'egoz*, where the meaning is quite clear and requires no elucidation.

Joseph Kara

Joseph Kara is less concerned with the meanings of individual words than are his northern French colleagues. He deals with only twenty-one words altogether and for most of these provides synonyms either in isolation or in the course of a comment on an entire verse.[14] For example, for the word *navokhah* (3:15), Kara provides an interpretation which, though perhaps not linguistically accurate, gives the reader a vivid image of the scene:

> *and the king and Haman sat down to drink.* Out of joy at having carried out their plans; and the Jews in the city were wandering aimlessly [*nevukhim*] out of distress, as in *navokhu 'edrei ha-ṣon* [*sic*] ("The herds of sheep [*sic*] are perplexed," Joel 1:18), because there is no pasture for them. They wander aimlessly for lack of pasture.[15]

"A"

The anonymous northern French exegete ("A") is more concerned with the meanings of words per se than are either Rashi or Joseph Kara.[16] He defines more words than either and uses biblical material to better advantage for exegetical purposes. Two examples illustrate this point:

> *To the wise men who know the times* (1:13). Who knew to give advice when it was necessary, as "Of Issachar, men who had understanding of the times to know what Israel ought to do" (1 Chr 12:33), to let Israel know what to do.[17]
>
> *Into the hands of those who have charge of the king's business* (3:9). Any man who is diligent and clever and who takes care of the king's affairs is called by Scripture *'oseh ha-melakhah.* Related to this is "when Solomon saw that the young man was industrious (*'oseh melakhah*) he gave him charge over all the forced labor of the house of Joseph" (1 Kgs 11:28). Because if you would say that *melakhah* here refers to actual labor what then is the meaning of "into the king's treasuries" (Est 3:9)? Rather, this is what he says: "I will weigh out [the silver] into the hands of the treasurers who look after the king's affairs so that they might deposit it into his treasuries."[18]

In both of these cases, "A" is the only exegete to point out these relevant parallels.

Rashbam

A major part of Samuel b. Meir's (Rashbam) commentary is devoted to word meanings and grammatical notes. Although his commentary, or at least what we have of it, is much shorter than the other three northern French commentaries under discussion, he deals with more individual words than any of the other three exegetes.[19] He devotes particular attention to the forms of verbs and the declensions (*mishqal*) of nouns.

He points out that *naton* (2:3), *gadol* (9:4), and *'amod* (9:16) are infinitive absolute forms (*leshon pa'ol*).[20] He discusses the noun forms of *manoteha* (2:9), *yeqar* (6:3) and *mishloaḥ* (9:19) and brings biblical parallels of words of the same declension. He suggests that *yuṣa'* (4:3) is a *pu'al* form, although it is more likely *hof'al*.[21] He considered *navokhah* (3:15) to derive from a biliteral root, *BKh*,[22] and perhaps considered *va-tithalhal* to derive from one as well, since he calls it a doubled word (*tevah kefulah*), i.e., the root is repeated twice. Another group of biliteral roots that he identifies is the group of weak verbs with *vav* or *yod* as the second letter, e.g., *yasuf* (9:8). He takes the root of this word to be *SF*. Of course, Rashbam was influenced here by Dunash ben Labrat and Menahem ben Saruk, his principal sources for grammatical matters, and had not yet been exposed to the work of Judah Ḥayyuj who established on a firm basis the triliteral structure of all Hebrew roots.[23]

The foregoing brief survey confirms D. Rosin's assertion that Rashbam was the most sophisticated grammarian among the northern French exegetes.[24] It also demonstrates how inferior to the Spanish school the best of the northern French exegetes was. A comparison with his contemporary, Abraham Ibn Ezra, will make this very clear.

Abraham Ibn Ezra

The exegetical methods and aims of Abraham Ibn Ezra were similar to those of the northern French School, although Ibn Ezra, who was able to draw upon the highly sophisticated body of grammatical and linguistic knowledge created by his predecessors in Spain and Babylonia, most of which was unavailable to his northern French brethren, displays a much higher degree of technical sophistication and refinement in his exegesis.

In both of his Esther commentaries, he cites many biblical parallels to clarify word meanings or grammatical points. He does this to a much greater extent than his northern French colleagues, even though they use similar methods and were no less familiar with the biblical text.[25] Ibn Ezra was very much aware that the vocabulary of the Bible represented only a small part of the Hebrew vocabulary in use at the time.[26] Nevertheless, he tried to use the Bible's internal resources to best advantage.

Ibn Ezra shows great concern for detail and scientific accuracy in his commentary. For example, he is not content to dismiss *ḥur*, *karpas*, and *tekhelet* (1:6) as different colors, as do Rashi and Joseph Kara, but tells us what colors they are. (*Ḥur* is white, *karpas* is the color of celery,[27] and *tekhelet* is found amidst royalty (*VA*).)[28] *Buṣ* (1:6) is not just flax,[29] but a fine flax found only in Egypt (*VA*). Ibn Ezra seems to apologize for not identifying the stones mentioned at the end of 1:6, because none of them is known to him except for *shesh* which is marble (*VA*). He struggles with the identification of *oil of myrrh* (2:12) rejecting the opinion that it is musk[30] or an oil containing musk and suggests that it might be the oil of the Jericho tree (*VA*).[31]

In explaining the word "royal stud" (*ramakhim*) (8:10), Ibn Ezra displays a knowledge of Arabic and contemporary science.

> *ha-'aḥashteranim*. These are mules. *Benei ha-ramakhim*. These are mares because every mule whose father was an ass and whose mother was a mare is better than one born of a stallion and a she-ass. And the author of the *Natural History* already mentioned this.[32] We know that *ramakhim* are mares from Arabic because the Holy Tongue is similar to it.[33]

Ibn Ezra's knowledge of Arabic and use of comparative philology on rare occasions actually led him astray. Relying on the fact that the Arabic word for city is *madina*, he interprets *medinah* in Esther as a walled city (1:1, *VA*) and follows this interpretation consistently throughout the book. To distinguish between *'ir* and *medinah*, he determines that the former is a general term for a settlement which includes *medinot* ("cities") and *kefarim* ("villages") (8:11, *VA*) but then must contradict himself at 9:2 where the text clearly states that the cities (*'arim*) are included in the *medinot*.[34]

Other Exegetes

The commentaries of Isaiah of Trani and Immanuel of Rome contain many word definitions but very few comments of a grammatical nature.[35] Gersonides in his comment to 1:6 does display familiarity with grammatical principles,[36] but shows little interest in grammar elsewhere. Joseph ibn Kaspi was very grammatically oriented and even composed a grammatical work, *Sharshot kesef*.[37] His commentary contains several remarks of a grammatical nature,[38] as does the commentary of his contemporary Shemariah b. Elijah.[39]

Use of Grammatical Treatises

The works of the great Spanish and Provençal grammarians such as Jonah Ibn Janaḥ[40] and the Kimḥi family[41] contain rich stores of important exegetical material which was utilized by several thirteenth-century Esther exegetes. One of the most popular interpretations derived from a grammatical work was the explanation of the three words of Persian origin beginning with *'aḥash-*: *'Aḥashverosh* (1:1), *'aḥashdarpanim* (3:12), and *'aḥashteranim* (8:10). Apparently, Saadiah Gaon was the first to suggest that these three words were compound words sharing the element *'aḥash-* which means "great." According to Saadiah, *'Aḥashverosh* means "great and a head," *'aḥashdarpanim* means "great one living inside" (*gadol dar panim*), i.e., someone close to the king, and *'aḥashteranim* means "great one of two species" (*gadol mi-terei minim*). This opinion was quoted in Saadiah's name by Joseph Kimḥi in his *Sefer ha-galui*,[42] and through Kimḥi it seems to have reached other medieval exegetes.[43]

David Kimḥi's interpretations of the three occurrences of the word *shoveh* were used by Isaiah of Trani, although without acknowledgement.

The fact that there are virtually no quotations of these grammatical works in commentaries written after the thirteenth century is another indication of the decline in interest in grammar after this period.

Est 7:4: A Crux Interpretum

Probably the most widely commented upon verse in the entire book of Esther is 7:4, especially the clause *'ein ha-ṣar shoveh be-nezeq ha-melekh.*[44] The main problem is the meaning of the two words *ha-ṣar* and *shoveh*. The majority interpreted *ṣar* as meaning enemy and referring to Haman. But many explained it as trouble or harm, damage or misfortune, referring to the calamity that was destined to befall the Jews. The greatest difficulty was presented by the word *shoveh*. This was usually interpreted as "equal to" (*shaveh*) or "worth," but several other connotations are provided as well. When it came to putting all this together, however, the variety of interpretations that emerged was almost as great as the number of exegetes.

One common reading of the phrase was "the enemy [i.e., Haman] was not concerned (*'ein shoveh*) about the loss or damage to the king."[45] Others interpreted *shoveh* as "equal to." For example, according to Immanuel of Rome (fol. 205r), Haman was not equal to the king with respect to the losses suffered, meaning that the losses were all the king's. David Kimḥi explains that the enemy, with all his gold and silver will not be able to compensate for the damage that will be caused to the king as a result of Israel's destruction.[46] Still others interpret *shoveh* as "to gain" or "benefit." For example, according to Isaac Arama (fol. 158r) the phrase means that the enemy who buys the Jews (as slaves) is not gaining at the expense of the king, but this is not the case if the Jews are destroyed.

Zechariah ben Saruḳ (p. 16b), looking at the phrase from a different angle, comments that Esther tells the king that if her people had been sold into slavery she would have kept silent since the enemy would have benefited from the harm caused to the king. But in this case, when the Jews are destined to be destroyed, no one benefits, and she could not keep silent in the face of such senseless destruction. Joseph Ḥayyun (fol. 83r) gives a different twist to the verse, reading it as "the enemy is not worth anything compared to the harm caused to us by the king."[47] Two exegetes offer midrashic interpretations of the phrase. Baḥya ben Asher, connects the verse with Dt 28:36, explaining that the damage caused by the enemy cannot be compared to the punishment the Jews deserve for having crowned a king to rule over them.[48] Joseph Ḥayyun (fol. 83v) offers the comment that the harm destined for the Jews by Haman's decree is far greater than that prescribed by the King (i.e., God) in the Torah (and therefore is unjustified).

The other comments on the phrase interpret *ṣar* as trouble, damage or misfortune, as in the phrase *ṣor u-maṣoq meṣa'uni* (Ps 119: 143). Ibn Ezra is the first to interpret the verse this way, explaining that Esther pleaded before the king that, had her people been sold into slavery, she would have kept silent because that trouble would have been as nothing to them if it would have meant saving the king from aggravation. More plausibly, Immanuel of Rome (fol. 205r) interprets as follows: "The misfortune of our destruction is not as difficult for me to tolerate as the damage caused to the king because of Haman's plot, since the king benefits from the presence of the Jews in his kingdom." Similarly, both Shemariah of Crete (fol. 2r) and Gersonides (p. 42v) interpret the phrase to mean that the suffering caused to the Jews by Haman's plot does not compare to the damage done to the king.

The comments gathered here on this problematic verse give some indication of the variety of interpretations possible for some verses, even when there was basic agreement as to the meanings of the difficult words in the text. They also demonstrate the relative independence of the various exegetes. Although two or three followed one of Ibn Ezra's interpretations, most developed their own interpretations that often differed radically from those of other exegetes.

The Lottery

The question of how Haman's lottery, referred to in 3:7, worked, is one of the cruxes of the Book of Esther. Only a few exegetes tried to elucidate the lottery's mechanism and their solutions are worth recording. According to some, Haman worked the lottery himself, while others were of the opinion that he sought professional help. Gersonides (p. 41a), for example, suggests that he consulted either an astrologer or someone versed in geomancy (*ḥokhmat he-ʿafar*).

The two exegetes to give the most detailed descriptions of the lottery mechanism were Jacob ben Reuben, a twelfth-century Karaite exegete, and Zechariah ben Saruḳ. According to Jacob ben Reuben, Haman brought in a magician to calculate the hours of the day. He then took slips of paper and wrote the name of a day on each one. He made thirty of these in all. He then put them all into a container, mixed them up, and said: "The day in my hand is the day on which to slaughter them." Then the sorcerer put his hand in the container and picked out a slip. The number on the slip was the day for the slaughter. Apparently, the month was chosen by a process of elimination.[49]

Zechariah ben Saruḳ's explanation is by far the most detailed and elaborate offered by any medieval exegete of Esther. According to R. Zechariah (p. 12b), Haman prepared 365 slips, one for each day of the solar year, or 354, one for each day of the lunar year. On each was written a day and a month, e.g., 1 Nisan, 2 Nisan, etc. On 354 other slips of paper were written the names of the months only, i.e., on thirty slips were written Nisan, on twenty-nine 'Iyyar, etc. He then put the 354 day slips in one box and the 354 month slips in another. He then picked a slip from each box until he got a match. Since unmatched slips were discarded, it was possible that he might go through all the slips of paper without getting a match. Therefore, when he did get a match—the thirteenth day of Adar—Haman was very pleased. Such an ingenious system would indeed work. Whether it fits the description of the lottery in the text is difficult to determine, especially since according to most modern commentaries, the text at this point is corrupt and needs to be amended according to the Septuagint.[50] Still, I have not encountered a more detailed or plausible explanation for the mechanism of the *pur*.[51]

Other Difficult Words

Several other words or phrases served as foci for spirited debate among the exegetes. For example, there was considerable controversy throughout the Middle Ages concerning the referent of the pronoun *hi'* in 1:20. The majority of exegetes explained it as referring to Ahasuerus' kingdom,[52] the immediate antecedent of the pronoun, but there were some who attributed it to Vashti,[53] or else, indecisively mentioned both alternatives.[54]

Another example is the clause *u-fenei Haman ḥafu* in 7:8. Most exegetes understood *ḥafu* as a transitive verb with the subject "servants" understood. The clause therefore meant that the king's servants covered Haman's face as a sign of the king's displeasure with him, or as a sign of his being condemned to death.[55] Others, however understood the verb as an intransitive one, referring to a transformation that occurred in Haman's face, i.e., it changed color out of shame or embarrassment.[56]

A third example is 9:25. The antecedent of the participle *u-ve-vo'ah* in the clause *u-ve-vo'ah lifnei ha-melekh* is unclear. The majority of exegetes applied the verse to Esther, explaining that when Esther came before the king, he was persuaded to send out new letters that would save the Jews. Ibn Ezra, in his second commentary, is the first to offer an alternative interpretation, explaining it as referring to Haman's decree or his deed (*VA*, 34). Joseph ibn Kaspi[57] concurs. It is only at the end of our period, however, that we find several other exegetes offering different interpretations. Isaac ben Joseph ha-Kohen (fol. 74v), Isaac Arama (fol. 162v), and Abraham Saba (*EKE*, 94) all explain the verse as referring to Haman's evil plot. Abraham Ḥadidah (fol. 49r) offers an entirely different interpretation, referring it to Mordecai's warning to the king concerning Bigthan and Teresh's plot against him.

In the three examples just quoted, it is not possible to trace any lines of development or influence in the comments of the individual exegetes. Only in the third case is there a clear chronological division. Saba's comment was probably borrowed from Isaac Arama. It is not clear whether Ibn Ezra's comment had any influence on this point.[58] Again, the relative independence of the exegetes is noteworthy.

Creative Philology

Isaak Heinemann devotes a substantial portion of his book on the methods of interpretation of the sages, *Darkhei ha-'aggadah*, to a discussion of what he calls "creative philology." This deals with the ways in which the sages handled individual words, sentences, or chapters according to their unique principles of exegesis.[59] In the medieval commentaries on Esther, there are several examples of a kind of creative philology different from that discussed by Heinemann. In these cases new connotations are given to difficult words often with very little linguistic support in order to suit an exegete's polemical or tendentious purposes. One could, using harsher language, call such comments "forced interpretations." For example, Joseph ibn Kaspi (*GK*, 35) offers a new interpretation of *le-hinnaqem*, "to avenge oneself" (8:13):

> Similarly, "to avenge themselves upon their enemies," to turn against their enemies who are besieging them, as in the phrase "for the people that fled to the wilderness turned back upon the pursuers" (Jos 8:20).[60] For someone who turns against an aggressor is called an avenger (*noqem*).

There seems to be no linguistic or midrashic basis for this interpretation, and the only plausible explanation for it is that it fits in well with the picture Kaspi is trying to give of the Jews acting purely in self-defense, only striking out after they had been attacked.[61]

Occasionally, however, exegetes would attempt to take a fresh look at a difficult verse solely out of a desire to come to a better understanding of a difficult passage. This seems to be the case in the following interpretations by Isaac ben Joseph ha-Kohen to 3:8, "*ve-la-melekh 'ein shoveh le-hanniḥam*". In contrast to all the other exegetes who comment on this verse, R. Isaac reads *shoveh* as a participle, rather than an adverb. Thus he explains:

> There is no one to place or put (*shoveh*) [the case] before the king that he should abandon them (*le-hanniḥam*) and that this people should not be protected by the crown. And *shoveh* and *mashveh* have the same meaning just like *poqed* and *mafqid*, both meaning placing or putting to rest, except that *shoveh* has a broader connotation of placing or settling down (*hannaḥah, hityashevut*).[62]

According to R. Isaac, therefore, Haman is saying that no one has ever tried to persuade the king to deprive of royal protection this wicked people, that he has just described, and surrender them to the mercy of their enemies.

R. Isaac (fol. 68r) also explains *shoveh* in 5:13 in a unique manner. *Ve-khol zeh 'einenu shoveh li* means, according to him, "all this does not calm him or bring him repose from his sadness and anguish as long as he sees Mordecai sitting at the king's gate." Again, he understands *shoveh* as a participle and not as an adjective, as it is usually taken. We see, then, that even in the late Middle Ages some exegetes still showed concern for grammatical and lexicographical matters.

MIDRASHIC LITERATURE

There exists a substantial body of midrashic literature pertaining to the Book of Esther,[63] and it is possible that even more was available in the Middle Ages.[64] Throughout the Middle Ages the exegetes of Esther drew upon the midrashic tradition as an authoritative source for their commentaries.

The Northern French School

The only exceptions to this rule might be those "pursuers of *peshaṭ*," Rashi's successors in the northern French School, but even their commentaries do not ignore rabbinic opinion entirely. At the very least, they display an awareness of the midrashic comments on the book and occasionally react to them.

For example, Joseph Kara, flying in the face of tradition, argues convincingly that the text never mentions Vashti being sentenced to death as the midrash claims.

> *That Vashti is to come no more before King Ahasuerus* (1:19). Just as she refused to come at the king's command conveyed by the eunuchs, similarly she may not come before him again and anyone who claims that she was sentenced to death misunderstands the text of Scripture (*shogeh hu' bi-feshuṭo shel Miqra'*),[65] for if they had killed her why was there any need to write this in the law books of Persia and Media as irrevocable? No reconciliation could bring her back from the dead. *But one does not argue with the words of the 'aggadah* [emphasis added].[66]

Kara's polite disclaimer, uttered at the end of his comment is a typical medieval expression of disagreement with the interpretation of the sages.[67]

Kara's second reference to a rabbinic tradition occurs in his comment at the end of chapter 2 where he describes the relation between chapters 2 and 3 as that of a remedy being provided before an illness has struck:[68] "This teaches you that he provided two remedies for the blow of Haman, the first that Esther became queen and the second that Mordecai saved the king from death."[69] Here, Kara approves of the rabbinic viewpoint, probably for theological reasons, but expands on it to include Esther's becoming queen as another remedy. This point is not mentioned in the midrash.[70]

The anonymous northern French commentary ("A") uses midrashic sources sparingly and without acknowledgement. An example is the following: "*When the virgins were gathered the second time* so that she would make known her kindred, because 'a woman is jealous only of the thigh of another woman.' "[71]

Similarly, Rashbam never refers directly to a rabbinic statement in his commentary. However, in his comment to "from India to Ethiopia" (1:1) he seems to be expressing his opinion with regard to the debate in the Talmud on this point: "India and Ethiopia are distant from each other and there are one-hundred and twenty-seven provinces between them."[72]

Rashi

Rashi, of course, is much more closely connected to the midrashic tradition. He is in constant dialogue with the sages, at times accepting their comments (with or without editorial changes), other times rejecting them out of hand, and yet other times quoting them as additional, supposedly acceptable, opinions. The following table illustrates Rashi's use of rabbinic material in his Esther commentary:

Table 3.

TYPE OF COMMENT	NUMBER OF OCCURRENCES
Original comments	94[73]
Midrash quoted as only comment	12[74]
Comments based on midrash but not acknowledged	18[75]
Midrashic source given as an alternative	7[76]
Existence of midrashic source mentioned but not quoted	5[77]
Total	136

Much recent scholarly attention has been devoted to the problem of determining Rashi's criteria for quoting rabbinic sources in his commentaries.[78] One fact that emerges quite clearly from this study is that Rashi did not choose his sources at random but rather exercised great care in their selection, often adapting and combining sources in order to suit his exegetical requirements. Rashi, it must be stressed, was first and foremost an exegete, whose primary aim was to elucidate the text in its context. Midrashic sources often used methods that were foreign to a medieval exegete,[79] and which therefore were not that helpful to an exegete wishing to come close to the original intent of the text. Still, Rashi, whose attachment to the rabbinic tradition was strong, tried to exploit this tradition to the best advantage through carefully and judiciously selecting and editing midrashic sources to meet his own needs. A few examples from his Esther commentary will illustrate Rashi's method of adapting these sources.

Verse 9:26 reads:

> For that reason these days were named Purim, after *pur*. In view then, of all the instructions in the said letter and of what they had experienced in that matter (*mah ra'u 'al kakhah*) and what had befallen them (*mah higgia' 'aleihem*), (9:27) the Jews undertook . . .

The problem in the text concerns the referents of phrases *mah ra'u* etc. and *mah higgia'* etc. Rashi, like most premodern exegetes, did not see verses 26 and 27 as being part of one sentence and therefore had to search elsewhere for antecedents for the verbs *ra'u* and *higgia'*. His comment to the verse reads as follows:

> *What they saw* [or, what caused or possessed] the doers of these deeds to do them. What did Ahasuerus see [what possessed him] to use the holy vessels and what became of them? Satan came and danced among them and killed Vashti. What did Haman see [what possessed him] to become jealous of Mordecai, and what became of him? He and his sons were hanged. What did Mordecai see [what possessed him] not to bow down and what did Esther see [what possessed her] to invite Haman?

The source upon which Rashi based his comment is found in B. T. Megillah 19a and reads as follows:

> *From where must a man read the Megillah etc.* . . . R. Huna said: They derived it [their lesson] from here: "And what did they see? For this reason. And what came upon them?" He who says that the whole of it must be read [interprets thus]: What had Ahasuerus seen to make him use the vessels of the Temple? It was for this reason, that he reckoned seventy years and they had not yet been redeemed; "And what came upon them?" that he put Vashti to death. He who says that it should be read from "there was a Jew" [interprets thus]: What had Mordecai seen that he picked a quarrel with Haman? It was for this reason, that he made himself an object of worship. "And what came upon them?" that a miracle was performed [for him]. He who says that it is to be read from "after these things" [interprets thus]: What did Haman see to make him pick a quarrel with all the Jews? It was for this reason, that Mordecai did not bow down or prostrate himself; "and what came upon him?" They hung him and his sons on the tree. He who says that it is to be read from "on that night" interprets thus: What did Ahasuerus see to make him order the book of chronicles to be brought? It was for this reason that Esther invited Haman with him. "And what came upon them?" A miracle was performed for them.

The talmudic source centers around a halakhic discussion of the question of how much of the Scroll of Esther must be read in order to fulfill one's religious obligation. The deeper implications of the discussion concern the theological significance of the book. According to the first opinion, Ahasuerus's desecration of the Temple vessels is primary and brought destruction in its wake. According to the second opinion, the threat of idolatry was the key issue, and Mordecai's refusal to bow down to Haman caused God to act on his behalf. According to the third opinion, Haman's antisemitism was the issue, and the outcome was death for him and his sons. According to the last opinion, God's providence is the main theme of the story, and this can be seen from the miracle of Ahasuerus's sleepless night. The midrash is skillfully built around the framework of Esther 9:26: "And what they had faced (*u-mah ra'u*) . . . in this matter (*'al kakhah*) . . . and what befell them (*u-mah higgia' 'aleihem*)."

But this midrash, while useful for homiletical purposes, is of limited use for the exegete, since, in its tripartite structure, it ignores the syntax of the verse. Rashi, in his comment, ignores the halakhic context of the talmudic passage and employs a bipartite structure—that of an action and its consequences—which is more in keeping with the syntax of the verse. Yet he does this only for two of the four cases mentioned in the Talmud. He mentions both the deeds of Ahasuerus and Haman and their consequences, but only the deeds of Mordecai and Esther and not their consequences. The reason for this imbalance is that Rashi had a theological motive in making this comment—the desire to demonstrate God's providence and justice in guiding the events of the story. Therefore, he wished to stress that the deeds of Ahasuerus and Haman were met with the proper consequences and that they were punished for their actions. The deeds of Mordecai and Esther, on the other hand, do not fit this pattern of misdeed and punishment, and therefore, he did not need to mention their outcome in this context.[80] He still included them because they were found in his source. Thus Rashi has taken a talmudic source and adapted it to his exegetical needs, enabling him to convey a theological message while preserving the syntactical integrity of the text.

Another example is Rashi's comment on Est 9:29. The verse reads as follows: "Then Queen Esther, daughter of Abihail, and Mordecai the Jew wrote with full authority (*toqef*) to confirm this second letter of Purim."[81] The problem in the text is the word *toqef.* This word literally means "power" or "might," but this meaning does not fit well in this context. Rashi comments: "The power of the miracle of Ahasuerus and Haman and of Mordecai and Esther." This comment is based on the passage in B. T. Megillah immediately preceding the one just discussed and deals with the same issue of determining the proper place from which to begin reading the scroll in order to fulfill one's religious obligation:

> He who says that the whole *Megillah* must be read refers this to the power of Ahasuerus; he who says it must be read from "there was a Jew" (2:5), to the power of Mordecai; he who says from "after these things" (3:1), to the power of Haman; and he who says from "on that night" (6:1), to the power of the miracle.

The passage from the Talmud quotes four separate opinions giving them equal weight. Once again, Rashi ignores the halakhic context of the original passage and telescopes the four opinions into one, stressing the miraculous nature of the events of the story. This too is in keeping with his tendency to emphasize God's intervention on behalf of the Jews and his guiding of the events of the story, which was one of his prime considerations in choosing rabbinic comments for use in his Esther commentary.

One final example is Rashi's comment to verse 4:1. The verse reads: "When Mordecai learned all that had happened, Mordecai tore his clothes and put on sackcloth and ashes." The phrase "when Mordecai learned" translates literally as "and Mordecai knew." The question arises as to how Mordecai knew, since the verb *yada'* implies immediate unmediated knowledge. This invited exegetes who were so inclined to seek a supernatural explanation for Mordecai's knowledge. Thus, Rashi comments: The dream-master (*ba'al ha-ḥalom*)[82] told him that angels (*'elyonim*) had agreed to this because they [i.e., the Israelites] had bowed down to a graven image in the days of Nebuchadnezzar and they had partaken of the banquet of Ahasuerus. In other words, according to Rashi, Mordecai had dreamed that the powers that be had decreed that Israel should be punished because of two sins that they had committed. The sources for this comment are found in rabbinic literature. Apparently, the sages felt the need to justify the magnitude of the calamity facing Israel and the Book of Esther itself does not really provide a reason. Haman's hatred of one Jew, Mordecai, because of his refusal to bow down to him, is not sufficient cause. Since God was seen as a just God who did not punish arbitrarily, a reason had to be found to justify his wrath against his people. Two causes were provided: (1) that the Jews had bowed down to an image in the time of Nebuchadnezzar and (2) that they had partaken of Ahasuerus's banquet.

Several rabbinic sources mention these two reasons for Israel's distress, but most do not connect them with our verse.[83] Two sources that do are the First Targum to Esther and *Midrash Panim 'aḥerim B*. The Targum comments:

> And Mordecai knew through Elijah, the High Priest, everything that happened in the heavens and how the people of the House of Israel were sentenced to destruction . . because they had partaken of Ahasuerus's banquet.

Midrash Panim 'aḥerim B (p. 69) to our verse reads as follows:

> What is: "he knew all that had happened?" Mordecai said, "I know that destruction was decreed against them from the day that they bowed down to the image of Nebuchadnezzar, as it is

written, 'Whoever sacrifices to a god other than the Lord alone shall be proscribed' (Ex 23:19)." Therefore it says "he knew."

The Targum attributes Mordecai's knowledge to Elijah, the High Priest, i.e., Elijah, the Prophet,[84] while according to the midrash, Mordecai already knew that the Israelites were in danger because of what they had done. Rashi takes elements from both of these comments and adds a third—the source of Mordecai's knowledge being a dream rather than Elijah.[85] He is thus able to explain the source of Mordecai's knowledge and the content of it in a way that does justice to the magnitude of the calamity facing Israel and is exegetically acceptable as well.

We see, then, how Rashi freely borrows from his rabbinic sources and weaves disparate elements together in order to produce comments that are exegetically sound according to his criteria.

German Pietists

The commentaries of the German Pietists (*Ḥasidei 'Ashkenaz*) draw heavily upon rabbinic sources, both midrashim and targumim, and many could be called with some justification mere compilations of midrashic material. A brief survey of the notes in Lehmann's edition of the commentary of Eleazar of Worms would readily confirm this statement. The commentaries of Avigdor ben Elijah and Eleazar been Moses, the Preacher, are of a similar nature. A few original comments are interspersed among a plethora of midrashic and targumic sources.

Abraham Ibn Ezra and Other Exegetes

The commentary of Abraham Ibn Ezra demonstrates a much more selective approach to the midrashic tradition. Although he treats the sages with great respect and often quotes their opinions, Ibn Ezra does not hesitate to reject rabbinic statements that he considers unreasonable or to explain midrashic statements rationally.[86] The same can be said of Isaiah of Trani who makes heavy use of rabbinic material but also does not hesitate to react to statements that do violence to the *peshaṭ*.[87]

In general, the exegetes of the late thirteenth to late fifteenth centuries borrow freely from the wealth of midrashic material available to them while avoiding the comments of a more fanciful nature. Baḥya ben Asher, it will be recalled, devotes an entire third of his commentary to midrash. Joseph Naḥmias, who incorporates a great deal of midrashic material in his commentary, does make some attempt to be selective and to distinguish between the terms *peshaṭ* and *derash*. At some points he quotes a rabbinic opinion and then offers an interpretation he feels is the contextual meaning (*peshaṭ*).[88] Concerning the rabbinic opinion that Mordecai's mother was from the tribe of Judah and his father from Benjamin, he comments that this is a *derash* which is close to the *peshaṭ*.[89] This would seem to suggest that for Naḥmias the distinction between *peshaṭ* and *derash* was a formal one only and had no bearing on the content of the material in question.

Reinterpretation of Rabbinic Sources

Aggadic statements in the Talmud were often a source of embarrassment for medieval Jewish scholars who were called upon to defend them against attacks by Karaites, Moslems, or Christians who were seeking either to ridicule the Jewish faith in its entirety or to undermine the authority of the sages.[90] Medieval scholars trained in philosophy often had difficulty in reconciling rabbinic statements with the philosophical doctrines they were convinced were true. Various tactics were used to defend the writings of the sages or to circumvent the problems raised by them. Scholars denied the authority of certain aggadic statements or of entire categories of problematic material, but for many, this approach was unacceptable. Instead, they sought to reinterpret the words of the sages in such a manner as to resolve the conflicts raised by polemicists or philosophical teachings, while at the same time maintaining the integrity of the teachings of the sages.[91]

Many aggadic statements on the Book of Esther must have troubled the medieval exegetes, but the most problematic ones were simply ignored. Still there were attempts on the part of several medievals to reinterpret certain aggadic statements rationally. The first to do this was Abraham Ibn Ezra. Ibn Ezra was engaged throughout his career in a polemic against the Karaites,[92] and it is likely that his defense of certain rabbinic statements by rational reinterpretation was part of that apologetic effort. For example, he explains the midrash that states Gabriel gave Vashti a tail to mean that he made her ugly in Ahasuerus's eyes. The sages identified Hathach with Daniel, explains Ibn Ezra, because he was as loyal to Esther as if he had been the righteous Daniel himself. Similarly, the identification of Harbona with Elijah merely means that Harbona did a good deed on Israel's behalf, similar to the deeds of Elijah.[93]

Moses ben Isaac Ḥalayo (fol. 7r), who was greatly influenced by Ibn Ezra quotes the latter's interpretation of "Gabriel came and gave her a tail" and then quotes other interpretations, one that he had heard attributed to "the doctors," according to which the tail was a type of disease which broke out on Vashti's skin and finally his own opinion that the tail was the quality of justice which was represented by Gabriel.

Zechariah ben Saruḳ (p. 8a) also provides an interpretation of this rabbinic statement. According to him, God gave Vashti the idea that the king had made a tail out of her by sending for the eunuchs to fetch her. Making her follow the eunuchs (i.e., as their tail) would have been insulting and degrading to her.

One rabbinic tradition that seems far-fetched and without textual foundation was nevertheless adopted by several medieval exegetes. This is the identification of Memucan, Ahasuerus's adviser responsible for deposing Vashti, with Haman.[94] This tradition was accepted by Moses b. Isaac Ḥalayo, Isaac ben Joseph ha-Kohen, Abraham Shalom, Zechariah ben Saruḳ, and Abraham Saba. For Isaac ben Joseph and Abraham Shalom, at least, this tradition was appealing because it provided a reason for Haman's sudden rise to power. Ahasuerus was so pleased with the way events had turned out after Vashti was removed that he rewarded Haman by raising him up above all his other officers.[95] The rabbinic tradition therefore provided a solution to a problem in the text which made it worthy of serious consideration.[96]

Shemariah ben Elijah's Commentary on the 'Aggadah

A body of medieval Jewish literature that has received little attention by scholars is the commentaries on the *'aggadot* of the Talmud and on midrashic compilations. Recently, however, the commentaries of a hitherto unknown scholar, Isaac ben Yedaiah, have been the subject of a detailed study.[97] The commentary of Shemariah ben Elijah on the first chapter of B. T. Megillah belongs to the same genre of literature as the commentaries of Isaac ben Yedaiah on *Midrash Rabbah* and the *'aggadot* of the Talmud. It would seem that R. Shemariah and R. Isaac were near contemporaries, no more than a generation or two apart,[98] and their commentaries are part of a substantial corpus of commentaries on the midrash and *'aggadot* of the Talmud which were composed in the thirteenth and early fourteenth centuries.[99] Apparently, the impetus for the composition of many of these commentaries came from attempts by Maimonides to explain certain problematic *'aggadot* rationally. The students of Maimonides set out to continue this work and carry it out systematically for the entire midrashic corpus.[100]

In his commentary, R. Shemariah is very concerned that his understanding of the text correspond with that of the sages. Time and again, he mentions the identity of his opinion with that of one sage or another. One of Shemariah's favorite ways of formulating this is "and my interpretation of this verse was not unknown to the sages."[101] For example, in explaining the reason for Ahasuerus's acquiescence to Haman's plot, R. Shemariah concludes his remarks as follows: "I know that the reasons for my interpretation were not missed by Rava, for just as they were revealed to me from Scripture, so were they revealed to him and to all the sages for it was they who stated that Haman made of himself a god."[102]

The attempt to demonstrate that one's interpretation is identical with that of the sages was quite common in the Middle Ages. In an age when tradition and authority were paramount, it was important to pay homage to the sages of yore even when introducing bold new ideas and new interpretations of sacred texts, for it was thought that, in this way, new teachings stood a better chance of being accepted[103] and that one could thereby protect oneself against charges of heresy.[104]

Abraham Saba

Of all the medieval exegetes who can be considered original (i.e., whose commentaries are not mere midrashic compilations), the one who makes the most extensive use of midrashic sources and methods is Abraham Saba. Not only does Saba quote extensively from rabbinic sources throughout his commentary, but he uses rabbinic methods of exegesis in elaborating his own comments.

One example is his use of the Psalms. The sages would often provide a historical context for psalms for which none is given in the biblical text.[105] This technique was already used in the Bible itself. The prayer in chapter 2 of Jonah, for example, seems to have been an occasional psalm which the author of the Book of Jonah appropriated for his work.[106] In his Esther commentary, Saba makes use of this method three times.[107] For example, in his opinion Ps 23 should be understood as having been spoken by Esther on the occasion of her appearance before Ahasuerus.[108] Thus, he associates the verse, "He makes me lie down in green pastures" (Ps 23:2) with the sages' description of Esther as greenish. The phrase "He leads me beside still waters (*mei menuḥot*)" is associated with the remission of taxes the king granted to the provinces in Esther's honor.[109] The lesson to be learnt from this is that, if the king were so kind and generous to others, he should certainly be so to Israel. "Even though I walk through the valley of the shadow of death" (23:4) refers to Esther's entering the presence of the king uninvited, thereby putting her life in danger. "My cup overflows" (23:5) refers to the banquet to which Esther invited Ahasuerus and Haman. The final verse of the psalm, which expresses the psalmist's wish to dwell in the house of the Lord, is interpreted by Saba as referring to Esther's hope to witness the rebuilding of the Temple.[110]

Saba, like the sages, was very sensitive to nuances and slight differences in wording in the text and often ascribes much significance to such phenomena. For example, he points out that in 5:4 and 5:7, after Ahasuerus asked Esther her desire, the text reads "and Esther said," while in 7:3, when Ahasuerus once more puts the question to her, it reads "Then Queen Esther answered." Saba explains the addition of the word "queen" in the last verse by referring to the nature of Esther's reply in each case. In chapter 5, she was merely inviting Ahasuerus and Haman to come to a banquet, while in chapter 7, she was pleading for the survival of her people. This was a cause worthy of a queen, and therefore, the author added the word "queen" at this point.[111]

Another example is his explanation of why, according to the text, the Jews of Susa made the fifteenth day of Adar a day of feasting and gladness, while the Jews of the villages declared the fourteenth day of Adar a holiday (*yom-ṭov*) as well as a day of feasting and gladness (9:19). Saba considers this proclamation of a holiday to be an error on the part of the village dwellers and attributes this to their lack of learning. However, Saba considers their ignorance in such matters to be a virtue because such people are often more zealous in their fulfillment of the commandments than are their urban brethren who through their superior learning and sophisticated rhetorical skills often find ways to circumvent their religious obligations. In this case, the village dwellers, having heard that their brethren in the cities had declared a day of feasting and rejoicing and wishing to fulfill the day properly and completely, observed it as a holiday as if it were ordained by the Torah.

In considering the context of Saba's comment at this point, one should keep in mind his background as an itinerant preacher in Spain.

Saba has a definite preference for the simple pious people, who observe their religious practices unquestioningly, over those of greater intellectual sophistication who might be led astray by too great a reliance on their own intellects. This attitude can be seen as part of the general antipathy displayed by traditionalists and kabbalists toward rationalists and intellectuals.[112] Furthermore, an audience in a small village might have been much encouraged and flattered to learn that it was precisely the Jews in the villages who were responsible for the institution of Purim as a holiday and had such a strong influence on the spread of Purim customs.

In general, Saba's attraction to the midrash is, of course, connected with his role as a homilist and the homiletic nature of his commentaries. Since he was strongly connected to the rabbinic tradition and saw himself, by virtue of his vocation as a preacher and homilist, as continuing that tradition, it was natural for him to look to the midrash both for the material to include in his homilies and for the methods and techniques that he could use to build upon and extend that tradition.

KABBALAH

The composition of the *Zohar*, or *Book of Splendor*, by Rabbi Moses de Leon or his circle[113] in the late thirteenth century gave a new impetus to the study of *kabbalah*, or Jewish mystical lore. This mystical commentary on the Pentateuch had a profound influence on succeeding generations of kabbalists[114] and helped bring *kabbalah* into the mainstream of Judaism. During the fourteenth and fifteenth centuries, the *Zohar* was studied and commented upon, and its teachings penetrated other areas of Jewish life and thought as well.[115]

Up to the end of the period covered by this study, we find only faint traces of kabbalistic influences on our Esther commentaries.[116] Even Baḥya ben Asher, who often quoted mystical texts in his Torah commentary, has no recourse to these in his Esther commentary, the third section of which is based on astrology.[117]

Isaac Arama quotes a kabbalistic source only once, at 5:1, commenting on the phrase "Esther put on royal apparel:"

> In the opinion of the adepts in truth (*ḥakhmei ha-'emet*, i.e., the kabbalists) this verse is not lacking in garments, but she [Esther] came as a pauper wrapped in the first *sefirah*, which is the point of

> entrance of the prayers, where the kingdom of heaven (*malkhut shamayim*) is located; and this is the quality of *'adonai* to which we direct our thoughts when we open our mouths in our prayers, saying "O Lord, open thou our lips" (Ps 51:17). (fol. 155r)

According to this interpretation, the phrase "Esther put on royal apparel means that Esther immersed herself in prayer and meditation and raised herself spiritually to the level of the tenth or lowest *sefirah*, which is *malkhut*. This *sefirah* connects the lower world with the upper and is thus the conduit through which prayers may reach the upper *sefirot* and ultimately influence events on both the cosmic and earthly planes.[118] This interpretation of the verse is not found in the *Zohar*,[119] but it is not incompatible with the general teaching of the *Zohar* on prayer.[120]

Recent scholarship in Jewish mysticism has begun to reveal the extent of kabbalistic activity in Spain in the fourteenth and fifteenth centuries, a period which up until recently was considered to have seen very little activity in this area.[121] It is important, however, to distinguish between scholars who were sympathetic to the *kabbalah*, studied it, and incorporated some of its teachings into their philosophic systems and those who were active kabbalists and made meditation and the study of Jewish mystical texts their principal preoccupation. Isaac Arama belonged to the first group of scholars,[122] while his contemporary Abraham Saba must be considered an authentic kabbalist.

Saba belonged to a small school of kabbalists active in the Iberian Peninsula at the time of the expulsion.[123] The fact that he wrote a commentary on the *sefirot* and a kabbalistic work on the *halakhah*, called *Ṣeror ha-kesef* leaves no doubt as to his basic kabbalistic orientation. He even earned a reputation in his later years as a miracle worker.[124] All of Saba's works show profound kabbalistic influence, and his Esther commentary is no exception. This is not to say that his entire commentary is kabbalistic. Rather, only certain sections of it are, while others are entirely free of such material.

An examination of the sections of Saba's commentary which he interprets kabbalistically shows that he is not the first to apply mystical teaching to the verses in question. The Talmud already interprets certain verses in which the word *melekh* ("king") appears alone without Ahasuerus as referring to God, king of the universe.[125] This tendency is elaborated upon in the *Zohar*,[126] one of Saba's main sources. Portions of the Book of Esther that lend themselves most readily to kabbalistic interpretation are chapters 2 and 5. It is these on which the *Zohar* focuses[127] and Saba follows suit. His treatment of the figure of Esther, while perhaps not entirely kabbalistically inspired, is certainly couched in very mystical and allusive language.

In his comments to 2:5, Saba describes Mordecai's bravery and royal lineage at great length. Yet, in commenting on "he had brought up Hadassah" (2:7), he says:

> This is written to teach us that although he was a brave man, and a son of kings and was raised among kings, despite all this, he had no power or dominion over Haman except by virtue of his having raised Hadassah, that is, Esther the righteous, who was hidden in her deeds and her modesty and did not see the face of any man. (*EKE*, 37)

Esther received the trait of modesty from Rachel and from Saul her ancestors. By virtue of having raised the modest and hidden Esther, Mordecai was able to vanquish Haman.

Esther here is the *shekhinah*,[128] the tenth or lowest *sefirah* and Haman would seem to represent the *siṭra' 'aḥra'*, or demonic forces of the universe. Mordecai derives his power over Haman by virtue of his having raised Esther to a higher level in the sefirotic realm.[129]

It is interesting to note that for Saba, Esther is more a spiritual reality than a physical one. From his comment, it would seem that Saba considers Mordecai to be the active character in the process of saving the Jews. True, he could not have done so without Esther's help, but it is by her very nature, by virtue of her modesty and her hiddenness, not by any active role she herself plays in the drama, that Esther helps save the Jews. The power that having Esther under his care brings him enables Mordecai to prevail over his enemy.

Another important feature of Esther's nature was the fact that she was an orphan. According to the midrash, the Jews at that time were orphans because of their sins. Therefore, it fulfilled a certain mystical requirement for symmetry that Esther who had no father or mother should save Israel who were without father and mother, from the hands of Amalek who also had no known mother or father (all of Esau's children were of dubious parentage).[130] Again, it is a feature of Esther's nature and not any active role she takes that is stressed as being important in effecting the salvation of the Jews.

The sages too were mystified by the figure of Esther and spoke of her in cryptic statements, such as: "Esther was greenish and a thread of grace was suspended over her,"[131] or "Esther was like the ground (*qarqaʿ ʿolam*)."[132] The former statement refers to her second name, Hadassah, which means "myrtle." The latter refers to her passivity while lying with Ahasuerus. Furthermore, her very name, Esther, although not of Hebrew origin, is very close to the Hebrew word *seter* which means "secret" or "hidden." All of these elements of Esther's mysterious nature are incorporated by Saba in the following homily about Esther:

> All this [Mordecai's being in Susa and Esther's being taken by Ahasuerus's men] was brought about by divine causation in order to save Israel. Therefore, we should not wonder how [this could have happened]. He [i.e., God] alone knows and bears witness [cf. Jer 29:23] and overturns the normal state of affairs in order to carry out his promises. And God arranged matters so that the rape of a Jewish woman was permitted. Nevertheless, Esther, out of righteousness said "'If I am to perish, I shall perish' (4:16) since I am going willingly to Ahasuerus." For it seems that at first she went against her will and later she went willingly. Nevertheless, it seems that she was entirely forced, since, having seen the affliction of her people she surrendered herself to die. In regard to this the sages said "Esther was like the ground."[133] *There is in this matter a great secret for those who know*, for like an eagle who rouses his nestlings, she flutters over her young to have mercy on them in their time of trouble. She is like *Keneset Yisra'el*[134] who has mercy on her children and is in exile with them, as it is written "and for your transgressions your mother was put away" (Is 50:1); and it is written "I will not reject them or spurn them so as to destroy them" (Lv 26:44). The word "to destroy them" [*lklwtm*] is written defective, i.e., *lkltm* meaning, for the sake of their bride (*klh*) who is *Keneset Yisra'el* who hides and is revealed to her sons, as it says, "You are indeed a God who concealed Himself (*'El mistater*) (Is 45:15). Nevertheless, you are "the God of Israel, who brings victory" (ibid.), who reveals himself to his people. This all happened at the time of Esther, when God hid (*histir*) his face from Israel. Therefore, the sages said that Esther was greenish, since she was called Hadassah (myrtle) and the myrtle is green. At the time of Haman she was greenish because her face was turning

> green, as it were, because of Israel's sins. But the Holy One blessed be He stretched out and drew a thread of grace over her. Were it not for God's grace which extends for all eternity and who is the place (*maqom*) of *Keneset Yisra'el* who is called the universe (*'olam*), then when Esther entered before the king on the third day of her fast her face would have been green because of Israel's sins and because of fasting. But God, may He be blessed, stretched a thread of grace over her, i.e., a red thread so that her face would blush out of embarrassment and fear. . . . This is the significance of "she was greenish" and of "she was like the ground" for she is called the lower world (*'olam taḥton*), and she is the mystery of the land of the living, in such a way that "the earth remains forever" (Eccl 1:4). Therefore, since she is like the ground of the universe, she does not become unclean in her place and anyone who removes anything from her is liable, according to the opinion of the House of Shammai, who said: "A beehive is like the ground" (*qarqa' 'olam*), and Esther is a beehive to sting Haman and his seed. . . . And according to the context of Scripture (*pishṭan shel devarim*), she was taken completely by force . . . and she went before Ahasuerus to deliver herself for the sake of her flock . . . and saving a life overrides every other consideration. This is what is meant by "Esther was like the ground," since Israel was called earth and ground and possession, as it is written "for you shall be the most desired of lands" (Mal 3:12). Therefore, the sages said: "Generations come and go" (Eccl 1:4)—this refers to the Gentiles; "but the earth remains forever" (ibid.)—this is Israel." Therefore, this is what they were referring to when they said that Esther was like the ground. Since she was the ground of the universe, the universe (i.e., Israel, *'olam*), would stay forever, protected by Esther.[135] [emphasis added]

In this passage as well, Esther's mystical nature is stressed above all else. Esther as the *shekhinah* is an instrument of divine providence or even an integral element in the divine order of things.[136] She is identified with the people of Israel, takes upon herself the sins of Israel and atones for them, fights Israel's enemies and protects her from harm. Her every act has great significance for the future of Israel and of the universe. Perhaps, like some of his predecessors, Saba was overly embarrassed by the thought of Esther being taken to live with a Gentile king. By shrouding her in a veil of mystery and speaking of her in impersonal mystical terms, he could avoid confronting this issue. But it is more likely that Saba, as a mystic, simply understood the world in these terms. The figure of Esther lent itself quite readily to mystical interpretation, as the rabbinic statements concerning her mentioned above already indicate. Saba, however, is the first exegete to incorporate her into a more fully developed kabbalistic scheme and portray her as an instrument for the protection of the divine order.

Even more daring than his exposition of Esther's role in Israel's redemption is Saba's introduction of allegory into his discussion of the scroll and of the roles of Mordecai and Esther in it. Not only does the scroll deal with our physical redemption at the hands of the Messiah, says Saba, but also with the redemption of our souls. For just as the Torah has a revealed and a hidden meaning so does this scroll. The revealed meaning is our physical redemption, but the hidden meaning is the redemption of the soul which is the true redemption that occurs after death. This redemption is symbolized by Mordecai and Esther. Mordecai alludes to the pure body free of all contamination[137] and Esther is the soul hidden (*nisteret*) in the body, which is called *yeḥidah.*[138] In mystical terms, this chapter is referring to the purification of the soul which takes place after death. This process takes twelve months, which is alluded to in the twelve months that each maiden had to spend in preparation before being allowed to enter into the presence of the king (i.e., God) (2:12, 13). The word *tamruqeihen* ("ointments") comes from the root *MRQ* which in rabbinic Hebrew often refers to the cleansing from sins.[139] Thus the twelve-month period was the time needed for the soul to be cleansed of its sins before being allowed to enter before God (2:13). The word *zeh,* in verse 13 has the numerical value of twelve, which alludes to these twelve months, i.e., after *zeh,* or twelve months, the maiden (i.e., the soul) comes before the king. Mordecai's walking in front of the court of the harem really alludes to his praying to God to perfect his soul, alluded to in the words *shelom 'Ester* ("Esther's welfare"). The twelve months of purification are each governed by one of the twelve tribes, whose merit enables the souls of persons under their care to be purified and elevated to the highest level in order to enter Paradise. Saba concludes this section with a lengthy exposition on the twelve tribes and the nature of the sources of their merit (*EKE,* 48–58).

The sources for much of what Saba says with regard to the soul in the context of chapter 2 can be found in earlier kabbalistic literature.[140] Saba's introduction of these ideas in the context of a homiletical discourse on Esther intended for a wide audience, though not without precedent,[141] is still significant.

The phrase "Esther put on her royal robes" (5:1) was interpreted in the Talmud as Esther clothed herself in the Holy Spirit.[142] But *malkhut* ("royalty") is the name of the tenth or lowest *sefirah* in the kabbalistic system, the one synonymous with the *shekhinah* or divine presence. Like Isaac Arama, Saba interprets this verse as describing Esther praying before God, clothing herself in the divine name which is the tenth *sefirah* called the *shekhinah* which is also the quality of divine mercy. With divine aid, therefore, Esther came before the earthly king and found favor in his eyes. The king stretched out his golden scepter which symbolized the quality of justice and alluded to the punishment awaiting Haman and his kin. Thus Esther had the quality of mercy on her side and Haman the quality of justice against him. With divine guidance, Esther was able to succeed in her mission and win over the king to do her bidding (*EKE*, 75–76).

Wine also plays a very important role in the Esther story, according to Saba. As mentioned above, the Jews sinned by drinking the wine at Ahasuerus's banquets and, as a result, caused the decree of destruction to be promulgated against them. But then, when they repented by fasting for three days and three nights and abstained from wine, God forgave them. God therefore wanted to reward them measure for measure by commemorating the days of Purim with wine. The miracle of Purim was accomplished by Mordecai and Esther who rose up through their prayers to the place of the supernal wine (*yayin shel ma'lah*), the wine that regales God and men and which is located in the *sefirah* of *binah*, or understanding. This is the wine which has been stored in its grapes since the six days of creation (*yayin ha-meshummar ba-'anavav mi-sheshet yemei bereshit*).[143] Esther in her request to the king, "Let your Majesty and Haman come today" (*yavo ha-melekh ve-Haman ha-yom*) (5:4) (the first letters of which spell out the divine name) invoked the God of mercy on behalf of herself and her people.

This formula alludes to the good wine, which partakes of the quality of mercy and the divine name *YHVH*. On the other hand, Haman brought down the full force of God's justice upon himself when he uttered *ve-khol zeh 'einenu shoveh li* ("yet all this does me no good," 5:13) the last letters of which spell out the Tetragrammaton backward. From the moment that he uttered those words and stirred up the quality of justice, his fortunes began to fall. Thus, in this way, the wine brought mercy upon Israel and justice against Haman (*EKE*, 20–21).[144]

Again, Saba tries to show how intimately and deeply involved God was in the events of the Esther story. Every act and every utterance had its effect in the upper spheres, and God, in his mercy, protected his people and saved them from harm. Thus we see again, though on a different level, how the story of Esther provides reassurance for Saba that God still watches over his people even when they are in exile and that he will eventually redeem them.[145]

THE BOOK OF JOSIPPON

Very little material was available to the medieval exegete who wished to gain further information of a historical nature about the Book of Esther in order to flesh out the story. The apocryphal additions to Esther and the *Antiquities* of Josephus were unknown at the time. Midrashic sources, while used by many, were used with caution and often were not considered historically reliable. The one source readily available to most medieval scholars was the *Book of Josippon*. This tenth-century Italian history of the Jewish people in the Second Temple period was universally attributed in the Middle Ages to Josephus Flavius and was considered a reliable historical source.[146] Its popularity was considerable, and it was distributed rapidly and widely throughout Western Europe and the Mediterranean region.[147] *Josippon* devotes one chapter (chapter 9) to the Purim story,[148] and this was frequently consulted by Esther exegetes.[149] Immanuel of Rome makes the most extensive use of the work in his commentary, quoting four sections of the book:

1. At 2:21, the story of Bigthan and Teresh's plot;[150]
2. At 3:2, Mordecai's prayer;[151]
3. At 3:7, the reason for Haman's hatred for the Jews;[152]
4. At 5:1, Esther's dramatic appearance before Ahasuerus.[153]

Immanuel's use of *Josippon* may be seen as another attempt to make his commentary more accessible to the ordinary reader in addition to his extensive use of paraphrase and offering alternative interpretations for different phrases and words. The four passages from *Josippon* that he includes in his commentary focus on four major points of interest in the Esther story:

1. the reason why Bigthan and Teresh plotted against the king;
2. Mordecai's reason for not bowing down to Haman which led to his entire people being threatened by annihilation;
3. the cause of Haman's hatred of the Jews—something that is never articulated in the story;
4. the climax of the story in which Esther puts her life in danger in order to save her people.

All of these sections would have been of great interest to Immanuel's readers, and elaboration of the story at these points would have heightened its appeal. Since throughout the Middle Ages *Josippon* was considered to be a reliable and accurate historical work, the quotes from it were considered to be true and authentic additions to the story as told in Esther.

CONCLUSION

We have seen that exegetes drew upon the sources at their disposal in a very selective manner. Grammatical works were popular through the thirteenth and on into the early fourteenth century after which time interest in grammar declined. Midrashic literature was seldom ignored, except by the northern French School of exegesis, but it was used very selectively and often reinterpreted to bring it into line with the sensibilities of philosophically trained medieval scholars. Aside from references in the *Zohar*, the only medieval exegete to use *kabbalah* extensively in his commentary was Abraham Saba. And *Josippon* was quoted at length only by Immanuel of Rome. Although they worked within a well-defined and well-established religious tradition, the medieval exegetes still had a great deal of room for individual self-expression. Furthermore, as we shall see in the next chapter, many exegetes chose to broaden their horizons still further by drawing upon the riches of secular culture to assist them in their endeavors.

2

NON-JEWISH SOURCES FOR EXEGESIS

In the later Middle Ages, especially in Spain, Jewish scholars were not only thoroughly grounded in the sources of the Jewish tradition but were also well-read in secular philosophical and scientific literature and valued the secular sciences highly. At the same time as specialized scientific and philosophical treatises were being composed, presumably for the more sophisticated reader, biblical commentaries were being peppered with philosophical and scientific ideas which would thereby reach a wider audience. The works of Aristotle, especially his *Nicomachean Ethics*, figure most prominently in our Esther commentaries, but we find as well clear traces of a familiarity with works of rhetoric and astrology.

ARISTOTELIAN ETHICS AND PHILOSOPHY

Aristotle's *Nicomachean Ethics* was translated from the Greek into Latin by Robert Grosseteste in 1246–47 and thereby became available to the Christian scholarly community.[1] The Jewish community had to wait some eighty or more years before a translation of Averroës' Middle Commentary on the *Ethics* was made available to them by the

Provençal scholar and translator Samuel ben Judah of Marseilles.[2] Shortly thereafter, Joseph ibn Kaspi prepared an epitome of R. Samuel's translation of the *Ethics* as well as of his translation of Averroës' commentary on Plato's *Republic*.[3] Samuel's translation has come down to us in several recensions done at various times in the fourteenth century, all of which enjoyed wide circulation.[4] In the late fourteenth century, Meir Alguadez prepared another translation of the *Ethics* based on the Latin version and this translation was widely circulated in the fifteenth century.[5] The publication of the *Ethics* of Aristotle had a profound impact on Jewish scholarship in the late Middle Ages.[6] Its influence can be seen quite clearly in most of the Esther commentaries written in the fourteenth and fifteenth centuries.

Gersonides does not quote Aristotle directly, but his emphasis in his commentaries on the moral lessons to be learnt from Scripture may reflect a growing awareness of the importance of the Bible as a source and authority for the dissemination of moral teachings.

Joseph ibn Kaspi is the first exegete of the Book of Esther to quote Aristotle directly, and he does so, as would be expected, from his own epitome of Samuel b. Judah's translation.[7] Kaspi first resorts to Aristotle's *Ethics* to explain the phrase "there was no compulsion" (1:8), commenting that compulsion is the opposite of free will "as was explained in Aristotle's *Book of Ethics*."[8] Kaspi also uses Aristotle to help him explain the meaning of "those who knew the times" (1:13). He takes this phrase to mean "those with experience who have witnessed a lot of events," or in other words, the elders of the community.[9] He then quotes Aristotle who was of the opinion that listening to elders with experience is almost as good as listening to oracles.[10]

Several other comments of Kaspi on this chapter show a political awareness most probably acquired through the influence of Aristotle. For example, he comments that 1:16 demonstrates that for a ruler the loss of political prestige is more serious than the loss of personal prestige, for "without a flock, what need is there for a shepherd?" and "because a disease in the body politic is more difficult to cure than one in the ruler." Kaspi is stressing here the need for the maintenance of the social order and the importance of preserving the king's honor in order to maintain that order. The point is made by other later exegetes, but Kaspi seems to be the first to put Vashti's rebellion in a political context. This change in emphasis would seem to be the result of Aristotle's influence.

Kaspi, admittedly, has difficulty in understanding Mordecai's reasons for not bowing down to Haman. He does, however, offer the opinion that Mordecai was possessed of the quality of greatness of soul or magnanimity[11] and quotes as a proof text 2 Chr 17:6: "His heart was courageous (*va-yigbah libbo*) in the ways of the Lord." Thus is this very Greek virtue given biblical sanction.[12] Kaspi's final reference to Aristotle's *Ethics* is rather abrupt. In commenting on the expression it is not for the king's profit" (*'ein shoveh*) (3:8), he states that the meaning of equity (*shivvui*) has already been explained in the *Book of Ethics*.[13]

The *Ethics* also plays a major role in the commentary of Abraham Ḥadidah. At several points in his commentary Ḥadidah quotes the *Ethics* at length, far in excess of what would be necessary for strictly exegetical purposes. In commenting on Ahasuerus's elaborate display of riches and the enormous banquet that he made, Ḥadidah explains that he did all this in order to show the world that he was of a magnanimous nature.[14] He then quotes at length Aristotle's *Ethics*, Book 4, on the nature of the magnanimous person (*gedol ha-nefesh*), contrasting him with the pusillanimous man (*qeṭan ha-nefesh*). According to Ḥadidah, Ahasuerus was anxious to demonstrate his honor and magnanimity to the people of his kingdom, so they would recognize that he was indeed worthy to be king and possessed the required attributes for this exalted position.[15]

We see then that in the process of elucidating Ahasuerus's character with the help of the *Nicomachean Ethics*, Ḥadidah has taught the reader a lesson in ethics as well, since the reader is now aware of the attributes of both the magnanimous and the pusillanimous person.

The subject of Vashti's removal from office and the severe punishment recommended by the king's advisers allows Ḥadidah to introduce the discussion in *Ethics* 1:4–5 on what is the highest of all practical goods. Ahasuerus, says Ḥadidah, must have been of the opinion that honor was the highest good, and therefore, he had Vashti removed in order to preserve his honor. His advisers must have concurred in this opinion.[16] Here again, Ḥadidah has introduced into his commentary a substantial quotation from the *Ethics*, much more than necessary to answer the question he posed for himself. Again, it would seem that Ḥadidah's intention was to give his readers a lesson in ethics in the course of their study of the Book of Esther with the help of his commentary.

As mentioned earlier, around the end of the fourteenth century, Meir Alguadez prepared a translation of Aristotle's *Ethics* from the

Latin. This translation gained a great deal of popularity which it maintained through several printings down to the last century.[17] The fifteenth century was also witness to a dramatic rise in popularity of Aristotle's moral writings in Spain, apparently due to the influence of the work of Italian humanists such as Leonardo Bruni (1374?-1444).[18] With several Hebrew versions of the *Ethics* in circulation and avid interest in the work in court circles, it is not surprising to find many fifteenth-century Jewish exegetes making extensive use of the *Ethics* in their commentaries.

Isaac Arama is a case in point.[19] Arama finds the last verse of Esther (10:3) a convenient focus for the expression of his views on government and the desired qualities a good leader should have in order to govern his people properly.[20] According to Arama, in order for a legislator to be effective, he should have the power to enforce his laws and punish transgressors, and he should be respected by his people because of his greatness. Otherwise, they would accept rule only by force and not by law, an undesirable situation. Mordecai possessed these two attributes. He was next in rank to the king and therefore was a very powerful person, almost as powerful as the king. Second, he was great among the Jews, which meant that they accepted his decrees not because they had no choice but to submit to his power but out of respect for him and his legislative skills.

Furthermore, in order for a legislator to succeed, the laws that he decrees must have certain qualities. First of all, the laws should be designed to benefit the people rather than the legislator. This is not what the tyrant does,[21] who strives to benefit himself alone. Second, the main purpose of the laws should be to lead the people to the absolute good. Third, the laws should guide the people toward peace and harmony and mutual agreement among all its members, which is the political ideal.

Now Mordecai possessed all the qualities necessary for good leadership. He was well liked by most of his brethren and therefore did not have to use force. Even his being popular with most but not all of his brethren was sufficient because this meant he could use force if necessary to enforce his decrees. Second, he sought the welfare of his people, which corresponds to the second quality of ideal legislation—leading the people to the absolute good. Third, he spoke peace to all his people, which corresponds to the third quality, that of bringing peace and harmony to society. Furthermore, the laws of Purim are also intended to fulfill the function of improving society and instilling peace and harmony among its members. For what could do this better than days of feasting and rejoicing, the giving of gifts to one another and giving charity to the poor? Thus, Mordecai, in his own person and through the laws that he legislated was behaving as the ideal ruler should. This passage amply illustrates Arama's skill as homilist and exegete. He has succeeded admirably in interpreting the biblical text in the light of a philosophical one without resorting to mental gymnastics, or straining the reader's credulity.

The last exegete to be discussed in this section is Zechariah ben Saruḳ. Zechariah's commentary is liberally spiced with quotations from Aristotle (whom he usually calls *ha-ḥoqer*, the philosopher, sometimes *ha-filosof* or just *'Arisṭo*). The work that Zechariah quotes most frequently is Aristotle's *Politics* (five times), but he also quotes his *Nicomachean Ethics* (twice), *De anima*, and the *Metaphysics*. Zechariah's use of the *Politics* is especially interesting since no Hebrew translation of this work was available.[22] This makes it likely that he knew Latin, since the translation of William of Moerbeke had been available for over two-hundred years.[23]

Zechariah feels quite at home in both the secular world of philosophy and the sciences and the religious world of the sages. His ability to integrate skillfully the two worlds he revolved in can best be illustrated by some examples of his exegesis. In explaining the use of the singular verb *qaṣaf* ("become angry") (2:21) in reference to Bigthan and Teresh, the king's eunuchs, he comments:

> The text uses *qaṣaf* ("he became angry") in the singular because they were of one mind in what they were plotting against the king and it is well known to anyone with a little philosophical training (*le-mi she-ra'ah me'aṭ be-ḥokhmah*) that union is a function of form just as multiplicity is a function of matter (*ha-ḥibbur ba' mi-ṣad ha-ṣurah kemo she-ha-ribbui ba' mi-ṣad ha-ḥomer*) and since these eunuchs were of one mind they were united by form, and therefore the text uses the singular. (p. 11b)

In commenting on 4:14 about the importance of Esther not remaining silent at this point and acting on behalf of the Jews, Zechariah paraphrases the text: "Who knows if all the events that occurred up till now from the death of Vashti to the king choosing you as his wife all were directed toward this point in time, that is, to save Israel and if the purpose is lost, the means to that purpose are of no use at all" (p. 14b).

In other words, says Zechariah, Esther, who is the means to achieving the purpose of saving Israel, would not survive if the purpose were not achieved. Zechariah gives the following analogy to this case: "If a man struggles to attain wisdom in order that he be wise but after he achieves wisdom does not continue studying but forgets all he learnt, then all his struggling was for naught since the end purpose was lost" (p. 14b).

There is nothing very unusual or nontraditional in either of these comments. The ideas expressed in them are basically the same as those of the sages, but in the course of each comment, Zechariah has introduced ideas and terminology from the world of philosophy. These passages illustrate how popular exegetical works could be used as a means for the dissemination of philosophical ideas. The practice of using commentaries on the Bible as a vehicle for the dissemination of philosophical teachings was quite common among medieval exegetes with philosophical leanings, and was especially so among exegetes in Provence in the twelfth and thirteenth centuries.[24]

However, it would seem that the more extreme philosophical tendency typified by Jacob Anatoli,[25] Levi ben Abraham ben Ḥayyim,[26] and David Ibn Bilia[27] (all late thirteenth and early fourteenth century), which tried to allegorize significant portions of the Bible, had died out by the end of the fifteenth century. Zechariah and Isaac Arama, who were both certainly at home in the realm of philosophy and used it extensively in their works, were much more conservative and cautious in its application.[28]

It is difficult to say whether or not this was done intentionally. At the very least, we can say that these exegetes avidly studied philosophy and valued it as a discipline and, therefore, naturally used it when discussing the Bible. The result of their introduction of philosophical ideas into their commentaries was the exposure of these ideas to a wider reading public.

The only medieval attempt to allegorize the Esther story philosophically was made by the Karaite Judah Gibbor who lived in Constantinople in the late fifteenth and early sixteenth centuries. Gibbor considers his interpretation a "mystery" (*sod*), and claims that it does not negate the literal meaning of the text, but only enhances it. According to Gibbor, Mordecai is the active intellect out of which emanates the force of understanding which is Esther. The emanating force is not self-sustaining and therefore must be feminine. Hadassah represents this force *in potentia* (*be-khoaḥ*), while Esther is the force in action (*be-fo'al*). Ahasuerus represents everyman, who is in a state of constant struggle with the forces of evil represented by Memucan and Haman. At first, he is seduced by wine and follows his evil inclination (*yeṣer ha-ra'*) and has Vashti killed. The Jews (*yehudim*) represent the inner spiritual and intellectual forces that strive to become united (*mityaḥadim*) with their creator. Haman is the *yeṣer ha-ra'*, or the force of evil personified, who tries to destroy these forces. The struggle between Mordecai and Haman is the ongoing struggle between the active intellect and the *yeṣer ha-ra'*. By his marriage to Esther, Ahasuerus becomes strengthened and is able to conquer the evil inclination, with all its forces (five internal and five external), which are represented by Haman's ten sons.[29] There is no extant precedent among the works of either Rabbanites or Karaites for such an interpretation. But it may very well have been allegorical exegesis along these lines which Zechariah ben Saruḳ was so exercised about and which he criticized so vehemently in his commentary.

RHETORIC

Education in the Latin world in the Middle Ages centered on the study of the seven liberal arts. These were divided into two groups: the *trivium*, which consisted of grammar, logic, and rhetoric, and the *quadrivium*, made up of arithmetic, geometry, astronomy, and music. This division of the sciences was restricted solely to the Latin world in the Middle Ages, and no equivalents for these terms exist in Arabic or Hebrew.[30] This is not to say, however, that these disciplines were neglected by Jewish and Moslem scholars. To take the *trivium* for example, both logic and grammar were studied intensively by Jews in the Middle Ages. Logic was considered a necessary propaedeutic to the study of metaphysics,[31] and grammar was closely allied with the study of Scripture.[32] There exist numerous logical and grammatical treatises from the medieval period that attest to this sustained interest.[33]

The evidence concerning the study of the third member of the *trivium* —rhetoric—is considerably harder but not impossible to come by.[34] Two major works of rhetoric were written in Hebrew in the fifteenth century. The first is an *ars praedicandi* called *'Ein ha-qore'*, written by Joseph ben Shem-Tov ibn Shem-Tov (d. 1480).[35] The second is the influential *ars rhetorica*, *Nofet ṣufim*, of Judah Messer Leon which dates from the late fifteenth century.[36] The only other evidence we possess for an interest in rhetoric among Jewish scholars is the first chapter of the *Kitāb al-Muḥāḍara wa-al mudhākara* ("Book of Discussion and Remembrance") by Moses ben Jacob Ibn Ezra (written ca. 1138),[37] which deals with homiletics and the translation of Averroës' commentary on Aristotle's *Rhetoric* by Todros Todrosi, which dates from the middle of the fourteenth century (1337).[38]

Although there are few Hebrew works devoted to rhetoric before the fifteenth century, there is evidence that the Bible, midrash collections, and collections of *adab* sayings such as *Mivḥar ha-peninim* served as sources for the writing of poetry and letters or for preaching sermons and filled the same function that manuals of rhetoric did from the fifteenth century on.[39] It is not altogether surprising then that, when we examine our Esther commentaries which date from the fourteenth and fifteenth centuries, we find that some of the exegetes do show a familiarity with rhetorical principles.[40] These are applied specifically to Esther's pleas before the king in an effort to demonstrate how rhetorically perfect they were, taking into account all the conditions necessary for a well-crafted speech.[41] One scholar who devoted much attention to this matter was Isaac Arama. He analyzes Esther's pleas in great detail, pointing out how carefully Esther in her wisdom timed and planned the presentation of her case to Ahasuerus (Est 7:3–4), taking into consideration five[42] factors:

1. Timing—she waited till after the third day of the fast which she had proclaimed. (This is why she had twice delayed putting the question to Ahasuerus.)
2. Location—she took care that she would put her request in her own home where there would be no one to speak out against her and her people.
3. Means (*'emṣa'i*)—Esther provided a proper setting for making her request by inviting Ahasuerus to a banquet and predisposing him favorably toward her.
4. The ordering and the phrasing of her question (*kivvun ha-devarim ve-riṣṣuyam*), which was perfectly worded.
5. The quality of the question—that it be suited to the person asked. By saying that the enemy does not consider the damage to the king, she implied that to do the opposite of what she requested would cause damage to the king.[43]

Arama seems to be using here the rhetorical device of classification of circumstances. This technique for the analysis of the components of actions originated in Cicero's *De inventione*[44] and became part of the university curriculum during the Middle Ages.[45] In discussing the procedure to be followed in composing a forensic discourse, Cicero lists attributes of persons and of actions that must be considered. The attributes of actions are the following: place, time, occasion, manner, and facilities. The subject is discussed frequently by Christian scholars in late antiquity and the early Middle Ages, by which time the attributes are called circumstances and are abbreviated into questions, such as *quis, quid, quo, ubi, quando, quomodo,* and *quibus auxiliis.*[46] In the Middle Ages, these questions appear in a variety of contexts, when analyzing the elements of an activity.[47] For example, William of Auvergne, in the introduction to his manual of preaching analyses the activity of preaching by means of the questions *quis, quibus, ubi, quando, quomodo,* and *quid.*[48]

It is difficult to know the source from which Arama derived his particular classification of circumstances. His usual source, Aristotle, does offer a classification in his discussion of voluntary and involuntary actions,[49] but it bears little resemblance to that of Cicero or of the more common series of questions popular in the Middle Ages. Arama's use of the circumstances is also different from that of his ancient predecessors. While they used these questions to analyze an action that had already been performed, Arama has Esther taking these attributes into consideration when planning the best way to perform her act of petition. This would seem to be part of the general medieval tendency to incorporate contemporary wisdom into biblical commentaries.

Esther's second request to the king (8:5), divided into four short parallel phrases, was also very popular among the later medieval exegetes who saw it as a model of how a subject should approach a ruler.[50] According to Isaac ben Joseph ha-Kohen (fol. 71r–v), a person might have four motivations for action on behalf of another: (1) because the person would benefit from such action, (2) because the deed in and of itself is a proper and fitting one, (3) because the plaintiff has found favor in the person's eyes, or (4) in order to repay a favor the person owes the plaintiff. Esther phrased her question so that it included within it each of these motivations and thereby offered the king the maximum number of reasons for granting her request.

Similarly, according to Joseph Ḥayyun, Esther gave the king four conditions which corresponded to the four reasons for which a king would grant a request:

1. It is for his own benefit ("if it please the king").
2. He likes the plaintiff ("if I have found favor in his sight").

3. The request is fitting and proper ("the thing seem right before the king").
4. The plaintiff has the quality of goodness and perfection in his being regardless of whether the king likes him or not ("I be pleasing in his eyes"). (fol. 84v)

Esther named all four reasons in order to enhance as much as possible the chances that the king would accede to her request.

Isaac Arama (fol. 159v) also points out the aptness and ideal formulation of Esther's request:

> These words were spoken with the utmost precision and pleasantness, for if the thing requested is good for the person being asked and is proper in and of itself, what would prevent him from doing it, unless he would reject what was good for him out of hatred for the person making the request or because the integrity and fitness of the person making the request was suspect. Therefore, she put the question to him beautifully by saying: "If the matter asked of the king is good, and I have found favor in your eyes" so that you won't reject what is good for you out of hatred for me, "and the matter is fitting in the king's eyes and I am pleasing to you," so that you don't suspect me of wickedness, then .

Finally, Zechariah ben Saruḳ (p. 17a) credits Esther with being a good stateswoman (*medinit*) for phrasing her request so skillfully.[51]

The passages quoted here bring to mind another rhetorical device—*captatio benevolentiae*, or gaining the good will of the reader or listener. This technique originated in relation to letter-writing but was also applied to oratory. In the Middle Ages it was associated with the *ars dictaminis*[52] and the *ars praedicandi*.[53] The discussions of this device concerned the methods and techniques one should use in beginning a letter or a speech in order to predispose favorably the reader or the listener to the writer or orator. In our Esther commentaries, we find similar discussions in a different context—that of making a request before a king or ruler. It is possible that our exegetes, familiar with the rhetorical device of *captatio benevolentiae*, adapted it to their own needs in the context of their discussion of Esther's skill as a petitioner and that it is not found elsewhere in such a context. This is another illustration of how the Book of Esther, like several other biblical books, was used as a guide for proper behavior and etiquette in a court setting.[54]

The later Middle Ages witnessed a proliferation of Jewish sermons and homiletical commentaries, particularly in Spain and Provence.[55] Since throughout the fourteenth and fifteenth centuries Jews were forced to attend sermons in churches, it is not unreasonable to expect that Jewish preachers in Spain were also influenced by their Christian counterparts in developing their homiletical techniques.[56] Besides this negative influence, one should note as well the general growth of interest in rhetoric in Spanish culture during the late fourteenth and fifteenth centuries, which was at least partly due to the influence of Italian humanists.[57]

ASTROLOGY

During the entire Middle Ages, astrology, the study of the supposed influence of the stars on human events, was a respected science among both Christians and Jews. In the Jewish world, Maimonides was one of the few uncompromising opponents and critics of astrology, calling it foolishness and not at all worthy of being called a science.[58] Of his successors among the Aristotelians, only Joseph b. Judah ibn Aknin, Yedaiah Bedersi, and Isaac Pulgar opposed astrology. Even the rationalist Gersonides, the most original Jewish thinker of the late Middle Ages, affirmed the validity of astrological beliefs.[59] In such a climate of general acceptance, it is therefore not surprising to find many references to astrology and its influences in our Esther commentaries.

The first verse in the Book of Esther that elicited references to astrology was 1:13. Several exegetes interpret *yode'ei ha-'ittim* (lit., "those who know the times") to mean astrologers.[60] Verse 3:7, which describes how Haman's lottery worked, also elicited comments of an astrological nature. Ibn Ezra (Version A, to 3:7) suggests that Haman chose the month of Adar for destroying the Jews because then the constellation of Capricorn was in conjunction with Aquarius, which is Israel's constellation. This was apparently an omen that this time would be propitious for punishing Israel. Gersonides (p. 41a) further explains that the astrological details that must have been taken into account were the planet (or constellation) governing Israel (*ha-mesharet ha-moshel ba-'am*) (i.e., Aquarius in Ibn Ezra's explanation) and the constellation in ascendance (*ha-mazzal ha-ṣomeaḥ*) (i.e., Capricorn, according to Ibn Ezra).

Similarly, Isaac ben Joseph ha-Kohen (fol. 61v) explains that Haman wished to carry out his plan in conjunction with the upper stellar patterns *be-haskamat ha-ma'arakhot ha-'elyonot*. To do this, he cast lots for all the days of the year to find the most suitable one. Even if a suitable day was found, it would be deemed unsuitable if the star governing the month with which that day was numbered was in opposition to that action. R. Isaac adds that there could be no doubt that this lot was based on astrological calculations which were infallibly accurate. Therefore, it was a great miracle that the lottery was overturned in Israel's favor.[61]

The prominence that R. Isaac gives to astrology in his commentary is an indication of the widespread acceptance of astrology as a true science in the late Middle Ages. Further evidence is provided by Abraham Shalom in his *Neveh Shalom.** Shalom explains that Mordecai refused to bow down to Haman because the latter was a descendant of Amalek and Amalek was "a nation who by its very nature hated Israel, being opposite to her in opinions and in qualities." Shalom goes on to explain that from the earliest times Amalek was an augur and a sorcerer who believed that the earth was eternal and that everything was governed by the movements of the stars. The exodus of the Israelites from Egypt and all the signs that God performed for them demonstrated that the world was created and that there is reward and punishment for one's deeds. When he heard about these events, all of which contradicted his beliefs, he decided to do battle with Israel and try to conquer her, hoping that he could then say that everything that happened to Israel in Egypt was the result of pure chance. With his astrological knowledge, Amalek decided on a suitable day to attack Israel. But despite the advantages of strength, superior numbers, and favorable constellations, Amalek was still defeated, because God rearranged the disposition of the stars (*shidded 'et ha-ma'arakhot*). Thus was God's providence for his people demonstrated.

Shalom explains that God declared everlasting war unto destruction against Amalek because they attacked the very foundations and basic premises of the Torah. Haman, like his ancestor Amalek, believed that everything was controlled by the stars "and every accident that occurred to a person from the day of his birth to the day of his death" was impossible to change under any circumstances (Shalom, 71a). He also believed that each and every person had a constellation up above which guided him, that people changed their stations in life because of the changes in these constellations, that people should be honored

---

* (Venice, 1575), 68b–72b.

or scorned according to the status of their constellations, and that a successful man should be honored because of the star which brings him honor. So Haman, whose advice it was to remove Vashti and who was in the king's favor, persuaded the king to honor him by commanding that his subjects bow down to him. In Haman's belief, anyone who honored or paid homage to a person of high rank was honoring his constellation as well. For this reason, Mordecai could not bow down to Haman, for this would have meant acknowledging his belief in the control of the stars over human lives and events and would have been tantamount to idol worship. For Shalom, astrology is Israel's arch-enemy—a pseudoscience that threatens to undermine the very foundations of the Jewish faith, especially the beliefs in providence and reward and punishment. Shalom is, in this case as in much else, a faithful adherent of Maimonides who also vigorously opposed astrological beliefs.

It may seem a bit surprising that Shalom gives astrology such a prominent place in his system and opposes it with such vigor. However, as we have already pointed out, during the fourteenth and fifteenth centuries, astrology had many adherents, and a lively debate concerning the validity of its claims was being waged. At the center of the controversy was the famous apostate Abner of Burgos (Alfonso de Valladolid) (1270–1349). Abner wrote his book *Minḥat qena'ot* ("Offering of Jealousy"), which deals with predestination and free will, in response to a book by R. Isaac Pulgar called *Hakḥashat ha-'iṣṭagninut* ("Refutation of Astrology").[62] Abner argues forcefully on behalf of predestination and the control of the stars over the lives of people, while Pulgar, in the book mentioned above and in his polemical treatise *'Ezer ha-dat*[63] ("Support of Faith"), argues equally forcefully against such beliefs. It should be pointed out that in neither of these books is astrology portrayed as denying the fundamental tenets of Judaism and as being tantamount to idol worship. Abner of Burgos and the astrologer in Pulgar's *'Ezer ha-dat* both claim that their astrological beliefs are the correct ones and compatible with the basic tenets of the faith. Pulgar naturally disagrees, but at no point does he accuse Abner or the astrologer of idolatry. Therefore, although the sources cited above are evidence of the debate being waged over astrology in the fourteenth and fifteenth centuries, they cannot be taken as the direct sources for Shalom's portrayal of Haman as an astrologer who denied God's providence and strove to undermine the Jewish faith.

Another battle, however, was being waged in the fifteenth

century by Jewish traditionalists, and this was against the Averroists, those intellectuals who placed philosophy and particularly the opinions of Averroës on a higher level than the tenets of Judaism. These people were often accused of undermining the faith of the Jewish community in Spain and leaving it exposed to the ravages of apostasy. R. Isaac Arama, in fact, blames the Averroist intellectuals, who explained Jewish history according to the laws of astrology, for undermining the faith:

> In their pride they make many calculations concerning the miraculous events which caused all the nations to marvel at us such as the exodus from Egypt, the downfall of Pharaoh. . . . All these they attribute to the heavenly constellations, their conjunctions and predictable positions, as is to be found in some of their books. [These intellectuals] have been a sinful obstacle in the way of our redemption for those who have been enticed by them into believing that all is the product not of good deeds or divine providence but of fate have ceased to practice the repentance that leads to redemption; rather, they fix their eyes on the heavens and wait upon the constellations great and small, for from them they expect redemption to proceed.[64]

Thus, according to Arama, astrology was one of the weapons in the Averroists' arsenal and contributed to the undermining of the faith of the Jewish community. Perhaps it is this group that Shalom had in mind when he drew his portrait of Haman and Amalek.[65]

One of the most unusual and imaginative uses of astrology is made by Baḥya ben Asher in the third section of his commentary, the section in which he interprets the book *'al derekh ha-sekhel.*[66] Baḥya begins by giving an astrological interpretation of the events of the Esther story based on the attributes of the seven planets. Of the seven, Saturn and Mars are known to be malevolent, and Venus and Jupiter, benevolent. The colors associated with these four planets are black and red for Saturn and Mars, and blue and green for Venus and Jupiter, respectively.[67] Baḥya shows how the names of Ahasuerus and Haman can be associated with Saturn and Mars, the forces of evil, and Mordecai and Esther with Venus and Jupiter, the forces of good.[68]

Here then is a medieval version of a futuristic space war film, with the forces of evil, Ahasuerus (Saturn) and Haman (Mars) in conjunction and aligned against the Jewish people, on whose side were the forces of good represented by Mordecai and Esther. Now this stellar struggle was a particularly fierce one, as Baḥya describes it:

> This celestial battle in the days of Mordecai and Esther was extremely fierce and forces of the good and evil stars were aligned against each other fighting and struggling with each other; mighty Saturn and Mars were on the verge of overpowering Israel and Jupiter and Venus were powerless and could not withstand them.[69]

In such a desperate situation, Israel's only hope was divine intervention. For God has the power to rearrange the stellar constellations and overpower the mightiest of heavenly forces. It is Esther who achieves the victory by clothing herself in the Holy Spirit.[70] Thus inspired, she invites Haman and Ahasuerus to a banquet, thereby initiating a realignment of forces (*shiddud ma'arakhot*), with Ahasuerus coming over to her side and leaving the isolated Haman an easy prey.

Baḥya then goes on to describe Haman's downfall in detail in the same terms. He concludes his exposition with the hope that the reversal of fortunes that took place in the Esther story is a sign that sometime in the future the wheel will revolve (*yit'happekh ha-galgal*) and those that were on the top will be on the bottom and those that were on the bottom will be on top: "In the future, instead of our being trampled under foot among the Gentiles they will honor and revere us."[71] He is alluding, of course, to the hope for Israel's redemption.

What is especially interesting about this exposition of the Esther story is Baḥya terming it *'al derekh ha-sekhel*. We see from this, that for Baḥya, the term *sekhel* ("reason" or "intellect") was not restricted to philosophy but included astrology (and other sciences) as well. This fits in with his declared intention in the introduction to his Pentateuch commentary to use the sciences, where possible, as handmaidens, always subordinate to faith, to assist in the elucidation of the scriptural message.

Besides Baḥya, several exegetes mention the revolution of the spheres which affect the fortunes of people, with reference to the respective rises and falls in the fortunes of Haman and Mordecai. Ibn Ezra, for example, questions the wisdom of Mordecai challenging Haman at the time when his fortunes were on the rise (*'aḥar she-ha-sha'ah mesaḥeqet lo*).[72]

In a similar vein, Zechariah ben Saruḳ answers the question of why Esther saw fit to invite Haman to the banquet she made for Ahasuerus, as follows:

> We can also say that Esther did this so that [Haman] would rise in a moment to the peak of his greatness which had been decreed according to his birth (*she-hayetah gezurah le-fi moladeto*) for it is well-known that when a man rises to the top of the wheel he must of necessity descend because the wheel does not rest. A demonstration of this point is that Saturn is the uppermost of the seven planets and it influences (*yoreh ʿal*) the nethermost which is earth. For Saturn is cold and dry and the earth is cold and dry through its power. This teaches us that whoever rises very high is called "a descender" [i.e., is destined to descend].[73]

R. Zechariah further explains that the sages interpreted the verse "you will always be at the top" (Dt 28:13) to mean that you should not rise to the highest level so that you will not descend. For this reason the sages commanded that at weddings people should not rejoice unrestrainedly but should break glass cups in order to temper their joy.

Elsewhere, along the same lines, Zechariah (p. 15a) comments on the futility of Haman's efforts to reverse his fortune and that of Mordecai by building the gallows on which he hoped to hang Mordecai. For he had seen, through his astrological calculations, that Mordecai's fortunes were on the rise and that he was destined to be "over his [i.e., Haman's] house," i.e., in charge of it. By building the gallows, he hoped to be able to ensure that Mordecai would literally be over his house. But of course, his efforts were of no avail.

Zechariah's comments contain an interesting blend of rabbinic and astrological beliefs. The sages in several places state the opinion that "there is a wheel that rotates in this world," which determines the rise and fall of the fortunes of men.[74] However, Zechariah's words are even more reminiscent of the medieval depictions of the wheel of Fortune, which is driven by a blind goddess who indiscriminately raises up and brings down the fortunes of individuals. The figure of Fortune, a pagan goddess, was first introduced to the medieval world in literary form by Boethius, who in the second book of his *Consolation of Philosophy*, portrays her as turning her wheel "with her proud right hand," oblivious to the changes and reversals she causes in the lives of men. During the Middle Ages the image of Fortune and her wheel became a famous one and was often depicted in manuscripts of *The Consolation of Philosophy* and in other works as well.[75]

CONCLUSION

We see, then, that medieval exegetes, especially in Spain, were fully aware of the intellectual currents in their host countries and did not hesitate to introduce ideas and teachings borrowed from non-Jewish sources into their exegesis. Indeed, many probably saw biblical commentary as a convenient vehicle for the dissemination of new ideas which they felt should be better known among scholars who sought the truth and were not merely unthinking slaves to tradition.

LITERARY CONCERNS

Medieval Jewish exegetes are noted for their keen literary sensibility and attention to details both linguistic and stylistic, as were their predecessors, the sages of the Midrash. The exegetes of Esther too give ample evidence of their sensitivity to the literary and stylistic features of the book.

STRUCTURAL PARALLELISM

One of the Book of Esther's most noteworthy stylistic features is the linguistic parallelism to be found in the recounting of events in chapters 3–4 and 8–9. This feature was noted by several exegetes, two of them of the northern French school. Joseph Kara observes in commenting on 8:15:

> *Then Mordecai went out from the presence of the king in royal robes of blue and white.* Just as it says above "and Mordecai learned all that had been done and Mordecai rent his clothes and put on sackcloth and ashes and went out into the midst of the city" (4:1), in the same language he now says "he went out from the presence of the king in royal robes." Similarly for the whole affair, the author *made a point of writing* (*natan da'ato li-khtov*) about the joy of the Jews when they were saved in the same language that he wrote about their punishment. Just as it says above "and the city of Susa was perplexed" (3:15) he repeats and says "and the

city of Susa shouted and rejoiced!" Just as it says above "there was great mourning among the Jews," (4:3), he repeats and says "there was gladness and joy among the Jews" (8:17). Just as he says above "most of them (*rabbim*) "lay in sackcloth and ashes" (4:3), now he says "and many (*rabbim*) from the peoples of the country declared themselves Jews."[1] [emphasis added]

Kara's emphasis on the author "making a point" of using the same language to describe the joy and triumph of the Jews as he did to describe their despair demonstrates his awareness of the skill and artistry of the author. This recognition of the role of the human author in the composition of a biblical book of divine origin is a relatively rare phenomenon in medieval exegesis.

The anonymous northern French exegete "A" also points out these and other parallels although, as usual, his style is much more telegraphic and he makes no mention of the role of the author:

> 8:15. *Mordecai went out from the presence of the king.* Instead of "he went out into the midst of the city wailing with a loud and bitter cry" (4:1); "in royal robes" (8:15) instead of "he put on sackcloth and ashes" (4:1); instead of "the city of Susa was perplexed" (3:15) [it is written] "the city of Susa shouted and rejoiced;" (8:15) instead of "there was great mourning among the Jews" (4:3), [it is written] "there was gladness and joy among the Jews" (8:17); and instead of "fasting and weeping and lamenting" (4:3) [it is written] "a feast and a holiday" (8:17).[2]

Joseph Kara points out several other literary parallels in the story. These are: "causing them to look with contempt upon their husbands" (1:17) "and all women will give honor to their husbands" (1:20);[3] the two instances of couriers being sent, first by Haman (3:13) then by Mordecai (8:10);[4] and the remission of taxes after Esther becomes queen (2:18) and the new tax Ahasuerus imposed at the end of the story (10:1).[5]

The most extensive list of parallels is provided by Abraham Saba. Some of these are identical with those pointed out by Kara and the other northern French exegetes, and others are unique to Saba.

3:10. The king gives Haman his ring.	8:2. The king gives Mordecai his ring.

3:12. The summoning of the kings's secretaries.	8:9. (The same.)
3:12. The letters were written and sealed with the king's ring.	8:10. (The same.)
3:13. Women and children were to be killed on one day.	8:11. The women and the children of the Jews' enemies were to be killed on one day.
3:14. "The text of the document . . . was to be publicly displayed to all the peoples."	8:13. "The text of the document . . . was to be publicly displayed to all the peoples."
3:15. "The couriers went out posthaste on the royal mission."	8:14. "The couriers . . . went out in urgent haste at the king's command."
3:15. "The city of Susa was dumbfounded."	8:15. "The city of Susa rang with joyous cries."
4:1. Mordecai . . "went through the city crying out loudly and bitterly."	8:15. "Mordecai left the king's presence in royal robes of blue and white."
4:1. Mordecai "went through the city crying out loudly and bitterly."	6:1. Haman proclaimed before him: "This is what is done for the man whom the king desires to honor!"
4:1. "Mordecai . . . put on sackcloth and ashes."	8:15. "Mordecai left the king's presence in royal robes of blue and white."

These examples amply illustrate that at least some medieval exegetes had a sense of an author's hand at work in determining the narrative structure of the Book of Esther.

ADDITIONS FOR DRAMATIC EFFECT

On several occasions, Joseph Kara adds details to the story in an attempt to solve exegetical problems. A case in point is verse 2:19: "When the virgins were assembled a second time, Mordecai sat in the palace gate." In this verse, the meaning of "a second time" (*shenit*) and the connection between the gathering of the virgins and Mordecai sitting in the palace gate are not at all clear.[6] Furthermore, the aside concerning Esther's concealment of her identity and her fidelity to

Mordecai (2:20) does not seem to fit into the story at this point. Kara attempts to weave all these elements into a coherent narrative.

> *When the virgins were assembled, etc.* When Ahasuerus saw that even after he made her queen she refused to reveal her people or her kindred he thought that perhaps she came from a family of slaves or one of lowly birth and was not worthy of the throne. He said to himself, "I will gather virgins a second time. Perhaps I will find among them one of royal lineage even prettier than this one and I will remove Esther and make her queen instead." Therefore it says "and when virgins were assembled a second time, Mordecai was sitting in the palace gate." This means that even though Esther saw what Ahasuerus was doing and that her position was in danger, nevertheless, she "did not reveal her kindred or her people." [Furthermore], even though she saw that Mordecai was so important in the king's eyes that he appointed him to sit at the king's gate as is the rule for officers who serve the throne and guard the king and it would be an honor for her, not a shame if she would tell the king how they were related, for Mordecai was descended from the house of Saul and Esther, his niece, was worthy of the throne [still she refused]. (3:90)

In other words, even though Esther saw that she was in danger (2:19a) and Mordecai was in a good position at court (2:19b), she still remained loyal to her promise to Mordecai not to reveal her identity to the king. This interpretation is not without its difficulties but is a credible attempt to come to grips with a difficult text.

On another occasion, Kara introduces a new element into the story in order to solve an exegetical problem and increase the scene's dramatic effect.

> 2:13. *When the maiden went into the king in this way* (*u-va-zeh*). This means, in this manner it was the maiden's custom to come to the king. "Whatever (*kol*) she desired to take with her," they would give, and each maiden, when her turn came to go to the king, would ask that an important man from her people and kindred be given to her to escort her from the harem to the king's palace. (3:89)

The idea of a male escort accompanying the maidens on their way from the harem to the king's chambers has no basis in the text and seems to be a product of the exegete's imagination.[7] The use of the word *la-vo'* ("to come") in the phrase *'et kol 'asher tomar yinnaten lah la-vo' 'immah,* which is usually associated with the motion of animate objects, may have suggested to Kara this line of interpretation.[8]

Kara uses this new element he has introduced into the story to inject tension and surprise into the scene.

> *When the turn came for Esther . . . to go into the king she did not ask* (2:15) that any man escort her except for the man whom Hegai, the king's eunuch, who had charge of the women, would advise. Now if someone should delve deeply to ask for what purpose these three verses (2:10, 13, 15) were written, the reply would be as follows: At the beginning of the incident it says that Esther did not reveal her people or kindred (2:10). When she was asked who her people and her kindred were and she refused to answer, her questioner said, "tomorrow her turn to go before the king would come and the man that she would request to accompany her from the harem to the king's palace would be of her people and kindred (2:13)." Therefore, it says: "When the turn came for Esther daughter of Abihail the uncle of Mordecai she asked for nothing except what Hegai the king's eunuch, who had charge of the women, advised" (2:15). (3:89–90)

By this device, Kara has not only added an element of suspense to the story but has also enhanced the figure of Esther who is portrayed as cleverly thwarting the gossips at the king's court.

In order to involve his readers in the excitement of the event, Kara provides a version of the letters that Mordecai sent out to the Jews in Ahasuerus's kingdom (9:24):

> A certain man named Haman rose up against us to destroy us in the days of King Ahasuerus. But we had a sister of the seed of Benjamin named Esther; and Esther was taken before the king; "and when she came before the king (9:24) etc." (3:94)

The description in the letters of Esther as a sister of the seed of Benjamin and the appeal to "our brethren, the House of Israel,"[9] add a familiar touch to the tone of the text which would have appealed to Kara's listeners or readers.[10]

Elsewhere, Kara uses his skill as storyteller to add drama and poignancy to Esther's entreaties to Ahasuerus.

> *Let my life be given at my petition and my people at my request* (7:3). You say that if I ask for up to half of the kingdom you will give it to me. I am not asking for half of the kingdom, nor for a tenth nor for a hundredth. All I have is a tiny request—that my life be given at my petition and my people at my request. (3:93)

In all of these examples, Kara displays a good sense of the dramatic and does not hesitate to add details to enhance the power and poignancy of the narrative.

ISAAC ARAMA'S RETELLING OF THE STORY

Without question, the most serious attempt by a medieval exegete to rewrite the plot of the entire Esther story was made by Isaac Arama. The focal point of Arama's retelling of the story is his interpretation of 2:10, which states that Esther did not reveal her people or her kindred when she was taken to the king's palace to participate in the contest to choose the new queen, because Mordecai had told her not to. Most exegetes understood this verse to mean that Esther concealed her Jewishness from the king. But Arama rejected this viewpoint, arguing that since all the other maidens were brought to the king's harem from their father's home, it was inconceivable that Esther had come alone, or, if she had come alone, that no one knew that she came from the house of Mordecai, the Jew who sat at the king's gate (Arama, 149r). What, then, is the meaning of 2:10? According to Arama this refers to her ancestry. Mordecai wished everyone to have the impression that Esther was of royal lineage. He also did not want it known that they were cousins. Therefore, he himself said that he did not know her ancestry and was merely her guardian. As a result, no one pressed Esther for this information. For if Mordecai did not know, who would?

Making this assumption enables Arama to solve several problems in the text. Mordecai's daily inquiries after Esther's welfare would have left no doubt in people's minds as to their relationship. At 7:3, when Esther makes her appeal to the king, she does not spell out who her people are. We can conclude, therefore, that the king must have known that she belonged to the Jewish people. Finally, in 8:1, when Mordecai comes before the king, the text states that Esther had told the king how they were related. This, according to Arama, was the only thing that was not known. The assumption that everyone knew that Esther was Jewish, while perhaps solving some problems, raised others. For how to explain Haman's action against the Jews if he himself knew that he was attacking the people of the queen. It is in his discussion of Haman's action against the Jews and his motives for it that Arama's exegetical creativity is most clearly manifested.

First Arama speculates as to why Mordecai did not bow down to Haman. Apparently, Arama felt that under such circumstances prudence is called for. He asks:

> Why did he not bow down or do obeisance? Is it not a tradition from the sages to follow the advice [in Is 26:20] "hide yourself for a little while until the wrath is past?" Not only that, but he was warned every day by the king's servants, "Why do you transgress the king's command?" (Est 3:3). But he did not listen to them. . . . The opinion of the sages that he had an idol attached to his garment is a *derash*, since the text says that the people bowed down and did obeisance to Haman and not to his idol.[11]

On this point, Arama places himself in opposition to the entire exegetical tradition that preceded him. Arama also rejects as far-fetched Gersonides' suggestion that the king had made a god of Haman, as the Babylonian kings were accustomed to do.

Why, then, did Mordecai refuse to bow down? Because, says Arama, he was a relative of the queen, and all relatives of the royal family were exempt from such decrees. Not only were they exempt, but they were strictly forbidden to bow down. Since he was sure that when the time was right his relationship to Esther would become known, he did not wish to endanger himself by transgressing an even stricter law of the king. But, since no one knew of his relationship to the queen, how could he justify his action to the king's servants? The best he could do was to offer the lame excuse that he was of Jewish ancestry and his religion forbade such actions. But this excuse was guaranteed not to sit well with the king's servants who would accuse him of pulling rank and using his Jewish ancestry which was the same as the queen's as an excuse to evade his civic duty.

According to Arama, Mordecai did not suspect that this action would have any serious repercussions. At worst, he thought, the matter would come before the king and then, he would reveal his connection to Esther, and the king would praise him for his wisdom. But as things turned out, Mordecai had not reckoned on Haman's overweening pride and his capacity for reckless and irrational behavior. For when Haman learned that Mordecai refused to bow down to him because of his Jewishness and that the Jews as a group kept themselves apart from other nations, he resolved immediately to get at the root of the problem and to wipe out the entire Jewish people. Now this was obviously a reckless and foolhardy thing to do, since the Jewish people at the time were a powerful and well-respected nation known for their wisdom and well-represented in the king's court. Furthermore, everyone knew that the queen herself belonged to this people. Therefore, how could anyone even think of harming them let alone destroying them completely? And certainly the king would never agree to such a thing!

But Haman was overcome by his evil desires and was incited by the king's servants. He thus put himself in a very precarious situation, banking on his own high position and the king's affection for him and hoping that eventually he would win the king over to his side. He began his plan of action by describing to the king, in base and despicable terms, an anonymous nation, hoping that the king would let him have his way without asking too many questions and that, eventually over the space of a few months, he would reveal his true intentions to the king and by then it would be too late to revoke the king's decree.

Arama is quite conscious that he is breaking sharply with the exegetical tradition on Esther with this line of interpretation but he feels he must in order to make sense of the behavior of the king, who in the traditional understanding of the book comes across as little less than a fool.

So, how does Arama explain Ahasuerus's behavior in this incident? He does his best to protect his image and put him in as favorable a light as possible. He explains the phrase "that they be destroyed" in 3:9 which is Haman's request concerning this nameless people, to mean not physical destruction, but rather expulsion or enslavement. So, when he removed his ring and gave it to Haman, Ahasuerus was not agreeing to their destruction.[12]

Haman, then, according to Arama, acted on his own initiative entirely in issuing the decrees as they were worded. Proof of this assertion is given in 3:12 which states that the king's secretaries wrote an edict "according to all that Haman commanded." This would indicate that the wording of the decree was Haman's, not the king's.

How, then, was it possible, for a decree such as this to be issued without the king's knowledge of its contents? "Do not be surprised at this," says Arama. For the kings in those days were quite sheltered in their palaces, and only a few high-ranking officers had access to them.

So it was possible for a favorite officer who had the king's ear to issue a decree in the king's name signed with his seal and for the king never to be aware of its exact contents. Again, we see that Arama tries to protect the king's image from accusations of gross wrongdoing.

Furthermore, Arama interprets the king's words "the people also to do with them as seems good to you" (3:11) to be a conditional agreement, dependent on the verification of Haman's assertions about this people. From this it is understood, claims Arama, that if his story were not corroborated the king would not go along with his plan. Arama supports this opinion by a comparison with his own experience. There are cases like this every day in kings' courts. Someone will come and make a request for a specific reason and his request will be granted provided that he is telling the truth. Then someone else will come along and interrogate him and nullify his statements (fol. 153r). Here, again, Arama is trying to make Ahasuerus fit his image of a reasonable and responsible monarch. It was inconceivable to him that Ahasuerus should act in any other fashion.

Now Mordecai learned of Haman's secret and realized that it would be best that his plot be revealed as quickly as possible so that he would not be able to make a special plea before the king. But Mordecai did not have direct access to the king (apparently he was not of a high enough rank), and so he had to resort to other methods to attract the king's attention. This is why he tore his clothes and put on sackcloth and ashes and walked about the city wailing and mourning (4:1). He hoped thereby to gain the king's attention and be summoned to him. When Esther heard of Mordecai's action, she sent Hathach out to him and Mordecai explained to him what he thought should be done. If the king had agreed to all of Haman's plan, then the Jews would really have been in dire straits. But since Haman was lying and deceiving the king, it would be quite easy to unmask him. Therefore, he urged Esther to go immediately to the king while the matter was still fresh in his mind and before Haman had a chance to win him over completely, for when he found out how Haman had tried to deceive him, he would be furious and would take immediate action to punish him. Otherwise, if they delayed, Haman would have a better chance to succeed in his design.

Three days later when Esther made her plea before the king, the king by his reaction showed that he did not know that Haman had meant to destroy the Jews. For he asks indignantly, "Who is he and where is he that would presume to do this?" (7:5). His strong reaction,

Arama believes, demonstrates his sincerity and the fact that he had no intention of harming the Jews and was not just saying this to pacify the queen. Furthermore, Haman's reaction proves even more decisively that the king had not known his true intentions. Otherwise, Haman could have pointed out to the king that he himself had agreed to this deed; and he knew no more than the king that the queen was one of them. But since this was not the case and he had been deceiving the king all along, he had nothing to say.

Now, with Haman out of the way, Esther reveals to the king her kinship to Mordecai. Arama believes that this was necessary in order to let the king know why Mordecai had not bowed down to Haman. As mentioned earlier, Arama stresses here, in keeping with his line of exegesis, that the fact that Mordecai and Esther are Jewish never comes into the discussion, which indicates to him that this was common knowledge.

Whether or not one is convinced by Arama's depiction of the plot-line of the Book of Esther, one cannot help but admire his ingenuity and thoroughness in accounting for nearly every turn in the story's plot. One motivating factor for him was almost certainly his desire to protect the image of the king, or rather to bring the portrayal of Ahasuerus in the book in line with his perception of how a king should behave. But this alone does not explain the need for such a thoroughgoing revision of the conventional reading of the book. It may very well be that the need for Arama was a purely internal one, influenced only incidentally by external factors, and this for him was in the main an intellectual exercise whose sole purpose was arriving at the truth and repairing the reputation of one of the books of Sacred Scripture which he felt had not been treated seriously enough by his predecessors.[13]

ISAAC ARAMA'S METAPHORICAL SUMMARY

A most imaginatively styled summary of the Esther story is provided by Isaac Arama at the end of chapter 8 of his commentary.[14] Although he does not point out linguistic parallels between the two parts of the story, as do other exegetes, his description clearly highlights the sequence of events and their dramatic effect. Because of the vividness of the passage's imagery and its clarity of style, it is worth quoting in full. It serves as a fitting epilogue to this section of our discussion.

For the sequence of events in this story can be compared to an evening. After sunset, it becomes darker and darker by degrees until midnight when the sun is in the depths of the sea and the darkness is most intense. From that point on, the sun turns eastward and the sky gradually becomes lighter and lighter until the sun rises over the earth and shines forth over the whole world. So it was for Israel in [this] exile. [At first] their day was quiet and serene, especially when Esther was taken into the royal palace. Then suddenly their sun began to set one degree after another counting off the hours till midnight. The parable and the metaphor follow the hours of a night which are equal to those of a day, that is twelve hours along.

The first [stage of sunset] is alluded to in 3:1, "After these things King Ahasuerus promoted Haman the Agagite, the son of Hammedatha," for the elevation of the enemy was the beginning of the downfall. The second [stage] is alluded to in 3:4, "they told Haman in order to see whether Mordecai's words would avail," for they kindled the fire and put evil thoughts in his mind, and so with this the night becomes darker. The third [stage] is alluded to in 3:6, "But he disdained to lay hands on Mordecai alone . . . Haman sought to destroy all the Jews," for this decree had already occurred to him, and the darkness was getting still deeper. The fourth [stage] is alluded to in 3:8 when "Haman said to King Ahasuerus: "there is a certain people scattered abroad," for then his evil plot began to be carried out and the darkest time of the night was beginning. The fifth [stage] is alluded to in the king's utterance: "The money is given to you and the people also, to do with them as it seems good to you" (3:11), for certainly with this the intensity of the darkness was increased manifold. The sixth [stage] is alluded to in (3:12–15) when "the king's secretaries were summoned" . . "and letters were sent by couriers" . . . the couriers went out post hoste . . . "and the decree was issued in Susa the capital . . . and the city of Susa was perplexed," for then they were terrified and confused, and their sun was sinking into the depths of the sea. This was midnight when their darkness was most intense, as it is written: "And in every province, wherever the king's command and his decree came there was great mourning among the Jews" (4:3); and this darkness was even thicker than the darkness of midnight.

However, from that hour, their sun began to turn eastward and travel up the six steps that it had descended: The first was that wise woman's pronouncement: "So gather all the Jews . . ." (4:16), for she [must have] said that salvation would spring forth as a result of returning to the Lord, may He be blessed. The second was the king's good will toward her and his holding out his scepter and his saying: "What is your request?" . . . (5:3) for the radiance of the king's countenance gives life, and his will is like a spring rain cloud. The third [stage] was "On that night the king could not sleep" (6:1), for the supernal will had already agreed to turn the tables by mentioning [Mordecai's] merit to him [the king]. The fourth [stage] was the king's saying: "Make haste, take the robes and horse as you have said . . ."(6:10), for after this [incident] Haman returned home "mourning and with his head covered." The fifth [stage] was when the king said: "Who is he and where is he that would presume to do this?" (7:5) . . "Then said Harbona" (7:9) . . . "and the king said: "Hang him on that" (7:10), for when [Haman] was suspended from the stake (*'ammud*), the morning star (*'ammud ha-shaḥar*) rose. The sixth [stage] was when [the king] said: "And you may write as you please with regard to the Jews" (8:8) and that whole account until "Then Mordecai went out from the presence of the king" (8:15), for this was certainly the time when [Israel's] sun rose, and from then on it became lighter and lighter until the day was bright. For this reason it is written: "The Jews had light" (8:16).

CONCLUSION

It is noteworthy that concern for literary features in the text seems to have been restricted to the exegetes of the northern French school and to several fifteenth-century Spanish exegetes, particularly Isaac Arama. It is quite likely that the northern French exegetes' fixation on text in its context predisposed them to the development of a critical eye and a greater awareness of the role of the human author in the composition of biblical narrative. Isaac Arama and Abraham Saba were both great preachers and their homiletical skills probably enabled them to focus on rhetorical features in the text which lent themselves to use in sermons. In Arama's case, his interests carried him further than anyone else in the Middle Ages, to the point where he had re-written almost the entire story of Esther, capping his work with an elegant metaphorical summary.

THEOLOGICAL ISSUES

While literary matters concerned relatively few of our exegetes, theological issues figured prominently in nearly all of the commentaries. The Book of Esther is the only biblical book which is totally devoid of references to God. This fact has perplexed readers of the book from the earliest times to the present.[1] For how to explain the inclusion in the canon of a book which was ostensibly so secular in nature? Furthermore, it is important to bear in mind the view of the Christian Church for whom the Book of Esther was, on the whole, an embarrassment. Most premodern Christian exegetes would probably have wished that it had never been included in the canon.[2] The Church Fathers ignored it completely, and in the Middle Ages it was commented upon very rarely. Those exegetes who did comment on it usually interpreted it allegorically.[3] Many Christian scholars and not a few Jews, even in our century, are offended by its particularistic, nationalistic tone and especially by the bloody scenes of revenge and the joyful triumph of the Jews over their enemies described in the book.[4]

Here, then, was a book the Church wanted no part of. One can surmise that this fact made it even more attractive to the Jews, and Jewish exegetes did their best to instill it with religious significance. Stressing the miraculous nature of the events described in the book and the special relationship between God and Israel that is made manifest in it would have heightened the appeal of the book for its Jewish readers and emphasized that this book was especially precious and significant for the Jews.

As we shall see, medieval Jewish scholars provided various solutions to the problem of God's seeming absence from the book, which tie in with the themes of God's providence over Israel, the role of miracles in the story, and God's redemptive role in Israelite history. All of these issues are discussed in this chapter.

THE ABSENCE OF GOD'S NAME

The problem of the absence of God's name from the book is aptly presented by Immanuel of Rome:

> It is necessary to investigate the reasons that none of the holy names appears in the book. This book by right should be full of thanksgiving and praises and the telling of God's acts of kindness for He was exceedingly kind to that generation by the miracles and wonders that He showed them and the causes that He effected to save them. (fol. 182v)

Various attempts were made by medieval exegetes to account for this seemingly strange phenomenon. Some addressed the problem directly, seeking to explain why God's name was omitted from the book, while others sought to show that, whether or not God's name appears in the book, his presence behind the scenes and his orchestration of the events in the story are easily demonstrable.

Saadiah Gaon uses both lines of argumentation in the introduction to his commentary. First, he tries to prove that the book was divinely inspired even though there are no explicit statements to that effect, such as "Thus says the Lord" or "And God said." He argues there are several places which require a knowledge of hidden things that only a divinely inspired author could have known. One example is "Haman said to himself" (6:6). Another is "Esther won the admiration of all who saw her" (2:15).[5] He also argues that if believers in God had used God's name in the scroll, heretics would have erased it and substituted the names of their gods. Believers would thus have been responsible for introducing the name of an idol into a historical chronicle.[6] For this reason, no mention was made of God in the entire scroll.

Abraham Ibn Ezra approaches the problem through Neoplatonism, the philosophical system he identified with. The introduction to his first commentary begins as follows:

> There is no relief [from distress] except through God who has engraved an everlasting law on the heart of the thinking man (*maskil*) when he is awake and speaks to him in dreams as well. He supports him when he sets out to do any task. [The *maskil*] will always have Him in mind before he makes an utterance (*gam yizkerenu tamid ṭerem moṣa'ei piv*).

For Ibn Ezra, the *maskil*, or thinking man, is a person striving to know God, first through self-understanding, then through the understanding of His works in nature and finally through the understanding of God Himself.[7] By "everlasting law," Ibn Ezra means the laws of nature that God implants in people's hearts and that maintain order in the world.[8] It is these laws that start people on the path to the full knowledge of God. But to truly come to an understanding of God's nature and essence, people must detach themselves as completely as possible from their senses and the sensible world and enter into a sort of ecstatic trance similar to that experienced by the prophets.[9] This is what is meant by "he speaks to him in dreams." Such a person, who has reached such a high level of perfection, must surely be very close to God, and God must support him in all his activities. It goes without saying that such a *maskil* will always have God in mind when he sets out to do any task.

Now since the Book of Esther is part of the Sacred Scriptures and is divinely inspired, its author, Mordecai, must have been at a very high spiritual level and must have qualified in Ibn Ezra's system as such a *maskil*. Therefore, there is no question about Mordecai's relation with God or his pious intent when writing the book. One must therefore look for another reason for the absence of God's name in the book.

Although Ibn Ezra does not quote Saadiah Gaon, the solution he offers to this problem is very similar to that offered by Saadiah[10] in the introduction to his commentary. According to Ibn Ezra, Mordecai, the author of the scroll,[11] was afraid that when the story would be recorded in the annals of the Persian kings the idolatrous scribes would substitute the name of one of their gods for God's name as the Samaritans had done in their version of the Bible.[12] Therefore, Mordecai did not mention God's name in the scroll in order to protect His honor.[13]

Immanuel of Rome adds several new nuances to the argument:

> This was all intentional. For the ancient kings in that generation were at the height of pride and would attribute events both good

> and bad that occurred in their time to their might, prowess, and wisdom and not to the first cause. You will find that some were considered divine, and people were commanded to worship them. Others, who were not so proud, would command at least that their gods be worshipped and that the good and evil in nature be attributed to them. Therefore, Mordecai, in his wisdom, saw fit to compose this scroll as a story as if there were no other cause and it were all an accident. For if he had wanted to attribute the events of the story to the Creator, may He be blessed, he might have angered the king. . . Therefore, in his wisdom, Mordecai saw fit to write the account of the events as if it were all a story that happened without any divine cause. (Immanuel, 182r)

The above citation stresses the fear that Mordecai had of angering the Persian king who might be insulted that the events described in the book were not credited to him or to the gods he worshipped. Immanuel is the only exegete to suggest that fear of antagonizing the ruling authorities may have played a role in the composition of the Book of Esther, and it is possible that this comment reflects his own fears and concerns.[14]

Zechariah ben Saruḳ essentially repeats Ibn Ezra's argument, although he adds the comment that God's name is alluded to in several places, both in a sequence of initial letters of consecutive words and a sequence of final letters. These interpretations seem to have originated in the school of the German Pietists who were very fond of such wordplays.[15] Finally, Zechariah quotes an opinion, which he attributes to the kabbalists, that the events in the story took place at a time of divine eclipse (*hastarat panim*). This is alluded to in the similarity between the name *'Ester* and the root *STR* (to hide) in the verse *ve-'anokhi haster 'astir panai* ("I will surely hide my face") (Dt 31:18).[16]

Isaac Arama offers a completely different explanation to the problem, explaining that, since the cessation of prophecy, God's providence is manifested through hidden miracles, and it is these which sustain the people of Israel in their long years of exile. Arama rejects Ibn Ezra's explanation, arguing that the deeds of Daniel and Ezra, who were certainly as great as Mordecai, were also recorded in the annals of the Gentile kings, and they were not concerned about any possible affront to God's honor. Rather, argues Arama, the Book of Esther contains a record of events as they were guided by divine providence in order to fulfill the divine purpose.[17]

These were some of the ways, then, that medieval Jews, for whom God's existence and providence were axiomatic and who accepted the divine inspiration of the canonical books of the Hebrew Bible, found to introduce a divine element into a story that at least on the surface seems completely secular.

PROVIDENCE

Isaac Arama's reference to hidden miracles as a manifestation of divine providence leads us into our discussion of the two other central themes connected with the Esther story, providence and miracles. For if God is assumed to be involved in the events of the Esther story, it is through His providence that His involvement is made manifest and miracles provide the mechanism for this involvement. The sages never directly broach the subject of the absence of God's name from the book. However, from numerous statements they make with regard to the Esther story, it is clear that they saw the divine hand guiding events, settling accounts, and assuring a favorable outcome for the Jews.

According to the sages, the Jews were deserving of destruction because they had bowed down to Nebuchadnezzar's idol.[18] They had further transgressed by partaking in Ahasuerus's feast, consuming forbidden food and drink.[19] In the first two chapters of the book, God orchestrates the events so that Ahasuerus deposes his queen and chooses a Jewess, Esther, to replace her. Furthermore, Esther's uncle Mordecai uncovers a plot by two of the king's bodyguards to kill him. These events are understood as prophylactic measures taken by God in order to assure Israel's survival:

> *After these things* (3:1). After what? Rava said: After the Holy One, blessed be He, created a remedy for the affliction, as Resh Lakish said: "The Holy One, blessed be He, does not smite Israel unless He creates a remedy for them in advance, as it is written, "When I would heal Israel, the corruption of Ephraim is revealed" (Hos 7:1).[20]

But it was still necessary for Esther and the Jews to pray and fast in order to avert the evil decree. According to one account, it was finally the outcries of the Jewish schoolchildren that moved God to rescind the decree of annihilation he had sealed against Israel.[21] On that night, Ahasuerus's sleep was disturbed, he was read to from the annals of the kings of Persia, he learned of the good service Mordecai had done him which had never been repaid, and he resolved to right the wrong. From this moment, the fortunes of the Jews began to rise and those of Haman to fall. Even at this juncture, miraculous events took place, for Shimshi, the scribe, who was Haman's son, was reading to Ahasuerus and tried to erase the passage concerning Mordecai. But the angel Gabriel filled in what he erased and so Ahasuerus found out despite his efforts.[22] By this time, Ahasuerus had begun to doubt Haman's loyalty, suspecting that he was plotting to overthrow him, and Haman's early morning visit and the reply he made to Ahasuerus's query only deepened the king's suspicions.[23] So, he was quite ready to dispose of him when Esther accused him of trying to destroy her people. We see, then, that in the midrashic account, God and his angels are present behind the scenes throughout, and the question of the absence of God's name is not at issue.

Following the rabbinic view, Rashi explains the connection between chapters 2 and 3 as the preparation of the remedy for Israel's affliction. Mordecai was informed in a dream that the celestial powers had agreed to go along with Ahasuerus's and Haman's decree because the Jews deserved punishment for having bowed down to a graven image in the days of Nebuchadnezzar and having partaken of Ahasuerus's feast.[24] Similarly, many other medieval exegetes stress the role God played in guiding the events of the story, although with less emphasis on rabbinic sources. For example, throughout his commentary, Zechariah ben Saruḳ stresses the role of God's providence in orchestrating events so that Israel would be saved.[25] This for him seems to be the meaning of the book and the hope that it holds out for the future redemption of the Jews.

Religious themes figure prominently in the *to'alot* or lessons of Gersonides. Gersonides, following the sages, sees the hand of providence guiding events at all the critical points in the story. The banquet at which Vashti was deposed set the stage for Esther's appointment as queen.[26] The first set of letters that Ahasuerus sent out had the effect of making the king look foolish, and this subsequently helped the cause of the Jews.[27] God gave Esther added charm so that the king would be captivated by her and choose her to be his queen.[28] God arranged that Bigthan and Teresh's plot be discovered by Mordecai so that this could serve to save Israel when the time came.[29] Although Haman had a powerful position and used persuasive arguments to win the king over to his side, in the end he was thwarted by God.[30] God, through his special providence was able to overcome the destiny of general providence so that on the very day that Israel was to have been destroyed, she was victorious over her enemies.[31] Haman's defeat at the hands of Mordecai is naturally seen as divinely ordained administration of justice.[32] God turned Haman's plea for his life before Esther into an instrument for his death.[33] Similarly, the stake that Haman had prepared for Mordecai was used in the end for him.[34] Even the letters that Haman sent out, in which were written the orders to kill the Jews, proved to be an instrument for their salvation according to Gersonides' reasoning, since, had the irrevocable decree not been promulgated, it would not have been necessary to send out the second letters allowing the Jews to resist their enemies and destroy them. Surely, reasons Gersonides, if there had been a way to save Israel without killing all those people, the king would certainly have preferred it. [35] It required a great deal of providence to win the king over so that he would agree to all of Esther's requests (9:13) since he did not seem to be too pleased with the death toll among his people.[36]

The importance of fasting and praying to God is also stressed several times by Gersonides in the *to'alot*. The mourning and fasting by Mordecai and other Jews after the evil decree was promulgated shows that it is proper to humble oneself before God in times of distress.[37] Mordecai's efforts to forestall the evil fate decreed for the Jews teaches us that we must never give up our efforts to work for our salvation in times of danger.[38] Finally, Esther's plea to the rest of the Jews to fast and pray for her shows us the importance of communal prayer in times of distress.[39]

Gersonides thus attempts to put the whole Esther story into a religious framework, stressing, on one hand, God's providential guiding of the events leading to Israel's salvation and, on the other hand, the role that the people played through their praying, fasting, and turning to God in effecting the desired result. Religious themes that lay beneath the surface of the story are thus brought into full relief.

Joseph ibn Kaspi never raises the question of the absence of God's name in the Book of Esther. From his comments, however, it is clear that, in his view, God played the major role in effecting Israel's salvation. The concluding sentence of his commentary stresses the point that one of the major lessons to be learned from this book is God's providence and His mercy for His people. He clearly sees God's hand guiding events throughout the story and does not shy away from describing the events as miraculous.

> I have no doubt that God, may He be blessed, performed a miracle thanks to the merit of Mordecai and Esther and the righteous who were there, and as a result of this miracle, He, may He be blessed, who is the cause of all things, put fear in the hearts of the nations, for they heard of the miracle and the news of the events of the month of Sivan—the kinship of Queen Esther and the stature of Mordecai her uncle—reached the far corners of the kingdom. And He informed the nations how the miracle He performed for the Jews unfolded. For it was His wish that the king be unable to fall asleep and for the scribes to be called and for all the other wondrous events to occur that finally led to Haman's hanging, Mordecai's coming to power as viceroy to the king, and Esther the Jewess becoming queen. (*GK*, 36)

Kaspi evokes God's role in the Esther story even more strongly by comparing it with two of the greatest events in biblical history, the Exodus and the conquest of Canaan, in both of which God's active role is mentioned explicitly.

> And when these nations heard the deeds and wonders that God, may He be blessed, performed, they all melted away and trembled before Him. Likewise, Moses wrote in his Torah concerning the miracle at the sea: "The peoples have heard, they tremble" (Ex 15:14). And Rahab said to Joshua's messengers, "I know that the Lord has given you the land, and that the fear of you has fallen upon us and that all the inhabitants of the land melt away before you" (Jos 2:9). . . . Here as well God put fear in the hearts of all the nations throughout that winter, and their fear intensified every day, for He, may He be blessed, was increasing Mordecai's power daily as Scripture states: "For Mordecai was great in the king's house and his fame spread throughout all the provinces; for the man Mordecai grew more and more powerful" (Est 9:4). (*GK*, 37)

Here, and in the following quotation, Kaspi rephrases the impersonal passive speech of the author into direct, active speech to bring out more clearly God's active role in the events described.

> Therefore when the appointed day came, i.e., the thirteenth day of Adar, which was the day on which the enemies of the Jews had

> hoped to get the mastery over them, the tables were turned and the Jews got the mastery over their enemies. . . . Now, the phrase "*the tables were turned*" (*ve-nahafokh hu'*) does not mean to say that the last letters were the opposite (*hefekh*) of the first ones,[40] but rather that the Lord, may He be blessed, brought about the opposite (*hefekh*) of what the peoples had hoped for. (Ibid.)

Kaspi also notes that the same language is used in Joshua and in Esther with reference to the Israelites' defeat of their enemies. Jos 10:8 states: "The Lord said to Joshua, 'Do not be afraid of them, for I will deliver them into your hands; not one of them shall withstand you.' " Similarly, in Jos 23:9, Joshua states: "The Lord has driven out great, powerful nations on your account, and not a man has withstood you to this day." In Esther 9:2, the same language is used: "And no one could withstand them for the fear of them had fallen on all the peoples." Since God figures prominently in the verses in Joshua, it is not difficult for Kaspi to include Him in his description of the course of events in the Book of Esther.

Finally, Kaspi sees as a great miracle the fact that, according to the story, the leaders and princes of the provinces supported the Jews. The extraordinary support of non-Jews for a Jewish cause could only be explained by him as another aspect of God's providence on behalf of the Jews (*GK*, 38).

MIRACLES

The question of miracles in Jewish theology is very closely connected to that of divine providence, for miracles are a direct open manifestation of God's providence. The first exegete to make specific mention of the miraculous nature of the events recounted in the Book of Esther is Joseph Kara. In trying to deal with the problem of why Esther did not reveal her origins to Ahasuerus, Kara comments:

> *For Esther obeyed Mordecai's bidding just as she had done when she was under his tutelage* (2:20). All this was written for us to make known the saving acts of the Lord. For if Esther had revealed her people or kindred after marrying Ahasuerus, Haman would not have become jealous of Mordecai and Ahasuerus would not have given him permission to do with the people as seemed good to him and there would have been no miracle in this affair. This therefore,

> comes to teach us the power of the miracle, that at first Esther married the king before Haman rose to power and the king did not know her people or kindred. Then along came Haman and become jealous of Mordecai and plotted to destroy all of the Jews, "and when she [Esther] came before the king," the king ordered that "the wicked plot which he had devised against the Jews should recoil upon his own head" (9:25). (Kara, 3:90)

According to Kara, the concealment by Esther of her identity is a crucial factor that determines the whole course of events as described in the book. Had she made her origins known after becoming queen, Haman would not have dared to plot against her people, and there would have been no threat to the Jewish people and hence no miraculous salvation. Thus the Jews would have been deprived, as it were, of a miracle.

At first blush, this argument seems very strange, for would it not be preferable to avoid danger rather than have to rely on God's intervention? There is even a talmudic maxim which states that "one does not rely on miracles,"[41] meaning that it is better not to put oneself in a dangerous situation and have to rely on God's intervention if the situation can be avoided. Kara himself gives voice to such sentiments when he explains that Mordecai was popular with only the majority of his brethren and not all of them because he had put the Jewish people in danger by his provocative behavior toward Haman.[42]

In order to put Kara's views on miracles in perspective, it is necessary to examine the views of the sages on the subject. There are differing attitudes to miracles in rabbinic literature. Some sages saw the miracles depicted in the Bible as manifestations of God's glory and might and therefore sometimes sought to magnify them so that they appeared even greater than they were described in the Bible.[43] On the other hand, there are several cases in which a definite attempt is made to subsume the miraculous events described in the Bible under the laws of nature and to claim that they were provided for at the time of creation.[44]

In the postbiblical period we see a tendency to deemphasize miraculous events. Although there are many stories of wonders performed by saintly rabbis and holy men, the importance of divine oracles for making halakhic decisions is effectively downplayed and eventually eliminated.[45]

In light of this rabbinic deemphasis of the miraculous, Kara's emphasis of the miraculous nature of the events in the story takes on greater significance. Words of comfort and encouragement were sorely needed by the Jews in northern France and Germany who were enduring persecutions and expulsions at this time. The events of the Bible were distant, but they provided reassurance that God was with his people and would help them in time of need.

> *For if you keep silent at such a time* (4:14). When the Holy One blessed be He sees that no one is praying on Israel's behalf, He, in His Glory, saves them in their times of trouble. (Kara, 3:92)

If, for a Christian reader, the events related in the Book of Esther were mundane and devoid of religious value, this was not the case for Kara.

> *All his mighty and powerful acts* (10:2a). This means, miracles and wonders that are necessary to advertise the miracle have I written for you in this book, and matters which are purely for amusement (*divrei ṭiyyulim*)[46] such as the mighty and powerful acts of Ahasuerus and the full account of the high honor of Mordecai to which the king advanced him, which are mundane matters, it is not worthwhile to write down here. For this scroll was written in the Holy Tongue and was included in our canon, and if you wish to amuse yourself (*le-ṭayyel*)[47] with mundane matters, with Ahasuerus's powerful and mighty deeds and the account of Mordecai's advancement, they are written in the Book of the Chronicles of the kings of Media and Persia. (Ibid., 3:95)

The Holy Tongue, says Kara, is not the vehicle and the Holy Bible not the place for royal annals, especially of Gentile kings. Rather than feel embarrassed about the inclusion of Esther in the canon, Kara is proud of the book and seeks to invest it with religious significance by stressing God's role in the story and the miraculous nature of the events therein described.

Joseph Kara, never having studied philosophy, based his understanding of miracles solely on the rabbinic tradition. The treatment of miracles in medieval Jewish philosophy is much more sophisticated and complex, for it was necessary for philosophers to reconcile the generally held view of a divinity who had set the universe in motion to work according to a fixed set of laws, with the possibility that these laws could be suspended by God at specific points in time. Various solutions were offered to this problem, most of them taking a naturalistic approach, attempting to subsume the occurrence of miracles under the natural order.[48] Maimonides, for instance, sought to maintain the inviolability of the natural order but attempted to circumvent the problem by positing that God's interventions in the course of nature were already predetermined at the time of creation and therefore were not really interruptions of the natural flow of events.[49]

Maimonides further distinguishes between miracles that are impossible in nature and those that are possible in nature. Examples of the former are the changing of Moses' rod into a serpent, the earth opening up to swallow Korah and his assembly, and the splitting of the Red Sea. Among the things possible in nature are the plagues of locusts, hail, and pestilence that fell on Egypt and the cracking of Jeroboam's altar (1 Kgs 13:3). What makes these possible events miraculous is either their timing (as with Jeroboam's altar), some unusual occurrence associated with them (as the extent of the plagues of locusts or hail), or their persistence and coincidence (as with the blessings and the curses described in the Pentateuch).[50]

Most other medieval philosophers follow the view of Avicenna in interpreting miracles naturalistically and identify human beings, usually in the guise of prophets, rather than God, as the immediate causes of miracles.[51] But this view was not held universally even among Aristotelians, some of whom, such as Gersonides, seek other means of explaining how miracles can be wrought within the natural order. Others, such as Ḥasdai Crescas, are not satisfied with any naturalistic explanation and try to argue that God can indeed interrupt the natural order when it suits his purpose.[52]

Zechariah ben Saruḳ is the only one of our exegetes to have an extensive philosophical discussion on miracles and their relation to the Book of Esther. He distinguishes three types of miracles: (1) things done in the secrets of nature (*ṭevaʿim*) such as things which act by virtue of their forms but in an inexplicable manner; examples include the attraction of a magnet to iron or of a diamond to straw; all this we see with our eye but we cannot grasp with our mind; (2) miracles that are supernatural (*le-maʿalah me-ha-ṭevaʿ*), as the signs of Moses in which the staff was turned into a serpent and the serpent into a staff; this conversion of elements one to the other would have been possible in nature in the course of two hundred years or more, but God did this in one minute;[53] this is what is called supernatural; and (3) miracles that are the opposite of nature, e.g., snow burning or fire cooling. This is what Yurqami [*sic*],[54] the angel of fire, did when he cooled the furnace in which Hananiah, Mishael, and Azariah were found.

Zechariah's second category would seem to correspond to Maimonides' category of things possible in nature,[55] but the other two categories are independent. Indeed, it seems difficult to see the first category as falling in the sphere of the miraculous at all, since such matters can be explained by the laws of nature even though we may not know them or they may not be immediately apparent.

Zechariah next applies his theory of miracles to the miracles in the Book of Esther and determines that the story contains examples of all three types of miracles mentioned above. An example of the first category of miracle is found in the grace that Esther found in the eyes of Ahasuerus over all the other maidens (2:17). This grace is hers because of her form, which meets the criterion for the first category of miracle.

The second type of miracle Zechariah finds in the book also pertains to Esther, in this case, to the grace she found in the eyes of all who beheld her (2:15). This second type of grace is divine rather than natural since, in order for a woman to please all who behold her, she would have to have some supernatural quality.

Zechariah finds the third type of miracle in the course of events that led to the king's edict against the Jews not being carried out even though it could not be rescinded. This is a case in which a particular nature—the king's edict—was abrogated in order that a more general nature—Israel—should survive.

Zechariah's discussion of miracles, though couched in scientific and philosophical terminology, does not seem particularly erudite or convincing. His attempts to impose his categories on specific events in the Book of Esther seem quite forced. Particularly unconvincing is his description of the events in the Book of Esther as being opposite to nature, in the same class as snow burning or fire cooling. On the contrary, it is the apparent naturalness of the course of events as described in the book that has drawn the attention of readers.

A more fruitful attempt, already mentioned above, at explaining the miraculous nature of the events in the Esther story is made by Isaac Arama who uses the category of hidden miracles to describe them.

The concept of hidden miracles was used by several Jewish philosophers in the Middle Ages, each one understanding it differently. The first seems to have been Nahmanides, who uses the term to describe the miraculous nature of all creation and the events that happen to men. This is another way of saying that God through special providence governs the actions of all men and that he is behind even those that seem to occur in the course of nature.[56]

Simeon ben Ẓemaḥ Duran (fifteenth century), a rationalist who adopted a naturalistic Maimonidean approach to miracles makes a very unusual distinction between revealed and hidden miracles. According to Duran, when a person is under God's special providence, this providence is seen as a continuing miracle and this continuity makes it a revealed miracle. On the other hand, miracles of this type which are not continuing are defined as hidden miracles since, because of their lack of continuity, they could be interpreted as accidental.[57]

A third interpretation of hidden miracles is given by Isaac Arama. Arama distinguishes between two types of nature both of which were established at the time of creation. One is a blind nature that works according to fixed laws without any thought or meditation, and the other is a kind of supernatural nature that operates by will and intellection. Miracles are manifestations of the working of this second supernatural nature. Indeed, every day, through the medium of the intelligent nature, hidden miracles are performed that seem to be perfectly natural events but that actually represent the overturning of the laws of nature. Conversely, events that seem contrary to nature are actually in accordance with this second, wise nature.[58] As Wilensky points out, Arama's theory of hidden miracles is similar to that of Naḥmanides, except that for him, instead of the *shekhinah* being the agent performing the hidden miracles, as it is for Naḥmanides, the agent is the intelligent or wise nature. During the biblical period and the age of prophecy, the people of Israel were blessed with revealed miracles, but since the cessation of prophecy, God's providence is manifested through hidden miracles whose beneficiaries cannot tell whether they occur as natural events or events contrary to nature.[59] Since the events described in the Book of Esther fall under the category of hidden miracles, the name of God was not mentioned in the book.

Arama gives a few examples of the hidden miracles that he discerns in the book. One is the circumstances surrounding Vashti's deposition and Esther's selection as her replacement which all bear the sign of God's guiding hand. For how else to explain that Vashti was removed from office for refusing to appear before the king while Esther, who went to see him unsolicited—an equally grave offense—was greeted with open arms.[60] God's hand was also evident in the process of selecting Esther as queen and in the shedding of His grace upon her.[61]

All in all, Arama's theory of hidden miracles is a most sophisticated and subtle attempt to explain the role of the divine in the Esther story.

REDEMPTION

The expulsion from Spain awakened anew Jewish hopes for the advent of the Messiah and the final redemption,[62] and this theme appears in several of the commentaries written at the time of the expulsion. Zechariah ben Saruḳ, in discussing the four fasts mentioned in 9:31, ends his commentary with a brief mention of the expulsion and the suffering it caused and offers a short prayer for redemption:

> These four fasts are because of the troubles which befell our forefathers and us and which are still occurring today. For this year there was an expulsion of all the communities of Spain, Sicily, Valencia, Sardinia and Catalonia, and in this year of 5253 [1492–93] some Jews converted for nothing, some were drowned at sea, some lost their wealth and were considered as dead, some were burnt on ship, some were taken captive. May the Lord in his mercy have pity on those who remain and rebuild the Temple for us and return the priests to their service and the Levites to their singing and playing and Israel to their homes. Amen. So may it be speedily in our time.[63]

As with most catastrophes that befell the Jews, their suffering was seen as a necessary preliminary to the advent of the Messiah and the restoration of the Jewish people to their homeland. In the commentary of Abraham Saba, the theme of redemption figures prominently and is tied in with Saba's theology of history and the role of Amalek in that history.

Already in the Midrash, Amalek is depicted as the eternal nemesis of the Jewish people, pursuing them relentlessly from the time both nations stepped onto the stage of history. The repeated triumphs of the Israelites over the Amalekites took on great significance for Jews in later generations and seemed to provide proof of God's saving grace for His people.

We find this motif recurring in various forms in the Middle Ages. A particularly interesting manifestation of it, in the medium of religious art, can be found in the British Library Miscellany (Add. 11,639). This thirteenth-century manuscript of northern French provenance, one of the most richly illustrated medieval Hebrew manuscripts extant, has three consecutive leaves which illustrate this motif. The first (fol. 525v) shows Aaron and Hur supporting Moses' arms during the battle between the Israelites and the Amalekites (Ex 17:8–16) (Figure 1). The

Figure 1. Aaron and Hur supporting Moses' arms. (From MS. BL (London) Add. 11,639, fol. 525v.)

Figure 2. Samuel beheading Agag. (From MS. BL (London) Add. 11,639, fol. 526v.)

second (fol. 526v) shows Samuel beheading Agag after the defeat of Amalek at the hands of Saul and his army (1 Sm 15:33) (Figure 2). The third (fol. 527v) shows Haman leading Mordecai through the streets of Susa (Est 6:11) (Figure 3). All three pictures, then, illustrate the triumph of Israel over Amalek, and the idea to juxtapose them could only have occurred to an artist familiar with the Jewish tradition concerning the struggle between the two nations.[64]

Saba takes up this theme in his depiction of Haman, the descendant

Figure 3. Haman leading Mordecai through the streets of Susa. (From MS. BL (London) Add. 11,639, fol. 527v.)

of Amalek. According to Saba, Haman was openly and knowingly continuing the evil work of his forefathers. Just as Amalek tried to set his hand on God's throne (Ex 17:16) and uproot the Israelites from this world, so Haman tried utterly to wipe out the Jewish people. The purpose of Amalek's attack on the Israelites in the desert was to prevent them from entering the Land of Israel and ultimately building their Temple. Similarly, Haman tried to persuade Ahasuerus not to let the Jews rebuild their Temple.[65]

The triumph of the Jews over Haman, the seed of Amalek, is seen by Saba as a foretaste of the final redemption at which time the seed of Amalek will be utterly destroyed and sinners will cease from the land.[66] In fact, Esther is seen as the foundation of all exiles and redemptions in Jewish history (Saba, *EKE*, 14). In this way, the events described in the Book of Esther take on cosmic significance, for not only does the book describe the salvation of the Jewish people at a particular point in their history, but it symbolizes the final redemption of the Jewish people at the end of days. This final redemption involves the ultimate defeat of the forces of evil symbolized by Amalek. Furthermore, since according to Saba the fortunes of the Jews were at the lowest point of their history and those of Haman (Amalek) at their highest, and yet they emerged victorious, their everlasting survival is assured (ibid., 95). The defeat of Amalek will be a victory not only for Israel, but for God as well for, ever since the Amalekites attacked the Israelites in the desert, the integrity of God's throne has been impaired. But in the end of days, when Amalek is utterly defeated, God and his throne will be whole once more.[67]

For Saba, the Esther story is not merely an isolated episode in Jewish history that affected the Jewish community in exile. Rather, it is organically connected to the most significant event of Jewish history, the giving of the Torah at Mount Sinai. There is a midrashic tradition that questions the sincerity of the Jewish people when they received the Torah at Mount Sinai and their motivations for believing in God at that time. The ideal would have been to believe and follow God because of His stature and exalted nature. But the Jews chose to follow Him because He had led them out of Egypt and had performed miracles for them. Their motive for belief in God was thus flawed and suspect.[68] This situation remained unchanged until the time of Mordecai and Esther when the Jews accepted the Torah sincerely and wholeheartedly without a hint of doubt or skepticism. This is what is meant by the phrase "the Jews ordained and took it upon themselves" (Est 9:27), i.e., they fulfilled what they had already received, meaning the Torah.[69] For it was only now at this point in time that Jews were able to receive the Torah sincerely out of recognition of God's greatness in his own right and not out of base motives of gratitude for favors done to them.[70]

We see, then, that in Saba's view, the Esther story plays a pivotal role in the course of Jewish history. On the one hand, it harks back to the events at Sinai and signifies the completion of the receiving of the Torah on the part of the Jewish people. On the other hand, it looks forward to the end of days and the final redemption at which time the forces of Amalek will be utterly destroyed.

In another sense, Saba sees the Esther story as a source of hope for the Jewish people in troubled times. Therefore, it was important for Mordecai and Esther to record the events of the story for posterity so that it would serve as a sign for the Jews and a source of encouragement. For just as they were saved in the time of Mordecai and Esther, so would they be saved from their present woes.[71]

CONCLUSION

In sum, while God's name may not have appeared in the Book of Esther, His presence was never questioned. Indeed, the evidence the book offered the medieval believer that God did intervene to save his people from disaster was a source of strength and inspiration to many Jewish exegetes and homilists, and undoubtedly to their readers and audience as well.

Part II

THE WORLD OF THE EXEGETE

We now leave the exegete's study and step out into the street. In every field of their creative endeavors the medievals depicted the Bible in contemporary terms. Medieval artists and illustrators portrayed biblical scenes using familiar landscapes and architecture and depicted biblical characters in medieval dress.[1] Literary authors often made biblical characters conform to the religious and moral standards of their own age.[2] The same holds true in the area of biblical exegesis, and the exegesis of the Book of Esther provides an excellent case in point. In an earlier chapter we saw how exegetes were influenced by the secular sources they were exposed to in the course of their studies and often included opinions and teachings from these sources in their commentaries. We now move into areas where medieval influences are not spelled out explicitly but are still readily discernible. In the following chapters we will see that the exegete's physical and cultural surroundings had a profound influence on his understanding of the Book of Esther. Chapter 5 examines how the exegete's environment influenced his grasp of the physical setting of the Esther story. We will even find attempts to read local events and customs into the book.

The remaining four chapters deal, in one way or another, with Jewish-Gentile relations. Chapter 6 deals with the exegetes' attitudes to Gentiles including their views on the marriage between Ahasuerus and Esther and the reasons why it was necessary for the Jews to slaughter their enemies. Chapter 7 examines the exegetes' perceptions of why the Gentiles hated them and wanted to destroy them, which emerge from an analysis of Haman's diatribe in Est 3:8.

The royal court, discussed in chapter 8 was a hotbed of intrigue and the Jewish courtier was always in a precarious position, vulnerable to attack from Gentile and sometimes Jewish enemies. Mordecai served as a fine model of the ideal courtier, and his actions in the Book of Esther are scrutinized and sometimes even criticized. Esther too is portrayed in her role as skilful courtier and earns much praise for her talents and dedication to her people.

Finally, the Jews' relation to the monarchy which was so crucial to Jewish survival in a hostile environment is examined in chapter 9. We will find some of our exegetes interpreting the text very creatively in order to ensure that it conforms with their image of how a king should behave.

PERSIA THROUGH EUROPEAN EYES: GEOGRAPHY, ARCHITECTURE, CUSTOMS, AND INSTITUTIONS

URBAN GEOGRAPHY—*SHUSHAN HA-BIRAH* AND *SHUSHAN HA-'IR*

The physical setting of the king's palace and his court was given considerable attention in the Esther commentaries. Many exegetes attempted to clarify the location of the king's palace in Susa and the relationship between *Shushan* (Susa) and *Shushan ha-birah*, or fortress Susa. The first exegete to distinguish between *Shushan* and *Shushan ha-birah* was Abraham Ibn Ezra, and as we shall see, this distinction has a major influence on his understanding of the Esther story.

The main points in Ibn Ezra's argument are summarized in the following quotation from version B to 1:2:

> *The capital* (*ha-birah*). A palace, as in "for the palace will not be for man" (1 Chr 29:1); and the plural is *biraniyyot* (2 Chr 17:12, 27:4). Now Susa the palace is not the city Susa because Susa the palace is the palace of the king in a walled city (*medinah*), as it is written, "I was in the palace of Susa which is in the city of Elam" (Dn 8:2).[1] The city of Susa, on the other hand, consisted of unwalled streets around Elam and this is where the Jews were. At this time Mordecai was the only Jew in the palace of Susa by virtue of his being a judge in the royal court before Esther was taken, as I shall explain below. Therefore Scripture says "the city of Susa was perplexed" (3:15), because the majority of the city's population was Jewish. Similarly, "the city of Susa shouted and rejoiced" (8:15). For how important were the Jews that the king's palace should be concerned about their misfortune or rejoice in their salvation. Similarly it is written "to the Jews in Susa" (9:13), and "the Jews who were in Susa, gathered" (9:15).[2]

Ibn Ezra's conception of the geography of the situation is based on three points. The first is his understanding, on the basis of the texts in Chronicles, of the word *birah* as "palace." The second is his identification of the Hebrew word *medinah*, "province," with the Arabic word *madīna*, "a walled city."[3] The third is the quotation from Dn 8:2 which, according to his understanding, placed Susa the palace within the confines of the city of Elam. The plan of the cities according to Ibn Ezra is shown in Figure 4.

This view of the situation is confirmed for him by verses 3:15 and 8:15, which refer to the confusion and subsequent rejoicing in the city of Susa. Ibn Ezra could not conceive that anyone other than the Jews themselves would be concerned for their welfare and would sympathize with their lot. This confirmed in his mind the separation between the Jewish and Gentile populations.

This distinction between *Shushan ha-birah* and *Shushan ha-ʿir* leads Ibn Ezra to a most unusual interpretation of verses 2:5 and 2:8. Since he had already established that the Jews were living in the city of Susa, the mention of a Jew in the palace of Susa takes on great significance. Ibn Ezra concludes that Mordecai must have been the only Jew living in the king's palace and was already established there before the competition to choose a new queen was announced (2:5A). Furthermore, as he was Esther's guardian, she must have been living in the king's palace together with him.

2:8. *So when the king's order was proclaimed and his edict* given in writing,[4] the palace officers put guards around Esther so that she would not hide. Her beauty had already been noticed, since she was living in the king's palace with the king's servants. (*VA*, 20)[5]

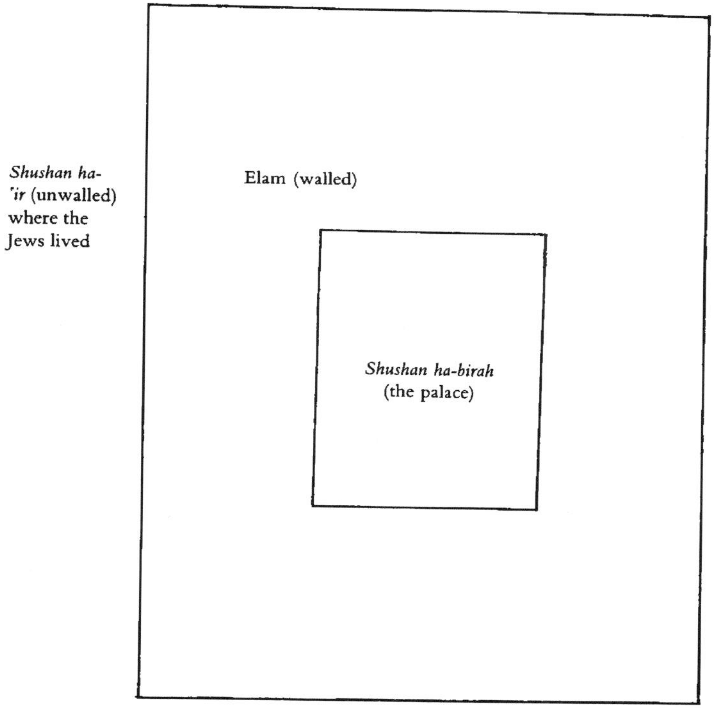

Figure 4.

This distinction between the city of Susa and Susa the palace is maintained by Ibn Ezra throughout his commentary.[6] He has some difficulty, however, in sustaining his argument at 9:12 and 9:14. In his first commentary (at 9:12) he seems to ignore the fact that the Jews are described as killing their enemies in the king's palace and explains the verse as referring to Susa itself. However, in his second commentary he corrects this discrepancy and explains the verse as indeed referring to the king's palace.

Just as Ibn Ezra's distinction between *medinah* and *'ir* has its origin in his familiarity with the Arabic language, so may the geography of Islamic Spain have had an influence on his distinction between *Shushan ha-birah* and *Shushan ha-'ir*, for the palaces of the caliphs in Andalusia were built at some distance from the cities. Ibn Ezra may have known of places such as the Madīnat al-Zahrā' built by the Caliph 'Abd al-Raḥmān III near Cordoba in 936 to house his residence and government,[7] and this information may have influenced him when he was writing his commentary. Furthermore, his own recollection of the Spanish town of Lucena, which was probably his last place of habitation in Spain,[8] may have predisposed him to making this distinction. Lucena was known in Islamic Spain as an entirely Jewish city, although in this case the Jews lived within the walls and the non-Jews outside them.[9]

Since Ibn Ezra's commentary was the most widely read commentary in the Middle Ages, many later exegetes dealt with his interpretation of *Shushan ha-'ir* and *Shushan ha-birah* in their commentaries. Moses ben Isaac Ḥalayo (fol. 4v) and Isaac Arama (fol. 147r, to 2:5) both accept Ibn Ezra's distinction. Many other exegetes do not, however, and offer other interpretations. Several explain that *Shushan* and *Shushan ha-birah* are the same place, the epithet *ha-birah* being added to it because the king's palace was located inside it.[10] Isaac ben Joseph ha-Kohen (fol. 64r, to 3:15) suggests that *Shushan* refers to the Jewish quarter of a larger city called *Shushan ha-birah*, where the king's palace was situated. His plan of the city is shown in Figure 5.[11]

If *Shushan* was inhabited only by Jews, then how did the Jews come to kill three hundred men there (9:15)? R. Isaac explains that the three hundred men were taken from *Shushan ha-birah* and brought to *Shushan* to be executed there. This was done with the blessing of the king who supported the elimination of the Jews' enemies whom he considered undesirable elements well worth being rid of. Thus R. Isaac avoids Ibn Ezra's problem of having to explain how the Jews could kill their enemies in *Shushan ha-birah* (9:12) (Ibid., 73r–v).

Another exegete who dissented from Ibn Ezra's geographical analysis was Immanuel of Rome, who rejected Ibn Ezra's definition of

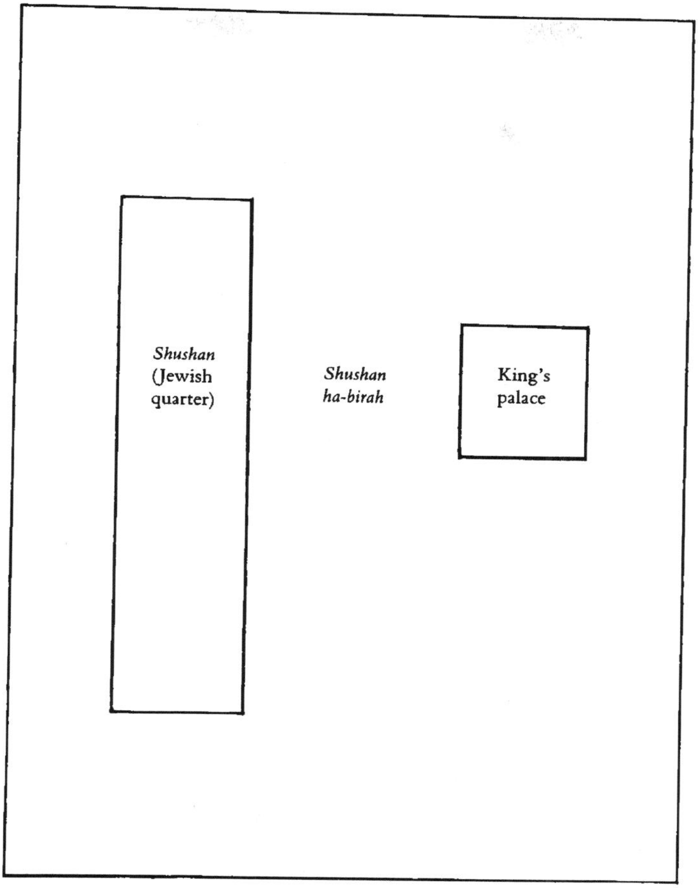

Figure 5.

the word *medinah* as "city,"[12] and instead defined it as a "territory" which includes within itself many "lands" (*'araṣot*) and is divided from its neighbor by "language and script" (*be-lashon uvi-khetav*).[13]

These divergent views of Ibn Ezra, Isaac ben Joseph, and Immanuel of Rome, who lived in different periods or countries, graphically illustrate how an exegete's immediate surroundings can influence his interpretation of a detail in the text.

PALACE ARCHITECTURE AND LANDSCAPING

Rabbi Shemariah ben Elijah of Crete was the only medieval exegete who displayed an interest in the architecture of the palace itself, and he furnished the following description of the relationship between the court, the garden, and the palace mentioned in 1:5:

> *Bitan.* This is a very large house which can sleep thousands of people, which is why it is called *bitan*. The garden was surrounded by a wall and there was a large courtyard around the garden and the king's palace was open to the courtyard and, similarly, the garden was open to the courtyard. In my opinion, they would eat in the courtyard and stroll in the garden and sleep in the palace. The courtyard was associated with the garden and the garden with the palace because the garden was planted for the sake of the palace and the courtyard was made for the sake of the garden, not for its own sake. This is why it is written "in the court of the garden of the king's palace." The king planted the garden close to the palace, so that he would be able to stroll in the garden at his pleasure and feast his eyes on various trees and plants. In order to prevent people from seeing him as he went in and out of the palace garden he surrounded it with a wall and surrounded the wall with a court. The court was adjacent to the palace. He would go out of the palace into the court and from the court into the garden. (fol. 65v)

R. Shemariah's portrayal of the king's palace and its relationship to the garden and courtyard is illustrated in Figure 6.

It is possible that Shemariah's depiction of the king's palace was influenced by his experience, but we have no concrete evidence for this. His description does bear some resemblance to the Moorish style of architecture as best exemplified by the palaces of the Moorish kings in

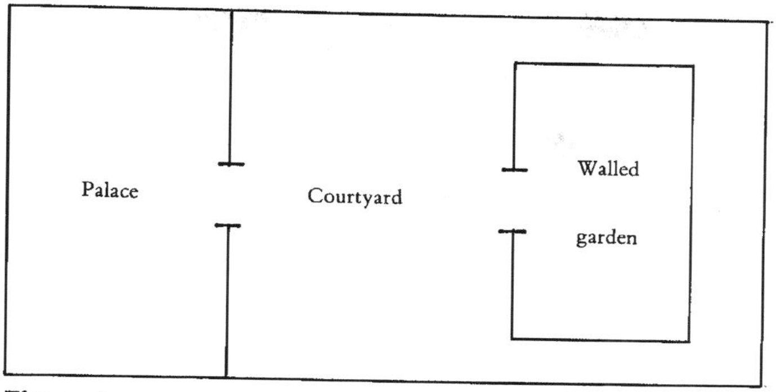

Figure 6.

Seville and Granada. Shemariah did spend some time in Spain in his later years,[14] so his exposure to Moorish architecture cannot be ruled out (see Figure 7).

THE BANQUET SCENE

Verse 1:6, which describes the decoration of the courtyard in rather vague terms,[15] elicited many attempts at clarification. According to Rashi, the words *ḥur*, *karpas*, and *tekhelet* referred to types of colored garments which were spread out as bed coverings. These were "embroidered" (Rashi's interpretation of the word *'aḥuz*)* with threads of fine linen and purple and were spread out on silver rods and marble columns.

According to Joseph Kara, the first three words of the verse refer to colored hangings (*cortines* in Old French) which were embroidered (*'aḥuz*) with flax and fine linen. The word *gelilei* refers to the wheel-like shape of the capitals of the pillars. The hangings were suspended from the capitals and the pillars (3:87). The practice of hanging tapestries on the walls for special occasions was widespread in the Middle Ages throughout western Europe,[16] and as we shall see below, nearly all of the remaining exegetes who describe the banquet scene in detail include hangings or partitions in their interpretation of 1:6 (see Figure 8).

The anonymous northern French exegete "A" (p. 26) explains the

* See above, p. 15

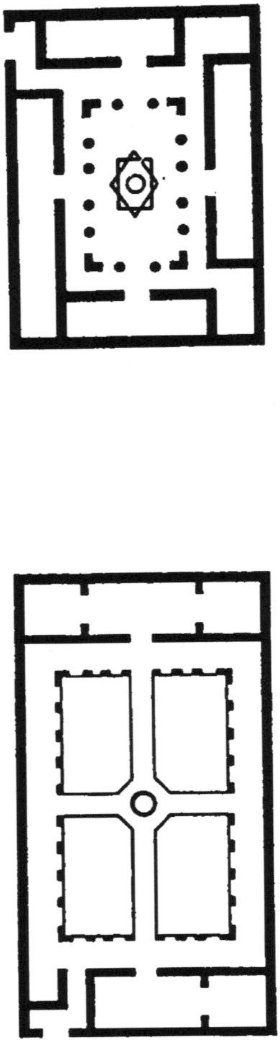

Figure 7. Examples of Moorish architecture: *Top*, house with inner court; *bottom*, house with inner garden. (From Titus Burckhardt, *Die Maurische Kultur in Spanien* [Munich, 1970], 190.)

Figure 8. A medieval banquet scene, showing hangings in the background. (From Robert Delort, *Life in the Middle Ages* [New York, 1973], 215.)

whole verse as referring to the couches (1:6): *ḥavlei buṣ ve-'argaman* refers to the cords of the couches, *gelilei khesef* refers to the planks of the couches, and *'ammudei shesh* refers to their legs. He explains the couches of gold and silver as being additional to these couches. Ibn Ezra explains *ḥur*, *karpas*, and *tekhelet* as three colors, white, green, and blue, respectively all associated with silk. In his second commentary he mentions that these colors refer to covers and curtains (*VA*, 1).[17]

Immanuel of Rome and Gersonides provide the most elaborate and imaginative descriptions of the banquet scene. According to Immanuel, the words *ḥur*, *karpas*, and *tekhelet* refer to white, green, and blue fabrics which were used to form a protective canopy over the courtyard to shield the guests from the sun and rain. This canopy was attached by ropes of purple silk (*ḥavlei buṣ ve-ʾargaman*) to pillars of marble on silver wheels (*ʿal gelilei khesef ve-ʿammudei shesh*). The purpose of the wheels was to enable the pillars to be shifted from place to place as the sun rose or set. One can only wonder whether Immanuel had actually seen such pillars on wheels or whether the idea was a product of his own imagination.[18]

Gersonides as well pictures white, green, and blue cloths suspended from cords of flax forming a canopy for protection from the elements. However, at this point, he makes a radical departure from the usual understanding of the text. Apparently troubled by the fact that *ʾargaman* ("purple") is a color and not a fabric, he finds it necessary to read the verse as if there were a pause after *buṣ*. Therefore, the second half of the verse reads *ve-ʾargaman ʿal gelilei khesef ve-ʿammudei shesh*. This he explains as follows:

> *ve-ʾargaman*. This is a cloth (*beged*) dyed red which was suspended like a curtain from *gelilei khesef ve-ʿammudei shesh*. Now *gelilei khesef* are cylinders (*ʿiggulim ki-demut ʿammudim*) and I would think that they leaned against the marble pillars and were like poles between them. The purple cloths were suspended from these cylinders and the multicolored cloths of the canopy were also attached to them.[19]

Gersonides pictured a completely sheltered enclosure covered by a canopy of multicolored fabrics and enclosed by purple curtains. He also points out, in commenting on the second half of the verse, that the description begins at the top of the room, with the canopy, pillars, and curtains, and then moves down to the bottom describing the bed and finally the floor. Thus it follows the path that an observer's eye would take when surveying a room upon entering it. In a similar vein, but with more concise expression, Isaiah of Trani (3:298) pictures three colored hangings tied with ropes of flax and purple attached to marble pillars by silver poles (*qelonsa'ot*), in order to form a canopy over the guests beneath.

Finally, according to Isaac Arama (fol. 144r), *ḥur*, *karpas*, and *tekhelet* refer to the partitions around the courtyard which were made of fabrics of those three colors and were suspended from marble columns by silver rings. Abraham Saba (*EKE*, 25) pictures a canopy (*sukkah*) of these garments stretching from the trees of the garden up to the marble columns.

DRINKING CUSTOMS

Verse 1:8 "and drinking was according to the law; no one was compelled" has puzzled exegetes through the ages and very few let it pass without comment. For the text is vague and gives no indication as to the law being referred to or what the people were not compelled to do.

Rashi, following the sages, mentions the ancient Persian custom of forcing guests at a banquet to drink a large vessel of wine.[20] Immanuel of Rome (fol. 186r) mentions the custom of the guest being required to drink as much as his host. According to one anonymous northern French exegete ("A", p. 26), no one was forced to drink a beverage he did not like. Another northern Frenchman, perhaps recalling a bad experience that he had had at some feast, comments that everyone had plenty to drink and that the glass was not snatched away from him as soon as he had emptied it for the first time.[21] In a similar vein, Gersonides (p. 40a) comments that no one was forced to deprive himself and do without as sometimes happens at large meals when food and drink are in short supply. Eleazar of Worms displays some cultural refinement and knowledge of banquet etiquette in explaining that the guests were given a choice between red and white wine (*SB*, 8).[22] Isaac Arama (fol. 144v) refers to the custom of letting the eldest at a gathering drink first. This would mean that the others could drink only as much as the eldest wished, since he would set the pace. According to him, at this banquet, such formal drinking etiquette was not observed. Finally, Abraham Ḥadidah (fol. 41v) quotes his teacher R. Shem Tov, as follows:

> Since in the law of the kings it is written that whoever gets drunk in the king's palace is liable to the death penalty, therefore it is written "drinking was according to the law. . . ." Anyone even if

> he became drunk would not be compelled at all, i.e., would not be punished, for this is a *taqqanah* ("statute") in the king's law.

It is difficult to determine if any of the practices mentioned here actually reflect medieval custom. I was unable to find precise parallels to any of them although it is quite likely that in some cases at least the authors' own experiences are reflected. For instance, being offered a choice between red wine and white is quite conceivable for medieval France or Germany where both types of wine were available and drunk in abundance.[23] Similarly, in northern France, it was the custom until the seventeenth century that drinking glasses were not allowed at the table. When a guest wished to drink, he summoned a valet who brought him a full goblet and then waited till he had emptied it before taking it back to a central table designated for drinking vessels and wine.[24] Since several guests usually shared one glass, it is possible that our anonymous French exegete ("A") did have an experience in which a harried valet snatched away his glass in order to refill it and offer it to another guest.

CORONATION PRACTICES

In the late Middle Ages, in the commentaries of certain Spanish exegetes we occasionally find that an exegete will read his own immediate experience into a text, perhaps without even realizing that he is doing so. A case in point is the following description of the king's coronation by Isaac ben Joseph ha-Kohen:

> 1:2. *In those days etc.* Now the text explains why the king made a feast for his servants, for it was the custom of kings *and still is today* that when a king comes to power as a leader and commander of his people, he still aspires for one more honor which both he and his people yearn for, since this would benefit the masses and bring honor and glory to the king [emphasis added]. This is receiving the crown and sitting on the throne of his predecessors. For the performance of this act there is a special location in the kingdom at which at that time all the counts of the counties (*medinot*) and their commanders and governors assemble in order to establish and found on a just basis matters dealing with the governing of the counties (*medinot*) and their laws [and to ensure] that the king agrees to their continuation. While the

> assembled are engaged in these matters, it is the established custom of the king to show them, in their honor, the vast riches of his kingdom by bringing out before them some of his finest treasures. He shows them the splendid glory of his majesty by performing before them all sorts of brave deeds and engaging in pleasurable activities which are appropriate for royalty.[25] After they have tarried there many days and have achieved their demands they crown him, and he, like a bridegroom, goes out and makes a one- or two-day feast for them and then gives them leave, and they return to their cities happy for the peace they have attained. (fol. 53r)

This passage contains a curious blend of facts based on R. Isaac's own knowledge of contemporary custom and other items taken from the passage in Esther that R. Isaac was commenting on. But R. Isaac does not differentiate between the two entirely different situations, for he says at the beginning that what he is about to describe is an ancient royal custom and one that is still followed today. The first point that R. Isaac makes is the distinction between a king coming to power and ruling, on one hand, and being crowned and sitting on his throne, on the other. This distinction would seem to be based on Esther 1:1–3. In the first verse, Ahasuerus is described as ruling over 127 provinces from India to Ethiopia; in the second verse he is said to be sitting on his throne; and in the third verse he makes a huge feast for his subjects. It would seem that R. Isaac concludes from these verses that Ahasuerus ruled for several years before being crowned and that the feast mentioned in the third verse describes a coronation feast.

There may be, in addition, a medieval component in R. Isaac's words, for there was considerable debate among medieval jurists as to the status of a king as ruler before his coronation and as to the effect of coronation upon his status. Lucas de Penna, a fourteenth-century Neapolitan scholar, maintained that before his coronation the only acts that a ruler may perform which have validity are those necessary for the maintenance of public order and discipline, i.e., of an administrative nature. But specific sovereign rights, such as new legislation, abrogation of laws, new fiscal policy, and the conferment of privileges, which must receive divine sanction, are not within the scope of his powers before coronation.[26]

Therefore, when R. Isaac says that the people yearn for the king to be crowned for their benefit and for his greater glory, he may be referring to the plenitude of temporal powers that a king receives only after his coronation. If this interpretation is correct, it shows how well-informed R. Isaac was concerning the theoretical foundations of the monarchy in his day.

R. Isaac next mentions that there is a special place in the kingdom designated for the coronation, and it is there that all the counts, governors, and officers assemble "to establish and found on a just basis matters dealing with the governing of the counties (*medinot*) and their laws and to ensure that the king agrees to their continuation."

This passage seems to give a fairly accurate description of the situation in fourteenth-century Aragon. The city of Saragossa was designated by Pope Innocent III in 1205 as the city in which kings were to be crowned. Although this designation met with some opposition in the thirteenth century, Pere III (or Pedro IV), of Aragon (1336–87), affirmed it as the "head of the kingdom" and was crowned there.[27]

The monarchy in Catalonia-Aragon was a limited one with the nobility having considerable control and leverage over the king. This had been the case since 1283 when the Aragonese nobles had become virtually independent of the Crown.[28] In 1300 the Courts had limited the right of the count of Barcelona to raise taxes to the districts under his jurisdiction.[29] When Pere III succeeded to his father's throne, the nobles and knights of Barcelona urged him to come to Barcelona to swear to their *Usatges* (legal code) and constitutions before being crowned king,[30] claiming this was the custom of all past kings. This Pere refused to do, proceeding straight to Saragossa to be crowned. But later in his reign before Pere could issue laws, he had to negotiate with the urban patriciate who constituted the ruling class.[31]

Thus, the situation of the king negotiating before his coronation with the nobles in order to ensure the rights of the latter seems quite appropriate for fourteenth-century Aragon. Had Pere allowed the nobles of Barcelona to have their way, this is exactly what would have happened.

It is unlikely, of course, that these negotiations would have lasted a full half-year as R. Isaac would have it, but here once again, he feels constrained by the text of Esther. He has to explain the reference to the 180 days in 1:4. It was simply unacceptable to him that this meant that the king gave a feast that lasted for 180 days as many people think:

> for this would have been superfluous and an act of foolishness, for every seemly and honorable act which a person does to show

> another his stature and honor should not properly be repeated many times, for as people see it more, it loses its spiritual quality and the wonder surrounding it is diminished, and it may in the end lead to boredom and revulsion. (Ibid.)

R. Isaac's own knowledge of contemporary practice seems to be coming into play here. Once again, we call Pere III to witness: "And that day [of Our coronation] and the two following We kept open house to any men who wished to eat, and, according to the scribe *de ració* and others of Our officials, there were some ten thousand persons who ate there on the first day."[32] Even if the figure of ten thousand is exaggerated,[33] we can imagine that Pere entertained quite a large crowd. But the festivities lasted only two or three days, and this would seem to have been decisive for R. Isaac, although he gives other reasons as well.

While we cannot be certain that R. Isaac knew Pere's chronicle, it is certainly possible, since the chronicle was written in the 1380s and R. Isaac's commentary around 1400. What seems indisputable is his familiarity with fourteenth-century Aragonese politics and the influence this knowledge had on his commentary.[34]

THE *AUDIENCIA* AND THE *UNIÓN*

Another commentary whose milieu is definitely fourteenth-century Aragonese is that of Solomon Astruc. At several points in his commentary, Astruc introduces *le'azim* or "vernacular words," not as is usually done, to explain difficult words in the text, but rather to help bring the text to life and make it more accessible to his contemporaries.

Astruc explains the king's consultation with his advisors (1:13) as follows:

> It was his custom not to do anything in his kingdom without his wise men and whatever would be decided when they were in council which is called *audiencia* he would do. Now *audiencia* is two words *audi ciencia*, i.e., to hear understanding in their tongue. (Astruc, 215)

It was the common practice of fourteenth-century rulers to seek out the counsel of their advisors.[35] Among other institutions established in the latter part of the fourteenth century was the *Audiencia*, or Royal

Court of Appeal, headed by the king. Enrique II of Castile published ordinances in 1371 to regularize the composition of the *Audiencia*,[36] and similar developments took place in Aragon, Portugal, and Navarre.[37] It seems likely, then, that the name *audiencia* would have been known to Astruc, who lived in Catalonia, although he may not have been altogether certain as to its function. The description of it that he provides in his commentary would seem to fit the Royal Council more closely.

Astruc uses the word *audiencia* one more time in his commentary, when referring to Mordecai's refusal to bow down to Haman. Mordecai had explained to the king's servants that he was Jewish and protected by the king's law from having to do anything against his faith. The king's servants saw that he was right and told Haman that, if Mordecai took his case before the King's council or the *Audiencia*, he would be vindicated because he was a Jew.[38] Here again, Astruc is equating the Royal Council with the *Audiencia*, or Royal Court of Appeal, although in this case the proper forum for discussing Mordecai's case would actually have been the *Audiencia* and not the Council.

A contemporary institution about which Astruc seems to have been better informed is the *Unión*. In continuing his comment on Haman's plot to destroy the Jews, he says:

> when Haman saw that the members of the Council would support his [Mordecai's] claim and that he would not be able to coerce him and that all the Jews would follow his advice, he decided to destroy the entire people through one act of informing (*malshinut*). He said there is one people—Israel—who have taken counsel together to rebel against him [the king] and to make a union (*yiḥud*) and a conspiracy called *Unión*. (Ibid, 216)

Unión is a word in Aragonese, the only *la'az* that Astruc uses which is not Catalan,[39] and indeed, the *Unión* was a predominantly Aragonese phenomenon. In 1283, the Aragonese nobles, fearful of the growing authority of Pedro III formed the Aragonese *Unión* to counteract royal power and were granted a general privilege which severely limited the Crown's authority over them. In 1301, Jaume II secured the legal condemnation of some leading nobles, and the *Unión* remained dormant from then until 1347, during the reign of Pere III (Pedro IV) of Aragon. When Pere sought to have his eldest daughter Constanza designated as the successor to his throne, the nobles of Aragon, backed by Pere's brother Jaume, who aspired to the throne, revived the *Unión* and openly rebelled against him.

A Valencian *Unión*, with a more popular base, soon arose as well. For a time the unionists had the advantage as civil war spread across Aragon in 1348. But by October 14 of that year, several events had transpired to give Pere the upper hand, and on that day following a meeting of the Aragonese Cortes, Pere formally dissolved the *Unión*, cutting to pieces its privileges and smashing its seal and bulls. On December 10, Valencia surrendered and Pere ordered a similar destruction of the records of the Valencian *Unión*.[40]

The revolt of the Aragonese and Valencian *Uniónes* against Pere III must have been one of the major events in Aragonese history in the fourteenth century, and so it is not surprising that it would have made a profound impression on Astruc's memory. His association of the *Unión* with rebellion and conspiracy is entirely accurate and may reflect popular usage, as does, apparently, his popular etymology of *audiencia* quoted above.

THE TRIAL OF VASHTI

Verses 1:13–15 describe Ahasuerus taking counsel with his advisors:

> Then the king consulted the sages learned in procedure (lit., "the times"). (For it was the royal practice [to turn] to all who were versed in law and precedent. . . .) "What," [he asked] "shall be done, according to law, to Queen Vashti for failing to obey the command of King Ahasuerus conveyed by the eunuchs?"

This passage elicited much comment in the Middle Ages and gave exegetes the opportunity to discuss issues concerning the administration of justice and the judicial system.

The question of the identity of the "wise men who knew the times" (1:13) was the focus of many comments, especially among exegetes in the High Middle Ages. The sages had already made the connection between this phrase and the description in 1 Chr 12:33 of men of Issachar "who had understanding of the times" (*yode'ei binah le-'ittim*) and identified Ahasuerus's advisors as Jews.[41] No medieval exegete accepted this interpretation. However, several northern French exegetes did interpret the phrase in the light of the verse in Chronicles, without making the identification with Issachar. According to Joseph

Kara, "This means he asked the wise men who knew the times, i.e., those who had understanding of the times (1 Chr 12:33); each and every time that an event would occur which required advice, he would ask those that knew how to give advice what to do" (3:88). In the view of another northern French exegete ("A"),[42] the phrase meant "those who knew how to give advice when it was needed" (i.e., at the right time), while a third simply equated the phrase with that in Chronicles.[43] Isaiah of Trani also made the connection between the verses in Esther and Chronicles, but he understood *'ittim* to mean laws.[44] According to him, the advisors in Esther knew the laws of the ancient kings and those in Chronicles knew the laws of the Torah.[45]

Ibn Ezra, in his first commentary, identifies *the wise men who know the times* as astrologers[46] or as historians "that know the times of the ancient kings."[47] Gersonides sees astrology as one of the skills that the king's wise men possessed which enabled them to be skilled advisors:

> These wise men were experts in the law and political philosophy[48] and therefore were able to judge matters properly and along with this they knew the times, i.e., they were well-versed in astrology for in this way they would be guided to decide matters according to the arrangement of the heavenly bodies (*le-fi mah she-ye'ot me-ha-mesuddar me-ha-geramim ha-shemeimiyyim*) and for this reason he said "before all those who know law and judgment."[49]

Several other exegetes understand the phrase in a legal context. Immanuel of Rome simply calls the wise men judges (fol. 187r, col. 1–2). Abraham Ibn Ezra (version B) and Moses Ḥalayo explain that these men knew the laws and statutes which it was proper to apply at various times as the circumstances changed.[50] Joseph Naḥmias explains the phrase as referring to those who know the customs of the times of the ancient kings.[51]

Later medievals who commented on this verse exhibit a very strong interest in procedural matters. They were interested in clarifying exactly whom it was that Ahasuerus would consult in such matters and according to what legal principles Vashti would be tried. Most of these exegetes, with the exception of Isaac Arama, keep their remarks within the framework of Jewish law.

According to Zechariah ben Saruḳ (p. 8b), for example, the reference to "times" (*'ittim*) is crucial because there are times when a man will sin and not deserve a severe punishment and other times when someone else might commit the same sinful act and be punished much more severely. This all depends on the "discretion of the judges" (*shuda' de-dayyanei*).[52] R. Zechariah then quotes the sages of the Talmud who, according to him, said: "A court may, when necessary, impose flagellation and pronounce capital sentences where it is warranted and where it is not warranted by the Torah, *all according to the season and the time* (*ha-kol le-fi ha-'et ve-ha-zeman*)"[53] [emphasis added]. An illustration is to be found in the case of R. Simeon b. Shetaḥ who hanged eighty witches in one day, thereby transgressing two laws—one, that one does not try more than one case in one day, and the second that women are not to be hanged.[54] The purpose of R. Zechariah's comment is to demonstrate that there are occasions when extraordinary circumstances require that the law as it stands be transgressed.[55]

Zechariah ben Saruḳ focuses his attention on the first part of verse 1:13, "the wise men who know the times." For him, the second part, "for this was royal practice [to turn] to all who were versed in law and precedent," merely indicates that it was not the king's custom to try cases in which he was directly involved himself. Other exegetes do comment on this part of the verse. Some, e.g., Immanuel of Rome, Joseph Naḥmias, and Solomon Astruc, make a distinction between *dat* and *din*, explaining the former as custom and the latter as law.

Abraham Saba makes a slightly different distinction which he elaborates in the following passage:

> For this reason [the fact that it was the beginning of his reign] Ahasuerus wished that Vashti be tried (*she-ya'asu din be-Vashti*). Therefore, you will find that he wished that the wise men who know the laws (*dinim*) be present, as well as the officers who know the customs and laws of the state (*she-yode'im be-datot u-ve-nimusei ha-melukhah*). For all kings would institute customs and edicts (*datot ve-taqqanot*) in their kingdoms which pertained to state law (*be-nimusei ha-melukhah*) in addition to the laws recorded in the books of the wise men. (*EKE*, 31–32)

Saba then draws an analogy between this situation and the situation in Jewish law. Aside from the explicit laws written in the Bible and Talmud, there are also "fences" (*seyagim*) and edicts (*taqqanot*) such as those of Ezra and Hillel which were enacted to meet the demands of specific situations at specific times.[56] Similarly, Ahasuerus gathered around him wise men versed in the laws which were written in the law books and officers who were familiar with state law which was created according to the need of the time and the season, i.e., "the wise men who knew the times" (1:13), or perhaps these were the same people, well-versed in both aspects of the law. Ahasuerus wished this case to be dealt with according to conventional law (*ha-dat ha-nimusit*)[57] so that he would be feared forever by all in his kingdom. According to Saba, the seven men mentioned in the following verse were well-versed in conventional law and therefore were the closest to the king, and their advice would take precedence even when it contradicted the law as written in the law books.

Saba then elaborates his interpretation of the word *dat*, meaning custom or convention and shows that it applies throughout the whole Bible. Indeed, he concludes from Dt 33:2 (*mi-yemino 'esh dat lamo*) that two types of Torah were given to Moses at Sinai, one consisting of absolute laws (*dinim*), the other conventional laws (*datot*)—the edicts and fences enacted to meet the specific needs of a community at a specific time.[58]

Saba points out that Ahasuerus in 1:13–14 asked for a verdict based on conventional law (*ke-dat mah la'asot*), since he knew that, strictly speaking, according to the absolute law (*din*), Vashti was not guilty. Since, however, this was the beginning of his reign, the exigencies of the time required that he rule according to conventional law and not according to absolute law. Vashti, as queen and the scion of a royal family, did not deserve such treatment. Nevertheless, since she disobeyed the king, who was a great and powerful man, she had to be punished. But the main consideration seems to be that she defied the king in public, before the officers. Had her defiance taken place in private, she would not have been punished so severely.

Saba also explains Memucan's statement (1:16) in this context. According to his understanding, Memucan who was of lower rank than the other officers, spoke before the others because the king had requested a verdict according to conventional law and not according to absolute law. Memucan felt better able to reply according to convention, since he knew there were greater experts in the law than he. His argument was that since the queen had defied the king openly, her action could not be overlooked, and she had to be punished as severely as possible so that she would serve as an example for all to see. Thus other wives would not be tempted to imitate her actions.

While for Zechariah ben Saruḳ and Abraham Saba, Jewish law in its medieval stage of development provided ample source material for the exegesis of these verses, there is also evidence that at least some of the later exegetes were influenced by non-Jewish sources, especially the discussion of justice in Aristotle's *Ethics* (Book V).[59] Allusions to this discussion can perhaps be found in "Ramah"'s assertion that those who know the times are those who know political philosophy[60] and can judge according to the time and the need of the hour.

Of particular interest is Isaac Arama's treatment of these verses (fol. 145r–v) which reveals a direct and detailed knowledge of the *Ethics*, especially Book V, chapter 10.[61] Arama distinguishes between conventional justice (*ṣedeq nimusi*) and situational justice (*ṣedeq ḥelqi*). The former is formulated in terms that are universal and immutable, while the latter changes according to particular circumstances. According to Arama, kings have in their palaces two types of judges—those who judge according to conventional justice and others above them, trained in logic and common sense, who judge according to situational justice. The function of the latter is that of the equitable man (*ḥasid*).[62] The former are referred to in the text of Esther as "those who are versed in law and precedent" and the latter as "the wise men who knew the times." The king wished to have the opinion of both sets of judges, which is why they are both mentioned in the verse. Indeed, Arama (fol. 145r) says that, according to conventional justice, Vashti would have been exonerated for the reasons mentioned above. But since he was more concerned with what the particular situation required, as indicated by his first approaching the "wise men who knew the times," he followed their opinion. This discussion owes much to Aristotle, who states:

> The explanation of this is that all law is universal and there are some things about which it is not possible to pronounce general terms; therefore, in cases where it is necessary to make a general pronouncement but impossible to do so rightly, the law takes account of the majority of cases, though not unaware that in this way errors are made. . . . So when the law states a general rule and a case arises under this that is exceptional, then it is right, where the legislator owing to the generality of his language has erred in not covering that case, to correct the omission by a ruling such as the legislator himself would have given if he had been present there, and as he would have enacted if he had been aware of the circumstances.[63]

According to Aristotle, the principle of equity serves to rectify the necessary defects in general laws when they come to be applied to specific cases. The rectification is made by a judge applying the law to a specific case, but it is made on the assumption that the legislator would have done the same had he been called upon to decide the case. Arama's two types of judges—those dealing in general principles and those deciding on specific cases—correspond to Aristotle's "legislators" and "adjudicators" or "judges."

However, we cannot draw too close an analogy between Arama and Aristotle because Arama apparently felt constrained by the biblical text to make a distinction that Aristotle did not make. For the functions of legislator and judge are quite separate, and it is the function of the judge to apply the laws set down by the legislator. In most cases, the law can be applied as it is without alteration, but there are some cases that involve exceptional circumstances and for which the principle of equity must be applied. But always, the one making the decisions is the judge, not the legislator who could also be called the legal theorist. Therefore, Arama's distinction between two types of judges—those who follow the general principles laid down by the legislators and those who deal with the exceptional cases according to the principle of equity—is not to be found in Aristotle and would seem to derive from his need to explain the two terms for advisors that appear in 1:13.[64]

Arama's Memucan continues the discussion of Vashti's case in 1:16. According to him, one does not even need to argue this case on the basis of situational justice, because in a case such as this, in which the transgression took place in public and would be publicized throughout the land, only adequate, universally applicable arguments (*ṭa'anot maspiqot u-mefursamot*), not particular specialized arguments (*ṭa'anot ḥelqiyyot peraṭiyyot*), can be used. This is because the gravity of the sin is known to all and the mitigating arguments are known only to the judges and not to the public. An analogous case would be that of a son smiting his father in public. Although he may have been justified in doing so and there may have been mitigating circumstances in the matter, the masses would not be aware of this and would only know that this person smote his father and was spared punishment. Therefore, for the welfare of society and in the interests of preserving the social order, he must be punished. The same argument applies to Vashti. In order to preserve the social order, Vashti must be punished. Otherwise, there would be a danger of undermining the authority of the king, and the result would be anarchy. The danger is articulated by

Memucan (1:16): "Queen Vashti has committed an offense not only against Your Majesty but also against all the officials and against all the peoples in all the provinces of King Ahasuerus." Therefore, exonerating her or treating her with leniency would constitute a danger to the common good and to the social order of the kingdom. Regardless of whether or not she had justice on her side, she must be punished because weightier considerations overrule the pursuit of absolute "abstract" justice.

Vashti was to be punished severely, according to Arama, because in committing her act in public she had brought shame and disgrace upon the king and his officers, thereby threatening to undermine the social order. It was, then, the circumstances under which Vashti committed her act and not so much the act itself which determined the severity of her punishment.[65] According to Arama's general law, Vashti should have been vindicated or, at most, suffered a light punishment. But, according to the particular law, she had to be punished severely for the good of the community as a whole and in the interests of maintaining the general social order. Thus, Saba and Arama come to the same conclusion following quite separate paths. While Saba uses only Jewish sources, Arama combines ideas from both Jewish and Aristotelian sources.

An interesting parallel to Arama's point is found in the fourteenth-century *Tractatus de legibus*, attributed to Durandus of St. Pourçain.[66] The author of the treatise distinguished between natural law and human or civil law. Disagreeing with Thomas Aquinas, who claimed that human law was derived from natural law, the author states that: "Civil law does not take nature (*natura rei*) as the foundation but rather public expediency, so that there public expediency occurs as the whole cause of establishing its conclusions."[67] As an example of this distinction, the author first refers to a point of penal practice. According to natural law, a criminal should be punished, but it does not specify the precise punishment. The specification of the punishment belongs to human law, and is to be determined solely on the basis of public expediency. "Human law measured punishment according to public expediency, divine law according to justice."[68]

This distinction between natural, or divine, law and public expediency, although not equivalent to Arama's distinction between conventional and situational justice, does show how legal theorists were expanding and adapting Aristotelian categories in the late Middle Ages. This is not to suggest, of course, that Arama was directly influenced by the *Tractatus de legibus* but rather to point out that similar distinctions were being made in the legal discussions of both Jewish and Christian legists of the late Middle Ages and that Jewish scholars such as Isaac Arama were familiar with intellectual currents and trends in the Christian world and drew from the same sources available to their Christian neighbors.

CONCLUSION

We have seen in this chapter how rooted the Jews were in their environment and how they did not hesitate to draw on their own experiences and first-hand knowledge in order to shed light on events that took place in another country 1500 years previously.

The treatment of the trial of Vashti in a medieval context is but one illustration of the positive influence that contacts with Gentiles had on the development of Jewish thought in various areas of scholarship. Unfortunately, the relations between Jews and Gentiles were not always so positive and fruitful and for the exegetes of Esther, at least, the negative far outweighed the positive. This will be clear from our discussion of Jewish-Gentile relations and antisemitism as they are reflected in the commentaries.

6

JEWISH-GENTILE RELATIONS AND JEWISH ATTITUDES TO GENTILES AS REFLECTED IN THE COMMENTARIES

The Book of Esther, as has been noted recently, presents a "life-style for the Diaspora."[1] One of the realities of Diaspora existence is the necessity for Jews to interact with the rulers and citizens of the various countries of their residence. While relations could be cordial, they were often hostile, and hardly a generation passed without a Jewish community somewhere being persecuted or threatened with expulsion. Indeed, the salvation described in the Book of Esther served as a paradigm for many Jewish communities in the Middle Ages who celebrated individual Purim holidays to commemorate the deliverance of their communities from serious threats to their existence.[2]

It is not surprising, then, that the events related in the Book of Esther struck many a responsive chord in the minds and hearts of our exegetes, and we find that their commentaries serve as sounding boards for the expression of opinions pertaining to the position of the Jews in the Gentile community, relations between Jews and Gentiles at court, Jewish attitudes to Gentiles and Jewish perceptions of their image in the eyes of the Gentiles.

ESTHER AND AHASUERUS: A MIXED MARRIAGE

One of the most troublesome features of the Esther story is the very fact that a Jewish woman married a Gentile, even if he was a king. The idea of a Jewish woman letting herself be taken, apparently without protest, into the harem of a Gentile king did not sit well with the sages or with many of our medieval exegetes.

The sages were the first to express their discomfort with Esther's role as Ahasuerus's queen, especially with the idea of her having sexual relations with the king. They insisted that she never did so willingly and thus retained her spiritual integrity.[3] This motif is given its most extreme expression in the *Zohar*, the thirteenth-century mystical work, which states that God sent down a female spirit in the guise of Esther to take her place with the king and that she never lived with Ahasuerus as his wife.[4]

Ibn Ezra (version B, *VA*, 20–21) points out that the passive form of the verb *va-tillaqaḥ* ("she was taken") indicates that she was taken against her will. Another imaginative expression of this uneasiness is the comment attributed to Rabbi Judah the Pious. He explains that Mordecai was sitting at the king's gate (verse 2:19) waiting for an opportunity to snatch Esther away from the king's palace and take her off to a safe place.[5] This is exactly what Abraham Saba, with the picture of hundreds of Jewish martyrs to the faith still fresh in his memory, faulted Mordecai for not doing. Saba could not help but wonder why Esther did not lay down her life for her faith[6] and why Mordecai did not do a better job of protecting her. His personal anguish and discomfort is evident as he asks:

> Now when Mordecai heard the king's herald announcing that whoever had a daughter or a sister should bring her to the king to have intercourse with an uncircumcised heathen, why did he not risk his life to take her to some deserted place to hide until the danger would pass or even to take her to another kingdom. And if he could do neither of these things, have we not seen with our

> own eyes during the expulsion from Portugal, when sons and daughters were taken by force and converted, that Jews strangled and slaughtered themselves and their wives? Especially during the first decree, which was directed only against the children, they would take their sons and daughters and fling them into pits to kill them or would strangle or slaughter them rather than see them committing idolatry. So why did Mordecai not do one of these things that the simplest Jews in Portugal did? He should have been killed rather than submit to such an act. . . . And why did he wait till they took her away? . . . This was a very strange thing. Why did Mordecai not keep righteous Esther from idol worship? Why was he not more careful? Where was his righteousness, his piety, and his valor? His heart was like a lion's and yet he surrendered to the enemy all that was dear to him. She too should by right have tried to commit suicide before allowing herself to have intercourse with him.[7]

After posing the question with so much emotion and at such great length, Saba finally bows to tradition by exonerating Mordecai and Esther. He himself does not seem completely convinced by his explanation that events moved so quickly that they did not have a chance to act. This ambivalent treatment suggests that he may not have been satisfied with the traditional answer to this problem, although out of respect for tradition he could not come out and say this openly. Furthermore, we may see reflected here Saba's anguish at his own personal catastrophe and at his own inability to save his family from forced conversion. As he describes in his account of his experiences in Portugal:

> Afterwards they gathered some ten thousand Jews into a courtyard and they forced them and enticed them to convert, and after four days no more than forty men or women were left. In the end they stripped me of my skin, and my sons and daughters and all that I owned remained there, and nothing was left me except my body.[8]

It would seem that, in his case as well, events transpired so quickly that he was unable to protect his children from their captors, and his harsh criticism of Mordecai may have been directed equally against himself.

But Saba's misgivings are the exception, and the general feeling among the exegetes is that Esther was placed in her royal position by an act of divine providence. So, according to Rashi (to 2:11) "Mordecai said that the only justification for this righteous woman to be taken to sleep with Ahasuerus was that she would eventually rise up to save Israel. Therefore, he used to keep coming back in order to learn what would happen to her in the end."

Closely related to this issue is the question of why Mordecai commanded Esther to conceal her identity. This is tied in with the traditional view that Esther was a descendant of King Saul and was thus of royal lineage and suited to be queen.

Rashi explains Mordecai's injunction to Esther not to reveal her origins as a strategy on his part to disqualify Esther for the monarchy:

> *not to make it known* (2:10). So that they will say she is of a despised family and will send her away. For if they knew that she was of King Saul's family they would keep her.

Rabbi Eleazar of Worms expressed the concern that if the king found out that Esther was Jewish he would order his officers to marry Jewish women as well. Apparently, in his view, one Jewess married to a Gentile was trouble enough.[9] His teacher, R. Judah the Pious, in keeping with his view, mentioned above, that Mordecai was waiting to snatch Esther away to safety, argued that if Ahasuerus knew that Esther was Jewish when Mordecai abducted her, he would keep all the Jews hostage until she was returned.[10]

These views contrast with those of other northern French exegetes. Joseph Kara (3:89), for instance, sensitive to anti-Jewish feeling among Gentiles, comments that if her origins were known and the king then wanted to make her queen, his officers and servants would not let him since all the nations hate Israel (2:10). The anonymous exegete, "A", expresses a similar opinion, pointing out that since Esther was so beautiful the king would certainly not refrain from sleeping with her. Then, if it became known that she was an Israelite, the king's officers would not let him take her as queen and she would find herself deflowered and shamed in public (2:10).[11]

Ibn Ezra sees the main motivation behind Mordecai's telling Esther to conceal her family's and people's identity the desire to enable her to continue her religious observance in secret.[12]

> In my opinion, the real reason that Mordecai did this was to enable Esther to observe God's Torah in secret so that she would

> not eat non-kosher meat (*nevelot*) and would observe the Sabbath without the servants' knowledge. For if the matter became known, the king might force her to transgress or even kill her since she was taken against her will. (2:10A)

Here for the first time in the Middle Ages, Esther is portrayed as a crypto-Jew forced to live openly as a Gentile while steadfastly maintaining her religious practices in secret. True, in this case Esther's crypto-Judaism was not imposed on her for religious reasons, but the fear is expressed by Ibn Ezra that, were her religion to be revealed, it would become an issue, and she would be forced to transgress it.[13] It is not surprising that in subsequent generations Esther and the Fast of Esther had a tremendous appeal for the Conversos in Spain and Portugal. Conversos could readily identify with Esther who would not reveal her race or her birth yet remained steadfast in the religion of her forefathers while living in alien surroundings.[14] The Fast of Esther took on an importance second to none in the Converso religious calendar being observed on the full moon of February and some Conversos even kept it as a three-day fast, a practice unknown to Rabbinic Judaism.[15]

Concerning the question of Esther's descent from King Saul,[16] mixed feelings are expressed in the commentaries. On the one hand, there is pride in Esther's royal descent and in her suitability, by lineage, to be queen, and on the other hand, a great reluctance to see her queen to a Gentile king regardless of her suitability for the position. Rashi is the only medieval who seems to take seriously Esther's alleged descent from King Saul and to think that knowledge of this fact would make a favorable impression on the king.[17]

In his second commentary, Ibn Ezra, in what could be a reaction to Rashi's statement, takes a more sober view of the situation and analyzes the king's motives quite differently:

> In my opinion, all the Jews were contemptible (*nivzim*) in the eyes of the throne as can be seen from Belshazzar's statement to Daniel calling him "one of the exiles of Judah" (Dn 5:13). It seems to me that Mordecai realized that the king was not interested in noble birth, but only in a beautiful woman regardless of her country of origin. He knew that Esther was very beautiful and feared that the king would find no one like her, and if she were to refuse to eat the king's food he would force her. But if she were queen she would be able to hide herself. (*VA*, 21; to 2:10)

According to this view, it mattered little what Esther's lineage was. Her beauty was what attracted the king's attention. If the king knew that she was Jewish, he might force her to transgress her religion. If she managed to conceal her origins till she became queen, then she would be able to keep her religious practices in secret.

For Rashi's northern French colleagues, Joseph Kara (3:89) and "A" (p. 27), Esther's royal descent was of little import. More significant for them was the very fact of her Jewishness which both felt would prevent her from becoming queen if it became known. Immanuel of Rome (fol. 192v) also felt that if the fact of her Jewish descent became known she would be reviled by the king and his officers.[18] Shemariah of Crete (fol. 73r) was concerned that, if she were known to be Jewish, Esther would be subject to scorn and derision at the hands of other women in the king's harem.

According to Isaac b. Joseph ha-Kohen (fol. 58v–59r), Mordecai was conscious of Israel's downtrodden state and fearful that the enemies that the Jews had in court, especially Haman's sons and other Amalekites who were in the king's favor, could easily prevent Esther from becoming queen if they wished to do so. Even after she became queen, he still feared for her safety and so continued to forbid her to reveal her origins.

Therefore, for many medieval Jewish exegetes the romantic view of Esther as a woman of royal descent who was worthy of being queen was overshadowed by the realities of medieval life in which Jews were despised and in which being Jewish was often a hindrance rather than an aid to one's advancement in court circles.[19]

In general, one sees in commentaries written in Spain, where Jews were often favored in court circles and enjoyed special privileges, less reluctance to entertain the thought of a Jewish woman being queen to a Gentile king than one does among the exegetes of northern France whose experiences with the temporal powers were neither as intimate nor as positive.

JEWS AND THEIR GENTILE NEIGHBORS—THE HUMAN DIMENSION

On occasion, it is possible to detect glimpses of the attitudes Jews had toward their Christian neighbors and of the expectations they had from the relations between the two communities. One verse that is relevant to this issue is 3:15, "But the city of Shushan was dumbfounded." The question is who is included in this statement. Were only the Jews, or were the Gentile neighbors of the Jews also disturbed by the promulgation of this wicked decree? Most exegetes understand the verse as referring only to the Jews.[20]

For some, such as Ibn Ezra, the interpretation of the verse is tied in with the geography of the situation. According to Ibn Ezra, the Jews lived in the city of Susa while the king's palace called *Shushan ha-birah* or "Susa the capital" was located in the city of Elam.[21] In this case, the phrase in 3:15 can refer only to the Jews since they were the only ones living there.

Others, however, are not exegetically constrained in this way and can consider the possibility that Gentiles might have shared in the anxiety of the Jews. Thus Gersonides (p. 41) comments that the Jews were perplexed and possibly the Gentiles as well. Immanuel of Rome (fol. 199r) says the text refers to the Jews and their admirers (*'ohaveihem*), while Joseph Ḥayyun (fol. 77v) suggests that there were many Gentiles who were also perplexed by and uncomfortable with the edict because of the great injustice involved.

Here again, we may see reflected the exegetes' personal attitudes to non-Jews. If an exegete had fairly friendly and civil relations with non-Jews, he might more easily entertain the thought that non-Jews would be distressed at his misfortune than if he had suffered a great deal from Gentiles or had had very little contact with them.

THE SECOND SET OF LETTERS AND THE SLAUGHTER OF THE ENEMIES OF THE JEWS

The dénouement of the Esther story (chapters 8 to 10) tells of Mordecai's rise in fortune and of the discomfiture of the Jews' enemies. The triumph of the Jews over their enemies as described in the Esther story must have seemed particularly satisfying to the Jews in the Middle Ages who suffered countless persecutions, massacres, and expulsions throughout their history and only very rarely were capable of putting up even the barest resistance. Reading the scroll not only filled them with pride at the glories of their ancestors in days gone by but must have given them hope for the future when Jews would once again be independent and able to defend themselves.

It is quite remarkable, then, that this triumphalist mood is not universal and one finds a significant number of exegetes questioning the necessity for sending out the second set of letters allowing the Jews to kill their enemies. Abraham Ibn Ezra is the first to raise the issue, asking: "Why did Mordecai write that the Jews should kill their enemies? Would it not be enough for him and for them that they [the Jews] should escape?" (first commentary, to 8:8). Ibn Ezra's reply is that Mordecai really had no choice since, according to Persian law, the king's decree was irrevocable. Mordecai's only recourse was to resort to subterfuge and to send out a second set of letters which would in effect undermine the first set.

> This is what Mordecai had to write: "Let it be known that the king ordered Haman, his vizier, to write an edict in the name of the king to be sealed with the king's ring which stated that the Jews should kill their enemies on the thirteenth day of Adar. And behold Haman wrote the opposite, that the Jews should be killed on that day. Now when his evil plot was revealed to the king he had him hanged on a gallows for having tried to harm the Jews against the king's will." . . . The surest proof [that this is true] is that Haman was hanged and the king ordered that new letters be written and sealed with his ring and these corresponded with his original wishes. (Ibid.)

So, according to Ibn Ezra, the only way for Mordecai to save the Jews from the king's first edict was to declare it a forgery, perpetrated by Haman unbeknownst to the king. In this way, Haman appears as the only villain of the piece and Ahasuerus's name is protected. Mordecai's image is also enhanced, as he is portrayed as the clever adviser who enables the king to emerge relatively unscathed from a potentially embarrassing situation. Furthermore, this solution assures that the integrity of the laws of Persia and Media is protected, since the original decree that Ahasuerus had wished to promulgate was in the end enacted. This is a very important point for Ibn Ezra, one which he spells out quite clearly in his second commentary: "It is inconceivable that the Jews could be saved if the king's decree were not carried out" (*VA*, 31). This comment of Ibn Ezra's, as we shall see, was to have greater repercussions in subsequent generations than perhaps any other in his commentary.

Immanuel of Rome is the next exegete to take up the question, asking if it would not have sufficed for Mordecai to write that the Jews not be killed. In his answer to this question, Immanuel approaches the problem from a different perspective. According to Ibn Ezra,

Mordecai's sole aim was to circumvent the Persian law which stated that "an edict written in the name of the king and sealed with the king's ring may not be revoked" (8:8). The only way to save the people therefore would be to prove that the first edict sent out by Haman was a forgery. Immanuel, on the other hand, seems more concerned with protecting the reputation of Persian and Median law, and portrays Mordecai as a loyal subject having the interests of his king uppermost in his thoughts.

> For Mordecai thought: If we write that the Jews not be killed this would disgrace and belittle the laws of Persia and Media because "an edict written in the name of the king and sealed with the king's ring may not be revoked" (8:8). Therefore, there was no choice but to write that the first letters that Haman dictated and sealed with the king's ring were by the king's order, but that Haman had forged these letters. For the king had ordered that the Jews kill their enemies as they wished. He did this out of love for his wife who was of the Jewish people and out of love for Mordecai who had revealed the plot of Bigthan and Teresh. Now Haman like a slanderer (*pasul*) and an informer (*masor*) wrote the opposite to what the king had intended, that is, that the Jews be killed. Therefore, the king commanded that he be hanged. This is the way that Mordecai considered to be more proper for, if not for the irrevocability of Persian laws, Mordecai would not have contemplated that the Jews should kill their enemies. (fol. 208r)

Immanuel elaborates on Ibn Ezra's comment and adds several new nuances to it. He stresses much more strongly Mordecai's reluctance to write those letters and his feeling that this was the only way that he could save his people. He also adds reasons for the king's willingness to allow the Jews to kill their enemies—his love for his wife Esther and for his faithful servant Mordecai who had saved his life. Apparently, Immanuel assumes that people who received the letters would not have known that Esther had not revealed her people or her family's identity to the king.

Joseph ibn Kaspi states that the main purpose of his commentary is to deal with this very question. Kaspi seeks to refute Ibn Ezra's interpretation on logical grounds. If, he argues, we have to beware of forgery, the whole force of the law that a king's edict cannot be revoked is vitiated. A king can argue at any time that a particular edict was forged and for that reason cancel it. Furthermore, how could the king compromise himself by lying, especially when everyone at court knew that the king had allowed Haman to send out his edict? Rather, the king's law must stand under any circumstances, and this applies to forgeries as well. The king, then, must carefully scrutinize anyone to whom he wishes to give his ring.

Kaspi (*GK*, 31–32), voicing a frequent criticism of his predecessors, attributes their failure to understand this passage to their lack of training in logic or at least to their failure to apply it to their exegesis. He then explains the principle of contradiction according to which two statements in order to be contradictory must have subjects and predicates identical in all respects and must differ only in that one is the negation of the other. If both statements are positive, they can still contradict each other if the predicates are mutually exclusive. But if neither of these conditions is fulfilled, the statements are not contradictory.

Kaspi then launches into a detailed analysis of the two verses in question (3:13, 8:10) to see whether they really do contradict each other. Needless to say, he finds many differences between the two decrees, the principal one being that they are directed to two different groups of people, the first one to the Gentiles, the second to the Jews. Therefore, there is no contradiction between the two decrees, for certainly the king can justifiably direct one decree to one group of subjects and another decree to a second group.

Kaspi makes the additional point that the first decree gave the Gentiles permission to kill the Jews, but it did not command them absolutely to do so. If the Jews were to defend themselves and prevent the Gentiles from killing them, the king's decree would still have been obeyed at least in spirit. Kaspi points out that the first letters ordered the Gentiles to kill the Jews but did not order the Jews to bare their necks to the sword and submit without a fight.

It seems possible to detect in Kaspi's argument an attempt to justify the actions taken that led to the slaughter of the Jews' enemies. Whatever his motivation, he does his best to defend the Jewish position and put the Jews in the best light possible. Here, for example, is how Kaspi imagines Ahasuerus exhorting the Jews:

> I command you to gather together and assemble in the towns on the appointed day to defend yourselves. And when the enemy, the forces of the many peoples, attack you as I commanded them to

> do on that day and lay siege to your city in order to trap you and kill you, rise up if you are able and turn the tables against these pursuers and avenge yourselves of those enemies who are coming against you. (*GK*, 34–35)

The Jews here are definitely the underdogs, besieged by forces greatly outnumbering them and acting purely in self-defense, in obedience to Ahasuerus's orders. The odds were against them, and Ahasuerus was not really doing anything to help them. He seems to be rather like a spectator at a gladiatorial contest or a tournament eagerly waiting to see if the underdog can muster the strength to turn the tables on his superior opponent.

Kaspi stresses that Mordecai chose the same day in the second letters as was mentioned in the first because he did not want the Jews to initiate the fighting even on the appointed day. Since the Jews were acting purely in self-defense it would not make sense to move the date ahead, and if it were postponed to a later date, then the Jews would be killed. To stress the Jews' defensive position even more, Kaspi states that if the Jews were not attacked on that day and if someone from their ranks would have killed a Gentile, he would have been liable to the death penalty. He even goes so far as to offer a new interpretation of the word "to avenge oneself" (*le-hinnaqem*, 8:13) so that it would fit in better with his general thesis (ibid., 35).[22]

Kaspi is one of the few exegetes to try to trace the course of events during the year between the time Haman's letters were sent out and the arrival of the appointed time for the slaughter. According to his reckoning, the first letters were sent out in Nisan (April) and the second ones in Sivan (June), two months later. Since the second letters were sent with swifter couriers both sets of letters probably reached the outlying areas by Tishri (September). When the letters reached the Jews, there was great rejoicing among them, while among the non-Jews there was fear and trembling for the next five months. Kaspi describes in detail the state of fear that the Gentiles were in all that winter as they waited for the appointed day and as Mordecai's reputation increased steadily. One would have expected that by the thirteenth of Adar the Gentiles would have been afraid to come near the Jews let alone think of doing them any harm. But this was not the case, for when the day did come, God hardened the hearts of the wicked of the Gentiles who, despite their fears, decided to attack the Jews who had gathered in the cities, in a desperate attempt to defeat them. But this was not God's will, and the Jews emerged victorious with God's help.[23]

Kaspi's point seems to be that the Jews could hardly be accused of ruthlessness or cruelty in dealing with their enemies. Had they left the Jews alone no blood would have been shed. It was their own perversity or (perhaps, more correctly) God's desire to punish them that caused them to attack the Jews and led to their massacre.[24]

Like Kaspi, Abraham Saba (*EKE*, 87) stresses that permission was given to the Jews only to defend themselves. He rejects Ibn Ezra's theory that Mordecai wrote that the first letters were a forgery and that the new letters ordered that the Jews should kill their enemies. It just did not make sense to him (*'eino mityashev 'al ha-lev*) that the king would command that the Jews should kill their enemies. Apparently, the idea of a king commanding Jews to kill Gentiles was totally unthinkable for Saba. He could imagine that the king would wish to protect his Jews but that he would allow them to attack Gentiles was inconceivable.

Several exegetes attempt to put the slaughter of the enemies in a more favorable light by identifying the enemies of the Jews with the Amalekites, their traditional foes. The first to do this is Gersonides, who explains that the Amalekites were still a serious threat to the existence of the Jewish people at that time.

> It is worthwhile for you to know that it is quite clear from here that the first letters that Haman sent in the king's name did not command that the Jews be destroyed, killed, wiped out, and looted, but only gave permission to their enemies who desired their death to destroy them and wipe them out. Now, it seems to me that Israel's enemies were all descendants of Amalek, who had been attempting to destroy Israel from the very beginning as is mentioned in the Torah. When they found Israel in a state of degradation, they attempted to destroy her. Since the desire of Amalek to destroy Israel was revealed to God, he therefore commanded in the Torah that the memory of Amalek be wiped out. Were it not for His providence, may He be blessed, Amalek would already have emerged victorious as we explained at the end of the portion *When Pharaoh let* [*Be-shalaḥ*] (Ex 17:8–16). It seems that our father Jacob prophesied about this war when he said concerning Benjamin, "in the morning he consumes the foe, and in the evening he divides the spoil" (Gn 49:27). The morning was

> Saul's war with Amalek, for that was the beginning of Israel's kingdom; and the evening was in the days of Mordecai when twilight and darkness fell on Israel's kingdom. (p. 42b)

Gersonides here seems to have based his comment on the following midrash:

> The patriarch Jacob also hinted at all this in the blessing of the tribes, as is written, "Benjamin is a ravenous wolf; in the morning he consumes the foe" (Gn 49:27); this refers to Saul who was the morning of Israel, being the first of the kings and who was from the tribe of Benjamin and smote Amalek and looted all their possessions; "and in the evening he divides the spoil" (ibid.), this refers to Mordecai and Esther who championed Israel in their exile which is like the shadows of the evening and divided the spoils of Haman who is compared to a wolf. For God raised him [i.e., Mordecai] up to oppose the wolf, namely the kings of Media and Persia who are compared to a wolf, as it is written, "and behold another beast, a second, like a wolf" (Dn 7:5).[25]

The parallel between this passage and Gersonides' comment is clear. But the latter has taken the analogy one step further. For him, the spoil at evening is neither Haman, nor the kings of Media and Persia, but the tribe of Amalek itself. Thus, it is not only a remnant of the perennial enemy of the Israelites that has returned to hound them but that enemy in full force.[26]

Gersonides' perception of the Amalekites as the sole enemies of the Jews also allows him to explain how Ahasuerus could have permitted the Jews to kill their enemies so freely.[27] The extra day requested in order to deal with the enemies in Susa is also explained by Gersonides with reference to the Amalekites. In his view, the heaviest concentration of Amalekites, including their leaders—presumably, the house of Haman—was in Susa, and so more time was needed in order to destroy their forces there.[28]

Gersonides' introduction of the people Amalek into the Esther story can be seen at least in part as an attempt to remove some of the opprobrium associated with the slaughter of the enemies of the Jews. In this view, the Jews were not killing indiscriminately among all the nations of the kingdom but were dealing with one specific age-old enemy with whom they were locked in continuous battle. Seen in this light, the final slaughter does not seem so objectionable.

Isaac ben Joseph ha-Kohen echoes this view of Gersonides, claiming that only Amalek opposed the Jews and desired their destruction and that no Gentile not of the seed of Amalek was killed in the skirmishes between the Jews and their enemies.[29] But it is Abraham Saba who gives this view the fullest expression and puts it into a broader theological context. Saba stresses that the only enemies the Jews had were the Amalekites[30] and that these people were universally hated. So, when the day of revenge came, no one supported them and the Jews could do with them what they pleased.[31]

Joseph Ḥayyun takes a much more rational approach to the issue. He cannot accept the view that all the Jews' enemies were Amalekites because the latter were not in exile and scattered as the Jews were. Rather the enemies were those

> that made public their desire and eagerness for the arrival of the day when they could take revenge on the Jews just as there are today in the cities in which we live in this exile certain Gentiles who hate us very much and we know who they are and there are many others who love us and would not speak wicked or hateful things against us.[32]

Ḥayyun's statement is significant for it reflects a climate of relative tolerance and mutual respect between Jews and Christians, which was characteristic of the situation in mid–fifteenth-century Portugal. Certainly, the Jews had enemies, but these were few (*meyuḥadim*) and easily identifiable, while the friends of the Jews were very numerous (*rabbim me'od*).[33]

Ḥayyun is also troubled by the extent of the Jews' massacre of their enemies, and he admits that the Jews exceeded the mandate given to them by the king in the second set of letters which Mordecai sent out. According to these letters, the Jews had permission only to defend themselves ("to assemble and fight for their lives," 8:11) and in so doing to destroy their enemies. But the Jews destroyed their enemies even though they met no opposition (9:2). They justified their more active role in seeking out and destroying their enemies through a careful, if somewhat forced, exegesis of the king's letter. According to their understanding, the king allowed them two things—first to gather and defend themselves, second to destroy, to slay, and to annihilate any armed force of any people or province that were their enemies,[34] i.e., those that made it known in public that they were their enemies and sought their destruction. Since, says Ḥayyun, there was some possibility of interpreting the letters in this way, therefore, they could justify the actions they took. For, he says, "It would have been a very strange thing for them to shed innocent blood."

Ḥayyun seems to be the exegete most disturbed by the slaughter, and his defense of it is rather weak in comparison to the others. Even Isaac Arama (fol. 161r), who also recognizes that the Jews were only given permission to defend themselves, justifies their action by explaining that when the appointed day arrived, the Gentiles followed the first set of letters and attacked the Jews, while the Jews followed the second set and defended themselves. This position is similar to that of Kaspi. It does not, however, seem defensible on strictly exegetical grounds, since the text does not mention that the Jews were attacked.

So, by and large, the exegetes, through various strategies, do their best to justify the actions of the Jews described in the Book of Esther. No one condemns the action outright, but several display manifest discomfort with the whole incident and try to portray the sequence of events in a way which puts the Jews' behavior in a more favorable light. Since their commentaries were written in countries in which the Jews were an insecure minority which had very little temporal power, their attempts to deal with this embarrassing text are not unreasonable and may reflect their uneasiness with a situation in which the Jews suddenly found themselves in control and able to take revenge on their enemies. As much as they may have relished the thought of revenge, the realities of their own situations made them temper their instincts and seek out ways to diminish the negative reactions that the telling of the incident might provoke among their Gentile hosts.[35]

EXPLICIT REFERENCES TO CHRISTIANS AND MOSLEMS IN THE COMMENTARIES

Direct references to Christians and Moslems are limited to two late fifteenth-century commentaries: those of Zechariah ben Saruḳ and Abraham Saba. In the introduction to his commentary, Zechariah in an autobiographical aside laments his misfortune:

> I used to teach the Torah in the most important communities in Spain [i.e., Castile] and Aragon. I left my home, abandoned my

> inheritance and came without money or [personal] worth to the land of Ishmael, a nation whose language I do not understand, "a ruthless nation that will show the old no regard and the young no mercy" (Dt 28:50). (p. 3a)

Although Zechariah is bitter about his present misfortune, he blames no one for it.[36] But he does have a very low opinion of the Moslems in the country (Algeria) in which he has settled. He is frustrated because he does not understand their language and considers them rather crude and uncivilized.

Abraham Saba also has very little good to say about the Moslems, but the Christians fare even worse in his opinion. In discussing the relative faults of Ahasuerus and Haman, Saba attributes the characteristics of each to their racial origins:

> All this can be attributed to the fact that Ahasuerus originated from Persia and Media, whose people were Ishmaelites, lacking in wisdom and science, counsel and speech and were a people unskilled in speaking (*ṭeme' sefatayim*). But Haman was a crafty villain from the family of Edom, possessors of wisdom and science. For Edom was clever in every type of wisdom as it is written: "I will make the wise vanish from Edom" (Ob 8), like the wicked Esau, father of Edom, who was a skilled huntsman, clever in deception and unlike Jacob who was a simple person. Similarly, Haman was a slanderer who knew how to present his arguments properly and forcefully with boasting tongue and flattering lips to follow counsel. This also came to him from Esau whose tongue was schooled in speaking clearly and smoothly in order to mislead his father and deceive him with his utterances. . . . Similarly, Haman would stalk Ahasuerus and seduce him with his carefully ordered speeches and smooth utterances which were softer than oil.[37]

This vivid comparison between Ishmaelites and Edomites must have been based on Saba's personal experiences with Moslems and Christians. Being exiled from a Christian country to a Moslem one whose language and culture were so completely different from those he was accustomed to must have had a traumatic effect on Saba. Apparently, he did not develop a very favorable impression of his Moslem hosts and considered them uncultured and unsophisticated in comparison with the Christians in Spain. This impression apparently influenced his description of Ishmaelite and Edomite characteristics in his Esther commentary.[38] As we just mentioned above, Saba's contemporary Zechariah ben Saruḳ, who was also exiled to North Africa, had a similarly negative impression of the inhabitants of his new host country. However, it should be noted that in Saba's eyes, the Ishmaelites, while slow-witted and uncultured, were not totally malevolent. The Christians or Edomites, on the other hand, were a clever people, skilled in all areas of scientific and intellectual endeavor and possessing great powers of speech and expression. But intelligence and morality are not linked of necessity, and the Edomites put their natural gifts to ill use. Because of their cleverness and smooth tongues, they were better equipped to carry out their evil designs and to do so craftily and deceptively.

Saba here seems to be giving voice to a distrust of intellectual sophistication and urbanity. Although he expresses considerable disdain for Ahasuerus, at this point, he does not put him in the same class as the thoroughly wicked, smooth-talking, and clever Haman. Similarly, though the Moslems are perhaps more vulgar and uncouth than the Christians, they would seem to be preferred as hosts to their intellectually superior and culturally more sophisticated neighbors.[39]

Saba continues this comparison between the two oppressors of the Jews in the following passage, which is based on Ps 120:

> [It is] as if two Jews in exile met each other and each one tells what befell him in his particular exile. One tells of the evil deeds that the Edomites committed against him and the other tells what the Ishmaelites did to him. Each one thinks his troubles are so great that he desires to be in the exile of the other and suffer what the other suffered. The man living under the exile of Edom says: "O Lord, save me from treacherous lips, from a deceitful tongue" (v. 2). This is an allusion to Edom who has power in his tongue to debase and scorn every living thing with his well-ordered speech and smooth talk . . . so that in their wisdom they commit every imaginable evil to Israel except kill them or do them bodily harm as the Ishmaelites do. His counterpart who came from the Ishmaelite exile replies to him, "What are you complaining about? What can you profit, what can you gain, O deceitful tongue?" (v. 3), i.e., what harm can they do to you with a deceitful tongue? If they do not hit you or kill you, what do you care about words

aimed at you, even if they be like "a warrior's sharp arrows, with hot coals of broom-wood" (v. 4). None of this is as bad as the exile of Ishmael. I have a right to complain since I have been under Ishmaelite exile. I have a right to mourn and cry "Woe, woe." This is referred to in the verse "Woe is me, that I live with Meshech" (v. 5). Another way of interpreting "a warrior's sharp arrows" is to explain it as the reply of the Jew under Edomite exile who says, "You say, 'what can you profit, what can you gain, O deceitful tongue?'" (v. 3). You should know that a sword wound heals more quickly than a tongue lashing which is like a warrior's sharp arrows. His counterpart replies to him: "Despite this, I deserve to be cried for because I sojourned in Meshech among 'a nation far and remote'[40] (Is 18:2, 7) who smites on the cheek and plucks out the hairs of one's beard and hand. 'I dwell among the clans of Qedar' (v. 5) who blacken and darken one's face with blows without speech, since no one understands their language. If this were for a short time I could endure it, but 'too long have I dwelt among those who hate peace' (v. 6), those who do not wish to be greeted, saying that it is not proper for a Jew to greet them nor for them to greet a Jew. Therefore, 'I am all peace' (v. 7), i.e., even though I speak of peace 'they are for war', to make war with me and smite me." (p. 66)

Saba's portrait of the Moslems is much harsher than that of Zechariah. While Zechariah felt lonely and isolated because he could not understand the language of his new host country and felt that the Moslems were cold, harsh, and merciless, Saba portrays them as a cruel and violent people who threaten the very lives of the Jews in their midst and subject them to constant harassment and humiliation.[41]

Yet the verbal abuse suffered under Christian rule could be no less painful and threatening, and Saba seems to be saying "a plague on both your houses." The two Jews in his parable may each wish to live in the exile of the other, but when all is said and done, there is not much to choose between them. No matter where in exile one lives, the heavy hand of the oppressor is sure to be felt in one way or another.[42]

It is likely that there is another factor involved in Saba's evaluation of Ahasuerus and Haman and their respective nations. That is his overall view of history and the roles he sees Edom (symbolized by Amalek and Haman) and Ishmael (symbolized, somewhat anomalously, by Ahasuerus) playing in that history. In Saba's worldview, Amalek and Edom are Israel's permanent nemeses and symbolize the forces of evil in the world, while Israel symbolizes the good.[43] However, his assessment of Ishmael is much more positive. For example, he says that because of his having been circumcised, Ishmael merited dominion over the land of Israel,[44] even though the rite that his descendants follow is imperfect.[45] Furthermore, because of Abraham's harsh treatment of Hagar and lack of compassion for her, his offspring was destined to be ruled by the descendants of Ishmael.[46]

Saba is not the only one of his contemporaries to speak bitterly about the Christians' oratorical and persuasive skills, and Ben-Sasson[47] is no doubt correct in understanding these references as pertaining to the skills of the Christian preachers who subjected the Jews of Spain to a constant barrage of sermons and diatribes aimed at convincing them to convert. The fact that they were often successful is attested to by Abraham Shalom in the following exegesis of Ps 124:

> *When men assailed us* (Ps 124:2). This refers to the dispute between us and Gentile scholars concerning religious opinions (*de'ot toriyyot*) as it is written, "and every tongue that contends with you at law you shall defeat" (Is 54:17). And since two evils result from this type [of oppressor]—either physical destruction . . . of those that oppose their false belief or spiritual demise as was the case with some of our people whose faith was spoiled and who exchanged their honor and their Torah—therefore, it is written "then they swallowed us up alive" (Ps 124:3) "and then the torrent swept over us" (Ps 124:4), and since many of our people have stumbled, he says "then over us the seething waters swept" (Ps 124:5).[48]

But Saba's and Shalom's views were not entirely representative. Despite the Christian oppression of Jews in Spain and the threat to their physical and spiritual existence, many Jewish scholars of the generation of the exile came away with a rather high opinion of Christian society and a certain envy of the values which they saw lacking in their own community.

Thus, Isaac Abravanel says of the level of learning in Christian society:

> The wisdom of the scholars of Edom [Christendom] is inestimable . . . whether in rhetoric . . . physics or metaphysics,

> and in all sciences . . . their wisdom exceeds that of all the ancients.[49]

And Joseph Jabez speaks enviously of their high morals:

> For their nobles take pride in the commandment of charity and in taking pity on the poor . . . out of their love for God. And their scholars are polite to each other (*noḥim zeh la-zeh*).[50]

These quotations illustrate the fact that many Jews had mixed feelings about the Christian society in which they lived, finding in it much that was worthy of admiration and emulation while at the same time deeply resenting the persecution and discrimination inflicted upon them by their Christian hosts.[51]

There are two other explicit references to Christians in Saba's commentary, one of which appears in his comment to 3:12.[52] Saba wonders why Haman was in such a hurry to send out his letters against the Jews since he had almost a year's time before they were to come into effect. He answers that he wanted to terrorize the Jews for a full year so that they "would die many deaths" out of fear and foreboding and that in order to save their lives many would apostatize because they took pity on their wives and children.

It is not difficult to draw a parallel between Saba's statement and the situation of the Jews in his own time in Spain and Portugal. But Saba makes the task even easier for us by spelling it out:

> This is clear from the text "and many of the people of the land professed to be Jews for the fear of the Jews had fallen upon them" (8:17). Now this is what was supposed to happen to Israel out of fear of the wicked Haman, and there is no clearer proof of this than the attempt we have seen with our own eyes, by the Edomites [i.e., Christians] to do all kinds of things to the Jews to frighten and confuse them so that they would take pity on their children and convert. This was Haman's intention and the Lord, may He be blessed, overturned his plan so that the fear of Mordecai fell over the rebels and they declared themselves Jews. (*EKE*, 68)

Here, Saba is using his own experience to confirm his exegesis. Having seen what the Christians did to the Jews in Spain and Portugal in their attempts to convert them, he then reads this experience back into the Esther story and concludes that Haman's intentions must have been similar to those of the Christians. For someone who had endured such hardship and sorrow because of his refusal to convert to Christianity, the turnabout described in the Esther story must have been especially comforting and the revenge especially sweet.

CONCLUSION

The situation described in the Book of Esther lent itself to comparison with the situation of the Jews in their various exiles. The state of their relations with their Gentile neighbors is often reflected in the comments made on various parts of the book and, in the cases of Abraham Saba and Zechariah ben Saruḳ, their immediate experiences evoked reflections on the nature of Christians and Moslems and the relative merits of living under their rule. The general absence of triumphalist expressions with regard to the Jews' victory over their foes is remarkable and unexpected, and could possibly derive from Jewish feelings of precariousness and oppression in exile. But we note that at least Saba and Zechariah did not hesitate to speak of their hosts albeit in other contexts, in very negative terms, and so there were exceptions to this general tendency.

One aspect of Jewish-Gentile relations which deserves special treatment is antisemitism and the perceptions of Jews of Gentile attitudes towards them. This topic is considered in the following chapter.

THE STATE OF THE JEWISH PEOPLE IN THE DIASPORA: PERCEPTIONS OF ANTISEMITISM

Several verses in the Book of Esther provide opportunities for the expression of opinions concerning the situation of the Jewish people in the Diaspora. One of the questions that puzzled many was why Haman decided to destroy all the Jews when he learned that Mordecai was one of them (3:6). The fact that Haman could devise such a plan and come so close to executing it raised serious questions about the status and security of the Jewish people. On the basis of this verse and others, the northern French exegetes expressed quite pessimistic views on this matter. According to Joseph Kara (3:91, to 3:8), for example, there was no nation as downtrodden as the Jews. If the king's servants had told Haman that Mordecai was from any other nation he would never have dreamed of destroying them.[1] But since there was no nation as weak as Israel at that time, Haman sought to destroy all the Jews in Ahasuerus's kingdom.[2] He also felt that if the king knew that Esther belonged to the lowly and persecuted Jewish people, he would never have taken her as his queen.[3]

On the other hand, there are some later medievals who have a more positive view of the position of the Jews in exile. Among these are Isaac Arama, Isaac ben Joseph, and Abraham Saba. Arguing on historical grounds, Arama (fols. 152r–v) says that everyone knew that during the entire Babylonian and Persian periods the Jews were highly regarded by the kings because of their wisdom and were present in the court of every king. Therefore, because of their high position, no one in his right mind would ever dare to try to harm them, and the king would certainly never agree to let them come to harm. Saba (p. 65) concurs with this view, referring to Daniel and his friends. The only way that Haman could get his way was to deceive the king, by describing the Jews anonymously in such a denigrating fashion that the king would readily agree to their destruction. Solomon Astruc depicts the Jews as a privileged minority who were fully protected by royal decree.[4] R. Isaac ben Joseph[5] has Haman pleading before the king that the Jews who now enjoy a special protected status in the kingdom do not deserve it and should be denied this status.

Jews in the later Middle Ages were often given the title of *servi camerae regis* ("serfs of the king's chamber") and were, in essence, the king's personal property subject to his benevolent protection and also vulnerable to his every whim.[6] In general, this arrangement worked to the Jews' benefit because it was usually in the king's best interests to protect them. There were also, however, cases in which a king would sell or transfer ownership of some of his Jews in order to pay off his debts or reward a loyal subject. Furthermore, the Jews were subjected to a seemingly endless barrage of expulsions in the fourteenth and fifteenth centuries against which they had no defense.[7]

"A PEOPLE SCATTERED AND DISPERSED"

Perhaps the most notorious and certainly the most commented upon verse in the entire Book of Esther is 3:8 in which Haman puts his case to the king:

> There is a certain people scattered and dispersed among the other peoples in all the provinces of your realm, whose laws are different from those of any other people, and who do not obey the king's laws; and it is not in Your Majesty's interest to tolerate them.

There is no question that this diatribe portrays the Jews in a very bad light. Furthermore, as a modern commentator has pointed out, it is very cleverly formulated, proceeding from truth ("scattered, yet unassimilated") to half-truth ("their laws are different") to outright lie ("they do not obey the king's laws"), the conclusion called for being their elimination.[8]

The medieval exegetes elaborated upon Haman's invective in various ways, putting a dazzling array of arguments in his mouth. These arguments can be categorized, along the lines used by modern scholars in discussing the phenomenon of antisemitism,[9] into those of a social, religious, economic, or political nature.

SOCIAL REASONS FOR ANTISEMITISM

Arguments of a social nature focused on the social isolation of the Jews from the rest of society. Thus Ibn Ezra comments, "*a people.* Who keeps to itself and does not mingle with the others" (*VA*, 24). Others added that they do not eat, drink, or intermarry with the Gentiles.[10] Such a group is naturally suspect. The Jews have been criticized and vilified repeatedly throughout the ages for their refusal to assimilate with the Gentiles. The most extreme view is voiced by Shemariah ben Elijah, who depicts the Jews as hating all other nations.[11] Looking at the Jews' isolation from a different point of view, Isaac Arama (fol. 153r) points out that because of their isolation, there is no need to worry that the nations among whom the Jews dwell will protect them; rather, they will lend a hand in destroying them.[12] Therefore, on the one hand, the Jews' isolation is seen as just and sufficient cause for eliminating them, and on the other, it facilitates the process of elimination.[13]

RELIGIOUS REASONS

The social separation of the Jews derives from their religious beliefs, which prevent them from mingling with the Gentiles. The laws and customs of Judaism figure prominently in the remarks placed in Haman's mouth by the authors of certain midrashim and especially in the Targum Sheni. The latter, an Aramaic translation and paraphrase of Esther, which probably dates from the late seventh or early eighth century[14] and contains a great deal of midrashic material, gives a most detailed description of Jewish customs and observances. In the course of a lengthy exposition of Est 3:8, Haman accuses the Jews of wasting their days in prayer and ceremony and using their numerous rituals and holiday observances in order to avoid having to do business with their Gentile neighbors. The fact that their religious services are recited in a foreign tongue arouses the suspicion that they are cursing the king and praying for his downfall. When they go to synagogue on the Sabbath or on holidays, the Jews "read their books, interpret their prophets, curse the king, imprecate the governors," and pray for the downfall of the king and their enemies. They mercilessly circumcise their male children on the eighth day and force their young children to fast on the Day of Atonement. For their Feast of Booths,

> they erect booths on the roofs of their houses, then they go into our orchards, cut down our palm leaves, pluck down our citrons, break our willows, destroy our gardens and our fences without any pity, and then they make *hosannas*[15] and say "As the king does among his arrayed army, so do we." Then they go to their synagogues, read their books, pray, rejoice, go around with their *hosannas,*[16] jump and dance like goats and we do not know whether they curse or bless us.[17]

This description of Jewish laws and customs is an interesting attempt by a Jew to look at his religion through non-Jewish eyes and seek out those aspects that could be held up to ridicule.[18]

The Targum Sheni and other midrashim focused on the laws and customs that distinguished the Jews from their Gentile neighbors and aroused their suspicions. But it was also possible to consider Judaism as an attractive option for some Gentiles and a threat to the state religion. This argument is presented by Shemariah of Crete:

> Why is it not worthwhile for the king to leave them alone? . . . These words [i.e., Haman's] are undoubtedly the words of a man who enacts legislation for the king and the entire kingdom, and all look to him to remove any obstacles which would stand in the way of the observance of any of the laws [including idol worship]. Therefore, he said to the king that it has come to his knowledge that there is one people in his kingdom which denies every religion and all the gods of the nations and scorns them all, and they do not follow the laws of the king, i.e., they do not worship and believe in the same gods that the king worships and believes in. Were they only in one place, perhaps I

> could tolerate and overlook them, but this nation is scattered and dispersed throughout the entire kingdom and constitutes a great stumbling block and obstacle for all the believers. Now, it would be extremely damaging to the king to leave them be because all the nations will learn to scorn idols and their worship and make light of them, and as a result their anger will be poured out on the kingdom and they will cause your enemies to overcome you. (fol. 52r–v)

This interpretation derives from R. Shemariah's understanding that Ahasuerus had made a god of Haman. Similar occurrences were quite common in the ancient world. It was a simple step to see Haman not just as an object of worship and reverence but as a sort of minister of state for religious affairs, responsible for propagating the state religion among the masses through legislation and institutions and for assuring that no forces external or internal threatened the well-being and success of this religion. In this context, the Jews, because of their distinct and unusual religious practices and their determined refusal to have anything to do with the state religion, could very easily be seen as a threat.

Indeed, it is true that Jews proselytized actively for their religion during the Roman period and not without success. Although many Roman writers mocked Jewish practices and resented the Jews' exclusiveness and obvious contempt for the Roman religion, there is evidence that certain Jewish practices, such as the observance of the Sabbath and the abstention from eating pork, were attractive to some Romans. The conversion of the royal house of Adiabene in the first century and Jesus' complaint against the Pharisees who "traverse sea and land to make a single proselyte" (Mt 23:15) are evidence of Jewish missionary activity in ancient times.[19] Even in the Middle Ages there are isolated incidents of Christians converting to Judaism, but once the Church was ascendant, it took drastic measures to see to it that Judaism could not compete with it on even terms, and the Jews never again pursued converts actively.[20] Understood in this context, R. Shemariah's interpretation is quite insightful, although it is difficult to know whether he was aware of the success and spread of Judaism in antiquity.

In several sources, midrashic and exegetical, one can see reflected signs of Christian anti-Jewish polemic. The earliest source that contains such arguments is *Midrash Panim 'aḥerim B* in which we find the following:

> [Haman] said to him: My Lord, come and see how different and perverted they are in comparison with all the other nations. Once a week they make a holiday[?][21] and call it the Sabbath. They open their synagogues and read things which can be heard clearly. They say, "Hear, O Israel, the Lord our God, the Lord is one." Then they stand up and pray, and they say in their prayer [i.e., the *'amidah*] "who humbles the wicked" and they say that we are the wicked. Afterwards they say "who loves righteousness and justice," and they hope that the Holy One, blessed be He, will bring us to justice. Then they take the Torah scroll and curse us falsely, saying, "may Your enemies cringe before You" (Dt 33:29).[22]

The Jewish emphasis in the *shema'* prayer on the oneness of God could easily be construed by Christians as a direct attack on the Christian belief in the Trinity. The blessing "who humbles the wicked," is the conclusion of the blessing against the heretics, or *birkat ha-minim*, which not surprisingly, Christians have always understood as referring to them.[23] The blessing which follows could also be easily interpreted by wary and insecure Christians as an affront to their faith and an expression of Jewish stubbornness and defiance. The same can be said for the verse in Deuteronomy. We seem to have here an early example of Christian anti-Jewish polemic as recorded by a Jewish witness.[24]

Other evidence of anti-Christian polemic being placed in Haman's mouth comes from a much later period, specifically, the Iberian Peninsula in the fifteenth century. According to Abraham Shalom, Haman warns that in addition to their basic moral and spiritual depravity, the Jews could undermine the whole kingdom, "for people will learn from their bad customs and laws and the evil will spread to the entire kingdom, and one of these days all of your people will be corrupted by their opinions and customs."[25] Furthermore, it is simply not proper for the king in his function as ruler of the people to allow the existence in his kingdom of a people who do not participate in the religion of the land,

> for the king should properly promote religion and not destroy it. Since the laws of this people are not one with those of the king, it is fitting to destroy them. For it is of the essence of the king's duty as king to unite his subjects in belief and not to allow

> differences of opinion with him, for this could lead to suspecting the king of heresy (*la-ḥashov ʿal ha-melekh toʿah*) and would cause people to speak out against him since [there were some people] who disagreed with him in religious matters.[26]

This last argument gives an accurate description of the situation in late fifteenth-century Spain. During this period the Catholic monarchs were uniting their country on national and religious grounds, thereby creating a climate in which Jews, as obstacles to religious unity, could no longer be tolerated.[27]

Still another echo of Christian polemic against Judaism can be found in the words put in Haman's mouth by Joseph Ḥayyun, who expresses the Christian denigration of the Jewish faith and their utter scorn for its believers:

> For they are more accursed than all the nations, the reason for this being their different religion. For their laws . . . are senseless. It is religion with its sense of order which preserves the people. Therefore, just as their laws are different from those of all the nations so are they different and more accursed than all the nations. (fol. 76v)

Furthermore, there is no hope that the Jews would convert because they stubbornly cling to their religion.

> Therefore this accursed people, so different in its religion, ought to be killed and destroyed, as the philosopher says—"kill him who has no religion." Since their religion is so strange and irrational it is as if they did not have a religion at all. (Ibid.)

Here, as Ben-Sasson[28] points out, can be seen reflected not only the growing Christian intolerance to outside influences that might interfere in the unification of the country under one religion, but the feeling among Christians that the very connection of the Jews with a religion as corrupt and baseless as Judaism was an abomination and an affront to reason and good sense. So, disregarding the argument for unification, Judaism ought to be eliminated and its adherents eradicated because of its debased nature.

It is intriguing that many Jewish scholars living at this time seemed on the whole to agree with the aims and methods (including the

Inquisition) of the Christians for achieving a united society, even though they thought that the purpose (Christianity) was false.[29] This is perhaps an indication of the degree of identification that some Spanish Jews had developed with their host country.

ECONOMIC REASONS

Several exegetes deal with economic reasons for antisemitism. According to Targum Sheni, Gentiles believe that the Jews sell everything at inflated prices and buy everything at prices below their market value.[30] Avigdor b. Elijah gives a true-to-life vignette of an encounter between a Jewish moneylender and a Gentile borrower.

> They make for themselves a day of rest which they call the Sabbath and if a Gentile comes to redeem his pawn he [the Jew] says to him "today is the Sabbath" and he holds onto the pawn in order to increase the interest [that the Gentile will have to pay] and the latter spends the money [he had saved up] and the pawn is forfeited to the Jew.[31]

It is a well-known fact that moneylending was one of the most widespread Jewish occupations in the Middle Ages and was also a cause of much animosity and ill feeling between Christians and Jews.[32] It is somewhat surprising therefore that this quote from Avigdor b. Elijah should be the only reference in all the medieval Esther commentaries to moneylending by Jews. The case mentioned here must have involved a farmer or small artisan who would have had to leave a pawn, since loans to noblemen or wealthy businessmen would have been secured by writs of indebtedness.[33] One can imagine that, on numerous occasions, borrowers unable to repay their loans would have had to default. The humiliation they suffered would have led to much ill feeling against Jewish moneylenders and Jews in general.[34] Even in the case mentioned by R. Avigdor, the accusation is that the Jew delayed returning the pawn to the borrower. Contrary to what one might expect, no mention is made of Jews' charging exorbitant interest rates.[35]

One accusation that does appear several times in medieval sources[36] is the failure of the Jews to pay their taxes. Several northern French sources (Rashi, and two anonymous exegetes) simply state that the Jews do not pay their taxes to the king. But the most interesting comment on the topic is by Isaac Arama:

> 3:8. *And it is not in Your Majesty's interest to tolerate them.* They are poor and impoverished and do not pay poll taxes and property taxes (*missim ve-'arnoniyyot*) at all and those which they do owe they use all sorts of tricks to avoid paying the tax collectors (*mithappekhim be-taḥbuloteihem le-havriaḥ 'oto min ha-mokhesim*) so that the gain derived from them is minimal and might even be close to a loss.[37]

It was through the payment of a variety of taxes to the authorities that the Jews in the Middle Ages assured their continued existence. Indeed, as Baron points out, next to the religious tradition, the main reason for the Jews being tolerated in the West was the rulers' self-interest in the revenue derived from them.[38] To accuse the Jews of not paying their taxes was tantamount to threatening them with expulsion. Indeed, one of the reasons for the expulsion of the Jews from England in 1290 was that they had been milked dry by the king and could not bear the burden of ever-increasing levies. Therefore, they were no longer of use to the king.[39]

Since the survival and security of the Jews depended on their paying their taxes faithfully, one would expect that they would be careful about fulfilling their obligations to the crown, although they would sometimes bargain, plead, or bribe in order to have excessive levies reduced.[40] Yet, we have, at least in Spain, considerable evidence that certain individuals were delinquent in paying their share of taxes and were punished accordingly.[41] Of course, the Jewish community itself was responsible for its members, and so communal leaders were sometimes involved along with the authorities in bringing delinquents to account.[42]

It is difficult to judge whether or not the situation described in Arama's remark accurately reflects the Spanish situation although it would seem to be plausible. In the fifteenth century, Jews were still responsible for a good percentage of the tax-farming in Castile,[43] although their share of it must have dwindled steadily toward the end of the century. Jews were squeezed economically, on one hand, by the rising Christian middle class and, on the other, by the Conversos who were competing with the Christians. Thus their economic situation declined steadily throughout the fifteenth century as conversions and stiff competition took their toll.[44] Since Arama was writing in the second half of the fifteenth century, the situation for many Jews must have already been quite serious. It is quite possible that Jews were having difficulty paying all the taxes required of them and many individuals may have attempted to avoid paying altogether.

Still another version of the economic argument is given by "Ramah" (fol. 8r), whose Haman argues that, since the Jews have their own laws, they need have no recourse to the king's courts. Therefore, the king's judges, scribes, and servants derive no benefit from them. Even in the cases when the king's law would apply (according to the principle of *dina' de-malkhuta' dina'*, "the law of the kingdom is law"), they do not obey the king's laws. Therefore, it is not worthwhile to let them be because they derive benefits from the kingdom and give nothing in return. Here is a fine example of the Jew-as-parasite argument, in which the Jews are depicted as sucking the lifeblood of their host society without benefiting the latter at all.

POLITICAL REASONS

A line of interpretation that appears in some of the later medieval commentaries concerns the possibility that the Jews, scattered as they were, were liable to engage in subversive activities and might constitute a threat to the stability of the kingdom. Gersonides is the first to interpret 3:8 in this manner.

> *There is a certain people etc.* He informed him that they were one people and for this reason he ought to fear them all the more because they were always of one mind. He also informed him that they were "scattered and dispersed among the other peoples" and because of this it would be more feasible for them to stir up trouble against the king because they could seduce the people among whom they lived away from the king. Furthermore, "their laws are different from those of any other people." This is to tell us that their customs and laws do not resemble those of any other nation which makes it easy for them to act against the kingdom and against the peoples in whose midst they live. He also informed him that they do not keep the king's laws, i.e., they do not carry out his decrees and for this reason they are like rebels against the kingdom. (p. 41a)

Solomon Astruc paints a very similar picture in his commentary:

> He said: "There is one people," meaning that the Jews have taken counsel together to rebel against the king and to make a union

(*yiḥud*) and plot called *unión*,[45] as it says [in the midrash] "they fritter away the whole year going from one holiday to the next."[46] Proof for this is that they have one teaching and one law and one [sage] will not permit what another has forbidden. . . . Furthermore, he said that they are "scattered and dispersed among the other peoples" so that no ruler can rule over them; they are in all the provinces of the kingdom and their laws are different from those of every other people. They do not eat and drink with us and do not worship like we do. They do not obey the laws of the king, even those which do not contradict their own faith. One must beware lest they multiply and when a war breaks out unite with our enemies and cause all the countries especially those farthest away from you to rebel. This would be easy for them because there are some of them in every city. If you plan to punish them, you will not be able to because they are found in every province. If you begin in one city, near or far, they will escape and rebel against you. They have already transgressed the king's command by not bowing down to the monument the king set up and have rebelled against you. (pp. 216–17)

In the same vein, Isaac ben Joseph ha-Kohen (fol. 63v) points out that Haman's words are maliciously deceptive in that they accurately describe the condition of the Jews but also of a group of spies and informers.

The main points of the political rationale are: (1) the unity and cohesiveness of the Jews, which made them an internal threat to the stability of the regime, since they could foment rebellion from within; (2) their dispersion throughout the kingdom, which made them a potential fifth column in time of war, since they could easily assist the enemy; (3) their refusal to obey the laws of the king, which was certain to arouse suspicion and cast doubts on their loyalty to the king. We find similar charges expressed against the Jews from time to time throughout the Middle Ages, not always without foundation. In 694 C.E. in Spain, the Visigothic authorities unearthed a plot by Jews who were preparing to overthrow the government. In 711, when the Berbers invaded Spain under their leader Tariq, the Jews joined forces with them, facilitating the overthrow of the oppressive Visigothic kingdom. In city after city, where it was possible, the Jews were drafted into the ranks of the conquering army. Several medieval Christian sources accused the Jews, apparently without foundation, of having opened the gates of Toledo before Tariq's army. But it was true that here again, the Moslems mounted a garrison from among the Jews. So the memory of Jewish sedition must have remained vivid in the medieval Spanish mind. Tales of Jewish plots to undermine Christianity and enslave the Christians occur frequently in medieval anti-Jewish tracts.* Several such tales appear in the *Fortalitium fidei* of Alonso de Espina.[47]

There is another political interpretation, favored by some exegetes, that is diametrically opposed to that discussed above. Rather than focusing on the unity of the Jews, it stresses that they are "scattered and dispersed" which is a sign of their internal weakness. Ibn Ezra simply comments that the Jews are so bad that they are divided among themselves while Abraham Saba in his usual colorful and prolix style laments:

> *There is one people.* That is, although it may seem that they are one people, in total harmony, nevertheless, they are scattered and divided—that is, they are divided against each other by needless hatred even though they are in exile among the nations. (p. 66)

Here Saba is expressing his outrage and grief at the sad situation in which he sees the Jewish community in his time. Even in a time of persecution, the Jews cannot stay united among themselves. Isaac Arama makes a similar point: "They are separated from each other and rejoice in each other's misfortune and therefore since they are so divided it will not be difficult to overcome them" (fol. 153r). Not only are the Jews not united as a group—a lamentable situation in and of itself—but their disunity facilitates the task of destroying them.

Finally, Abraham Shalom has Haman argue that internal division and anarchy among the Jews are the factors that have prevented them from establishing a political entity of their own. This again is a sign of their worthlessness. Furthermore, the generations spent in exile have rendered them powerless and cowardly, so that "the sound of a driven leaf shall put them to flight" (Lv 26:36). If they were to join the people in battle, they would put fear in the hearts of the strong because of their own cowardice. Indeed, it would seem that their centuries in exile have

* See, e.g., Jeremy Cohen, *The Friars and the Jews: The Evolution of Medieval Anti-Judaism* (Ithaca, N.Y., 1982), 91–96, 239–41.

altered their national character and made them weak, unwilling, and incapable of governing themselves.[48]

Here again, we find echoed the mood of fifteenth-century Christian Spain: the Christians were becoming less and less tolerant of the Jews, and the Jews were feeling the increasing weight of Christian disdain and disapproval as the century drew to its tragic close.

CONCLUSION

Thus, we see clearly how the commentators' particular situations and perceptions of their relationship with their Christian environment influenced their exegesis. These factors are also reflected in the reasons they gave for the Gentiles hating them and wanting to expel them from their midst. Haman's diatribe became for them a vehicle for stock-taking and self-analysis, and their commentaries provided a forum for the expression of their views.

Although antisemitism was a very real and significant aspect of Jewish life in the Middle Ages, relationships were often more complex and many a significant drama in Jewish-Christian relations was played out in the royal court. It is to this arena that we now turn.

8

THE ROYAL COURT

One of the most pervasive influences in medieval life was the royal court. The Book of Esther provides a rich and vivid description of court life in the palace of a Persian king. The author of the Book of Esther was obviously very familiar with the structure and composition of the Persian court, and he describes many aspects of court life in great detail. In the Middle Ages, we find that many of our exegetes drew upon their own experiences or those of their fellow Jews when commenting upon court behavior and etiquette, and many of their comments can be understood only in their medieval context.

COURT LIFE AND THE COURTIER

Some exegetes, in commenting on the text of Esther, make specific reference to court practices in their own times. In the case of Abraham Ibn Ezra, the allusions are more subtle and must be teased out of his comments, many of which make sense only when their medieval background is clarified. Although Ibn Ezra wrote his biblical commentaries in Italy and France, he lived most of his life in Islamic Spain, and it is there that we must look for clues to help us understand some of his comments on court practices and behavior.

The power of the Moslem rulers of Spain in Ibn Ezra's own day, though more limited than that of their Umayyad predecessors of the tenth century, was still, in theory, absolute.[1] Although the caliphate had a highly developed and diversified administrative, civil, and judicial system, the ultimate authority rested in the hands of the caliph, and his officers and advisers were there only to carry out his wishes and desires.[2]

Ibn Ezra's views concerning the authority and power of the king are compatible with the situation in Islamic Spain. The king's law is absolute, he says, not to be added to or subtracted from (1:8B).[3] After the king sleeps with a woman, no one else is allowed to sleep with her, since this would be an insult to the king (2:14A/B; *VA*, 22). Haman was standing in the courtyard, because royal etiquette requires that an officer stand even when he is not in the presence of the king (6:5B; *VA*, 28).

Similarly, Ibn Ezra's comments on the internal organization of Ahasuerus's court illustrate his familiarity with the caliphate. Ibn Ezra wonders why Mordecai, when put into a compromising position by Haman, did not leave the gate of the palace but instead chose to stay and endanger his life and the lives of the Jews (3:4A/B).

A

One can ask why did Mordecai put himself and the rest of the Jewish people in danger? He should have requested that Esther have him removed from the palace gate so that he would not irritate Haman who was enjoying a rise in his fortunes at the time. The answer is that he could not leave the palace gate without permission, and if he did so, he would be liable to the death penalty.

B

Someone might ask why did Mordecai not leave the palace gate before Haman saw him rather than put himself in grave danger? The answer to this is that Mordecai could not leave the palace gate because he was placed there by order of the king. Furthermore, this was a great honor and if he would transgress the king's command he would be killed.

There are several differences in nuance between these parallel comments. From *A*, one has the impression that, according to Ibn Ezra, Mordecai was sitting in the palace gate by sufferance of the king and that this was not necessarily a desirable thing, since limitations were placed on his freedom. As the king's subject he had to obey him under penalty of death. According to *B*, on the other hand, it seems that Mordecai is privileged to be at the palace gate. Leaving would mean jeopardizing his position in the king's court. Two points emerge from this comment: the emphasis on total obedience to the king on pain of death and the opportunity for success and advancement that being stationed in the king's court permits.

Once again, a comparison of these comments with the situation in the courts of Islamic Spain at the time of Ibn Ezra can shed considerable light on his portrayal of Mordecai's position in court. The caliph in tenth-century Spain had absolute authority in making all appointments of functionaries and magistrates, and these could be revoked at will.[4] It was inconceivable that a court official should consider leaving the court of his own volition. Only the caliph could hire or dismiss him. Resigning was out of the question. The personal officers of the king's household had to be at the palace at all times.[5] The chief of police, a somewhat lesser official, sat at the gate of the imperial palace surrounded by subordinates who remained seated and left their places only to carry out specific orders.[6] This strengthens the impression that the movements of court officials were under the control of their superiors.

Mordecai's position at Ahasuerus's court was never explicitly stated in Esther. However, one may assume that Ibn Ezra considered that he held a higher, rather than a lesser, position, one that would give him a little more freedom of movement, at least within the palace compound, "for if Mordecai were not an officer of the king before the Esther affair, the other officers would not have allowed him to walk around in the court of the harem" (2:10A).

It can be assumed that faithful performance of one's duties would enhance one's possibilities for promotion. In the court of the caliph the office of chief of police was awarded only to important personages for whom it could serve as a stepping stone to a higher position such as *ḥādjib* or *wazīr*.[7] In this context, Mordecai's later promotion to an office equivalent to *wazīr* in Ahasuerus's court seems natural, a reward for his good service to the throne.

Ibn Ezra's explanations of the phrase "who saw the king's face" (1:14) shows that he had a clear picture of the internal organization of a king's court:

A	*B*
Who saw the king's face. There are places where the king does not appear before all his subjects and in the books of the Persian kings it is written that	*The men next to him.* The "next to" refers to the custom of Persian kings for the king to sit alone in his row. In the first row nearest to him sit the most

there are four levels of officers, the first row sitting up front facing the king and this is the meaning of "sat first in the kingdom"—in the row of royalty.	important officers and after them there is another row. The meaning of "in the kingdom" is in the row of royalty.[8]

Ibn Ezra interprets the phrase "who saw the king's face" literally, taking it to mean that the highest ranking officers had an unobstructed view of the king's face. One can compare this description with the point made by Lévi-Provençal that the officers of the caliph's household formed his personal entourage and were on a level with the principal dignitaries of the central administration.[9] To be among the king's inner circle was to enjoy a very prestigious position. When Haman's promotion is mentioned (3:1), Ibn Ezra points out again that proper protocol in the king's court requires that all officers have seats. Ibn Ezra does not try to belittle Haman's status in the king's court as did Joseph Kara (3:97, to 3:10), but points out that being given the king's signet ring is a very great honor (*VA*, 24, to 3:10). Aside from this, however, Ibn Ezra plays down the role of Haman and has very little to say about him.

As did Ibn Ezra with Islamic Spain, other exegetes in Christian Spain and Provence drew on their personal experience in royal courts and made frequent references to contemporary court practices. Gersonides (p. 42b), in explaining why Haman's face was covered, compares this custom with what happens in royal courts in his own time—when an officer becomes angry with someone standing before him, he commands that the latter be removed from his presence.

In the following comment to 3:11, Isaac Arama refers to the process through which day-to-day requests are handled in court:

> We see from [the king's] words that if the matter turned out not to be the way that Haman described it, the king would not agree with him, and there are cases every day in the courts of kings in which someone will come and ask for something for such and such a reason and they [the judges] will grant his request in writing on condition that his words can be verified. Later, someone else might come and question him and nullify his request. (fol. 153r)

On the basis of what he knows to be contemporary court practice, Arama argues that the king did not grant Haman unconditional permission to destroy the people he described.

A final example can be found in the commentary of Abraham Saba (*EKE*, 60, to 3:2), who suggests, in agreement with the Targum, that Haman had an image on his breast to which his servants bowed down. He compares this with the practice of Christian kings whose officials have crosses on their garments so that whoever sees them would bow down. Of course, the knightly cross was intended as a means of identification and not as an instrument of religious coercion. That Saba should see it this way would probably indicate that he did not regularly frequent court circles and had little first-hand contact with Gentiles. Still, his awareness of the phenomenon and mention of it in his commentary is significant.

COURT INTRIGUES

One of the most fascinating aspects of court life has always been the interpersonal relationships and rivalries, the struggles for power and influence among the courtiers. The Book of Esther, which vividly portrays the precipitous rise and fall of an ambitious courtier, Haman, and the equally spectacular rise to power of a Jewish courtier, Mordecai, offers many opportunities for the exegete to expatiate upon the various turns taken by the events described. This is especially true for the exegetes in Spain and Provence, who were closer to the royal courts, but it also pertains to at least one of our northern French exegetes ("A") who shows some familiarity with the nature of power struggles in court circles. This anonymous exegete offers a most unusual comment to 1:13–14:

> *For it was the royal practice [to turn] to all who were versed in law and precedent.* Even though the king has it in his power to do whatever he desires without a trial, nevertheless, it is the king's practice to place the matter before all who are versed in law, judgment, and justice and to judge according to their advice, regardless of whether they are unrelated or related to him. Now, some relatives of his, members of his household, were there—Carshena, Shethar (1:14)—and they did not wait until those who knew the times decided the law, because they knew that they would not have

> sentenced her to death. One of them—Memucan—jumped in and spoke to the king according to his desire.[10]

The textual basis for our exegete's comment is the word *qarov* ("close"). This is usually understood to refer to the advisers closest to the king, those who had his ear. Our exegete however understood the word *qarov* in another sense, that of blood relative, and does not take the word as referring to the wise men mentioned in 1:13. This allows him to portray the following scenario. The relatives of the king, presumably noblemen, were Vashti's enemies and saw an opportunity to bring about her downfall. The king's legal advisers would probably not have dealt so harshly with Vashti because they were on her side. Therefore, in order to achieve their goal, the king's relatives, led by Memucan, intervened before the king's advisers had a chance to speak and portrayed Vashti's actions in very grave terms urging the king to depose her. The king listened to their advice and Vashti was put to death. What confirms this interpretation for him is 1:21, "The proposal was approved by the king and the ministers." Our exegete assumes that "the ministers" refers to the king's relatives and concludes that this implies that the outcome of the affair was not pleasing to "the wise men who know the times," i.e., the king's advisers.[11]

ESTHER AS MASTER OF INTRIGUE

Many exegetes felt uncomfortable with the idea of a Jewish woman being married to a Gentile and would have preferred that Esther had somehow managed to avoid being chosen as queen.[12] However, once having been made queen and being called to act on behalf of her people in a time of crisis, Esther was the recipient of universal praise for the skill and intelligence she displayed in orchestrating Haman's downfall. She was seen as a master of court intrigue, cleverly outmaneuvering Haman and thwarting him at every turn.

Esther's strategy in not presenting her case to Ahasuerus immediately but rather inviting the king and Haman to a banquet (5:4) on their behalf, suggested to the exegetes many intriguing possibilities. Already the sages, in the oldest midrash, suggested—among others—the following reasons for Esther's action:

> R. Eleazar said: "She set a trap for him, as it says, 'May their table be a trap for them' (Ps 69:23)." . . . R. Meir said: "so that he

should not form a conspiracy and rebel (*she-lo' yittol 'esah ve-yimrod*)." R. Judah said: "So that they should not discover that she was Jewish." . . . R. Jose said: "So that he should always be at hand for her." . . . R. Joshua b. Korha said: "She said: 'I will encourage him so that he may be killed, both he and I.' "[13] . . . R. Eliezer of Modi'im says: "She made the king jealous of him and she made the princes jealous of him."[14]

R. Shemariah b. Elijah in his commentary on this talmudic midrash elaborates on several of these comments of the sages. With regard to R. Eleazar's statement that Esther set a trap for Haman, he explains that Esther realized that Haman was the king's closest adviser, and therefore, she wished to do him a great honor by inviting only him along with the king. Now, Esther knew that the king would ask her at the banquet what her request was and he would sing her praises to Haman, who would feel obliged to join the king in praising Esther in order to please the king and show his appreciation to her for inviting him. He might say to the king such things as "she is the finest of all the women ever created," or "the grace that you have found before the idols that you worship [caused them] to create her for you from an honorable race that they favor, one that is beyond compare in the whole world."[15] Haman would be especially interested in building up Esther's worth, since it was he who had advised the king to depose Vashti. Thus, by heaping praise on Esther, he was also emphasizing the value of his advice. After all this, what would Haman be able to say when Esther finally accused him of plotting to destroy her people? As we see, he was speechless. Furthermore, claims R. Shemariah, if Esther would have complained against Haman when she first went to the king, the king might have easily rejected her plea by reassuring her that Haman had not intended that she be included in the decree, and might have said to her "Why are you so worried about this wretched people? They do not do you honor. I will decree that no harm will come to your entire family" (Shemariah, 91r–92v).

R. Shemariah surmises that if Esther would have complained about Haman in his absence, he would have had a better chance to prepare a defense before he appeared before the king. Furthermore, many other officers might have spoken on his behalf in the hope that he would do the same for them in the future. For all these reasons, Esther sought to isolate Haman, so that the element of surprise would be overwhelming.

R. Shemariah goes on to speculate why R. Judah said that she invited Haman in order to conceal her Jewishness. How was this possible, when the very purpose of her inviting the king and Haman was to reveal her Jewishness? He answers that Esther arranged the situation so that as few people as possible would be present when she revealed herself to the king and accused Haman. Any servants there would have been her own and therefore Jews. Indeed, even at this point it would have been dangerous if Esther's Jewishness were to become known to the general public. Better that people think that Haman was killed for having tried to seduce the queen and having plotted to kill Mordecai who had saved the king's life,

> for if it became known that she was Jewish, everyone would think that she was behind the king's actions and that the king acted unjustly out of love for his wife. It would make matters very difficult for the king's officers to say that the king chose as his queen a Jewish woman, a member of a people who hated all other peoples, and out of love for her ordered that his best officers such as Haman and his sons be hanged and that his wife's relatives kill among the nations at will. (Shemariah, 93v)

R. Shemariah's opinion that Esther's Jewishness was not generally known even after chapter 7 is the polar opposite to that of Isaac Arama, according to whom it was known even before she became queen.[16]

Gersonides, in treating the same topic, looks at Esther's strategy from the viewpoint of a courtier who must intercede before a ruler on an urgent matter. Esther's strategy is depicted as a model of courtly behavior.

> Someone who needs to intercede in an urgent matter,[17] in order to prevent a great evil from befalling him, should do so in such a way that in the course of events no opening for intercession should be closed to him. . . .

In keeping with this advice, Esther entered the king's inner court wearing royal garments, in order to find favor in the king's eyes. She did not immediately plead for the salvation of her people, since she feared that Haman would oppose her. Rather, she tried to win Haman over to her side by inviting him to a banquet along with the king. She hoped that if Haman could be won over, and peace made between him and Mordecai, she could enlist his help on behalf of Israel against the king. On the other hand, Esther's action could work against Haman, since her invitation to him would make the other officers in court jealous of his power and influence. Then, when she invited Haman a second time, she seemed to be indicating that Haman was more powerful than the king since she hesitated to make a request of the king without first winning over Haman to her side.[18] This made the officers even more jealous. Gersonides also stresses Esther's wisdom in coming before the king at the peak of her fast when she was weak and faint from hunger.[19] The king felt pity for her and was moved to offer her half his kingdom. He further speculates that it was his distress over Esther's weak condition and his perplexity over her attention to Haman that kept Ahasuerus up that fateful night (6:1).[20]

Gersonides incorporates many midrashic viewpoints into his comment, but of special interest is his portrayal of Esther as a wily, clever, and skillful courtier adept at playing off rival factions in court against each other to her advantage. Her every move was calculated for effect and succeeded in producing the desired result. Particularly intriguing is his suggestion that Esther was also considering making overtures to Haman, while exploring the possibility of joining up with him and Mordecai against the king. Haman is here portrayed as a powerful and ambitious courtier who might possibly be won over to Esther's side if it would serve his interests. His role as archenemy of the Jews is not stressed at all in this context. Esther's ploy in inviting him is thus an excellent tactic. On the one hand, it puts her in his favor and leaves the possibility open of enlisting his help on her behalf if this would prove to be necessary. On the other hand, it stirs up the jealousy of the king and the other courtiers and serves to undermine Haman's position at court.

Two northern French exegetes stressed the pitfalls that Esther would have faced had she made her plea before the king immediately. According to Joseph Kara (3:92), had she made her plea before the officers, her words would have been undermined, because Haman had many friends at court and Israel many enemies. "A"[21] voices a similar opinion, adding that if she had spoken to the king alone, he would have had to send men to search for Haman, and, in the interval, he could have changed his mind. Therefore, it was important that Haman be present when she made her accusation.

Isaac Arama (fol. 155v) adds the consideration that she wanted to allow an interval between her illegal approach to the king and the making of her request to make sure that the king was well-disposed toward her. Furthermore, she felt safer making her request in her own chambers where she was certain that none of her enemies was present, "for if she would ask him in his palace she was afraid of the trouble-makers (*meqaṭregim*) who were there, for a ruler listens to the lies of all his wicked servants." This last comment is either a proverb Arama has picked up or his own comment on the foibles and weaknesses of kings and rulers.

Finally, Isaac ben Joseph ha-Kohen reminds the reader that Esther was actually informing against Haman and even though he deserved it, she hesitated to invite a person to a banquet in order to inform against him. This may explain why she procrastinated and did not make her request at the first banquet but waited till the following day.

INFORMERS

R. Isaac's comment leads us into a discussion of informers and informing as they figure in our commentaries. Informing against a fellow courtier and thereby bringing about his downfall was a favorite method of those skilled in intrigue. Within the Jewish communities of Spain in the Middle Ages, informing against a fellow Jew was considered the gravest of offenses and, in extreme cases, was punishable by death.[22] This may explain R. Isaac's hypersensitivity to the question, for the case mentioned here is not even one of a Jew informing against a fellow Jew but rather of a Jew informing against a Gentile who was a sworn enemy of the Jews.

The issue of informing (*malshinut*) also comes up in the following passage from the commentary of Solomon Astruc which deals with Haman's frustration at Mordecai's continued defiance of him despite all of his successes (5:9). Astruc's Haman asks his family to help him figure out the basis for Mordecai's self-confidence, and asks their advice on how best to present his case against Mordecai before the king. Haman points out that he has more wealth than Mordecai and more friends in court. The king certainly has favored him more than Mordecai and has bestowed much honor upon him. He has the power to appoint people to the king's court and remove them. His authority is unchallenged. Even the queen is on his side, even though she is not of his people, because he enabled her to become queen.[23] His being invited to Esther's banquet along with Ahasuerus as the sole guests is further proof of her favorable inclination towards him (Est 5:11–12). "Yet," says Haman,

" 'all this means nothing to me' (5:13), i.e., all this honor and respect that I have is nothing to me compared to the jealousy I feel against him for scorning me in the king's court. I am afraid to know what he could be relying on and my sole desire is to bring him down completely from his high position" (p. 219).

Haman is thus shown to have everything that is needed to succeed in court—wealth, friends, influence, and the favor of the king and queen. He therefore cannot understand how Mordecai could have the audacity to defy him so openly. Mordecai's brazenness has completely unnerved him and he must enumerate his assets in order to bolster his sinking self-confidence.

But his wife Zeresh and his advisers are not impressed by Haman's long list of virtues and successes:

> *Then his wife Zeresh and all his friends said to him* (5:14): We have heard all your arguments and they are all worthless. If Mordecai will come to the king's court and plead his case before the king his arguments will be justified before all who are versed in law and judgment. . Therefore, since as long as Mordecai is alive you will not be able to best him, do this and save yourself. Speak to the king in the morning before going to the banquet and tell him that Mordecai rebelled against him and scorned you and ask him to give him to you to do with as you please. . . . He will not deny him from you. Mordecai will not come before him to plead his case because a rebel is not allowed to do so. Then you can hang him from a tall gallows so that he will be a sign against all those that cross you. Then all of the Jews will see that their leader is dead and will be silent.[24] Then you will not have to fear any troublemaker, and you will be able to go joyfully with the king to the dinner. (p. 220)

Here again, Astruc stresses the strength of the Jewish position in the court. Mordecai was perfectly within his rights not to bow down to Haman. Any court would agree. Therefore, the only way for Haman to eliminate him would be to accuse him of treason. In this way, it would be possible to circumvent the normal legal channels and to punish Mordecai without a trial. But Haman was overconfident and overplayed his hand. He immediately set up the stake before he had asked the king about it, confident in his stature and honor. He did not understand what his wife meant when she said: "ask the king to have

Mordecai impaled on it" (5:14), i.e., that the king's servants should impale him at his command. He did not think of this, but rather expected that the king would give him the authority[25] to impale him (Ibid.). But Haman's confidence in his stature was unfounded, as we know, since there were other forces at work behind the scenes.

It is interesting to note that Haman and his enmity toward the Jews is discussed by Astruc almost totally within the context of the court. The fact that Haman descends from Amalek, the age-old enemy of the Jewish people, is mentioned only a couple of times in passing and is not ascribed much significance. Haman is driven by blind ambition as well as jealousy. On his instigation (as Memucan), Vashti was removed from her throne and he was given authority over her domain.[26] His campaign against Mordecai and the Jews was motivated purely by his desire for revenge for the humiliation caused him by Mordecai's defiance. His position at the court was not as strong as one would think at first, since the Jews, and Mordecai in particular, were protected by the Crown and did not have to transgress the laws of their religion for any reason. Haman could use only underhanded methods to achieve his end, and he was therefore doomed to failure.

The advice that Zeresh gives to Haman strikes one as being quite unusual. Where did Astruc get the idea that a rebel could be summarily executed at the hands of an officer without the king hearing his case or even finding out the person's name? As it happens, such events did occur in medieval Spain, if only rarely. The case that comes most readily to mind occurred in Astruc's own time and bears a striking similarity to Zeresh's plan for eliminating Mordecai. Don Juzaf Pichon (Joseph Picho), an influential Jew, had been the chief accountant of Enrique of Castile. He had enemies among the Jews in King Enrique's court who had accused him and had him arrested. The king released him and he then accused the other Jews. During the coronation celebrations of Juan I in 1379, Pichon's enemies asked the king for letters patent authorizing the city governor to execute a Jewish *malsin* ("informer") whom they would designate "for, they said, they were bound by custom to kill any Jew who acted as a *malsin*." The king who was preoccupied with his coronation festivities granted them the writ they desired, not thinking that they might have sinister motives. Pichon's enemies then proceeded with a government official to Pichon's house and killed him on the spot. When the king heard what had happened, he was very annoyed, because Don Juzaf Pichon had served as an official in his father's household. The upshot of the affair was that the king had Pichon's murderers executed and decreed that "from that day on the Jews should not have the power of blood justice over any Jew as they had had up to that time, having executed this power according to their laws and ordinances."[27]

We see then that it was possible for someone in court to engineer the execution of another courtier with the king's permission and without the king knowing the identity of the accused. It should be stressed that the case of Juzaf Pichon was a unique incident[28] and that, as a result of it, the Jews no longer were allowed to execute informers on their own. However, since the event did occur in Spain in Astruc's time, it is not unreasonable to suggest that he was familiar with the case in all its details and that on some level—conscious or subconscious—it influenced his understanding of the Esther story.

COURT ETIQUETTE—GERSONIDES' INSTRUCTIONS FOR PROPER CONDUCT

In the later Middle Ages, with the spread of secular learning among Jewish scholars, the Bible, whose authority was, of course, unquestioned, came to be looked at as an adjunct to the study of the secular sciences. Scholars sought verification in the Bible for the truths they were learning from the works of the ancient Greeks and Romans and their medieval Arab interpreters and became quite adept at doing so. There was also an increasing interest in ethics and rules for proper conduct, probably the result of the introduction of Aristotle's *Nicomachean Ethics* into the medieval curriculum in the thirteenth century.[29]

The first exegete to devote himself to deriving rules for proper conduct from the Bible seriously and systematically was Gersonides, who devoted a significant portion of each of his biblical commentaries to a discussion of the *to'alot* or moral lessons to be derived from each passage under discussion. In his Esther commentary, the fifty-one lessons he lists make up more than half the commentary. Most of these pertain to court etiquette and when compiled and classified comprise a veritable manual of behavior and etiquette for the courtier, and not necessarily a Jewish one at that.[30]

Several lessons pertain to the importance of obtaining good advice from one's advisers. A king should consult his advisers even when angry, as Ahasuerus did (1:13).[31] He should consult the lower-ranking advisers first, as Ahasuerus did (1:14, 16), so that they too would get a chance to speak.[32] It is important for an adviser to provide all the facts to the person being advised so that he would be able to decide what action to take. This is what Mordecai did for Esther (4:7).[33] Finally, even Haman becomes a model for proper behavior for Gersonides. The fact that Haman consulted his wife as well as his wise men (5:10) teaches us that when we need advice we should consult anyone who might possibly be of assistance.[34]

With regard to giving and receiving favors, Gersonides advises that someone who does another person a good turn should be sure that the beneficiary knows about it so that he does not ascribe it to chance. This also ensures that he is repaid for his favor. This is why Esther made sure that Ahasuerus knew that Mordecai had saved his life (2:22).[35] By the same token, a person receiving a favor should remember it so that he will be able to repay his benefactor. For this reason, Mordecai's good deed was recorded in the king's annals (2:23).[36] And eventually, of course, he should repay his benefactor, as Ahasuerus did to Mordecai (6:3).[37]

From the requests that Esther and Haman made to the king, Gersonides derives several lessons with regard to the proper procedure to follow when making a request before the king. For one thing, one should not ask for more than the lord is able to give. Haman overstepped his limits when he asked for everything short of the throne, for the "man whom the king desires to honor" (6:6).[38] Esther, on the other hand, presented her case with consummate skill and ingenuity, first asking for something the king could not possibly deny—her life—and then asking for the salvation of her people. She also made it clear that Haman's request was not in the best interests of the king and was made out of hatred, selfishness, and jealousy. Esther's tactic was to ask for what she wanted in stages, gradually leading up to her ultimate desire—the cancellation of the decree.[39] Esther's other encounters with the king were also handled with great skill and are worthy of emulation.[40] For example, she waited several months before approaching the king again in order not to give the impression that she was pestering him with her requests.[41]

Gersonides, apparently influenced by Esther's treatment of Mordecai (8:2), sees nepotism as a virtue. He suggests that it is proper to benefit one's relative as much as one is able, especially to repay a favor.[42] However, he cautions that in doing this one must take care not to overstep the limits and antagonize the ruler. Esther was careful not to appoint Mordecai over Haman's house until the king had given

Mordecai his ring, thereby putting him in charge of his kingdom. By waiting, Esther avoided putting herself under suspicion of giving Crown funds to her relatives.[43]

Finally, Gersonides offers a general piece of advice to courtiers—that they be alert and abreast of current affairs in order to be ready to take appropriate action when the need arises. This we learn from Mordecai who kept himself well-informed of palace news and so knew immediately of the decree against the Jews and was able to take swift action.[44]

As mentioned above, the suggestions and advice that Gersonides derives from the Esther story are primarily general in nature. They would apply to any courtier, not necessarily court Jews. Gersonides, however, clearly had his Jewish readers in mind when writing his commentary, and one cannot help but surmise that he was speaking from his own experience. Joseph Shatzmiller has cited evidence indicating that Gersonides had contacts with the papal court in Avignon.[45] It is uncertain to what extent he was involved in court affairs, but he certainly displays a keen understanding of and sensitivity to the workings of the court and the effective procedures to be used in achieving one's goals.

Gersonides also derives a few general lessons in behavior and ethics from the Esther story. Ahasuerus's banquet, which was made to celebrate his wealth and good fortune, teaches us to rejoice in our good fortune when we are blessed with it.[46] Perhaps he sees this as a sign from God that our deeds are pleasing to him. The banquet itself and the way it was conducted can teach us the proper protocol in such matters. It is important to note that all of the guests, whether of greater or lesser importance, were treated the same without any exception.[47] This is proper procedure on all occasions. In order to avoid embarrassing one's guests or making them feel uncomfortable, the servants at such an affair, like those of Ahasuerus (1:8), should try to anticipate the needs of the guests and provide for them without their having to make special requests.[48]

Gersonides also stresses the importance of keeping men and women separate at public gatherings, especially drinking parties, on the premise that mixed seating would lead to promiscuity. Another advantage to separate seating is that the women would not be inhibited by the men's presence and would not hesitate to ask for what they wanted. Therefore, Vashti's separate banquet for women was a most desirable thing.[49] Finally, Vashti's refusal to accede to Ahasuerus's demand and the dire consequences she suffered show us what happens when a woman does not submit to her husband's will as the Bible prescribes.[50]

The topic of court etiquette as it is treated in the commentaries naturally leads us into the question of the role of the Jewish courtier in the royal court and his relationship to the Jewish community. Discussion of this topic in the Esther commentaries centers around the role of Mordecai.

MORDECAI AS THE IDEAL JEWISH COURTIER

The phenomenon of a Jew attaining a position of great power and influence in the court of a Gentile king, as did Mordecai in the Book of Esther, was paralleled nowhere as closely in the Middle Ages as in both Islamic and Christian Spain. Jewish courtiership seems to have been a uniquely Spanish phenomenon in the Middle Ages,[51] and although we occasionally find among the writings of the moralists of different periods criticisms of the excesses of certain courtiers,[52] there is little criticism of the institution in and of itself.[53] The question of the Jewish courtier and his role in the community became an important issue in the internal relations of the Jewish community in the later Middle Ages, especially in Spain and southern France where Jews were much more involved in the secular government than they were in northern France and Germany. For many Jews, having one or several of their brethren in the king's court was seen as a great boon to the community, since these Jews, who were often trusted advisers of the king, had the king's ear and were able to intercede on behalf of their brethren when the community was threatened physically or economically.[54] Indeed, there are many instances in the annals of Jewish history in which court Jews did help their communities immensely.[55] This fact may account for the particular attention paid by certain exegetes to the roles played by Mordecai and Esther in the king's court.

Abraham Ibn Ezra, a product of Islamic Spain, had no difficulty in seeing Mordecai as a trusted adviser in Ahasuerus's court, for he knew of several such cases from the history of Spanish Jewry. The most prominent among these were Ḥasdai ibn Shaprut in tenth-century Cordoba and Samuel ibn Nagrela in Granada in the eleventh century.[56] In fact, the family of Ibn Ezra himself had a long history of communal leadership and enjoyed a favored position in the royal court as far back as the reign of Baddis and his father Habbus, kings of the Berbers.[57]

Therefore, it is not surprising that in version A of his commentary, Ibn Ezra interprets verse 10:1 as an indication that Ahasuerus succeeded and prospered as a result of having appointed Mordecai as his vizier. The message is that it pays for the king to have a Jewish adviser and, of course, that this is also good for the Jews.

In version B he suggests the possibility that it was Mordecai who gave the king the idea to levy the tax on his subjects and that perhaps the tax was brought to him when it was collected. The handling of a ruler's finances was a traditional Jewish occupation since the Islamic period. É. Lévi-Provençal mentions that the positions of *kātib al-ẓimām*, "secretary of income and expenditures," and of *ṣāḥib al-'ashghāl al-kharādjīya*, "secretary of taxation affairs," in the Caliph's court were often held by a Christian or a Jew.[58] Therefore, it would be natural for a medieval Spanish Jew to imagine Mordecai as a tax collector.

Solomon Astruc, writing a couple of centuries later, stressed the importance of the Jews as a source of revenue, suggesting that Mordecai proposed to the king to raise a levy against the Jews in order to remind the king how valuable an asset to his kingdom they were.[59]

For Gersonides, Mordecai was the ideal wise courtier who could do no wrong. Alert and well-informed, he kept himself abreast of palace events. He was therefore able to take swift action immediately after the decree against the Jews was promulgated.[60] It was because of his wisdom that he sat as a judge at the king's gate and was able to discover Bigthan and Teresh's plot.[61] His handling of the whole affair was exemplary. By promptly reporting his discovery, Mordecai helped to preserve the welfare of the monarchy and with it the state. In addition, he earned for himself a handsome reward.[62] Mordecai's behavior as well as his decisions were correct in every respect. Although Esther's union with the king was a transgression of the Torah, it was justified by the great benefit that the Jews derived from it, especially considering the lowly state that they were in at the time.[63] His advice that Esther not reveal her people and her birthplace (2:10) prevented her from being rejected as queen because of her origins, in which case she would still have had the shame of being a concubine.[64] Mordecai acted correctly in not bowing down to Haman because doing so would have meant transgressing God's command.[65] But this was the only justification for doing so.[66] He displayed his piety and faith by praying for the revocation of the king's decree against the Jews even though it was supposed to be irrevocable.[67] Mordecai's adoption of Esther was most praiseworthy[68] and helped bring about Israel's salvation. Finally, he set an example worthy of emulation by his concern for his people. Gersonides even goes so far as to attribute Mordecai's success in public life to his demonstration of care and concern for his people.[69] In sum, Mordecai is not only the ideal courtier but also the ideal leader of his people whose character and conduct are exemplary in every way. He is careful to act both on behalf of the king, thus preserving the welfare of the state, and on behalf of his people, thereby saving them from destruction and maintaining their security.

Although court Jews were in general highly regarded and valued for their service to the community, they were sometimes criticized by the more pious elements of the Jewish community for compromising their religious beliefs and practices, either in order to remain in the king's court or simply out of indifference and a desire to conform to the mores of the dominant culture.

Rabbi Solomon Alami subjects such courtiers to scathing criticism in his *'Iggeret musar* ("Ethical Epistle") written toward the end of the fourteenth century.[70] Alami laments the general low moral and spiritual state of the people, claiming that the majority have lost their faith. He lays a considerable part of the blame for this sad state of affairs at the feet of the communal leaders who showed no concern for the people's trespasses and were themselves guilty of many sins:

> When the Jews were well established in the king's court they would order cocks to be roasted on the Lord's Sabbath . . . and the officers and the deputies [i.e., communal leaders] lent a hand in this dastardly deed and other such despicable acts, and they spoke harshly and conspired against those who chastised them for their abominable misdeeds.[71]

Although the Jewish community could derive many benefits from having its members in high positions at court, these courtiers could threaten the spiritual welfare of the community since, by their example, they could lead others to laxity in observance of the commandments and even to apostasy. For pious Jews who were willing to grant the importance of having Jews in the king's court,[72] the ideal courtier was one who remained steadfast in his Judaism and compromised his beliefs as little as possible for the sake of conforming to the practices of the royal court.

This is the way that Mordecai is portrayed by Abraham Saba.[73] Saba is very understanding of the position of Jews in exile under harsh rulers, noting that it is impossible for them to keep the Torah and the commandments. In halakhic terms he likens them to servants who are exempt from fulfilling most commandments.[74] Therefore, the behavior of Jews such as Joseph in Egypt and Hananiah, Mishael, and Azariah in Babylonia and, of course, Mordecai, who occupied high positions in Gentile courts, is most praiseworthy indeed. According to Saba, Joseph was praised for following the ways of the Torah and avoiding all temptation including nonkosher food while a slave in Egypt. He was so strict in this regard that he would eat only dry bread.[75] Despite this, he maintained his comely appearance, as if he were enjoying the food of the king's table. In a similar situation was Mordecai who, though in exile, maintained his Jewishness as he had done in Jerusalem. For this reason, says Saba, the verse does not say "and there was a Jew"[76] but rather "a *Jew* was,"[77] with the emphasis on Jew, stressing that it was a marvelous thing that there was an observant Jew in the fortress of Susa who stood at the palace gate as an important officer in the royal court. Despite the manifold temptations of the court and his high position in it, Mordecai stayed pure and avoided all things unclean just as Joseph had done when he was king [i.e., viceroy].[78]

Although in the passage just referred to Saba likens Mordecai to Joseph, elsewhere he emphasizes that Mordecai's rise to power was even more remarkable than Joseph's:

> Perhaps the verse, "For Mordecai the Jew ranked next to King Ahasuerus" (10:3) is connected with the verse "are recorded in the annals of the kings of Media and Persia" (10:2), for it was written there that "Mordecai the Jew ranked next to King Ahasuerus" and this was one of the greatest and most marvelous things found in the annals of all the ancient kings. For indeed Pharaoh made Joseph his viceroy because of his wisdom, but this was not such a great thing at that time, for Israel was not yet in such a state of degradation. On the contrary, Pharaoh recognized and knew of the stature of our father Abraham, and the whole world knew of his great strength, since he conquered kings and was called father of a multitude of nations. Therefore, it was not so surprising that Joseph was his viceroy. But now, at a time when Israel was in exile and in a state of degradation, it is a remarkable thing to see written in the annals of the kings of Media and Persia that Mordecai the Jew, *wrapped in prayer shawl and phylacteries*, was the viceroy to King Ahasuerus, the greatest among the kings of Persia

> [emphasis added]. Now if he would only have spent his time occupied with affairs of state and government, this again would not have been so noteworthy. But he was so pious and saintly that even though he was viceroy he was great among the Jews, busying himself with their affairs in order to teach them the law and the commandments. Not only did he reply to all those who approached him with requests, but he even would go out of his way to seek the welfare of his people and to familiarize himself with their affairs and would try to make peace among them.[79]

The comparison of Mordecai and Joseph in this passage is noteworthy because through it Saba sets up an implicit analogy with his own times which he carries through in the rest of the passage. For Saba, Joseph seems to be of less interest as an example for his contemporaries because he lived in a period in which circumstances for Jews were significantly different. Jews were respected and a force to be reckoned with in his view, since Pharaoh himself knew of and respected his ancestor Abraham. But Mordecai's situation was different. In his time the Jews were in exile and degraded. Therefore, it was all the more remarkable that a Jew should reach such a high position in the king's court. The analogy to Saba's own times is quite obvious.

This brings us to the next point. What kind of Jew was Mordecai? For Saba the epithet *yehudi* has the connotation of piety and religious observance.[80] Not only was Mordecai an observant Jew, but he was also not ashamed to appear in court wrapped in his prayer shawl with phylacteries displayed prominently on his head and arm! He was not willing to compromise his religious beliefs one iota in order to advance himself in public office, and yet he succeeded. Saba here seems to be pointing a finger at his contemporaries who frequented the courts of kings and were attracted by their manifold allurements. He seems to be holding up Mordecai as an example to those people who were compromising their religious beliefs and practices in order to advance their careers in court.[81] Mordecai was a Jew who did not compromise and yet still managed to succeed in a very impressive fashion.

This picture of Mordecai as the ideal courtier is enhanced by his concern for his fellow Jews. Saba portrays Mordecai as being totally involved in his community providing leadership and guidance in social and economic as well as in religious and spiritual matters. He was a rabbi and teacher as well as a successful courtier. And lest one get the impression that Mordecai did not use his position in court to the best advantage of his fellow Jews, Saba informs us that the tribute that Ahasuerus laid upon the land and the isles of the sea did not include the Jews thanks to Mordecai, who was powerful and influential enough to persuade the king to exempt his Jewish brethren.[82]

The overwhelming reverence for the courtier and the recognition of the important role he played on behalf of the Jewish community generally overrode all other concerns of a moral or religious nature. Indeed, the Book of Esther could be readily adduced as a supporting document, if one were needed, to demonstrate the desirability of having Jews well-placed in court circles. Saba's emphasis on Mordecai's piety and observance may have been his attempt to set a standard which, however unattainable in real life, could nevertheless serve as a model for the sincerely religious courtier.[83]

BIGTHAN AND TERESH'S MOTIVES FOR PLOTTING TO KILL THE KING

The Book of Esther itself offers no reason for Bigthan and Teresh's desire to kill the king. Later midrashic and medieval sources did their best to make up for his deficiency.[84] Some of these sources connect the anger of those two servants with the promotion of Mordecai to a position in the king's court. The Septuagint at 2:21 reads: "the chiefs of the body-guard were grieved because Mordecai was promoted, and they sought to kill the king." According to other sources, they had been replaced by Mordecai and wished to take revenge against the king for their humiliation.[85] In the version of *Panim 'aḥerim B*, one can detect an element of jealousy as well as antisemitism:

> They said: "since the king has removed us from our positions, let us kill him stealthily, so that everyone will say that when Bigthan and Teresh were guarding the king they did a good job; now after he appointed a Jew to the position, he was killed."

Few of the medieval exegetes take up this point, but those that do (Zechariah ben Saruḳ and Isaac Arama) echo the Septuagint, probably unwittingly, in saying that Bigthan and Teresh resented the fact that a Jew had been appointed to a high position in court.[86] These two exegetes, court-conscious as they were, would naturally imagine that Mordecai's presence in a favored position in court would be a source of vexation to other courtiers. The jealousy of other courtiers often led to the downfall of court Jews in the Middle Ages. Arama's and Zechariah's contemporary, the famous statesman and scholar Isaac Abravanel, is a case in point. In the introduction to his Joshua commentary, he explains why he was forced to flee from Portugal where he had once been among the king's favorites at court: "Wicked men who tried to trip me up, and to take everything I possessed, plotted . . . and accused me of things which I had never dreamed of doing."[87] Isaac ben Yedaiah's observation that "every Jew close to the royal court loses his wealth before his death," and that even if he manages to survive and avoid punishment, his son or grandson will not be so fortunate, seems to be borne out by the historical record.[88]

MORDECAI'S REFUSAL TO BOW DOWN BEFORE HAMAN

It is noteworthy that despite Mordecai's image as the ideal courtier, exegetes of all periods and locations question his prudence in refusing to bow down to Haman. Joseph Kara (3:95) is the first to raise the issue, although he does it rather indirectly in commenting on the last verse of the Scroll (10:3).

> *popular with the multitude of his brethren.* This teaches you that there were some of his brethren among whom he was not popular and who used to malign him by saying: "Look what Mordecai did to us, for he baited Haman at whose hand we were sold to be destroyed, slain, and annihilated which would have happened were it not for God, who is master of the hearts of kings, taking our part and inclining the king to command that the Jews should get the mastery over their foes."

Although Kara does not criticize Mordecai directly, he does indicate that there is some room for questioning the wisdom of his actions in this matter. The implication seems to be that Mordecai was a bit rash in challenging Haman so demonstratively and directly.

Abraham Ibn Ezra, in his comment to 3:4 (version A), openly asks why Mordecai endangered his life and the lives of his people by confronting Haman. He does not question whether or not Mordecai should have bowed down to Haman. He seems to feel he should not have. He only wonders why he did not leave his place at the palace gate rather than challenge Haman openly at a time when he was at the height of his power. Had he avoided making a scene, the whole nearly catastrophic incident that followed might have been avoided.[89]

Abraham Shalom puts the question most clearly: "One might wonder about Mordecai and his perfection and ask why he did not bow down to Haman just as other princes and even more respected men had done, [to other officers] even though there must have been among them some who hated them and wished them harm. But, nevertheless, they subordinated their will to the king's command."[90] The issue in question here is obedience to the king's command.[91] Under ordinary circumstances, the king's command must be obeyed, according to the principle of *dina' de-malkhuta' dina'*, "the law of the kingdom is law," i.e., binding on its Jewish inhabitants.[92] Also, there were precedents for Jews bowing down before Gentile kings and leaders, two examples being Abraham to the Hittites (Gn 23:6) and Jacob to Esau (Gn 33:3). Therefore, why did Mordecai refuse?

The answer that most of the exegetes give (even those that do not explicitly ask the question) is that bowing down would have involved some form of idolatry. Ibn Ezra (versions A and B) and Saba follow the midrash [93] in saying that Haman had an image affixed to his clothing or his turban. According to Rashi, who also follows a midrashic source,[94] Haman made a god of himself, while Gersonides (p. 41a) and Joseph Ḥayyun (fol. 75r) say that the king made a god out of Haman in the manner that Nebuchadnezzar[95] had wished to do with Daniel (Dn 2:46). For Abraham Shalom, who considered Haman and Amalek to be astrologers who denied God's providence, Haman's beliefs were heretical and therefore bowing down to him would be tantamount to idolatry.[96]

Isaac ben Joseph ha-Kohen (fols. 60v–61r) and Abraham Saba recall the relationship between Mordecai and Haman and their ancestors. According to R. Isaac, Mordecai felt that in view of the punishment Saul had received for not wiping out all of Amalek, his paying homage to Haman would be equally reproachable, and he did not wish to repeat Saul's mistakes. Saba recalls that Mordecai was a descendant of Benjamin who had not bowed down to Amalek's ancestor Esau (since he had not been born yet!). Therefore, it was not proper for him to bow down to Haman.[97] Isaac Arama (fols. 151v–152r), following his own unique interpretive path, explains that since Mordecai was Esther's uncle, he was part of the royal family and therefore exempt from the decree. No one knew this at the time, but he thought that, when the relationship between himself and Esther became known, he would be subject to punishment for having bowed down. He had no inkling that his actions would have such a disastrous effect on the Jews.

Aside from Arama, who is in a class by himself, most of the exegetes (except, perhaps, Saba and Isaac ben Joseph) seem to agree that had Mordecai's bowing down to Haman not entailed idolatry, he should have done so in order to avoid provoking him and stirring up jealousy among the other courtiers. We see then that survival and protecting the Jewish people from potential threats to their safety were primary concerns for our exegetes. A general sense of respect for temporal power and royal authority is also indicated in many of these statements.[98]

MORDECAI'S ENCOUNTER WITH THE KING'S SERVANTS (3:3–4): JEALOUSY AND RIVALRY IN THE ROYAL COURT

Est 3:3–4 describes an encounter between Mordecai and other servants of the king who apparently rebuked him for not obeying the king's command and finally informed on him to Haman to see whether Mordecai would continue to resist. This incident would seem to be typical of any royal court. One courtier singled himself out for special privilege without any apparent justification. The only reason Mordecai gave was his Jewishness. He seemed to be inviting trouble, and as we mentioned above, several exegetes[99] question the prudence of his action. The anonymous French exegete, "A" (p. 28), asserts that Mordecai would have been better off not revealing his Jewishness to the other courtiers, because this only aroused their jealousy against him. Joseph Kara (3:90) points out that had they not brought the matter to Haman's attention, he probably would not have noticed that Mordecai was not bowing down to him.

According to Abraham Saba (*EKE*, 60), the other servants were jealous because they saw no justification for Mordecai singling himself out for special privilege since they had equal status in court. He also suggests that his being Jewish added an extra dimension to their jealousy, and in fact, had he not been Jewish, they might not have bothered to protest to Haman at all. Isaac Arama (fol. 152r), following his unique understanding of the story, considers that the servants thought that Mordecai was using his Jewishness as an excuse for getting special privileges, since the queen was Jewish. They resented this and spoke to Haman to see if Mordecai would prevail.

Not all the exegetes, however, see the king's servants as Mordecai's enemies. Several depict them as being on friendly terms with Mordecai and looking out for his best interests. According to Isaac ben Joseph ha-Kohen (fol. 61r), all the servants loved Mordecai and were jealous of Haman's position in court. They were hoping that Mordecai would prevail and that Haman would receive his just deserts. Similarly, Abraham Shalom believed that the servants loved Mordecai and had his best interests in mind. That is why they asked him why he transgressed the king's command and not why he refused to bow down to Haman. They tried to impress upon him that he was defying the king's wishes. Even when they told Haman about this, they were not acting against Mordecai but hoped that they would help him by explaining to Haman that Mordecai was not bowing down for religious reasons and not out of pure spite. They also saw this as a test of Mordecai's faith, since if he prevailed the truth of Judaism would be evident before all.[100]

These remarks reflect a very tolerant atmosphere in which Jews are respected members of society and in which confessional differences are also treated with respect. Such an atmosphere is portrayed nowhere more clearly than in the comments of Solomon Astruc to this verse:

> *They told Haman to see if Mordecai's words would stand* (3:4). That is, when the king's servants would ask Mordecai to bow down he would excuse himself by saying that he was a Jew and a Jew does not bow down to an idol or to any form. This is the command of the King who is greater than all other kings. Furthermore, he is not scorning or transgressing the king's command at all in this matter, because the king himself has legislated that the Jews should not be forced to do anything which contravenes their religion. This is what is meant by "for he told them that he was a Jew." For this reason the king's servants saw that his arguments were valid and they said to Haman, if Mordecai were to take his case before the king's council, i.e., the *audiencia*, they would vindicate him because he is a Jew. (p. 216)

Here, then, the Jews are depicted as a privileged minority with full legal rights to practice their religion as they see fit and who are allowed to disobey the king's orders if these would cause them to transgress their religious practices or beliefs.

The situation that Astruc describes in his commentary resembles very much the state of affairs in Aragon under the relatively enlightened reign of Pere III (Pedro IV) (1336–87).[101] According to Yitzhak Baer, Jewish financiers enjoyed intimate personal relations with Pere and other members of the royal family that were not influenced by confessional differences. They were regarded as loyal counselors of the king and his family.[102] Although Baer makes no specific mention of their religion being protected by the king, one can assume that in such an atmosphere the Jewish religion was respected and tolerated.

Indeed the very fact that many exegetes, e.g., Gersonides, felt that Mordecai's Jewishness was an adequate justification for his not bowing down to Haman is significant in and of itself, because their remarks presuppose an atmosphere in which such a claim would be respected.

CONCLUSION

In conclusion, our exegetes' comments on courtiership and court life display an active interest in the institution and keen awareness of its importance for Jewish survival. The roles of Mordecai and Esther were obviously very much admired by the exegetes. But it is interesting to note that in their commentaries these characters are treated with a mixture of respect and suspicion by the Gentiles in court. This reflects the medieval reality in which Jews were key players in many a royal court. On the Jewish side, their presence there was for the most part not only tolerated by Jewish leaders but advocated and encouraged. The Book of Esther gave exegetes an opportunity to reflect on the Jewish position in the royal court and the figures of Mordecai and Esther served as role models for good Jewish courtiership.

While relations with other courtiers were important for Jewish survival, the key relationship was that with the king. The role of King Ahasuerus in the Book of Esther is the focus of the next chapter.

9

THE JEWS AND THE MONARCHY: THE ROLE OF AHASUERUS IN THE BOOK OF ESTHER

One cannot discuss court life and Jewish-Gentile relations as reflected in the medieval Esther commentaries without giving special attention to the question of Ahasuerus's behavior toward the Jews. The character and behavior of the king has always been puzzling for readers of the book, especially those for whom its historical veracity is axiomatic.[1] For in chapter 3, Ahasuerus readily and unquestioningly agrees to Haman's plan to eradicate this "scattered and dispersed people" from their midst. Yet in chapter 7 and following, he becomes a great friend and advocate of the Jewish cause. One is therefore confronted with the need to explain this seeming about-face. One possible explanation is that Ahasuerus was a weak, fickle, and malevolent ruler easily influenced by his powerful advisers. When he was under Haman's influence he readily agreed to whatever he asked of him and did not give it much thought. In other words, he was either quite indifferent to the Jews, or hated them as much as Haman did and happily went along with his plan. But, when, through Esther's maneuvering, Haman fell out of favor and Mordecai and Esther gained control, they had virtually a free hand as far as the Jews were concerned.

The other possible explanation of Ahasuerus's behavior is that Ahasuerus was a weak and benevolent ruler. He never intended the Jews any harm, but he had no idea of what Haman was planning to do. When he found out, he was justly outraged and punished Haman and his cohorts as they deserved and from then on did whatever he could to benefit Mordecai, Esther, and the Jews.

The first opinion is, in general, characteristic of the majority of the sages and has a few advocates in the Middle Ages. Rashi follows the rabbinic line quite closely. Quoting the Talmud (without acknowledgement), he refers to Ahasuerus as a thoroughly wicked king who was not even of royal ancestry.[2] Ahasuerus himself had issued the decree against the Jews and was fully cognizant of it.[3] He was not sensitive at all to the Jews' plight, and wondered why Esther should care so much for her people's welfare.[4]

Joseph Kara too, has nothing good to say about Ahasuerus. In the Vashti affair, Ahasuerus reveals himself as quick to anger, "and unrefined in manner."[5] Vashti was quite justified in opposing him.[6] He readily agrees to the destruction of the Jews.[7] He was fickle and unreliable and might change his mind at any time. Therefore, it was necessary for Mordecai and Esther to act quickly while he was still favorably inclined toward them.[8] "A," the third northern French exegete, describes him as a weak king who could not control his drink. In addition, "A" adds a new dimension which will recur in later commentaries, although with a different slant—Ahasuerus's susceptibility to pressures by other members of the royal family and the officers at court.[9]

At the other end of our time span, two Iberian exegetes, Joseph Ḥayyun and Zechariah ben Saruḳ, both heavily influenced by rabbinic opinion, are also quite negative in their assessment of Ahasuerus. According to Ḥayyun (fol. 77r), Ahasuerus hated the Jews just as much as Haman did. He did not take the bribe from Haman because of his strong feeling of hatred, apparently not needing the monetary incentive. He gave Haman permission to do what he wished with the Jews, and this included plundering their property. According to R. Zechariah, Ahasuerus had declared himself a god as had Nebuchadnezzar before him,[10] and the image which was affixed to Haman's breast was that of Ahasuerus himself. He gave Haman permission to destroy, kill and annihilate the Jews, and although the destruction of the Jews was instigated by Haman, Ahasuerus cooperated with him fully:

> *If it please Your Majesty, let an edict be drawn for their destruction* (3:9) and I [Haman] will pay the perpetrators. Immediately "the king removed his signet ring from his hand" (3:10), "and letters were sent" (3:13). Note that the wicked Haman at first only asked that the Jewish religion be obliterated, as I have said.[11] After that he made a further request that their money be confiscated.[12] And when he sent out the letters he wrote in them that [the Jews] should be destroyed, killed and annihilated. Now if you should ask how did he do what the king did not command him to, I would reply that when he [Ahasuerus] said, "and the people to do with as you please," he gave him permission to destroy, kill and annihilate. (p. 13a)

EXEGESIS IN DEFENSE OF THE KING

In contrast to this negative attitude, most other medieval exegetes try to put Ahasuerus in a more favorable light. This tendency is seen nowhere more clearly than in the attempts by several Spanish exegetes to minimize Ahasuerus's role in Haman's plot to destroy the Jews.

One point made in defense of Ahasuerus's actions is that he was not fully aware of Haman's intentions and that he gave Haman permission only to confiscate the Jews' money. This is based on the assumption that the words *le-'abbed* (3:13, "to annihilate") and *le-'abbedam* (3:9, "that they be destroyed") refer to the wealth of the Jews, not to their physical destruction.[13] Thus, Abraham Ḥadidah:

> It is possible that when Haman said, "If it please Your Majesty let an edict be drawn for their destruction" (3:9), [the king] thought that this referred to the confiscation of their money and for this he gave him permission, and he [Haman] added on his own "to destroy, massacre" (3:13); and for this reason he [the king] said, "'Who is he and where is he who dared to do this' (7:5) for he decreed to slay all the Jews and I only gave permission to take all or part of their money but not to kill them." (fol. 45 v)

The rationale for this interpretation would appear to be the following: each of the words *le-hashmid, la-harog, le-'abbed* (to destroy, to massacre, to annihilate, 3:13) must have a different connotation. When Haman spoke to the king he used one word—*le-'abbedam* ("to annihilate them")—but when he wrote the decrees he wrote in them more than the king had agreed to. Since the king would never have agreed to destroy the people Haman was referring to, *le-'abbedam* cannot mean to destroy or annihilate but must have a less severe connotation, such as destruction or confiscation of their money and resources. It is plausible that this the king would agree to. The clinching argument in this line of interpretation is the fact that the king in 7:5 seems to know nothing about Haman's plot and asks in righteous indignation, "*Who is he and where is he who dared to do this*?" Therefore, the conclusion to be drawn is that Haman acted wholly on his own initiative and the king was totally in the dark.

Several exegetes demonstrate their awareness that the Jews were a valuable source of revenue for the king. Thus, an anonymous northern French exegete glosses 7:4 "the enemy does not consider the loss to the king"[14] as follows: "[this means] to cause him to lose the tax revenues that they [the Jews] provided each year."[15]

No one expresses this more clearly than Solomon Astruc in his comment to Est 10:1:

> *King Ahasuerus imposed tribute on the mainland.* Perhaps this was Mordecai's advice to the king so that he should appreciate the benefit deriving from allowing Jews to remain, to wit, what he takes from them year after year. For there would have been no point to write this here unless Mordecai had done this so that the king would no longer listen to bad advisers, for he could see with his own eyes the advantage deriving from their existence. (p. 223)

In contrast to most exegetes, who comment that because of Mordecai's presence in the court the king taxed his kingdom heavily (Kara, Ibn Ezra, Naḥmias, Isaac ben Joseph) but exempted the Jews (Arama, Saba), Astruc suggests that it was precisely at Mordecai's instigation that the king raised a levy against the Jews, so that the king would be reminded of how valuable the Jews were to him as a source of needed income and never again consider destroying or expelling them.

At 3:10–11, Astruc has his Haman assure the king that ten thousand talents of silver would end up in his coffers to compensate for the loss in tax revenues that the king would suffer as a result of the Jews' elimination. Astruc does not think that Haman would have suggested paying the ten thousand talents out of his pocket because this would have made him look too eager to be rid of the Jews out of his hatred for them. But, in his view, Haman assured the king that he would take in more revenue from the Jews on this one occasion than he would gain from them in his whole lifetime.[16]

Along similar lines, "Ramah" asks: "Why did the king not answer [Haman] that it would be proper to take their wealth and expel them which would be better than killing them (fol. 8 v)?" He answers that it seems to him that Haman suggested that the king confiscate the wealth of the Jews (*sha'al 'ibbud ha-mamon she-lahem la-melekh*) and offered to give an additional ten thousand talents of silver on top of that. But when the king replied, "The money is given to you, the people also etc." (3:11), he immediately wrote *to destroy, massacre, and exterminate* (3:13) saying: "I will count out the money, but I will not give it immediately." He also adds the following rather cynical comment at 3:11: "I know that the Jews will give you the money first as a bribe, and after that, you can do with them as you please" ("Ramah," ibid.).

Bribery was a way of life for Jews in the Middle Ages and served various functions. Quite often it was necessary for a community to guarantee its security in the face of a threatened massacre or expulsion by means of bribery, and even then, as "Ramah" suggests above, they were not always assured that the bribe would have the desired results.[17]

Following a line similar to that of "Ramah," Isaac Arama writes, "His saying 'let an edict be drawn for their destruction' (3:9) does not mean to destroy, massacre, and exterminate (3:13), for *this is something that human nature could not tolerate*, but it means that they should be expelled or enslaved" [emphasis added] (fol. 153 r). Arama's defense also focuses on the word *le-'abbedam* ("for their destruction") (3:9), but he, without any apparent foundation except his conviction that the very idea is contrary to human nature, states that it must mean to expel or enslave.

It is not very difficult to understand why some exegetes could more easily entertain the idea of expulsion of the Jews than their destruction. Expulsion of Jewish communities was an all too common occurrence in Europe in the late Middle Ages. England, in 1290, was the first country to expel its Jewish community. The Jews were expelled from and recalled back to France several times in the fourteenth century. The final expulsion of French Jewry occurred in 1394. Germany also witnessed numerous massacres and local expulsions throughout the fourteenth and fifteenth centuries.[18] The motivations for these expulsions varied. Although fiscal reasons—i.e., the need to fill empty coffers—were almost always involved, the rising tide of nationalism which brought with it increased feelings of hostility among the populace toward Jews and other foreign elements in society was certainly a contributing factor.[19] Of course, in the context that we are dealing with, the monetary factor is the one that is paramount in the minds of the exegetes. Indeed, it would seem likely that, for most medievals, this would be the case. Furthermore, if the king's main goal is to acquire the Jews' wealth, expulsion is just as efficient a method as destruction and leaves open the possibility of recalling the Jews at a later date.

The second exegetical line of defense of Ahasuerus's reputation is based on the words in 3:11, "the people also, to do with them as it seems good to you."[20] The first exegete to use this line is Solomon Astruc whose comment to 3:11 reads as follows:

> He said: "The money is given to you." The king meant by this that he is not concerned with [material] damage or benefit and that if Haman could see any benefit deriving from reproving them and punishing them so that they would not rebel against him, that money [that he would take from them] would be his either to do with as he pleased or to give all or part of it into the king's treasury. With regard to the people he should do whatever he sees as fitting and proper in order to foil their rebellion. This is what is meant by "as it seems good to you," i.e., that he should choose the good and the fitting. *By this he demonstrated that he did not want to destroy them but only to subjugate and enslave them.* This is the reason why, when the king said: "Who is he and where is he who dared to do this?" (7:5), no one replied to him: "You, my lord, agreed to destroy them." For the king had told him "*as it seems good to you.*" . . . In this regard our sages said: "Hatred upsets the normal order of things."[21] Haman's hatred prevented him from understanding what the king meant when he said "as it seems good to you." [emphasis added] (p. 217)

According to Astruc, the king never intended to give Haman permission to destroy the Jews. The phrase "as it seems good to you" is understood by him to mean that the king intended that Haman should do what was good and proper, i.e., whatever would remove the danger to the kingdom and the possibility of a rebellion. The word "good" is taken to mean "what is best for all concerned" and "to you" (literally, "in your eyes")—"that you should work out the most convenient way to do good for all concerned." All the king wanted to do was to subdue and subjugate the rebellious Jewish population and so preserve order in his kingdom.

Abraham Saba, like Astruc, understood the phrase "the people also, to do with them as it seems good to you" (3:11) to imply that the king did not wish to destroy the Jews,

> for this would be a very shameful act to smite for no reason the people that came to his land at the command of an ancient king . . . and Ahasuerus thought that after he delivered [the Jews] into [Haman's] hands he would have mercy on them, and it never occurred to him that he would perpetrate such a cruel act as killing an entire nation, for the blame would all fall on the king, and Haman as his servant should have avoided this. (*EKE*, 67)

But, says Saba, Ahasuerus did not realize the depth of Haman's hatred for the Jews. And Haman, when he saw that Ahasuerus gullibly accepted all he said without question, simply went ahead with his evil plan.

Saba is perhaps the most ambivalent of all the exegetes in his attitude to the king. He is unwilling to see him as a coconspirator with Haman and generally attributes good intentions to him. Nevertheless, Ahasuerus was to blame for being so foolish and gullible in so readily acquiescing to Haman's plan. In Saba's commentary, one can clearly see the tension between the midrashic and medieval views of Ahasuerus, for he was strongly influenced by both. His views of Ahasuerus are worth examining in greater detail.

According to Saba, Ahasuerus was a great king and he goes to great lengths to build up the evidence to support this claim. First of all he was one of the kings of Persia and Media, who were all close to God and treated the Jews respectfully.[22] Furthermore, it is well known that even the most vicious of Israel's enemies would never agree to destroy the Jews in order not to be called a barbarous kingdom.[23]

Saba explains the necessity for including the verses describing Ahasuerus's prowess and the majesty of his banquet by the need to establish that he was a great and important king and not a minor monarch of little importance:

> For this reason, he said that it is not so [that Ahasuerus was unimportant], for he is a great king, the Ahasuerus of renown, who rules from India to Ethiopia, and he was a famous man, a giant among giants, who emerged victorious; with his great might he captured 127 provinces from India to Ethiopia thereby adding onto the Persian kingdom. This is what is meant by "he raised himself up to his throne,"[24] with his strength and might, something that the other kings of Persia had not done. This is attested to at the end of the scroll, where it is written "all his mighty and powerful acts . . . are recorded etc." (10:2). . . . At the end he mentioned that he taxed the mainland and the islands, thereby showing his great strength and might. (pp. 23–24)

Besides portraying him as a great and powerful king in temporal terms, Saba also considers him righteous in the eyes of God, classing him with the likes of Abraham, Perez (son of Judah) and Terah (Abraham's father). Because of the great good that he did for Mordecai and all of Israel he is included among the righteous of the nations of the world who have a share in the world to come (p. 24).

In view of all this, Saba finds it difficult to understand how Ahasuerus could acquiesce to the destruction of this great nation taking shelter under his wing. This seems to him to be totally incomprehensible. Saba seems to be torn between his idea of how a good king should behave and the poor image of Ahasuerus that emerges from the scroll. He feels he must defend Ahasuerus's reputation, and the best he can do is portray him as a well-intentioned but gullible and fickle person who was easily deceived by those more clever than he. This was why the sages called him a foolish king (p. 28). He himself did not want work on the Temple to be stopped, but he listened to Vashti's advice (ibid.). He had good intentions and conducted his affairs properly, but he was surrounded by poor advisers and was often led astray by their advice (p. 29).

In another way, Ahasuerus was really an instrument of God's design. The Jews had sinned by bowing to the idol of Nebuchadnezzar and by partaking in the banquet of Ahasuerus and therefore deserved to be punished.[25] God, therefore, inclined Ahasuerus's heart to listen to Vashti's advice about not rebuilding the Temple and to Haman's advice about the Jews.

As Saba was favorably inclined toward Ahasuerus (p. 28), it was only with great reluctance that he called him a wicked king and in the one place where he does heavily criticize his character he takes care not to place him in the same class as Haman.

> We have already explained that although Ahasuerus was a wicked person, his wickedness is not to be compared with that of Haman. Rather he was a foolish, gullible simple person (Prv 14:15), confused, unstable, and fickle. He did not possess the knowledge to distinguish between good and evil and truth and falsehood. This resulted in his acquiescing to unjust causes as readily as to just ones. The builders of the tower [of Babel] behaved in a similar fashion, agreeing to falsehood as readily as they did to truth. (p. 65)

Rather, he attributes his dull-wittedness and poor performance as king to his racial origin. According to Saba, Ahasuerus, being of Persian origin was an Ishmaelite, while Haman was an Edomite. The Ishmaelites were rather dull-witted, ignorant people with little rhetorical skill. The Edomites on the other hand were clever, learned, and shrewd and were very gifted and smooth talkers who did not hesitate to use their skills for the practice of slander and deception.[26] Thus Saba finds a genetic justification for Ahasuerus's behavior. As he was of Ishmaelite origin, one could not expect any better from him. He fell easy prey to the smooth-talking and clever Haman.

One can see in all of these exegetes a definite desire to protect the reputation of the office of the king and portray Ahasuerus in a better light than it would seem the plain meaning of the biblical text would warrant. What could have been the motivation behind this desire? The answer might be found in the ideal of the gracious king which was so prevalent in certain circles of Spanish Jewry in the Middle Ages.[27] According to this view, which was expressed nowhere better than in the *Shevet Yehudah* of Solomon Ibn Verga, the king is the constant and faithful protector and benefactor of the Jews. The king is never responsible for the calamities that befall the Jews over the generations. In fact, he always does his utmost to protect the Jews from the masses and lower clergy, their traditional enemies.

But sometimes, if the people rise up against the Jews, the king, with all his good will cannot save them. In Ibn Verga's words:

> For as a rule, the kings of Spain and France and the princes and those who know and all the nobility loved the Jews and hatred

> was to be found only among the masses who were jealous of the Jews. And if the king guarantees our security and the people [still] rise up, how can we be secure, especially, as we have seen in the past so many expulsions that were brought upon us by the people? To what avail is the king's grace and that of the judges of the land if the will of the people is not with us and they constantly wish us evil?[28]

Though the position of the Jews might still be precarious, their ties to the monarchy could not be broken. The Jewish courtier class in Spain felt that it had a special relationship with the Spanish monarchy, and their view of the uniqueness of this relationship became a guiding myth for them right up until the eve of the expulsion.[29] These Jews gave themselves over body and soul to their protector monarchs and saw themselves as virtually indispensable to their rulers. It was therefore inconceivable to these people that a king would agree to or even contemplate the wholesale destruction of his Jewish subjects. In this view, the few monarchs who broke faith with the Jews and treated them with undue cruelty and harshness were soon punished.[30]

But even in the eyes of so stalwart a supporter of the monarchy as Ibn Verga, the Spanish kings could be seen to be susceptible to the machinations of unscrupulous counselors and were not always able to discern what was in the best interests of their kingdom. Consider the following incident related in *Shevet Yehudah*,[31] which is strikingly reminiscent in language and circumstances of the Esther story. The incident takes place in the mid–fourteenth century during the reign of Alfonso XI of Castile who ruled from 1312–50. In 1339, Abu Malik, son of Abu'l Hasan, Emir of Morocco, attacked Castile with a large force.[32] One of the king's advisers, Gonzalo Martinez de Oviedo, an avowed enemy of the Jews, advised the king to confiscate the money of the Jews and expel them from the country. He even offered to see to it that the inhabitants of the provinces would make up for the four million *marvedis* in taxes that the Jews provided. In support of his advice, Gonzalo argues that the king has nothing to fear from Israel's God, since he has forsaken them in anger. He calls Israel a rebellious people who do not help the king. When the king goes out to do battle against his enemies the Jews stay home eating and drinking. He urges the king to send letters ordering that the Jews in his kingdom be expelled and allowing anyone who finds a Jew in his house to confiscate his money and kill him. The king should appoint officers to guard all the gold and silver plunder in order to bring it to the king's treasury.

When the king heard all this he was silent. But some of those close to the king raged at Gonzalo saying: "This piece of advice is ill-timed. For it is the custom of Castile and her kings to love her Jews and protect them. Who will listen to you in this matter?" The archbishop of Toledo, "Don Gil" (Aegidius Albornoz), protested vehemently, calling Gonzalo's advice disgraceful and ill-conceived, "For the Jews are a treasure to the king, a goodly treasure. But you seek to destroy them and urge the king to do what his fathers did not. You are not an enemy of the Jews, but of the king!"

Gonzalo's diatribe against the Jews contains some of the traditional arguments which appear in the targumim and midrashim to Esther. The Jews are described as being of no use to the king, shirking duty in his service.[33] Furthermore, there is no need to fear retaliation from their God, because He has long since abandoned them.[34] The king here, as in our commentaries, appears to be weak-minded and susceptible to poor advisers. He seems ready to acquiesce to Gonzalo's evil plan and is only prevented from doing so by some of his advisers and the archbishop who step in and speak up on behalf of the Jews. The advisers speak of the traditional good relations between the Jews and the Crown that have existed for so long. The king has always protected his Jews. But it is the archbishop who provides the ultimate justification. The Jews are a treasure of the king. Anyone who wishes to destroy them does not have the best interests of the kingdom at heart. To be an enemy of the Jews is also to be an enemy of the Crown.

Therefore, if harm sometimes does befall the Jews of a given kingdom, the king is never to blame, for it is in his best interests to protect the Jews, and he would never desire such a thing to happen. Kings are subject to many pressures from advisers, clergy, and the masses, and not every king is endowed with the strength of character needed to stand up to these pressures. In the case quoted above, Alfonso would have probably gone along with Gonzalo Martinez's advice were it not for his other advisers who strongly argued on behalf of the Jews.[35]

The ideal of the gracious king is expressed most clearly in Ibn Verga's description of the Lisbon massacre of 1506.[36] I would argue that the same factors that were at play in influencing Ibn Verga's portrayal of King Manuel of Portugal and other kings in *Sheveṭ Yehudah* also influenced the portrayal of King Ahasuerus at the hands of the

Spanish exegetes mentioned above. We see a reluctance to ascribe any evil intent toward the Jews on the part of Ahasuerus and a refusal to consider that the king would even contemplate outright destruction of the Jews.[37] The generally weak exegetical underpinnings that the various commentators provide for their arguments only reinforce the impression that we have here a clear case in which an exegete's own experience and his perception of reality impose themselves upon the text in such a way as to hamper the exegetical process. In other words, the exegete tries to force his view of reality on the text rather than try to determine the text's meaning by letting the text speak for itself.

That this was not an isolated phenomenon in medieval exegesis can be demonstrated by an examination of some comments to passages in Mishnah 'Avot which deal with the related subject of relations between Jews and the secular authorities.

'Avot 1:10 enjoins the reader: "seek not acquaintance with the ruling power."[38] One would think that this rabbinic injunction would give our medieval courtiers and those that revered them pause for reflection and reconsideration of their positions. This was so in some cases,[39] but many chose to ignore it. Rabbi Joseph Naḥmias's comment to this verse is instructive:

> The king is called the authority because in him is invested the authority to do what he pleases . . . while the servants of the ruling powers are always in a state of utmost terror and fear for their lives which are constantly in danger; in any case, at this time it is necessary for us that Jews be present in the courts of kings, "seeking the good of their people and interceding for the welfare of all their kindred" (Est 10:3). We must pray for their welfare for if all is well with them so shall it be with us.[40]

'Avot 2:3 is even more outspoken in its condemnation and mistrust of imperial powers: "Be heedful of the ruling power for they bring no man nigh to them save for their own need; they seem to be friends such time as it is their gain but they stand not with a man in his time of stress."[41] This is a damning statement which seems to discredit kings in unequivocal terms. Yet this statement was totally unacceptable to R. Jonah Gerondi who states:

> The simplest sense of this mishnah would seem to speak to the discredit of kings. But Heaven forbid, Heaven forbid, this thing

> cannot be nor can it stand! For it is through them that the whole world is preserved. They execute judgment and justice, and there is no man on earth who can be as truthful as they. For being unafraid, they need not fawn upon people. And nothing prevents them from following a straight path.[42]

It is difficult to characterize the comments of R. Joseph and R. Jonah as exegesis. Neither of them actually interprets the text as it stands, apparently because it flies in the face of reality as they know it. R. Joseph ignores the statement in 'Avot or at best acknowledges it by implication, saying that the advice given in this statement is simply not appropriate for his situation in which it is necessary for Jews to be present in the courts of kings in order to preserve the welfare of their communities.[43] R. Jonah simply rejects the statement in 'Avot as totally unacceptable without trying to justify his position on exegetical grounds. Therefore, it is difficult to characterize this comment as "a forced interpretation."[44] It is more a reaction to the text than an interpretation of it. It does seem likely, as Septimus suggests, that R. Jonah's enthusiasm for royalty and royal justice stemmed in part from his own reassuring experiences with the royal powers,[45] and this experience colored his understanding of the text.

THE VASHTI AFFAIR

The generally high opinion that the medievals had of Ahasuerus and of the position of the king in general, is also seen in their treatment of the Vashti affair. Admittedly there is considerable criticism of Ahasuerus's initial action in summoning Vashti to appear before him,[46] but it was generally felt that, once Vashti had defied him in public, he had no choice but to act as he did, in order to protect the dignity of his office.

Consider Joseph Kara's elaboration on Memucan's argument (1:16):

> In ordinary circumstances, when a queen upsets the king, it is between him and her, and since no permanent breach is caused by this, it is worthwhile that anger should be contained, but here, in this case, "Queen Vashti has committed an offense not only against Your Majesty." (3:88)

Isaac Arama argues that Ahasuerus had to do what he did for the welfare of the kingdom,[47] and Abraham Saba (pp. 31–32) maintains that Ahasuerus had to deal severely with Vashti since he had to assert his authority at the beginning of his reign if he did not wish to be plagued constantly by insubordination and rebellion.

All in all, there is complete unanimity among the exegetes all through the Middle Ages that, considering the circumstances, Ahasuerus's punishment of Vashti was quite justified. An additional consideration for some (e.g., Saba and Immanuel of Rome) is that this was all part of God's plan to save the Jews and that Vashti had to be eliminated in order to make it possible for Esther to be chosen queen.

THE KING'S REACTION TO THE KILLING OF HIS SUBJECTS BY THE JEWS

Another passage which can be used to evaluate the attitude of the exegetes to Ahasuerus and their perceptions of his relations with the Jews is 9:12–13 in which Ahasuerus reports to Esther the casualty figures among the enemies of the Jews. One might expect Ahasuerus to feel more than a little uncomfortable about the carnage being wrought upon his subjects, and this discomfort is expressed in some of our early commentaries.

According to Joseph Kara, Ahasuerus was not too pleased with the situation but still stood by his promise to Esther.

> *In the fortress Shushan alone the Jews have killed . . . What then must they have done in the provinces of the realm!* (9:12) As if he regretted the matter and out of concern used an *a fortiori* argument: "If in the fortress Shushan, where the Jews should have been afraid to kill the king's people, out of fear of the king, the Jews have killed five hundred men, *a fortiori*, how many more must they have killed in the other provinces of the king where the king was not present? And lest you [Esther] say that I regret what I said to you at the feast, 'What is your wish now? It shall be granted you;' even now I stand firm in my offer: 'What is your wish now? It shall be granted you. And what else is your request? It shall be fulfilled.' " (3:94)

Similarly, "A" sees Ahasuerus as acquiescing to Esther's request only reluctantly and with much sorrow.

> *In the fortress Shushan* (9:12), where they should have been afraid and concerned about me [i.e., about my reaction] the Jews killed

> five hundred men, *a fortiori*, what then have they done in the rest of the king's provinces? And although this is a very difficult matter for me, still "what else is your request? It shall be fulfilled." (p. 31)

The sages also had difficulty in explaining Ahasuerus's action in light of his general lack of enthusiasm for the Jewish cause and his ready acquiescence to Haman's plot. They postulate divine intervention in order to make sense of the scene: "R. Abbahu said, 'This teaches us that an angel came and slapped him on his mouth,'"[48] which Rashi glosses "He began to speak in anger, and in the end he said: 'What is your wish now?'" The sages seemed to detect a change in mood from the first part of the verse to the second. In the first part, Ahasuerus seems to be angry and upset over the loss of so many of his subjects. Yet in the second part of the verse, he is conciliatory and asks Esther what else he can do for her. They could explain this seemingly instantaneous change of attitude on the part of Ahasuerus only by postulating the intervention of an angel who forced Ahasuerus to say what he said.

Gersonides must have had this rabbinic comment in mind when he wrote the fiftieth "lesson" in his Esther commentary:

> This is to make known the strength of God's providence for Israel in its ability to incline the king's heart to everything that Queen Esther requested. For one can see that from Ahasuerus's words to Queen Esther it was obvious that the killing of those men was difficult for the king to bear and for this reason he said: "In the fortress Shushan etc.," and yet despite this he said to her: "And what else is your request? It shall be fulfilled." (p. 48b)

However, those exegetes who were of the opinion that Ahasuerus was wholeheartedly behind Esther and the Jews and supported them without reservations interpret the verse quite differently. According to Isaac ben Joseph ha-Kohen, for instance, Ahasuerus complains about the low casualty figures:

> He said to her: "If in Shushan the capital, which is a populous city, the Jews killed only five hundred of their enemies and Haman's ten sons who were already frightened to death, while they [the Jews] knew that you and I were supporting them, who knows what they did in the other provinces which are far from us. This means, that I consider that they did very little in the other

> provinces." . . . What led me to interpret in this way is the fact that it would reflect badly on Esther's manners and great intelligence if she felt that the king, in telling her the numbers of dead and what the Jews did in the other provinces, felt anguished about the great carnage that had been caused, and only agreed to it out of his great love for her, telling her out of politeness that if she wanted anything else he would give it to her. It would not have been proper for her to ask for another day for the Jews of Susa to do what they had done the previous day. Therefore, it would seem that the king wanted very much to destroy those wicked men. For perhaps, after the death of Haman's sons, he had learnt about acts of informing and harmful deeds against the king and violence against the people which had been carried out with the help of Haman's sons. Besides, he wanted the whole world to acknowledge that the queen's people are valiant fighters. What confirms this interpretation is that when Esther asked for another day she did not ask for it in a supplicative manner . . . and her speech implied an apology for Israel for having held back and been reluctant to destroy their enemies out of fear that the king might be distressed by this. But since the king has made his opinion known in this matter, it could still be corrected by having the Jews continue what they did today on the morrow. (fol. 73r–v)

In a similar vein, Abraham Saba sees the king as quite satisfied with the killings since he considered the people killed by the Jews to be undesirable elements who needed to be eliminated, and he readily acquiesced to Esther's request for another day to continue the carnage.

Saba quotes another opinion even more similar to that of Isaac b. Joseph ha-Kohen:

> There are those that say that the king was angry that they did not kill more in Susa and he was also angry that Haman's ten sons were only killed and not impaled on stakes as had been done with their father. Therefore, the king said to Esther: "In the fortress Shushan, the Jews, in their weakness killed five hundred men," whereas they should have killed more since the king and the queen were helping them, and the ten sons of Haman who were as good as dead they [merely] killed. Therefore, in other provinces where the king and queen were not present for support what

> could they have done? Certainly, they must have left rebels and traitors. Therefore, "What is your wish now? It shall be granted you." Since she understood his words, she said, "Let the Jews in Susa be permitted to act tomorrow as they did today. (p. 91)

The opinions of Isaac ha-Kohen and Abraham Saba can be seen as fitting into the school of thought which saw Ahasuerus as entirely sympathetic to the Jews. Since he valued and respected the Jews as a people and considered them an asset to his kingdom, even without considering that they were the people of his queen, he was very interested in assuring their survival and success against their enemies. Therefore, it would be natural for him to consider the enemies of the Jews as undesirable elements best eliminated from his kingdom. This view, typical of the Spanish exegetes, contrasts sharply with that of the northern French who seemed to view the king as their natural enemy.

CONCLUSION

In conclusion, we have seen how the exegetes' experiences, this time with the ruling authorities, colored their views of the character and behavior of Ahasuerus and took some of them on tortuous and precarious exegetical flights of fancy. These may not do justice to the plain meaning of the text, but offer important insights into the thought processes of the medieval exegete.

CONCLUDING REMARKS

Our study of the Jewish exegesis of the Book of Esther in the Middle Ages is now drawing to a close. We have encountered a colorful array of exegetes spanning several centuries and hailing from countries all over the European continent. We have examined the sources they used and discussed their commentaries against their medieval background. We have seen how the exegetes brought their education and intellectual predilections to bear on their exegetical work. Those trained in Hebrew and Arabic grammar and lexicography applied these disciplines to their study of the book in an attempt to elucidate the *peshaṭ* or contextual meaning of the text. For many, the midrashic tradition of exegesis was still paramount and dominated their exegesis. Others who were more involved with the intellectual currents of their times explained the text in terms of these currents, whether philosophical or kabbalistic, or tried to use the biblical text as a vehicle for the dissemination of new ideas which they adopted from these schools of thought. Finally, in the exegesis of this book, perhaps more than in any other, the exegetes' personal experiences and attitudes figured prominently in their commentaries.

While the acronym PaRDeS, which signifies the four levels or methods of interpretation used by the medieval exegetes,[1] more or less accurately describes the various approaches to the biblical text found in our commentaries, only one Esther exegete, Baḥya ben Asher, actually employed a multilevel structure in his commentary on the book.[2] For Esther he provided only a threefold interpretation. Other exegetes interpreted according to their inclinations and interests drawing on a variety of sources in a more or less random fashion. While there may have been the sense among certain exegetes that the text had different levels of meaning, this was seldom made explicit or formally set out in the commentaries on the Book of Esther. Nevertheless, several interpretations were often given to a verse on an individual, ad hoc basis.

What conclusions may be drawn from our study with regard to the place of the Book of Esther in medieval Judaism? May we extend any of these conclusions to the Bible as a whole? The Book of Esther, in some ways, was unique, in that it was a historical book set in the Diaspora that described a situation that had an uncommon immediacy to medieval Jews who found themselves in situations similar to that described in the book. The story of a beautiful and clever Jewish woman marrying a Gentile king was a source of pride and encouragement for Jews, a reminder of better times past. In fact, it is remarkable to note how positively inclined toward Esther our medieval exegetes are. They take great pride in her wisdom and wit and lovingly describe in great detail her every action.[3] Mordecai's meteoric rise to power and his success in court would also have served as a much-needed boost to the sagging self-image of many medieval Jews, discouraged by a long and seemingly endless history of persecution and exile. The happy ending of the story helped strengthen the faith of Jewish communities during the Middle Ages and gave them hope that they too would soon be redeemed from their exile. Theologically, the book was an important buttress for the people's faith in divine providence and in the promise of ultimate redemption. Furthermore, as we have seen, the book, especially verse 3:8, served as a vehicle for the expression of the Jews' feelings about their own situation in the Diaspora and their relations with the Gentile community. In their comments on Haman's diatribe we see reflected their own impressions of how they were perceived by their Gentile neighbors.

With regard to the Bible as a whole, we can only raise some questions at this point that require further research to answer. One question that needs to be asked is how did the Jews in the Middle Ages read the Bible? The Bible is not cut of a single cloth. It contains narratives describing the early history of the Jewish people, collections of laws considered to be of divine origin and eternally binding on the Jewish community, prophetic works, prayers, and wisdom literature dealing with ultimate issues such as theodicy and humanity's role in the universe. The exegesis of each of these types of literature needs to be studied independently before one can arrive at a clear picture of the role that the Bible played in the intellectual and spiritual life of the Jewish community.[4]

Related to this question is the question of the role that the Bible played in the lives of the Jewish people. To answer this it is necessary to examine its use in other forms of literary and spiritual expression such as religious poetry (*piyyuṭ*) sermons, parodies, satires, and halakhic works. The Book of Esther, for example, figured in many *piyyuṭim* for Purim and Shabbat Zakhor and is the subject of many sermons for these two occasions as well. To what extent, if at all, were such works influenced by exegesis, either earlier or contemporary? What liberties did the authors take with the text, and is there any exegesis to be found in their works? These are questions only touched upon occasionally in this work but which deserve further consideration and fuller treatment.

Many exegetes, like artists and poets in the Middle Ages, portrayed events and scenes in the Bible in terms of their own background and culture because this was the only world that they knew. This approach often had the effect of bringing the text to life for their readers and making it more accessible to them. Can we say with certainty that exegetes who took this approach had a wider audience in mind? Or did they do their work ingenuously, following their natural inclinations? The Bible at all times was seen through a medieval prism which colored the exegetes' understanding of the text and limited the possibilities for interpretation. Often, interpretations suggested themselves to an exegete because the text spoke to his particular situation. One would expect that such comments would have been meaningful to his contemporary readers whose situation was similar or at least familiar.

This leads us to the question of the role of exegesis in the cultural and intellectual life of medieval Jewry. Was it the sole preserve of an intellectual elite, or were exegetical works read by a wider readership? Obviously, some commentaries were more popular than others. What factors contributed to the popularity of certain commentaries and to the neglect of others? Was this neglect always justified? Many of the exegetes included in this study are virtually unknown in Jewish history. Their works survive in manuscript, sometimes only in single copies. Some are not very original and probably deserve their obscurity and lack of fame. Yet, many have interesting things to say and contribute immeasurably to our appreciation of the medieval imagination. Therefore, it is important to study these minor figures in order to see the whole picture in all its hues and shades. It is no longer sufficient to rely on the famous figures whose works have already been printed when doing studies of this nature.

The modern study of medieval Jewish biblical exegesis has seldom gone beyond the thirteenth century, with most of the studies concentrating on Rashi and the northern French school, Abraham Ibn Ezra, and the Kimḥi family.[5] Furthermore, most of these studies have been carried out by biblicists, whose primary interest is in gleaning information from medieval commentaries which could aid in the elucidation of the biblical text.[6] This fact also explains why studies were seldom carried past the thirteenth century, since after this point interest in grammar and in elucidating the *peshaṭ* of the biblical text waned. Scholars are now beginning to change the focus of study of medieval exegesis and to place it in the context of medieval intellectual history.[7] The Bible, as the foundational text of the Jewish faith, could not be ignored by the medieval scholar. In order for his teachings to be accepted by the community, support for them had to be found in the Bible. Thus we see the Bible being searched diligently for sources of moral instruction and verses useful for the dissemination of philosophical or mystical ideas. Of course, not all medieval scholars were either philosophically or mystically inclined, and those who were not chose to adhere to the rabbinic tradition and continued to disseminate the views and interpretations found in the works of the sages.

The Bible played a pivotal role in the life of medieval Jews, and an understanding of their view of the Bible is necessary in order to get a complete picture of their worldview. The contribution of an exegete's exegesis to our understanding of the biblical text should not, however, be the sole criterion in determining the value of his commentaries. This is not to say that medieval exegesis has little to contribute to our understanding of the Bible, just that it should not be the be-all and end-all of the subject. The wealth of information gleaned from our examination of the exegesis of the Book of Esther and the variety of viewpoints expressed concerning the major issues of interest in the book have made this point abundantly clear.

The Bible as the central sacred text of the Jewish people speaks to each new generation in a new voice and needs to be interpreted afresh for each generation. It is time that the voices of the medieval scholars who studied and interpreted the books of the Bible for their own times be heard and understood in the context of those times.

APPENDIX I
THE EXEGETES OF THE BOOK OF ESTHER: A BIO-BIBLIOGRAPHICAL SURVEY WITH TEXTUAL EXCURSUSES

(Bibliographic citations are for the most part abbreviated. For full information consult the bibliographies at the end of the book.)

Saadiah ben Joseph Gaon (882–942)

Until recently, Saadiah's commentary, written in Judeo-Arabic, was known only from references to it in other sources, including his commentary on Daniel. But now, Professor Yehuda Ratzaby has published several fairly substantial fragments of Saadiah's commentary which enable us to get some insight into its nature and character. (See his "Mi-peirush R. Se'adyah li-Megillat 'Ester" in Esther bibliography under Saadiah.) The majority of the fragments are from the introduction, which must have been of considerable length. The other fragments include comments on 1:1–2, 4:5, 7:5–6, 8:1–4, 9:13–19. These fragments also would indicate that the entire commentary was very lengthy and rambling, including numerous excursuses on various topics of related interest.

Saadiah's commentary was known to Abraham Ibn Ezra, who quoted it twice in his Esther commentary. It was probably known to other exegetes as well, although direct evidence for this is lacking. Saadiah's translation or *tafsir* to Esther has been published by Joseph Kafiḥ in *Ḥamesh Megillot . . . 'im peirushim 'attiqim* (Jerusalem, 1961–62), 297–322.

Rashi (1040–1105)

The text of Rashi's commentary exists in over one hundred manuscripts and numerous printed editions. It was first printed in Bologna in 1487. No critical edition exists. The text of Rashi in the standard Rabbinic Bibles is marked by several inaccuracies, the most serious of which are the inclusion of eleven comments which are not Rashi's. These are:

2:3. ויפקד המלך פקידים. לפי שכל פקיד ופקיד ידועות לו נשים היפות במדינתו.
8:10. ביד הרצים. רוכבי סוסים שצוה להם לרוץ.
8:11. ושללם לבוז. כאשר נכתב בראשונות והם בבזה לא שלחו את ידם שהראו לכל שלא נעשה לשם ממון.
8:13. פתשגן. אגרת מפורש.
8:14. מבוהלים. ממהרים אותם לעשות מהרה לפי שלא היה להם פנאי, שהיה להם להקדים רצים הראשונים להעבירם.
8:15. תכריך בוץ. מעטה בוץ; טלית העשוי להתעטף.
(only the last three words are not Rashi)
8:17. מתיהדים. מתניירים.
9:3. ועושי המלאכה. אותם שהיו ממונים לעשות צרכי המלך.
9:28. ונעשים. משתה ושמחה ויום טוב לתת מנות ומתנות.
____. משפחה ומשפחה. מתאספין יחד ואוכלין ושותין יחד וכך קבלו עליהם שימי הפורים לא יעברו.

All of these comments except for the last are wanting in the three MSS checked, BA (Vatican) Ebr. 94, BL (Oxford) Opp. 34 (Ol. 63) (Neubauer 186) and BN (Paris) héb. 164, and are present in the MS. BP (Parma) 2203 and its sisters. (The last comment is found neither in the Rashi manuscripts checked nor in "A.") Therefore, the number of comments that I count as definitely Rashi's is 136 rather than 147 as in the printed versions. This number may have to be revised again once a critical edition of the text has been prepared. In addition, other variant readings are found in the manuscripts that help elucidate the text. A critical edition of this and other parts of Rashi's Bible commentary is still a desideratum. Concerning the problems and pitfalls involved in editing Rashi's commentaries, especially the Torah commentary, see Eleazar Touitou, "ʿAl gilgulei ha-nosaḥ."

A great deal has been written about Rashi's biblical exegesis. The most recent monographs are by Banitt, Gelles, Kamin, Leibowitz and Ahrend, and Shereshevsky (see especially pp. 73–152). See also Kamin, "Rashi's Exegetical Categorization," and Shereshevsky, "Significance."

Heide, "Rashi's Biblical Exegesis," is a very useful summary which also contains an extensive bibliography. Still of great value is the monograph by E. M. Lipschütz, *Rashi*. Several jubilee volumes have been published this century in commemoration of Rashi's birth or death and each contains articles pertaining to Rashi's exegesis. Among these are: The American Academy for Jewish Research, *Rashi Anniversary Volume* (New York, 1941); *Sefer Rashi*, ed. Y. L. Maimon (Jerusalem, 1955), *Rashi: His Teachings and Personality: Essays on the 850th Anniversary of His Death*, ed. Simon Federbush (New York, 1958); *Rachi: Ouvrage collectif*, ed. Manes Sperber (Paris, 1974).

Joseph ben Simeon Kara (b. ca. 1060)

An exhaustive annotated bibliography on Kara appears in the recently published study by M. M. Ahrend, *Le commentaire sur Job de Rabbi Yoséph Qara* (Hildesheim, Germany, 1978), 177–84, which contains a very detailed analysis of Kara's exegetical methods. I mention here only a few of the more important works on Kara published prior to Ahrend's study: Berthold Einstein, *R. Josef Kara*, Martin Littmann, *Josef ben Simeon Kara*, Simon Eppenstein, "Studien über Joseph ben Simon Kara als Exeget;" the last article was published in Hebrew as the introduction to Eppenstein's edition of Kara's commentary on the Former Prophets, *Peirushei Rabbi Yosef Qara' li-Nevi'im rishonim* (Jerusalem, 1972), which appeared some fifty years after the editor's death. See also Samuel Poznanski's "Mavo'," published as the introduction to his edition of Eliezer of Beaugency, *Kommentar zu Ezechiel*, and most recently Michael A. Signer, "Exégèse et enseignement," A. Grossman, "Ha-Polmos ha-Yehudi-ha-Noṣri," 29–60, and Gershon Brin, *Meḥqarim be-feirusho shel R. Yosef Qara'* (Tel Aviv, 1990).

Kara was a pupil of Menaḥem ben Ḥelbo, the first northern French exegete about whom we have any record. Kara is known to have commented on most of the Bible although only his commentaries to the Prophets, Job, and some of the Five Scrolls are extant. (For a complete list, see Ahrend, *Commentaire*, 180–84. To this should now be added Ahrend's edition of Kara's Job commentary: *Peirush Rabbi Yosef Qara' le-sefer 'Iyyov* [Jerusalem, 1988]).

The identification of the Esther commentary assumed to be his is not absolutely certain, although most scholars of the nineteenth and early twentieth centuries considered it to be genuine.[1] The text of the commentary has been published three times, first by Adolph Jellinek from MS. SUB (Hamburg) Cod. Hebr. 32, fols. 95r–100v, in *Peirushim 'al 'Ester* [*etc.*], 1–22. In this manuscript, the commentaries of two rabbis, Joseph and Samuel, are interwoven with some anonymous comments apparently by the compiler. Most scholars have assumed that the Joseph referred to is Joseph Kara and the Samuel is Rashbam.

Ten years after Jellinek published his manuscript, Adolph Hübsch published an edition of the Five Scrolls with the Peshitta Syriac translation under the title: *Ḥamesh Megillot 'im targum suri*. He included a commentary which he had found in a Maḥzor at the Prague University Library and which had belonged to the Eger Synagogue in Prague. He had no idea of the authorship of the commentaries, but scholars soon noticed that the commentaries to Ruth and Esther corresponded with those published by Jellinek.[2] This commentary was published a third time, by J. Gad, as an appendix to his edition of Joseph Bekhor Shor's commentary on the Torah (*Peirush 'al ha-Torah*, 3 vols. [Jerusalem, 1959], 3:88–97). He gives no indication of which manuscript or printed text he used. In general, his text is closer to that published by Hübsch. Using the MSS on which Jellinek and Hübsch based their editions, one can reconstruct a fairly accurate version of the text, although some questionable spots remain. Another witness is MS. UB (Erlangen) 1263, which has comments by Kara and Rashbam as well as others not hitherto identified.

Although the evidence seems to indicate that the commentary published by Jellinek and Hübsch is that of Joseph Kara, the attribution is not absolutely certain. S. Poznanski, ("Mavo," xxx), mentions that he did not find in the commentary expressions peculiar to Kara, but still he does not seem to doubt that the commentary is Kara's. There are no quotations in the commentary of Menahem ben Ḥelbo, Kara's teacher, or others which would help in the identification.

This lack of terminology typical of Kara's other commentaries is one reason for my hesitation in concurring wholeheartedly with the other scholars who identified this commentary as Kara's. The other is the fact that the anonymous commentary, called "A" in this study, shares several characteristics with Kara's other commentaries. At several points "A" uses principles of exegesis which are characteristic of Kara's commentaries. For example, at 7:5, "A" comments:

> *And King Ahasuerus said, he said to Queen Esther*. [If at] any place in the Bible two identical words are found together in the same verse, their meaning is to be found in the verse itself, each word referring to a different part of the verse.

"A" then gives examples of this phenomenon from Lv 26:43, Is 3:5, Is 22:16, and Ez 10:2, and explains the recurrence of "and he said" as referring to the two parts of Ahasuerus's questions, "and he said 'who is he?' and he said 'where is he?'"

Kara, in his Isaiah commentary (see Littmann, *Kara*, 27) formulates the rule in a slightly different fashion: "wherever you find two difficult words next to each other you will find their meaning beside them." This refers to difficult words that are not necessarily identical. Among the examples that Kara quotes are Lv 26:43 *ya'an u-ve-ya'an*, also quoted by "A," and Is 3:1 *mash'en u-mash'enah*.

It is interesting to note that although Kara gives a similar interpretation to the verse as "A," he neither formulates the rule nor brings other biblical parallels for this phenomenon.

Another comment of "A"'s that is suggestive is his interpretation of *'oseh ha-melakhah* in 3:9. "A" comments:

> Any man who is quick (*zariz*) and intelligent and fulfills the king's needs is called in the Bible *'oseh ha-melakhah*; it is related to (1 Kgs 11:28), "and when Solomon saw that the young man was industrious (*'oseh melakhah*) he gave him charge over all the forced labor of the house of Joseph." For if you were to understand *melakhah* in this context as actual work what would "into the king's treasuries" mean? But rather, this is what he says: "I will pay into the hands of the treasurers who have charge of the king's business that they may put it into the king's treasuries."

Now Joseph Kara comments on *'oseh melakhah* in 1 Kgs 11:28 as follows: "quick (*mahir*) in his work and efficient (*zariz*) in all things" (Kara, *Peirush Nevi'im rishonim*, 135). Thus he uses the same word, *zariz*, in his comment to 1 Kgs 11:28, as does "A" in his comment to Est 3:9, and in general, the two comments are quite compatible. In the commentary commonly attributed to Joseph Kara, the comment is quite different: "those that make silver and gold vessels for the king."

There are several possible conclusions to be drawn from this parallel: If Kara is the author of the Esther commentary attributed to him and of the commentary on Kings, then he is inconsistent in his interpretation of a word that appears quite rarely in the Bible. Or, Kara is not the author of the commentary commonly attributed to him, and the commentary we have been referring to as "A" is actually Kara's. This possibility, while quite attractive, is not without its problems.

First of all, it is possible to say that Kara was indeed not always consistent in his interpretation of words in different parts of the Bible. Also, one could argue that the parallel cited only shows that "A" was familiar with Kara's commentary on Kings and borrowed from it, as he seems to have done from his Esther commentary as well. Furthermore, if we were to assume that the R. Joseph of the Hamburg MS is not Joseph Kara, then who would he be? The only other Joseph we know of from this school is Joseph Bekhor Shor. Unfortunately, the one comment of his commentary that has survived bears no resemblance to either of the comments in MSS. SUB (Hamburg) Cod. Hebr. 32 or BP (Parma) 2203 (see below p. 212). Therefore, we are at a stalemate.[3] Since there is no conclusive evidence to the contrary, it would seem to be advisable to maintain the attribution of the commentary in the Hamburg MS to Joseph Kara.

Samuel ben Meir (ca. 1080–1174)

The major work on Rashbam's exegesis is still Rosin, *Rabbi Samuel ben Meir*; see also Rosin's introduction to Rashbam's Torah commentary, *Peirush ha-Torah*. Recently, he has been the subject of renewed scholarly interest. Cf. Samuel ben Meir, *The Commentary of Samuel ben Meir Rashbam on Qoheleth*; idem, *Rabbi Samuel ben Meir's Commentary on Genesis*; Sara Japhet, "Peirush ha-Rashbam ʿal Megillat Qohelet," (twice); Abraham Grossman, "ʿOd ʿal peirush ha-Rashbam li-Qohelet;" Moshe Ahrend, "Peirush Rashbam le-'Iyyov?"; E. Touitou, "ʿAl shiṭato shel Rashbam be-feirusho la-Torah,"; idem, "Peshaṭ ve-'apologeṭiqah;" idem, "Shiṭato ha-parshanit shel Rashbam;" Salters, "Observations on the Commentary on Qohelet by R. Samuel ben Meir."

Samuel, the grandson of Rashi, was a distinguished talmudist and one of the most important biblical exegetes of the northern French school. He commented on most of the Bible, although only his commentaries to the Torah and some of the Five Scrolls are extant (for a complete discussion, see Rosin, *Samuel b. Meir*, 12–22). His extant comments to Esther are found in MS. SUB (Hamburg) Cod. Hebr. 32, interspersed with those of Joseph Kara, and were published by Adolph Jellinek in 1855 (see above p. 208). It is possible that this manuscript does not contain the complete commentary of Rashbam, because there is very little overlap between the two commentaries. Only in five places does the compiler quote the comments of both Rashbam and Kara to the same verse (1:1, 1:22, 3:15, 4:2, 10:3). For Rashbam, there is no check on the completeness of the commentary as there is for Kara (Prague MS published by Hübsch).

Abraham Geiger in *Nit'ei na'amanim*, 9a–10b, published some comments to Esther, gathered from various Rashi manuscripts. There is some overlap between these comments and the Samuel comments in MS. SUB (Hamburg) Cod. Hebr. 32, but the material Geiger brings has many comments that are Kara's or that cannot be identified at all.[4] Another witness is MS. BN (Paris) 50, which is listed as Rashi's in the Zotenberg catalogue but which contains many comments identical with those attributed to Samuel in the Hamburg MS as well as other comments hitherto unknown. The whole question requires further research and may never be completely resolved.

"A" (thirteenth century?)

The third commentary of this school postdates that attributed to Kara, from which it appears to have taken some material. It is anonymous and will henceforth be referred to as "A." It was published by Abraham Berliner in *'Oṣar tov* (1878): 26–32, from MS. BP (Parma) 2203 (De Rossi 456), fols. 29v–33v. It exists in at least twelve other manuscripts which can be divided into two families as follows: The first group contains the Parma and BL (Oxford) Opp. Add. 4° 52 MSS and the second group all the rest (for a complete listing, see Esther Bibliography). The thirteenth manuscript is JTS (Breslau) 104 (= Saraval 27). This manuscript, along with the whole Breslau Seminary collection, has officially been missing since the beginning of World War II when the Seminary Library was sacked by the Nazis. The second half of this manuscript was recently rediscovered by the late Professor Gérard Weil of the Université de Lyons, France, and is now available on microfilm. (See Gérard E. Weil, "Sur une bibliothèque," 591, 593, 597). However, according to Professor Weil, the first half of this manuscript, which includes the commentary on Esther, is still lost. The catalogue to the Breslau collection published by D. S. Loewinger and B. D. Weinryb includes the incipit and last words of the manuscript (see p. 23). These are identical with those of the other manuscripts in the group in question. The catalogue attributes this commentary to Joseph Kara, but gives no indication whether this attribution is actually written in the manuscript or was supplied by the editors of the catalogue. It seems likely that the attribution was supplied since none of the nineteenth- and early twentieth-century literature which deals with this commentary mentions the appearance of Joseph Kara's name in association with it.

This question must wait until this manuscript is rediscovered. In general, the text of the MSS of the second group is more accurate, although some MSS have later interpolations. The Parma manuscript published by Berliner is relatively late (fifteenth century) and contains many difficult passages, which can be corrected by comparison with MSS of group II. Since the majority of manuscripts belong to the group which differs significantly from the Parma MS, Berliner's choice of text to publish turns out to be a poor one. A new edition of this text would be desirable. In the nineteenth century, this commentary was attributed by some scholars, e.g., A. Geiger, (in *'Oṣar neḥmad*, 4:43) to Joseph Kara. This attribution was rejected after comparison with MS. SUB (Hamburg) Cod. Hebr. 32 which, it is generally accepted, contains Kara's commentary. (See above and see also Poznanski, "Mavo," xi; S. D. Luzzatto, *Kerem ḥemed* 7 [1843]: 68.)

Joseph Bekhor Shor (twelfth century)

His commentary is no longer extant. One comment (to 1:7) from it has survived and appears in the commentary of Avigdor b. Elijah, MS. SUB (Hamburg) Cod. Hebr. 235, fol. 130r:

שונים. לשון שנים [קבל?] כל אחד ואחד מהן ב׳ כוסות מלאים; כששתה אחד מהן . . . בין [הביא] לפניו מלא מזומן אחריו וחוזרין וממלאין [?] את הריקים ואם כן והשתיה כדת אין אונס כי לעולם היה כוס מלא לפניו ולא היה צריך לשאול לשתות.

Ashkenaz

There are three full commentaries of known authorship that originate in Ashkenaz in this period. The most significant is that of Eleazar ben Judah of Worms (ca. 1165–ca. 1230). Eleazar was a student of R. Judah the Pious and one of the most prominent and prolific members of the group. His commentary was recently published by Manfred Lehmann from a unique manuscript. A second commentary from the school of the German Pietists is that of Eleazar ben Moses, the Preacher, who lived in Würzburg in the mid-thirteenth century. His commentary has survived only in a unique manuscript. Both commentaries use the methods of *gemaṭria*, letter combinations, and acrostics. They also incorporate much rabbinic material as well as philological exegesis.

A third commentary of Ashkenazic, though not necessarily of German Pietist origin, is that of Avigdor ben Elijah, ha-Kohen (Kohen-Ṣedeq) who lived in Germany in the thirteenth century (ca. 1200–75). Concerning R. Avigdor, see Hamburger, *'Avigdor Kohen Ṣedeq*, Zimmels, "Le-toledot R. 'Avigdor." His commentary, like that of Eleazar ben Moses, is found only in manuscript. On this manuscript see Zimmels, "Ketav-yad Hamburg." It is primarily a compilation of rabbinic material with a few original comments. In addition to these three commentaries, there are several comments from the school of the German Pietists which were published by I. S. Lange in his edition of a Torah commentary from this group (*Perushei ha-Torah le-R. Yehudah he-Ḥasid* (Jerusalem, 1974), 133–34. As Lange himself admits, not all the comments he has published can be definitely attributed to Rabbi Judah the Pious (ca. 1150–1217), the founder of the German Pietist movement, but they definitely derive from his school and many were probably recorded by his son R. Moses Zaltman. Most of the comments on Esther are from MS. BL (Oxford) Opp. 31 (Ol. 260) (Neubauer 271), fols. 79v–81r.

On the exegesis of Ḥasidei 'Ashkenaz, see Gershon Brin, "R. Judah he-Hasid"; idem, "Qavvim le-feirush ha-Torah," and Ivan Marcus, "Exegesis for the Few and for the Many."

Tobias ben Eliezer (eleventh century)

Tobias ben Eliezer lived in Castoria and Thessalonica in the late eleventh century. He composed a midrashic commentary on the Pentateuch and Five Scrolls called *Midrash Leqaḥ ṭov*. On him and his commentaries, see *Encyclopaedia Judaica* (Jerusalem, 1971), s.v. "Midrash Lekaḥ Tov." The commentary on Esther was published by Salomon Buber as part of *Sifrei de-'aggadeta' 'al Megillat 'Ester*, 83–112. His commentaries, while drawing heavily on midrashic sources are more than mere anthologies and include a great deal of original exegesis as well as Greek words and contemporary allusions. Tobias was heavily involved in polemical activities against the burgeoning Karaite community in Byzantium and much evidence of these activities can be found in his commentaries, especially to the Pentateuch. See Zvi Ankori, *Karaites in Byzantium*, index, under "Tobias b. Eliezer of Castoria."

Abraham ben Meir Ibn Ezra (ca. 1089–ca. 1164)

Ibn Ezra was a colorful transitional figure whose career marked the culmination of the Golden Age of Spanish Jewry under Moslem rule. He was born in Spain and lived there most of his life. However, most of his literary output was produced after 1140. This was the year in which he left his native land and embarked on an odyssey which lasted almost twenty-five years and took him through much of Western Europe. Beginning in Rome he moved northward through Italy, into Provence and northern France and finally arrived in England. It is thought by some scholars that he returned to Narbonne before he died. On his life, see Israel Levin, *Rabbeinu 'Avraham 'Ibn 'Ezra'*; also articles by J. L. Fleischer (cited in bibliography). A recent, more accessible summary which, however, adds nothing new can be found in Asher Weiser, "Raba'."

In the course of his wanderings, Ibn Ezra produced many works, including biblical commentaries, grammatical, philosophic, and scientific treatises. Ibn Ezra began his exegetical work in 1140 with his commentary to Ecclesiastes, and it seems likely that he commented on the other four scrolls before moving on to other books of the Bible. (Cf. Fleischer, "Rabbeinu 'Avraham 'Ibn 'Ezra' ba-'ir Roma'," 97–98, 152–55). For some biblical books Ibn Ezra produced two commentaries, one usually much longer than the other. Such is the case with Esther. The first commentary (*A*) was written in Italy in 1142, not long before his departure from Rome. His second commentary (*B*) was most likely written in France, probably in Rouen, in 1155 or 1156. The complex question of the relationship between the two commentaries is considered in Tmima Davidovitz, "Peirushei ha-Raba' le-'Ester," and in Walfish, "The Two Commentaries of Abraham Ibn Ezra."

For Ibn Ezra's exegesis the best introduction is still the monograph by Michael Friedländer, *Essays on the Writings of Abraham Ibn Ezra* (London, 1877). See also *'Enṣiqlopedyah Miqra'it*, 8:671–80, s.v. "Tanakh-Parshanut" (vol. 8, col. 671–80) and accompanying bibliography, cols. 681–83 (published separately as *Parshanut ha-Miqra' ha-Yehudit: Pirqei mavo'*, ed. Moshe Greenberg [Jerusalem, 1983], 47–60); Uriel Simon, *'Arba' gishot le-sefer Tehillim*, 121–236; idem, *Four Approaches to the Book of Psalms*, 144–295; idem, "R. 'Avraham 'Ibn 'Ezra'—Bein ha-mefaresh le-qor'av," 23–42. Quotations from commentary *A* follow the text in the standard editions of the Rabbinic Bible and no pagination is given. Commentary *B*, unless otherwise indicated, is quoted from the printed edition published by Joseph Zedner under the title *Va-yosef 'Avraham* (London, 1850) (henceforth *VA*). Zedner's edition was based on MS. BL (London) Harley 269 (Margoliouth 235), fols. 210r–218v. However, this manuscript lacks the comments to verses 1:7–20 and these were published by Leopold Dukes in *Literaturblatt des Orients*, 11(1850): 341, on the basis of MS. BN (Paris) héb. 334, fols. 75v–76r. References in the text will be to the Paris MS. This manuscript is being used as the base text for the critical edition of Ibn Ezra's second commentary which is being prepared by the Institute for the Study of Medieval Biblical Exegesis at Bar-Ilan University. Other MSS that contain the second version are listed in the bibliography of Esther commentaries.

Isaiah ben Mali of Trani (ca. 1200–ca. 1260)

The earliest Italian commentator on Esther is Isaiah ben Mali of Trani. For his biography, see A. J. Wertheimer's introduction to his edition of Isaiah's commentaries, *Peirush Nevi'im u-Khetuvim le-Rabbeinu Yesha'yah ha-rishon mi-Ṭrani*, 3 vols. (Jerusalem, 1959–77): 1:17–56. Very little has been written on R. Isaiah as an exegete. See now the article by E. Z. Melamed, "Le-feirush Nakh shel R. Yesha'yah mi-Ṭrani," which is a useful classified compilation of R. Isaiah's comments to the Prophets and Psalms but contains no attempt at analysis. His commentary, noteworthy for its clarity and conciseness, makes heavy, though unacknowledged, use of the Talmud and Midrash as well as the grammatical works of Jonah Ibn Janaḥ and David Kimḥi. Often a comment of his can be seen to be a clear reaction to a statement of the sages or of Ibn Ezra. Isaiah will also occasionally resort to the vernacular (Italian) to help clarify a comment (see above, pp. 19–20).

Moses ben Isaac Ḥalayo (thirteenth century?)

The name Ḥalayo is quite similar to the name Ḥalavah which is found a few times in Spain, especially in the name of Baḥya ben Asher ben Ḥalavah, on whom see below p. 216. But all the manuscripts consistently give his name as Ḥalayo (חלאיו) so there may be no connection. The name may be pronounced "Ḥalayu," since at least one manuscript rhymes his name with the word *yishlayu*.

We possess no biographical information for Rabbi Moses and

must therefore rely on circumstantial evidence for dating and locating him.

Ḥalayo's commentary, which exists only in manuscript (see Bibliography), is a straightforward verse-by-verse commentary which would seem to point to a relatively early date. The sources he quotes include Saadiah Gaon, Jonah Ibn Janaḥ, Rashi, Abraham Ibn Ezra, Maimonides, Joseph Kimḥi, and David Kimḥi. He shows some interest in grammatical questions and word meanings, topics that were of less concern to exegetes in the fourteenth and fifteenth centuries but that were still of importance in the thirteenth century. It seems likely, then, that he lived some time in the thirteenth century, probably in its latter part. As for his home, it could be almost anywhere in Western Europe or even Byzantium.[5] The one foreign word in his commentary is possibly Italian. The word is פְּרֶימְרֵי which seems closest to the Italian *premere* which means press. This *la'az* was given to explain the word *va-yazar* (Jgs 6:38), fol. 8r.

No other exegete except Immanuel of Rome quotes or uses Ibn Ezra as much as Ḥalayo, although the latter uses the *B* version rather than the *A* version which was available to Immanuel. Ḥalayo quotes Ibn Ezra at least sixty-two times, twenty-three times by name. In other instances, he introduces his comment by the words, "there are those who interpret," or "there are those who say," and on still other occasions, he gives no indication that the interpretation is not his. At several points, he cites Ibn Ezra's interpretation and then rejects it in favor of his own. He quotes rabbinic sources extensively, but like other medievals he tries to provide rational explanations for some midrashic statements which seem to contradict reason.

Baḥya ben Asher (thirteenth century)

Baḥya ben Asher lived in Saragossa in the second half of the thirteenth century, where he served as a judge and preacher in the Jewish community. Very little is known about R. Baḥya's life. See summaries in *Encyclopaedia Judaica* (Jerusalem), s.v. "Baḥya ben Asher ben Ḥlava," C. B. Chavel's introduction to his edition of Baḥya's *Bei'ur 'al ha-Torah,* 1:1–10, and Reifmann, "Toledot Rabbeinu Baḥya," 69–101. For his exegesis, see Chavel's introduction, 1:10–18, and especially B. Bernstein, *Die Schrifterklärung des Bachja b. Asher.* R. Baḥya was a disciple of Solomon ben Abraham Adret and Naḥmanides from whom he received his training in kabbalistic lore. R. Baḥya's fame derives mainly from his commentary to the Pentateuch, which has been very popular among Jews throughout the ages. In addition, he composed an alphabetically arranged treatise on the principles of Judaism, called *Kad ha-qemaḥ*, a commentary on the tractate *'Avot*, and *Shulḥan shel 'arba'*, which deals with the rules of conduct for various meals. All three works were recently edited by C. B. Chavel, *Kitvei Rabbeinu Baḥya* (Jerusalem, 1969–70). It is in *Kad ha-qemaḥ*, under the entry *Purim*, that his commentary to Esther is found (see Bibliography). The importance of Baḥya's commentaries lies in their encyclopedic nature. They contain comments from a wide range of sources—exegetical, midrashic, philosophical, and kabbalistic —for many of which his commentary is the only source extant.

Immanuel ben Solomon, of Rome (ca. 1261–after 1328)

Immanuel achieved his fame and in some circles, notoriety, as a secular poet. His *Maḥbarot* or "Cantos" (latest edition by Dov Jarden, 2 vols. [Jerusalem, 1957]) give a vivid description of the life of the nobility in Italy in the early fourteenth century and are noted for their skillful use of biblical language. A prolific biblical exegete, he took great pride in his exegetical works which covered most of the books of the Bible (with the exception of the Former and the Minor Prophets; see *Maḥbarot*, I, lines 318–43; XXI, lines 191–97; XXVIII, lines 627–52 and 833–901). In his own estimation, Immanuel surpassed all his predecessors in revealing the mysteries of the biblical text. (See *Maḥbarot*, XVIII, lines 833–92.) Future generations, however, did not seem to share Immanuel's high opinion of his exegetical achievements. Only his commentary to Proverbs was published in its entirety and that only once (*Sefer Mishlei 'im peirush 'Imanu'el ha-Romi* [Naples, 1487]; repr. with introduction by David Goldstein, [Jerusalem, 1981]).

Of his other commentaries, those to the Pentateuch, Psalms, Job, and the Five Scrolls survive in manuscript. Citations from Immanuel's commentary are from MS. BP (Parma) 2843 (De Rossi 615), fols. 182r–214v. Parts of his Genesis and Song of Songs commentaries have been published in recent times. For Genesis 1, see *Il commento di Emanuele Romano al capitolo I della Genesi*, ed. Franco M. Tocci (Rome, 1963). The word meanings and contextual interpretations to Song of Songs, were published by S. B. Eschwege, under the title *Der Kommentar des Immanuel ben Salomon zum Hohenliede* (Frankfurt am Main, 1908), and Pietro Perreau reproduced autographically in a limited edition of sixty copies the commentaries to Ruth, Lamentations, Esther, and part of Psalms from MS. BP (Parma) 2843. These were published in Parma between 1879 and 1884.

Shemariah ben Elijah of Crete (1275–1355)

Shemariah was born in Rome but his family moved to Crete when he was a child, whence his appellation *'Iqriṭi* (of Crete). He received a good secular education and knew Greek, Latin, and Italian. According to Moritz Steinschneider, *Die hebraïschen Übersetzungen*, 499, he is distinguished as the first medieval Jew to translate Greek works from the original into Latin. He apparently spent some time in the court of Robert of Naples (1309–43) where he was engaged in the writing of biblical and philosophical commentaries. After 1343 he apparently became involved in messianic speculation and began wandering through northern Italy and Spain. In 1352, while in Spain, he proclaimed himself to be the Messiah and in the ensuing uproar he was thrown into prison where he died several years later. Adolf Neubauer, "Documents inédits," 86–92, has published a poem by Moses b. Samuel of Roquemaure describing Shemariah's ill-fated career as messianic pretender. The poem is reprinted by Aescoly, *Tenu'ot*, 218–20, with notes. Aescoly points out that the evidence for Shemariah's messianic inclinations and career is quite flimsy and is based mainly on this poem. Furthermore, the author, Moses of Roquemaure, converted to Christianity a few years after this incident allegedly took place, which renders his testimony suspect. It is even conceivable that another Shemariah is referred to as there seem to have been several alive at this time. See Abraham Geiger, "Nosafot 'al devar R. Shemaryah ha-'Iqriṭi," 158–60.

There is much confusion in the literature about Shemariah's life. Colette Sirat, in the most recent study of Shemariah, "Mikhtav 'al ḥiddush ha-'olam," 200, n. 1, takes an extreme reductionist position, and points out several errors that were perpetuated in the nineteenth-century literature. The most complete survey of Shemariah's life and works can be found in the doctoral thesis of Shalom Rosenberg, "Logiqah ve-'onṭologyah," 1:94–100, 2:78–87. Other works dealing with Shemariah are: Vogelstein and Rieger, *Geschichte der Juden in Rom*, 1:446–50; Aescoly, *Tenu'ot*, 218–22.

Shemariah's Esther commentary is impossible to date. Neubauer's assertion that it was written in 1309 is based on a misreading of Schiller-Szinessy's catalogue of the manuscripts of the Cambridge University Library. (See Sirat, "Mikhtav," 200.) Only part of it (from 6:3 to the end) survives in one Cambridge manuscript. Other fragments can be found in Shemariah's *'Elef ha-magen*, his commentary on the aggadic portions of the Talmud, the only extant part of which is the section on B.T. Megillah, chapter 1, (found in the same Cambridge MS) and in the commentaries of later exegetes, especially Solomon Alkabez's *Menot ha-Levi* (Lwow, 1911; repr. Brooklyn, N.Y., 1976), 25b, 28a, 31a, 33b, 45b, 47a, 30b, 129b, 132a, and 134b.

Joseph ibn Kaspi (1280–1340)

Joseph ibn Kaspi, of Argentière in Provence, was a prolific and eclectic author who wrote many works in the areas of biblical exegesis, philosophy, grammar, and philology. (For a list of Kaspi's works, see Barry Mesch, *Studies in Joseph ibn Kaspi*, 7–42, 50–55, which contains an analysis and translation of Kaspi's own bibliography of his works, *Qevuṣat kesef*).

Although his work was in the mainstream of Jewish intellectual life for several centuries after his death, it has been given short shrift by modern scholars. The publication in recent years of several studies indicates a revival of interest in this colorful medieval thinker. Besides Mesch's study see Shlomo Pines, "Histabberut ha-tequmah me-ḥadash," Twersky, "Joseph ibn Kaspi," 185–204; Idem, "Joseph ibn Kaspi: Portrait of a Medieval Jewish Intellectual," 231–257; Basil Herring, *Joseph ibn Kaspi's "Gevia' Kesef"*; Hannah Kasher, "Pitronot balshaniyyim," 91–96; Shalom Rosenberg, "Higgayon, safah u-farshanut ha-Miqra'," 105–13.

Kaspi's Esther commentary called *Gelilei kesef* was published by Isaac Last in *'Asarah kelei kesef*, 2:29–39. Although Kaspi states explicitly on three separate occasions[6] that he intends to discuss in his commentary only the question raised by Ibn Ezra, he must have changed his mind in his later years and decided to write a fuller commentary after all. The single extant copy of this addition, is in MS. BL (Oxford) Opp. 211 (Ol. 272) (Neubauer 362), fols. 26r–28r, which was published by Last in a supplement to *'Asarah kelei kesef* (see Bibliography). In the first part of this addition, Kaspi summarizes the main points of his commentary and then continues with a brief verse-by-verse consideration of the book, as he does in his other commentaries, quoting Aristotle's *Ethics* at several points.

Gersonides (1288–1344)

For bibliographical information on Gersonides, see Kellner, "R. Levi ben Gerson." Levi ben Gershom, also known as Ralbag or Gersonides, was the major exponent of Jewish Aristotelianism in the late Middle Ages. Although he was a compatriot and contemporary of Joseph ibn Kaspi, there is no evidence that the two ever met. Although his works were widely distributed and frequently quoted by supporters and detractors alike, very little biographical information is known to us. For an outline of Gersonides' life, see Charles Touati, *La pensée théologique et philosophique de Gersonide* (Paris, 1973), 33–48, and now Seymour Feldman's introduction to his translation of Gersonides' *The Wars of the Lord*, 1:3–8. He was probably born in Bagnols, Provence, and spent most of his life in Orange.[7] Unlike Kaspi, who traveled a great deal, Gersonides never left Provence. He seems to have had contacts in his later years with the papal court at Avignon,[8] and may even have spent some time there.[9] Besides his major philosophical work, *The Wars of the Lord*, Gersonides composed commentaries on most of the books of the Bible[10] as well as fourteen philosophical works, most of them commentaries on the works of Averroës.[11] Gersonides' Esther commentary was first published in Riva da Trento in 1560 and most recently in Königsberg, 1860, along with his commentaries on Song of Songs, Ruth, and Ecclesiastes under the title *Peirush Ralbag 'al Ḥamesh Megillot.* No commentary on Lamentations survives.

Joseph ben Joseph Naḥmias (fourteenth century)

Joseph ben Joseph Naḥmias lived in Toledo in the first half of the fourteenth century. He was a member of a distinguished Spanish family whose earliest known ancestors lived in the early twelfth century. Apart from the fact that he was a pupil of Rabbi Asher ben Jeḥiel, little is known of his life. Although his Esther commentary is one of the few to have been published in a scholarly edition (see Bibliography), it is not particularly original. It is comprised largely of midrashic and targumic material and quotations, mostly unacknowledged, from the commentaries of Rashi and Ibn Ezra. (For a list of the sources he quotes, see Bamberger's introduction, 8–9.) Some of his other works show evidence of outside, non-Jewish influence—that he had a much more rounded education, and that he knew Arabic and was familiar with both secular and Jewish philosophical works—but there is little indication of this in his Esther commentary. It should be mentioned that the commentary is incomplete, as several lines were illegible to the editor and one page is wanting entirely. From 9:27 to the end, the text is, word for word, that of Ibn Ezra's commentary.

For summaries of his life and works see *Encyclopaedia Judaica* (Jerusalem), s.v. "Naḥmias, Joseph ben Joseph," and the introductions to his commentaries on Esther, Proverbs, and Jeremiah published by M. L. Bamberger. Bamberger also published Naḥmias' *Peirush Pirqei 'Avot*, and his commentary to a *piyyuṭ* for the Day of Atonement, "'Attah konanta," "Peirush seder ʿavodah le-R. Yosef ben Naḥmias." For a fuller bibliography, see the introduction to Naḥmias's Jeremiah commentary, 6–7. His commentary to B.T. Nedarim remains in manuscript.

Solomon Astruc (fourteenth century)

Solomon Astruc lived in Barcelona in the second half of the fourteenth century. The little that is known about his personal life is summarized by Simon Eppenstein in the introduction to his edition of R. Solomon's commentaries on the Pentateuch, Isaiah 53, Psalm 139, and Esther, entitled *Midreshei ha-Torah* (Berlin, 1899), IX–XII. See there for a bibliography up to the end of the nineteenth century. R. Solomon has been virtually neglected by twentieth-century scholarship. Eppenstein himself admits to several shortcomings in his edition (ibid., xii). The manuscript was copied for him, sometimes inaccurately, and he had to emend the text based on his own judgment. He was not able to compare the text with the manuscripts found in the Bodleian Library in Oxford and the Montefiore Library, then located in Ramsgate, now Jews' College, London. He also notes that many of the comments were not in their proper order, but because of the trouble involved, he did not rearrange them. For want of Spanish dictionaries, he was unable to translate the *leʿazim* or vernacular words found in the text. In actual fact, after having compared Eppenstein's text on Esther with the manuscripts, I can attest to its general accuracy. There are only a few minor errors in transcription. Several *leʿazim* were discussed above, pp. 111–13, 168.

Astruc's commentary to Esther is written in expository style and deals only with selected points in the text. It is somewhat disjointed and is probably not complete. Like other exegetes of his era, he quotes the sages (1:13, p. 215; 2:15, p. 216; 3:4, p. 216; 4:4, p. 218; 5:8, p. 219) and Ibn Ezra (5:8, p. 218) as well as an otherwise unknown Spanish exegete, Astruc Dernegra.

Tamakh, Abraham ben Isaac, ha-Levi (fourteenth century)

Some twenty-five years ago L. A. Feldman published fragments of a commentary to Esther which he attributed to Abraham ben Isaac ha-Levi Tamakh, a fourteenth-century Spanish-Jewish exegete (see Bibliography). The fragments consist of comments to six verses and appear in two separate manuscripts after commentaries by the aforementioned Rabbi Abraham. The first two are found in a MS. Wertheimer, after the commentary to Lamentations, the latter four in MS. JTSA (New York) L1052, after Rabbi Abraham's commentary to Song of Songs.

In the course of my research on the medieval commentaries to Esther, I was struck by the similarity between the comments published by Feldman and those in the commentary of Solomon Astruc, which was published by Simon Eppenstein from a manuscript in Milan's Ambrosiana Library. An examination of these two sets of comments reveals that each pair is basically identical in meaning and that they share many words and phrases in common. In fact, in the case of the fourth passage, the two comments are nearly identical, word for word. This seems to be a clear case of direct influence. The question that needs to be asked is who borrowed from whom. If we assume that the identity of the commentary as Solomon Astruc's is firmly established, as I believe it is, then we can assume that the author of the other comments borrowed from him. But is this author to be identified as Abraham ben Isaac ha-Levi Tamakh? Feldman based his identification on the fact that the excerpts in question were located after commentaries definitely known to be Tamakh's, in the case of the Wertheimer manuscript after his Lamentations commentary, and in the case of the JTSA manuscript after his commentary on Song of Songs. I was unable to examine the Wertheimer manuscript, since a microfilm of it was not available at the Institute of Microfilmed Hebrew Manuscripts at the Jewish National and University Library in Jerusalem. (I have since learnt that it is in Professor Feldman's possession). However, I was able to examine the JTSA manuscript and found that the section in question is at the end of the manuscript (fols. 130r–131v) and is written in a different hand from the commentary of Abraham ben Isaac ha-Levi on Song of Songs which immediately precedes it. Thus it is conceivable that this section was added much later by another scribe and that it has no connection with R. Abraham at all.

There is another section of text in the JTSA manuscript which Feldman neglected to include. This section is also quite similar to the commentary of Solomon Astruc. It would seem, then, that the author of the fragments in the JTSA and Wertheimer manuscripts based his commentary on that of Solomon Astruc. But that this author was Abraham ben Isaac ha-Levi Tamakh, as Feldman claims, still remains to be conclusively demonstrated. Since these comments do not add anything of substance to the body of medieval Esther commentary they have not been included in our study.

Isaac ben Joseph ha-Kohen (late fourteenth to early fifteenth century)

R. Isaac is another exegete about whom we possess next to no biographical information. From the introduction to his commentary on Ruth we learn that R. Isaac ben Joseph's family name is Emoilah or Amoilah, that he was of priestly lineage, and that he lived in the land of a nobleman called count (*'ereṣ 'aḥad ha-sarim di peḥah shemeih*)* who was kind to the Jews and allowed them to enter and settle in his territory. See MS. IZH (Warsaw) 259, which contains a more complete text than the printed version or any of the other manuscripts. The first item does not help us very much since the name Amoilah or Emoilah is unknown in other sources. In the introduction to his work *'Eṣ ḥayyim*, his great grandson Isaac ben Ḥayyim also mentions the name *'Emoilah*:

אלה תולדות יצחק בן חיים בן אברהם, אברהם הוליד את יצחק בן יוסף מן הכהנים אשר מאז לאמוילה לפנחס בן אלעזר בן אהרון הכהן מתיחסים.

See MS. BL (Oxford) Heb.f.16 (Neubauer 2770), fol. 1r. See also Mordekhai Dreksler, *Meqonen 'evleinu* (Seini, Romania, 1932). This passage as well would seem to indicate a family and not a place name. The second item is also not very helpful since priestly families were not uncommon. The third item is potentially the most helpful, but it is

* The use of the word *peḥah* for count is well established in medieval sources. See Joseph Shatzmiller, "Terminologie politique en hébreu médiéval: jalons pour un glossaire," *Revue des études juives* 142(1983): 135–37.

problematic as well. The term *'ereṣ 'aḥad ha-sarim* would seem to refer to a county, the term *sar* meaning "count." This matter requires further research.

R. Isaac can be dated to the turn of the fifteenth century. His commentary to Ecclesiastes (MS. JTSA [New York] L1052, fol. 50r) has a colophon which states that it was written in 1394 or 1395. This point is further corroborated by the testimony of his great-grandson Isaac ben Ḥayyim ha-Kohen who in the introduction to his commentary on Song of Songs refers to the commentary of his great-grandfather. See MS. BL (London) Add. 26,960 (Margoliouth 230), fol. 5r. He probably lived in Valencia. R. Isaac ben Ḥayyim lived in Jativa in Valencia around the time of the expulsion from Spain. See MS. BL (Oxford) Heb.f.16, fol. 1r: קהילתי שטיבה החרוצה.[12] If Isaac ben Joseph's great-grandson lived in Valencia, it is not unreasonable to assume that he himself also lived there or close by. Since he attests that he lived in a county, the most likely place to look for such a county would be Catalonia or Provence, since the counties there enjoyed considerable independence. Another piece of evidence to suggest a Catalan or Valencian provenance for R. Isaac is the presence of a Catalan *la'az* in his commentary. The word is *els majorals* (see MS. JTSA L1052, fol. 64v) which he uses to translate *la-rabbim* (4:3), understanding it to be the leaders of the community. See A.M. Alcover Sureda, *Diccionari Català-Valencià-Balear*, s.v. "majoral." The fact that this word is missing from the other two MSS of R. Isaac's commentary (RSL [Moscow] Guenzburg 154 and SUB [Frankfurt] hebr. 8° 124) does not rule out its authenticity, as a scribe not understanding Catalan might have left it out.

Abraham ben Judah Ḥadidah (late fourteenth to early fifteenth century)

Abraham ben Judah Ḥadidah lived in Spain in the late fourteenth or early fifteenth century.[13] Little else is known about him. All his extant works—his commentaries to Esther, Ecclesiastes, and the Passover Haggadah—appear in one manuscript: MS. BP (Parma) 2211 (De Rossi, 177). The manuscript is very difficult to read in places because of ink stains, and this hampered somewhat the study of Ḥadidah's work.

"Ramah" (fifteenth century?)

If little is known about Abraham ben Judah, Isaac ben Joseph, and Solomon Astruc, even less is known about "Ramah." In fact, all that we know about the author of this commentary are his initials *RMH*, given in the title at the head of the text. However, there are some hints in his commentary which can help to date and locate him. Since he quotes Gersonides, the terminus a quo for his period of activity is the mid–fourteenth century. The fact that he includes a Spanish proverb in his commentary[14] suggests that he is of Spanish provenance. Finally, his silence concerning the expulsion in his commentary suggests that he antedated this traumatic event.[15]

"Ramah"'s favorite sources are Abraham Ibn Ezra (whom he quotes ten times, always version *A*) and Gersonides (whom he quotes seven times). He also makes frequent use of traditional rabbinic sources including the Talmud (Babylonian and Palestinian), Midrash, and Seder ʿOlam. While he quotes no philosophic or kabbalistic sources, his language does indicate a familiarity with philosophic terminology.[16]

Abraham Shalom (fifteenth century)

Abraham Shalom was a fifteenth-century philosopher and homilist who lived in Catalonia and is reported to have died in 1492. The only work of significance on Shalom is the monograph by Herbert Davidson, *The Philosophy of Abraham Shalom*. He has gathered what little biographical information there is to be found about Shalom, ibid., p. 1. Shalom earns a place in our gallery of exegetes by virtue of a rather lengthy homily on the Book of Esther which is found in his major work, *Neveh Shalom* (Venice, 1575), V:6, 68b–72b.

Isaac Arama (1420–1494)

Shalom's contemporary, Isaac Arama,[17] was born in northern Spain in the year 1420. He served the community of Zamora as head of its *yeshivah* (talmudic academy) and later moved to Aragon where he served the communities of Tarragona and Borja as spiritual leader. It was in these communities that he developed his skills as a preacher, delivering in the synagogue every Sabbath sermons which dealt with the principles of the Jewish faith. In the 1480s he was invited to become rabbi of the larger community of Calatayud. When the Jews were expelled from Spain in 1492, he and his family fled to Naples where he died two years later.

In Calatayud, Arama wrote his major works, *ʿAqeidat Yiṣḥaq*, a commentary on the Torah, commentaries on the Five Scrolls, *Yad*

'Avshalom, a commentary on Proverbs, and *Ḥazut qashah*, an antiphilosophical polemic. Arama's commentaries on the Five Scrolls are philosophical and homiletical in nature, each one focusing on a specific religious theme which seemed to him to be central to the text of the Scroll. In the case of Esther, the central theme of Arama's commentary is divine providence.

Arama's commentary to Esther was published only once, in Constantinople in 1518. Although the commentaries to the Five Scrolls were also included in subsequent editions of *'Aqeidat Yiṣḥaq*, beginning with the Riva da Trento edition of 1561, for reasons unknown, the commentary to Esther that was printed was always that of Arama's son Meir and not his own. Curiously, the introductions to the Esther commentary and to the other scrolls published in the Riva da Trento edition of 1561 are neither by Isaac Arama nor his son Meir, but rather by Joseph b. David Ibn Yaḥya. See Isaiah Sonne, "Tokh kedei qeri'ah, III," 279–81; Joseph Hacker, "Defusei Qushṭa ba-me'ah ha-16," 478 and M. B. Lerner, "Tashlum peirush R. Yiṣḥaq 'Aramah li-Megillat Rut, 105–23. Since the sixteenth-century edition is quite rare, Arama's Esther commentary is not very well known. Substantial excerpts from it, however, were quoted by Solomon Alkabez (sixteenth century) in his compendious commentary *Menot ha-Levi*. It exists, in addition, in several manuscripts. The text of the Constantinople edition is very poor and contains several large gaps. Of the three manuscripts extant, the text of MS. JTSA (New York) L462 seems to be the most reliable. All citations are from this manuscript.*

Joseph ben Abraham Ḥayyun (fifteenth century)

Joseph ben Abraham Ḥayyun was one of the last rabbis of the Jewish community of Lisbon before the expulsion. It was once thought by scholars that he fled from Portugal after the expulsion decree was promulgated, but recent research suggests that he died in Portugal well before the expulsion from Spain. See Joseph Hacker, "R. Yosef Ḥayyun ve-dor ha-geirush mi-Porṭugal," *Zion* 48 (1982–83): 273–80. His commentaries were written in the third quarter of the fifteenth century. (Avraham Gross informs me that he wrote nothing after 1475.) A highly respected scholar and community leader, Ḥayyun

*I am preparing an edition of this commentary.

served as head of the *yeshivah* in Lisbon and was responsible for founding the charitable institutions in his community. Very little has been written about Ḥayyun and the Jewish community of Lisbon, but this gap will soon be filled with the publication by Bar-Ilan University Press of the monograph by Avraham Gross, entitled *Rabbi Yosef Ḥayyun u-qehilat Lisbon 'asher bi-qeṣeh ha-ma'arav*.

Of his extant works only two—the commentaries on the Mishnah Tractate *'Avot* and on Psalms—have been published (Psalms [Salonika, 1523], *'Avot* [Constantinople, 1578]). Others that remain in manuscript include commentaries to Song of Songs (MS. BL [London] Or. 1004 [Margoliouth 240], fols. 1–56a); Jeremiah (MS. BL [London] Add. 27,560 [Margoliouth 228]; the entire manuscript, covering Jer 2:29 to end) and Esther (MS. RSL [Moscow] Guenzburg 168, fols. 60r–97v).

Abraham Saba (mid-fifteenth to early sixteenth century)

One of the most colorful characters of the expulsion period is Abraham Saba, a homilist, exegete, and kabbalist, who lived in Spain in the latter half of the fifteenth century. For background literature on Saba, see N. S. Libowitz, *Rabbi 'Avraham Saba' u-sefarav* (Brooklyn, 1936); Gedaliah Nigal, "Pereq be-haguto shel dor geirush Sefarad," *Sinai* 74 (1973–74): 67–80; and, most recently, articles by Dan Manor and Avraham Gross (see Bibliography).

Saba was expelled from Spain in 1492 along with the rest of the Jewish community and made his way to Portugal, settling in Guimaraẽs in the province of Porto. In 1497 he was expelled from Portugal rather than undergo forced conversion to Christianity and ended up in Alcazarquivir (Ksar el-Kbir), Morocco, in poor physical condition. After regaining his health, he began to reconstruct from memory his biblical commentaries which he had first written in Portugal and had been forced to abandon. Sometime in 1499, after completing the first four parts of *Ṣeror ha-mor*, Saba moved to Fez[18] and in the following year, 1500, he completed this work.[19] He then continued to write his commentaries on the tractate *'Avot*, called *Ṣeror ha-ḥayyim* and on the Five Scrolls called *'Eshkol ha-kofer*, finishing the commentaries on Ruth, Esther, and Lamentations[20] by the fall of 1500. Apparently, these were all the commentaries on the scrolls he was able to complete. Aside from these works, he also wrote a commentary on the *sefirot*,[21] called *Ṣeror ha-kesef*, a kabbalistic commentary on the commandments and a kabbalistic commentary on the prayer book.[22]

It would appear that in the last years of his life he moved from Fez to Tlemcen, still in Morocco. There is also some evidence that he may have migrated to Turkey settling in Adrianople.[23] A legendary account tells of his dying at sea en route to France and being buried in Verona.[24]

Zechariah ben Joshua ben Saruḳ (fifteenth century)

Zechariah was a contemporary and compatriot of Abraham Saba. The little we know about his life is found in the introduction to his Esther commentary, his only extant work. Like Saba, Zechariah was a preacher, who "spread the Torah in the most important communities of Spain and Aragon," (ibid., 3a) and eventually emigrated to North Africa, settling in the city of Algiers (ibid.). Zechariah's commentary was completed on the second day of Nisan, 5253, or March twentieth, 1493 (ibid., 19b) and was apparently written out of gratitude to the Jewish community of Algiers for the hospitality they had shown him.

The two sources that Zechariah relies on most heavily are the sages and Aristotle, whom he quotes with almost equal frequency. (On his use of Aristotle, see pp. 49–50 above). In addition, Zechariah draws on a wide variety of Jewish sources, including Gersonides (8b, 16b), Judah Halevi (9a), Solomon Ibn Gabirol (10a), Josippon (ibid), David Kimḥi (16b), Joseph Albo (18a), Abudraham (ibid.), Maimonides,(19a), and Eleazar of Worms (ibid.).

Samuel de Vidas (fifteenth century)

In his commentary Zechariah makes reference to the otherwise unknown commentary of Samuel de Vidas. In the last section of his introduction, Zechariah castigates Rabbi Samuel de Vidas for criticizing some of his eminent predecessors in an improper fashion. He would not have mentioned this here, says Zechariah, but for the fact that he was shown a commentary to Esther by this same Samuel de Vidas, which presumably suffered from the same defect. This is the only evidence we have concerning the existence of this commentary. We know very little about Rabbi Samuel. He seems to have been an elder contemporary of Zechariah who was already dead when Zechariah was writing, since Zechariah refers to him as deceased. A Rabbi Symuel de Vidas is to be found in Segovia in 1485 (see Baer, *Juden im Christlichen Spanien*, 2:365). It is impossible to determine whether he is the same one referred to by Zechariah, but the possibility exists. In 1595 a commentary to

Lamentations by a Samuel de Vidas was published in Salonika. See Israel Mehlman, "Peraqim be-toledot ha-defus be-Saloniqi," in his *Genuzot sefarim* (Jerusalem, 1976), 79. In the introduction to the book the publisher recounts the great difficulties and hardships he underwent until he found in his birthplace, Fez, the books of Samuel de Vidas. According to the author's introduction, the Lamentations commentary was written in the city of Modiojar [perhaps Mogador?] This would seem to be the only extant work of R. Samuel.

Karaites

Since the Book of Esther is the basis for the observance of the Feast of Purim, which is also included in the Karaite calendar, one would expect to find Karaite exegetes engaging in polemical discussions of Rabbanite practices. Surprisingly this is not the case.[25] The first Karaite commentary on the book is by Japheth ben Eli, the dean of Karaite exegetes, who lived in Jerusalem in the tenth century. His commentary (see Bibliography) is quite straightforward, containing very little that is original or unusual. The same is true of the other Karaite discussions, by Judah Hadassi (twelfth century) and Elijah Bashyazi (fifteenth century), who devote sections to the book in their major works, (*'Eshkol ha-kofer*, 93a-94b, and *'Adderet 'Eliyahu*, 79a, respectively). Jacob ben Reuben (twelfth century) has a short commentary on Esther in his *Sefer ha-'osher*. It is probably based on the commentaries of previous Karaite exegetes, as are most of his other commentaries. One passage of particular interest is his explanation of the mechanism of the *pur* which was discussed above (p. 22).

Two other Karaite exegetes who commented on the book are Abraham ben Judah (fifteenth century, Constantinople) (see MS. BR (Leiden) Or. 4739, fols. 234r–35v) and Judah ben Meir Tawrīzī (seventeenth century, Jerusalem) mentioned here only for the sake of completeness. His commentary exists in two manuscripts: MS. BL (London) Or. 2517, fols. 108r–46v; MS. Kaufmann (Budapest) A29, p. 205–55. Finally, it should be mentioned that the distinction of being the only medieval author to offer an allegorical interpretation of the Esther story belongs to the Byzantine Karaite Judah Gibbor who flourished in the latter half of the fifteenth century (see pp. 50–51 above).

APPENDIX II
IMMANUEL OF ROME AND DANTE ON THE DIFFERENTIATION OF LANGUAGES AND THE DATING OF IMMANUEL'S COMMENTARY ON THE BOOK OF ESTHER

In this appendix, a comparison will be made between the views expressed by Immanuel of Rome on the differentiation of languages with those of his contemporary Dante Alighieri on this subject in order to demonstrate that Immanuel's view was influenced by Dante.

Very early in his commentary to the Book of Esther (at verse 1:1), Immanuel makes a very lengthy comment on the word *medinah*. He first rejects the definition offered by Abraham Ibn Ezra[1] and then continues:

> A *medinah* includes within itself many lands (*'araṣot*) and each *medinah* is divided from its neighbor by language and script (*be-lashon uvi-khetav*). This means that although originally they may have had one alphabet (*ketav*) and one language, nevertheless, because of the distance separating the *medinot* from each other, some differences in language developed among them. For example, the languages of the Spaniards and of the French and of other nations [of the Romance group] differ from one another although they all derive from one language [i.e., Latin]. Similarly with regard to script (*ketav*). Even though they all have basically the same alphabet (*mikhtav*), nevertheless there are differences in the form of the letters written in different *medinot* even though the

> letters are the same. We see, for example, that the letters written by our Spanish brethren differ somewhat in form from the letters that we write even though the alphabet (*mikhtav*) is the same. Evidence to support my statement that every *medinah* differs from the others in script (*ketav*) and language is found in this book: "and he sent letters to all the royal provinces to every province in its own script and to every people in its own language" (Est 1:22). This shows that there are slight differences in the form of the letters and in the language of the various *medinot.*[2]

Except for the statement at the beginning of this passage that a *medinah* includes many lands (*'araṣot*),[3] Immanuel's definition is fairly clear. A *medinah* in his view is a region differentiated in language and script. Western Europe, on the basis of this definition, would be divided into several *medinot* each using a different language derived from Latin, e.g., French, Spanish, Italian, Portuguese, Catalan, and Provençal. He does not indicate whether a *medinah* includes several peoples speaking several different languages but using the same script or whether one people might be divided into several *medinot* each one with local differences in script. In his discussion of differences in language, he definitely seems to be referring to European vernaculars, while in his discussion of scripts, he seems to be referring to local differences in the writing of Hebrew script.

Immanuel's observation that the language of the Spaniards, French, and other nationalities derive from one language is worthy of note. It raises the question of how aware people in the Middle Ages were of the similarities between the various Romance languages and how they explained their origin and diversification. It seems that the first scholar to attempt to account for the diversification of European languages was Immanuel's contemporary, Dante Alighieri.

Writing in his *De vulgari eloquentia* in 1305, Dante divides the languages of Europe into three distinct groups: (1) the northern Europeans, consisting of the Slavs, Ungars, Teutons, Angles, and Saxons, (2) the Greeks, and (3) the southern Europeans. Of the latter groups he says:

> In the rest of Europe outside of these regions a third language dominates which itself seems to be tri-form. For certain people in order to say yes use *oc*, others *oïl*, and still others *sì*, as do for example the Spaniards, the French, and the Italians. The sign that

> the vernaculars of these three nations derive from one and the same idiom is evident since they name many things with the same words, such as *Deus* (God), *celum* (heaven), *amor* (love), *mare* (sea), *terra* (land), *est* (is), *vivit* (lives), *moritur* (dies), *amat* (loves), and many others.[4]

It is clear that Dante groups all of the Romance languages together, recognizing their derivation from one mother tongue, Latin. Dante's originality on this point has been attested to by several modern scholars.[5] Therefore, the fact that Immanuel alludes to the same matter makes it almost certain that he was borrowing here from Dante.

Scholars have long been aware of Immanuel's literary dependence on Dante in many of his cantos.[6] More recently, F. Tocci has pointed to some influences of Dante on Immanuel's Genesis commentary.[7] However, I believe that Immanuel's familiarity with Dante's Latin works has never before been demonstrated. The *De vulgari eloquentia* was written in 1305. We can conclude then that Immanuel wrote his Esther commentary sometime after this date. It may indeed have been his contact with this work, whether directly or by word of mouth, which prompted him to write such a lengthy comment on the first verse in Esther.

NOTES

Introduction

1. Among the Five Scrolls, only on the Song of Songs was more attention lavished.

2. The work by M. H. Segal, *Parshanut ha-Miqra'*, 2nd ed. (Jerusalem, 1971), while still useful, is dated and full of value judgments that can no longer be sustained.

3. See the several recent studies of Rashi cited in Appendix I and the ground-breaking study by Frank Talmage, *David Kimhi: The Man and the Commentaries* (Cambridge, Mass., 1975).

4. Two recent efforts are D. R. G. Beattie, *Jewish Exegesis of the Book of Ruth*, Journal for the Study of the Old Testament, Supplement Series, 2 (Sheffield, 1977), and, of a different order, Uriel Simon, *Four Approaches to the Book of Psalms: From Saadiah Gaon to Abraham Ibn Ezra*, trans. from the Hebrew by Lenn J. Schramm (Albany, N.Y., 1991) (originally appeared as: *'Arba' gishot le-Sefer Tehillim* (Ramat-Gan, 1982). The former deals with the commentaries of Salmon ben Yeroḥam, the Karaite, Rashi, an anonymous exegete, (actually Isaiah di Trani), Abraham Ibn Ezra, and David Kimḥi; the latter with the commentaries on Psalms of Saadiah Gaon, Moses ibn Gikatilla, Abraham Ibn Ezra, and the Karaites Salmon ben Yeroḥam and Japheth ben Eli. Both works focus on the early medieval exegetes. Siegmund Salfeld's, *Das Hohelied Salomo's bei den jüdischen Erklärern des Mittelalters* (Berlin, 1879) (originally published in *Magazin für die Wissenschaft des Judenthums* 5 (1878): 110–78; 6 (1879): 20–48, 129–169, 189–209) is a useful survey of the commentaries on Song of Songs known at the time, but it is dated and sketchy. A model study of this nature based on Christian (mainly patristic) sources is Yves-Marie Duval, *Le Livre de Jonas dans la littérature chrétienne grecque et latine: sources et influence du commentaire sur Jonas de saint Jérôme*, 2 vols. (Paris, 1973). Cf. the more sketchy

but most provocative study by R. H. Bowers, *The Legend of Jonah* (The Hague, 1971). See also Jack P. Lewis, *A Study of the Interpretation of Noah and the Flood in Jewish and Christian Literature* (Leiden, 1968). Mention should also here be made of the study of the exegesis of Gn 1:28 by Jeremy Cohen, *"Be Fertile and Increase, Fill the Earth and Master It": The Ancient and Medieval Career of a Biblical Text* (Ithaca, N.Y., 1989). Although it deals with the career of only one verse, the breadth of sources consulted is truly impressive, and the author's scholarship impeccable.

5. A complete bibliography of Esther commentaries both in print and in manuscript is included at the end of this study.

6. For further biographical and bibliographical information, see Appendix I.

7. Aside from the Judeo-Arabic commentary of Saadiah, other Judeo-Arabic commentaries that exist are by the Karaite Japheth ben Eli (tenth century) and Tanḥum ben Joseph Yerushalmi (thirteenth century). I was also unable to consult the Hebrew commentary of the fifteenth-century Karaite Abraham ben Judah. See Bibliography for details.

8. Concerning Rashi's Esther commentary in particular, see Sarah Kamin-Rozik, " 'Sibbatiyyut kefulah' be-feirush Rashi li-Megillat 'Ester: ʿiyyun be-shiqqulav shel Rashi bi-veḥirat peirushei Ḥazal," in *Sefer Yiṣḥaq 'Aryeh Zeligman: ma'amarim ba-Miqra' u-va-ʿolam ha-ʿatiq*, ed. Yair Zakovitch, Alexander Rofé, 3 vols. (Jerusalem, 1982), 2: 547–58 (Hebrew section).

9. See, for instance, Abraham Ibn Ezra's introduction to his *Commentary on the Pentateuch*. Of course, the sages of the Talmud and Midrash had their own rules of interpretation based on quite different presuppositions than those a Western, philosophically trained mind would be accustomed to. See Isaak Heinemann, *Darkhei ha-'Aggadah*, 2nd ed. (Jerusalem, 1954); Max Kadushin, *Organic Thinking* (New York, 1938; reprint: New York, 1976); and most recently, Howard Eilberg-Schwartz, "Who's Kidding Whom?: A Serious Reading of Rabbinic Word-Plays," *Journal of the American Academy of Religion* 55 (1987): 765–88.

10. Cf. Frank Talmage, "Keep Your Sons From Scripture: The Bible in Medieval Jewish Scholarship and Spirituality," in *Understanding Scripture*, ed. Clemens Thoma and Michael Wyschogrod (New York, 1987), 84–88, who points out the decline in biblical studies in the Christian universities as the curriculum expanded to include philosophy and theology and suggests that a parallel development on the Jewish side—the increased involvement in talmudic studies in the Tosafist school in northern France—left the scholars less time for biblical studies.

11. E.g., MS. UB (Erlangen) 1263, fols. 151r–153v.

12. Both versions of his commentary were circulated, although version A seems to have been more popular as is evidenced by the far greater number of manuscripts of this version that are extant and by the greater number of exegetes quoting it. The following exegetes quote version A: Immanuel of Rome, Joseph ibn Kaspi, Baḥya ben Asher, Joseph Naḥmias, Solomon Astruc, "Ramah," Isaac Arama, Joseph Ḥayyun, and Abraham Saba. The following quote version B: Moses Ḥalayo and Abraham Ḥadidah. Although he never quotes Ibn Ezra directly, Isaiah of Trani also indicates at several points that he was familiar with his commentary. The commentaries of Immanuel, Baḥya, Kaspi, and Naḥmias are especially laden with quotes from Ibn Ezra. In Kaspi's case, a comment of Ibn Ezra's is the whole raison d'être of his commentary. See below, pp. 129–32. This is further evidence of the active interest in the works of Ibn Ezra in the fourteenth century, pointed out by Alexander Altmann, "Moses Narboni's 'Epistle on *Shi'ur Qoma*,'" in *Jewish Medieval and Renaissance Studies*, ed. Alexander Altmann (Cambridge, Mass., 1967), 241–42. (Repr. in his *Studies in Religious Philosophy and Mysticism* [Ithaca, N.Y., 1969], 196–97).

13. For background on the development of homiletics in fifteenth-century Spain, see Mordekhai Pakhter, "Sifrut ha-derush ve-ha-musar shel ḥakhmei Ṣefat ba-me'ah ha-16 u-ma'arekhet ra'yonoteha ha-'iqqariyyim" (Ph.D. diss., Hebrew University, Jerusalem, 1976), chap. 1–2. Pakhter sees fifteenth-century Spain as the source of the homiletical movement that flowered in Safed in the mid–sixteenth century, and preachers such as Isaac Arama and Abraham Saba as two of its most prominent figures.

14. For a bibliography of Esther commentaries published in the sixteenth century, see Yosef Kohen, "Megillat 'Ester ba-'aspaqlaryah shel ḥakhmei Ṣefat ba-me'ah ha-16," *She'arim* 4, 6 March 1966. The list includes twenty commentaries. There are several more in manuscript. In other words, in the sixteenth century nearly as many major Esther commentaries were produced as in all the preceding centuries, and these were all very lengthy.

15. *GK*, 31. Kaspi's predecessor is Abraham Ibn Ezra and the question he deals with pertains to Ibn Ezra's explanation of the content of the second set of letters that Mordecai sent out to the Jews (8:10). This point is taken up in Chapter 6. Although he says here and elsewhere that he would write nothing else on Esther, he must have changed his mind at some later date. See p. 219 below.

16. Cf. The introductions of Zechariah ben Saruḳ and Isaac Arama to their commentaries.

17. See p. 53 below, for his use of rhetoric.

18. His commentary as well does not live up to the expectations raised in the introduction.

19. See Maimonides, *Guide of the Perplexed,* trans. Shlomo Pines (Chicago, 1963), 3.27, p. 510.

20. One cannot completely rule out Christian influence in the case of Gersonides, as one of the senses of the fourfold system of interpretation of scripture elaborated by Christian scholars was the tropological, or moral. But perhaps it is more prudent to stress with A. van der Heide, "PARDES: Methodological Reflections on the Theory of the Four Senses," *Journal of Jewish Studies* 34 (1983): 155, n. 25, "the common cultural milieu which favored such distinctions."

21. He interpreted most verses according to the *peshaṭ* and midrashic methods, many verses according to the kabbalistic method, and relatively few according to the philosophic method. In his application of the method of *sekhel,* Baḥya included the opinions of philosophers and scientists insofar as they helped explain matters in the world outside the divine. For understanding the latter, the fourth, or mystical, method was called into play. He applies all four methods to the same verse twenty-two times. See Bela Bernstein, "Die Schrifterklärung des Bachja b. Asher ibn Chalawa und ihre Quellen," *Magazin für die Wissenschaft der Judenthums* 18 (1891): 36–37, n. 17.

22. In his *peshaṭ* commentary, Baḥya followed closely the commentary of Abraham Ibn Ezra, which he calls "the most correct of all the commentaries which were composed on this Scroll" (*Kitvei Rabbeinu Baḥya,* 330). In fact, he held Ibn Ezra in such high esteem that he occasionally paid him the highest compliment by using his commentary without acknowledgement. The midrashic commentary consists of comments on the text taken from various rabbinic sources, chiefly B. T. Megillah, chap. 1, and *Midrash Esther Rabbah,* but it does include comments of unknown origin. The third section offers an astrological interpretation of the Book of Esther, a unique and novel occurrence in the history of the medieval exegesis of the book. See below, pp. 58–59.

23. This is the same method he uses in his *'Aqeidat Yiṣḥaq* and is also used by Isaac Abravanel in his biblical commentaries. For Arama's influence on Abravanel, see Wilensky, *R. Yiṣḥaq 'Aramah,* 50–57.

24. See below, pp. 68–72.

25. The tragedy of the expulsion is still fresh in Zechariah's mind as he comments on Mordecai's exile from Jerusalem, "And so are we, plundered and driven from our country and our homes. All this has befallen us, yet we have not forgotten Him nor broken His covenant" (p. 11a).

26. Sara Japhet, "Kivvunei meḥqar ve-hilkhei ruaḥ be-ḥeqer parshanut yemei ha-beinayim bi-Ṣefon Ṣarefat," in *Yedi'on ha-'Iggud ha-'olami le-mada'ei ha-Yahadut (Newsletter of the World Union of Jewish Studies)* 25 (1984–85): 18; also published in *Meḥqarim ba-Miqra' u-va-Talmud*, edited by Sara Japhet (Jerusalem, 1987), 38–39.

Chapter 1. Jewish Sources for Exegesis

1. Cf. the following statements by Kaspi: "Let no man believe the lie that he will be able to understand the words of our Torah and the other books of the Bible without prior knowledge of grammar and logic." (*Mishneh kesef* (also called *Tirat kesef*) ed. I. Last, 2 vols. [Pressburg, Czechoslovakia, 1905], 1:10.) And: "Know this important matter: There is no thing or event in all the books of the Prophets that is not written in the Torah, even the coming of the Messiah which we are expecting today. However, only someone who is thoroughly familiar with the Hebrew language and the science of logic can know this, since only such a person will understand completely the words and sentences written in the Torah and will understand how the particular is found potentially within the general and the conclusions within the premises. These are delicate and important matters. In this regard, Isaiah, after recounting the fall of the nations had this to say: 'Search and read it in the scroll of the Lord: Not one of these shall be absent' (Is 34:16). The book of the Lord is the Torah of Moses. Remember this" (*Mishneh kesef*, 2:40–41). Kaspi's stress on logic is reminiscent of the emphasis put on this discipline by Shemariah b. Elijah who stated: "In all the wonderful secrets that I interpreted I did not force one letter from Scripture in order to establish that secret on the basis of the text. Rather the text itself according to its logical meaning and the true laws of logic (*ḥokhmat ha-mivṭa'*) and grammar supports that secret interpretation and testifies that this is its true intent more than it supports the plain corporeal meaning by which the masses understand it"(*'Oṣar neḥmad*, 2:91). Unfortunately, not enough of Shemariah's œuvre has survived to enable us to see whether he was as consistent in applying his principles as Kaspi. The two share other qualities, as Isadore Twersky points out, "Joseph ibn Kaspi: Portrait of a Medieval Jewish Intellectual," in *Studies in Medieval Jewish History and Literature*, ed. Isadore Twersky (Cambridge, Mass., 1979), 251–52.

2. Perhaps because the exegetes in these times felt they could add nothing to what had already been stated by their predecessors or simply that by then their interests lay in other areas. See above, Introduction, n. 11.

3. E.g.: *tor* (2:12). Time (Rashi, Rashbam); *ki khen yissad ha-melekh* (1:8). This means: so did the king advise (*ya'aṣ* for *yissad*) all the important men of his household (Kara).

4. E.g.: *'avetah* (1:16). This word has the same connotation (*lashon*) as wrongdoing (*'avon*) (Rashi); *meruqeihen* (2:12). Like cosmetics (*tamruqeihen*) (Rashbam).

5. E.g.: *ve-nishloaḥ* (3:13). Like *ve-nishloaḥ sefarim* ("letters were sent speedily"); this is an elliptical expression (*miqra' qaṣar hu'*), and its meaning is like that of a repeated word (*lashon kefel*), like *nish'ol nish'al David* ("David earnestly asked leave"; 1 Sm 20:28) or *'im nilḥom nilḥam bam* ("did he ever go to war"; Jgs 11:25) (Rashbam). (Apparently, according to Rashbam, our text should read *ve-nishloaḥ nishlaḥ sefarim*.)

6. E.g.: *deḥufim* (3:15). This has a connotation of haste (*'inyan behalah*) (Rashbam); *ha-partemim* (1:3). This has a connotation of greatness (*leshon gedullah*) ("A").

7. E.g.: *tamruqeihen* (2:3). Things with which one cleanses and rubs the skin in order to remove hair and soften the skin, as "It shall be both scoured and rinsed in water" (*u-moraq ve-shuṭṭaf ba-mayim*; Lv 6:21) ("A"); *ha-'aḥashteranim* (8:10). A species of camel that runs quickly (Rashi).

8. See example in n. 5, above.

9. E.g.: *Ke-ṭov* (1:10). Like "joyful and glad of heart" (*semeḥim ve-ṭovei lev*; 1 Kgs 8:66) (Kara); *va-titḥalḥal ha-malkah* (4:4). Like, "my loins are filled with anguish" (*ḥalḥalah*) (Is 21:3) ("A").

10. E.g.: *Va-yit'appaq* (5:10). He made an effort to control his anger because he was afraid to take revenge without permission (*e se retint* in Old French) (Rashi). I have found only six vernacular translations in the Ashkenazic commentaries I have studied. In addition to *e se retint*, Rashi has the following *le'azim*: *ve-nishloaḥ* (3:13)—*estre tramis*; *patshegen* (3:14)—*disreinement*. See Arsène Darmesteter, "Les gloses françaises de Raschi dans la Bible," *Revue des études juives* 56 (1908): 87–88, and now Moche Catane, *'Oṣar ha-le'azim: ha-milim ha-Ṣarefatiyyot she-be-feirushei Rashi 'al ha-Tanakh* (Jerusalem, 1990), 74. Catane corrects Darmesteter in many places. My thanks to him for identifying the *la'az* to 4:13. I found two other *le'azim* in some Rashi manuscripts, one at *yissad* (1:8), the other at *'al tedammi* (cuider) (4:13), but these may well be scribal interpolations, as they do not appear in all manuscripts. Finally, Joseph Kara has the word *cortines*, meaning hangings or tapestries at 1:6 (3:87).

11. There seems to be no linguistic basis for such a definition. Cf. the various connotations given for *'aḥaz* in Avraham Even-Shoshan, *Qonqordanṣyah ḥadashah le-Torah Nevi'im u-Khetuvim*, (Jerusalem, 1988), 37. All the other exegetes understand the word to mean "attached by" or "caught up with."

12. At Jb 33:27, *ve-lo' shavah li*, Rashi comments: "I did not receive any gain (*sakhar*)." Yitzhak Avineri in his *Millon peirushei Rashi la-Miqra' ve-la-Talmud Bavli* (Tel-Aviv, 1949; reprinted in his *Heikhal Rashi*, vol. 2 [Jerusalem, 1985]), 332, notes that the connotation Rashi gave for the word in Job would be more appropriate for the words in Esther.

13. It is interesting to note that Rashi comments on verse 3:8 in two places in his Talmud commentary. At B.T. Megillah 13b he comments: אין שווה. אין נאה ואין חשש להניחן, i.e., there is no benefit [I suspect that one should read הנאה for נאה; cf. Targum Rishon ad loc.: ומה הנאה אית ליה בהון אין ישבקינון על אפי ארעא] and no concern for leaving them. This comment is equivalent to that in his Esther commentary. However at Sanhedrin 39a he comments: דשויא לתרייהו. שתהא מועלת לשניהם כמו אין שוה להניחם, i.e., that benefits both of them, as in "there is no benefit to leave them be." It is difficult to imagine that Rashi considered the root *ḤShSh* to mean "benefit." I could find no linguistic basis for such a connotation. Perhaps he felt he had to use this root at 3:8 for the sake of consistency but did not feel comfortable with it. By the time he arrived at Tractate Sanhedrin in his Talmud commentary he was convinced that this word was inappropriate in this context and therefore dropped it. Cf. the comments of Yoel Florsheim, *Rashi la-Miqra' be-feirusho la-Talmud*, vol. 3, *Ketuvim* (Jerusalem, 1989), 242–43.

14. Cf. table on p. 15 above.

15. Kara, 3:91.

16. Cf. table on p. 15 above.

17. *'Oṣar ṭov* (1878): 27.

18. Ibid., 28.

19. Cf. table on p. 15 above.

20. See D. Rosin, *Samuel b. Meir*, 135–36.

21. Ibid., 136.

22. Ibid., 139.

23. Ibid., 133.

24. Ibid., 128.

25. He cites verses from other biblical books sixty-two times in his first commentary and fifty-eight times in the second. Compare this with the Ashkenazic commentators, listed above, p. 15.

26. See his comment to Song of Songs 8:11 in the Rabbinic Bible (Miqra'ot gedolot):

והעומד על זה החבור אולי יתמה למה אומר כאן בלשון ישמעאל בעבור קוצר דעתנו כי לא נדע מלשון הקדש כי אם הכתוב במקרא שהוצרכו הנביאים לדבר ומה שלא הוצרכו לא נדע שמו.

27. As in the Arabic word *karfas*.

28. I.e., royal blue. Cf. his comment to the word at Ex 25:4 in his short commentary, *Sefer 'Ibn 'Ezra' le-sefer Shemot*, ed. J. L. Fleischer (Vienna, 1926), 226, where he describes it as close to black, although somewhat similar to the sky.

29. So Kara.

30. So Saadiah Gaon, *'Egron*, ed. Nehemiah Allony (Jerusalem, 1969), 288. See Jonah Ibn Janaḥ, *Sefer ha-shorashim*, ed. Wilhelm Bacher (Berlin, 1896), 256, who also rejects this view and leans toward that of Hai Gaon who identifies it with a resin called in Arabic *labna rahaban*, a pleasant smelling liquid suited to the verse in Song 5:1. *Mor* is now generally accepted to be the perfume extracted from the myrrh plant, *Commiphora abyssinica*. See Jehuda Feliks, *'Olam ha-ṣomeaḥ ha-miqra'i*, 2nd ed. rev. (Ramat-Gan, 1968), 252–54; Michael Zohary, *Plants of the Bible* (Cambridge, 1982), 200. But see Harold N. Moldenke and Alma L. Moldenke, *Plants of the Bible* (Waltham, Mass., 1952), 82–84, who insist that the plant in question is *Commiphora myrrha* or possibly *Commiphora kataf*.

31. This is possibly the Jericho balsam, *Balanites aegyptiaca*, which is identified by some as the balm (*ṣori*) of Jer 8:22, 56:11, and 51:8 and of Gn 37:25. See Moldenke, *Plants*, 55; but cf. Feliks, *'Olam ha-ṣomeaḥ*, 248, who considers this unlikely. In his comment on the latter verse, Ibn Ezra refers to the opinion of Joseph ben Gorion in *Josippon* that *ṣori* refers to the fruit or the oil of the tree brought from Jericho to Egypt, although he does not accept this view. In any case, his identification of *mor* with the Jericho tree seems even more unlikely.

32. Cf. Aristotle, *Historia animalium*, trans. D. W. Thompson (Oxford, 1910), 6:23, p. 577.

33. Cf. the Arabic word *ramaka* which means a common stud mare. On the usefulness of Arabic for the study of the Bible, Ibn Ezra has this to say (at Song 8:11):

ובעבור היות לשון ישמעאל קרוב מאר ללשון הקדש כי בנייניו ואותיות יה״וא והמשרתים ונפעל והתפעל והסמיכות דרך אחת לשתיהן וכן בחשבון ויותר מחצי הלשון ימצא כמוהו בלשון הקדש על כן כל מלה שלא נמצא לה חבר במקרא ויש דומה בלשון ישמעאל נאמר אולי פירושה כן אע״פ שהדבר בספק.

34. "הנה נתברר כי הערים בכלל המדינות כי כתוב "בעריהם בכל מדינות. It should be noted that the reading adopted here (*he-'arim bi-khelal ha-medinot*) is found only in MS. BC (Verona, Italy) 204. All the other manuscripts read *ha-medinot bi-khelal he-'arim*, i.e., the walled cities are included within the settlements (in Ibn Ezra's opinion) which does not make sense in the context, although it does fit in with Ibn Ezra's overall scheme. See also below, pp. 97–100.

35. Isaiah uses two Italian *le'azim* in his commentary: *verdura* = vegetation (1:5); *statuti* = laws, statutes (1:13). For examples from Isaiah's other commentaries, see E.Z. Melamed, "Le-feirush Nakh shel R. Yesha'yah mi-Ṭrani," in *Meḥqarim ba-Miqra' u-va-Mizraḥ ha-qadmon muggashim li-Shemu'el A. Livenshṭam [Loewenstamm] bi-melot lo shiv'im shanah* (Jerusalem, 1978), 299–300.

36. This passage is quoted and discussed below, p. 106.

37. This work is still in manuscript. Part of it was published by I. Last in *Jewish Quarterly Review*, o.s.19 (1906–07): 651–87 (repr. along with Kaspi's *Tam ha-kesef*, ed. I. Last [London, 1913]).

38. E.g., at 1:1, concerning the initial *vav*; at 4:14, concerning the *kaf* of *ka-zot*.

39. See his comments to *ve-naton* (6:9), *ve-nahafokh* (9:1), *holekh ve-gadol* (9:4), *haregu ve-'abbed* (9:5).

40. Immanuel of Rome quotes Ibn Janaḥ three times: 1:3, *ha-partemim*; 1:5, *bitan*; and 2:9, *va-yevahel*. Moses Ḥalayo also quotes Ibn Janaḥ once (fol. 5r, on *'argaman*).

41. Moses Ḥalayo quotes David Kimḥi for the interpretation of *'argaman* and Joseph Kimḥi (apparently his *Sefer ha-galui*) for *'aḥashdarpanim* and *ramakhim*. See below.

42. Joseph Kimḥi, *Sefer ha-galui*, edited by H. J. Mathews (Berlin, 1887; repr. Jerusalem, 1966–67), 70.

43. Moses Ḥalayo, fol. 5r. quotes this interpretation in the name of Kimḥi without mentioning Saadiah. Isaiah of Trani, *Peirush*, 3:301, 303, gives this same interpretation without acknowledging its source. It is interesting to note that Ibn Janaḥ's interpretation of the word *'aḥashdarpanim* as a compound of *'aḥashdar* and *panim* meaning the officers of the king's face, i.e., those that were closest to him and saw his face, does not seem to have been accepted by any other exegete. See Jonah Ibn Janaḥ, *Sefer ha-riqmah*, ed. Michael Wilensky, 2nd ed., 2 vols. (Jerusalem, 1964), 1:122–23.

44. See L. B. Paton, *A Critical and Exegetical Commentary on the Book of*

Esther, The International Critical Commentary (New York, 1908), 258, 261–62; Carey A. Moore, trans., *Esther*, The Anchor Bible, 7B (Garden City, N.Y., 1971), 70. Moore calls this clause "undoubtedly the most difficult clause to translate in all of Esther, primarily because the meanings of three of the six words in it are uncertain, namely, *haṣṣar . . . šōweh . . . benezeq*."

45. So Rashi, Ibn Ezra (one of several alternatives offered), Isaac ben Joseph, fol. 70r, Joseph Naḥmias, p. 29, and Ḥayyun, fol. 83r–v.

46. See David Kimḥi, *Sefer ha-shorashim*, ed. J. H. R. Biesenthal and F. Lebrecht (Berlin, 1847; repr. Jerusalem, 1966–67), 374. Isaiah of Trani follows his interpretation, *Peirush* 3:301, 302. Cf. Tobias ben Eliezer, *Midrash Leqaḥ ṭov*, 108, who reads the verse as follows: "the gain that this enemy shall bring to the king is not worth the damage he will cause."

47. Cf. Immanuel of Rome, fol. 205r.

48. *Kitvei Rabbeinu Baḥya*, 332; paradoxically, this interpretation is given in the *peshaṭ* section of Baḥya's commentary.

49. See Jacob b. Reuben, *Sefer ha-ʿosher* (Eupatoria, 1836), 17a.

50. See, e.g., Moore, *Esther*, 33, 38; Paton, *Esther*, 200–202.

51. Most modern scholars plead ignorance. Cf. Moore, *Esther*, 38.

52. So Rashbam, Ibn Ezra, Moses b. Isaac Ḥalayo, Naḥmias, Ḥadidah, and Arama.

53. Abraham Saba; Naḥmias suggests that it might refer to Vashti's shame.

54. Ḥayyun, "Ramah."

55. So Saadiah (in Ratzaby, 1168, 1177), Ibn Ezra, Gersonides, and Naḥmias.

56. E.g., David Kimḥi, *Sefer ha-shorashim*, 113; Isaiah of Trani; Jacob b. Reuben, *Sefer ha-ʿosher*, 17b; Ḥayyun, and the anonymous French exegete in *Niṭʿei naʿamanim*, 11a. Incidentally, the Septuagint gives a similar translation: *Aman de akousas dietrapē tōi prosōpōi*, i.e., he changed countenance.

57. Last, *Millu'im*, 20.

58. In general, the question of influence, except in a few very clear-cut cases, was very difficult to determine. It is noteworthy, that Rashi and the other northern French exegetes on Esther are seldom, if ever, quoted by later exegetes.

59. See Heinemann, *Darkhei ha-'aggadah*, 96–164. For a recent reexami-

nation of the rabbinic understanding of the Hebrew language and its use for exegesis, see Eilberg-Schwartz, "Who's Kidding Whom?" 765–88.

60. *NJV* has: "The people who had been fleeing to the wilderness now became the pursuers."

61. In this category we could also include the new interpretations given to *le-'abbedam* ("to confiscate the Jews' money"; 3:9) (see below) and *ke-ṭov be-ʿeinekha* ("to do what is best," or "as you see fit"; 3:11) (see below pp. 185–89), which seem to have been made by exegetes in the later Middle Ages in an attempt to bring events in the Esther story closer in line with their own experience.

62. IbJ, fol. 63v. I have emended *mefaqqed* to *mafqid*, since the latter parallels *mashveh* and makes better sense in the context.

63. These include B.T. Megillah, Chapter 1, pp. 10b–17a; *Midrash Esther Rabbah* (for chap. 1–7), *Midrash 'Abba' Guryon* (for chap. 1–7), *Midrash Panim 'aḥerim* in two versions, the first covering selected verses in chap. 1 and 3–7, the second, chap. 1–7; *Midrash Leqaḥ ṭov*, compiled by Tobias ben Eliezer (eleventh century); the latter three were published by Salomon Buber under the title *Sifrei de-'aggadeta' ʿal Megillat 'Ester* (Vilna, 1886); *Yalquṭ Shimʿoni*, 1044–59; *Midrash Megillat 'Ester* in *'Aguddat 'aggadot*, ed. Chaim M. Horowitz (Berlin, 1881), 47–75; "The Oldest Version of Midrash Megillah," in Moses Gaster, *Studies and Texts in Folklore, Magic, Medieval Romance, Hebrew Apocrypha and Samaritan Archaeology*, 3 vols. (London, 1925–28; repr. New York, 1970), 3:44–49 (on chap. 1–6); *'Aggadat 'Ester*, ed. S. Buber (Lwow, 1897); *Pirqei de-Rabbi 'Eliʿezer*, Chapter 49–50. In addition, see Z. M. Rabinowitz, ed., *Ginzei Midrash* (Tel-Aviv, 1977), 155–178. The sermons (*Derashot*) of Joshua ibn Shuʿaib (Constantinople, 1523), 36a–37b, also contain a midrashic commentary on Esther. There also exist two targumim to Esther, the second of which is essentially a midrashic compilation in Aramaic. For a digest of midrashic commentary on the book, see Louis Ginzberg, *Legends of the Jews*, 7 vols. (Philadelphia, 1913–38), 4:363–448.

64. For example, Abraham Saba sometimes quotes rabbinic sources that are untraceable. His commentaries have preserved numerous lost rabbinic sources, and Ginzberg uses him as a source in his compilation, *Legends of the Jews*. Furthermore, there are a number of anonymous manuscripts of commentaries on Esther which are essentially midrashic compilations on the book. A study of these texts would undoubtedly uncover still more midrashic sources for the Book of Esther.

65. For evidence supporting the meaning of *peshuṭo shel Miqra'* as "text of Scripture," see Menahem Banitt, *Rashi: Interpreter of the Biblical Letter* (Tel

Aviv, 1985), 1–2, n. 6. For an exhaustive discussion of the term in rabbinical literature and in Rashi's commentaries, see Sarah Kamin, *Rashi: peshuṭo shel Miqra' u-midrasho shel Miqra'* (Jerusalem, 1986). According to Kamin, the term means "the literal meaning of the text" (p. 115, 265), which Banitt points out corresponds to the Latin expression *ad litteram*.

66. Kara, 3:88; Kara's fiercely independent tone still rankles certain pious readers and caused the most recent editor of his commentary to defend the well-established rabbinic tradition. See the comment by J. Gad in Kara, 3:88–89, n. 9. Rashi quoted this tradition which is found in *Pirqei de-Rabbi 'Eli'ezer* 49, *Esther Rabbah* 4 and other sources. He interprets *'asher lo' tavo'* as referring to the past. Vashti did not come, and therefore she was slain. Although most exegetes follow the rabbinic tradition on this point, many others do not. According to Immanuel of Rome she was kept imprisoned until she died. Isaac Arama comments that she was not allowed before the king again and Joseph Ḥayyun says that she was banished from the throne. According to Isaac ben Joseph ha-Kohen, she was not killed by Ahasuerus's decree, but consumed with jealousy and anger at having been replaced, she soon died. Joseph Naḥmias points out that the text does not mention she was killed but that this is what the rabbinic tradition asserts. We see then that Joseph Kara was in good company.

67. Cf. Rashi, *rabboteinu dareshu bo mah she-dareshu*, to Est 1:7 and 2:5, or Ibn Ezra, *ve-da'atam reḥavah mi-da'ateinu*. Cf. Simon, *Four Approaches*, 158–59.

68. Rashi quoted this same midrash, which is found in B.T. Megillah 13b, in his comment to 3:1. See Kamin-Rozik, " 'Sibbatiyyut kefulah' ", 2:553.

69. Kara, 3:90 to 2:21.

70. See B.T. Megillah 13b.

71. *'Osar ṭov* (1878): 28. Cf. Rashi ad loc. and B.T. Megillah 13a.

72. MS. SUB (Hamburg) 32, fol. 95r; Jellinek's edition has R. Yosef after this remark, which is an error. Cf. B.T. Megillah 11a and Rashi ad loc.

73. This figure shows that over two-thirds (68%) of Rashi's comments are original (at least I could find no midrashic source for them).

74. In these cases, a midrashic source is quoted, prefaced by a phrase such as "our sages said" (1:12), "our sages explained" (2:2), or "so our sages have derived and learnt" (9:19).

75. In these cases, Rashi bases his comment on a midrashic source, which is often adapted and abbreviated but is not acknowledged:, e.g.: *That Ahasuerus* (1:1). He in his wickedness from beginning to end (See B.T. Megillah 11a); *In the tenth month* (2:16). A cold season when one body enjoys another; the Holy

One, blessed be He, provided the cold season in order to endear her to him. (See B.T. Megillah 13a; only the first half of the comment is found there).

76. In these cases, Rashi gives his own interpretation and then quotes the sages introducing their comments either by "Our sages said," or "A *midrash 'aggadah.*"

77. In these cases, Rashi acknowledges the existence of a midrashic comment to the verse but does not deem it worthy of quotation. His usual formula of dismissal is "Our sages interpreted this verse after their fashion (*Rabboteinu dareshu bo mah she-dareshu*)."

78. See in this regard, Nechama Leibowitz, "Darko shel Rashi be-hava'at midrashim be-feirusho la-Torah," in her *'Iyyunim ḥadashim be-sefer Shemot be-'iqvot parshaneinu ha-rishonim ve-ha-'aḥaronim*, 2nd ed. (Jerusalem, 1970), 495–524. Cf. also Sarah Kamin, *Rashi*, 158–262; Kamin-Rozik, "'Sibbatiyyut kefulah'," 547–58; Yosefah Raḥaman, "Bei'ur derekh ha-limmud shel ha-midrash be-feirush Rashi la-Torah," in *'Iyyunim ba-Miqra': sefer zikkaron li-Yehoshu'a Me'ir Grinṣ [Y. M. Grintz]*, ed. Benjamin Uffenheimer, Te'udah, 2 (Tel-Aviv, 1982), 111–27; id., "'Ibbud midrashim be-feirusho shel Rashi la-Torah," in *Meḥqarim be-sifrut ha-Talmud, bi-leshon Ḥazal u-ve-farshanut ha-Miqra'*, ed. Mordechai Akiva Friedman, Avraham Tal, Gershon Brin, Te'udah, 3 (Tel Aviv, 1983), 261–68; Benjamin J. Gelles, *Peshat and Derash in the Exegesis of Rashi* (Leiden, 1981) and the compilation by Ḥayyim Zohari, *Midreshei 'aggadah ve-halakhah be-feirush Rashi la-Torah (be-hashva'ah la-meqorot)*, 2 vols. (Jerusalem, 1978).

79. See Heinemann, *Darkhei ha-'aggadah*, esp. part 2 (*Darkhei ha-filologyah ha-yoṣeret*), 96–164.

80. See Kamin-Rozik, "'Sibbatiyyut kefulah'," 549–50.

81. NJV notes that the meaning of this verse is uncertain in part. The translation given here is the "literal" one given in a note in the NJV.

82. I.e., an angel. Cf. B.T. Berakhot 10b where the term *ba'al ha-ḥalomot* is used.

83. E.g., B.T. Megillah 12a mentions Ahasuerus's feast and the sin of bowing down to the image, and *Esther Rabbah* 7:13 mentions Ahasuerus's feast. But neither passage refers these events specifically to our verse, although the latter does refer to it peripherally. See Kamin-Rozik, "'Sibbatiyyut kefulah'," 550–51.

84. Elijah is identified as a priest in several midrashic sources. See Aharon Wiener, *The Prophet Elijah in the Development of Judaism* (London, 1978), 45.

The tradition stems from his identification with the Aaronide priest Phinehas, concerning which see also Abraham Spiro, "The Ascension of Phinehas," *Proceedings of the American Academy for Jewish Research* 22 (1953): 91–114.

85. Mordecai's dream in which he envisions a dire threat to Israel's existence and then her ultimate salvation is an important element in apocryphal and midrashic literature on the Book of Esther. See, for example, *Esther Rabbah* 8:5. Of course, its content is quite different from that of Rashi's comment.

86. I have dealt with his treatment of rabbinic material in greater detail in my "The Two Commentaries of Abraham Ibn Ezra on the Book of Esther," *Jewish Quarterly Review* 79 (1988–89): 335–43. He rejects or reinterprets 55% of rabbinic statements quoted in his first commentary, and 74% in his second.

87. E.g., to 2:7, "Mordecai adopted her as his daughter"—the plain meaning is that he did not take her to wife (vs. B.T. Megillah 13a); 5:3, "even to the half of my kingdom"—its plain meaning is the same as its literal meaning (vs. B.T. Megillah 15b).

88. To 1:4 (p. 8), 2:7 (twice) (p. 17), 2:9 (p. 18), 3:2 (p. 30), and 5:3 (p. 26).

89. To 2:5 (p. 16).

90. For an excellent survey and analysis of the issue of *'aggadah* in the Middle Ages, see Saperstein, *Decoding the Rabbis*, 1–20.

91. Ibid., 11–14.

92. See, for example his comment to Esther 9:31, where he mentions the "deniers" (*makḥishim*). See also, Simon, *Four Approaches*, 211–16.

93. *VA*, 30 (to 7:9). For the sources of these and other comments that Ibn Ezra explains rationally, see Walfish, "Two Commentaries," 340.

94. See B.T. Megillah 12b. On the rabbinic practice of identifying characters and filling in details of the lives of biblical figures, see Heinemann, *Darkhei ha-'aggadah*, 29.

95. See R. Isaac's comment to 3:1, IbJ, fol. 60v; Abraham Shalom, *Neveh Shalom*, 71a.

96. Not everyone felt this way, of course. Joseph Naḥmias politely demurs with the comment, "Their words are the words of the living God, but my task is to interpret the text of Scripture (*le-faresh peshuṭo shel Miqra'*)" (pp. 12–13, to 1:16).

97. Saperstein, *Decoding the Rabbis*. This is the first monographic study devoted to an exegete of the *'aggadah*.

98. R. Isaac wrote his commentary in the 1270s, and R. Shemariah lived from 1275 to 1355.

99. Some others are those of Azriel of Gerona (thirteenth century), Moses ibn Tibbon (d. ca. 1283), Todros Abulafia (ca. 1220–98), Solomon Ibn Adret (1235–1310), Yedaiah Bedersi (ca. 1270–ca. 1340), and Shem Tov ibn Shaprut (fourteenth to fifteenth centuries). See ibid., 256.

100. See ibid., 20, 221. The commentaries of R. Azriel and Todros Abulafia are mystical.

101. MS. CUL (Cambridge) Mm. 6.26.2, fol. 67v.

102. Ibid., fol. 53r.

103. Cf. Saperstein, *Decoding the Rabbis*, 15.

104. For this phenomenon in Christian medieval society, see James S. Preus, "Theological Legitimation for Innovation in the Middle Ages," *Viator* 3 (1972): 1–26; for references to other Jewish sources, see Elliott R. Wolfson, "By Way of Truth: Aspects of Naḥmanides' Kabbalistic Hermeneutics," *AJS Review* 14 (1989): 154–57. My thanks to Elliott Wolfson for these references.

105. One example relevant to our study is the application of Ps 22 to Esther in *Midrash Tehillim*. See *Midrash Tehillim*, ed. Salomon Buber (Vilna, 1891) 180–97; *Midrash on Psalms*, trans. William Braude (New Haven, Conn., 1959), 297–326; cf. Saba, *EKE*, 15–17, who also applies this psalm to Esther.

106. See, e.g., R. H. Pfeiffer, *Introduction to the Old Testament* (New York, 1941), 589.

107. Besides Ps 22 and Ps 23, Saba provides a new context for Ps 120 which he reads as a dialogue between two Jews comparing life in exile in an Islamic country with life in a Christian one. This psalm is discussed in Chapter 6 below, pp. 137–38.

108. *EKE*, 77.

109. *Hanaḥah*, a remission from taxes, has the same root *NWḤ*, as *menuḥah* in *mei menuḥot*.

110. This is an allusion to the association made in the midrash between Ahasuerus's reply and the rebuilding of the Temple. According to the midrash, Ahasuerus gave Esther permission to ask for half his kingdom but not something that would divide his kingdom, i.e., the rebuilding of the Temple: *ḥaṣi ha-malkhut ve-lo . . . davar she-hoṣeṣ la-malkhut; u-mai nihu—binyan beit ha-miqdash.* See B.T. Megillah 15b.

111. *EKE*, 83.

112. Ibid., 92. Cf. Solomon Alami, *'Iggeret musar*, ed. A. M. Habermann Sifriyat meqorot, 8 (Jerusalem, 1945–46), 40–41, who almost a century earlier expressed similar views.

113. Recently, Yehuda Liebes has called into question the De Leon theory of authorship, established by Gershom Scholem in his *Major Trends in Jewish Mysticism* (New York, 1938), chap. 5, pp. 156–204. In a lengthy article entitled "Keiṣad nitḥabber Sefer ha-Zohar," *Meḥqerei Yerushalayim be-maḥashevet Yisra'el* 8 (1989): 1–72, Liebes marshals a considerable amount of evidence that would indicate that there were several other hands involved in the composition of the *Zohar*. De Leon is still a central figure in the process, but the picture is much more complex than what was once thought, and the whole question requires further study.

114. Beginning with R. David ben Judah, he-Ḥasid (ca. 1240–ca. 1320) whose *Book of Mirrors* or *Mar'ot ha-ṣove'ot*, which was written in the early fourteenth century, contains large sections of the *Zohar* in Hebrew translation. See D. C. Matt, introduction to *The Book of Mirrors* by David ben Judah, he-Ḥasid, Brown Judaic Studies, 30 (Chico, Calif., 1982), 13–17. Even Baḥya ben Asher who wrote his encyclopedic commentary to the Torah only slightly after the time that the *Zohar* was being published includes in it some Zoharic material. See Ephraim Gottlieb, *Ha-Qabbalah be-khitvei Baḥya ben 'Asher* (Jerusalem, 1970), 167–93, 264–74.

115. Especially *halakhah*. Cf. Meir Benayahu, "Vikkuaḥ ha-qabbalah 'im ha-halakhah," *Da'at* 5 (Summer, 1980): 61–67; Jacob Katz, *Halakhah ve-qabbalah* (Jerusalem, 1984), 9–124.

116. Zechariah ben Saruḳ mentions the *mequbbalim* twice in his commentary. In discussing the absence of God's name in the scroll he mentions the opinion of the kabbalists that the Jews at the time were in a state of divine eclipse (*hastarat panim*), which is alluded to in Esther's name (p. 13b). At the end of his commentary, he offers an interpretation of the blessing said after reading the scroll which he attributes to the "sages of the *kabbalah*," including R. Eleazar of Worms [whom he mistakenly called], the rabbi of Naḥmanides (ibid., p. 19a). I have found no other references to *kabbalah* or kabbalists except those mentioned in this chapter.

117. See below, pp. 58–59.

118. Concerning prayer in the *Zohar*, see *Mishnat ha-Zohar*, ed. and trans. F. Lachower and I. Tishby, 2 vols. (Jerusalem, 1948/49–1961; vol. 1, 3rd ed., 1971), 2:247–280; now available in English, *The Wisdom of the Zohar*, trans. David Goldstein, 3 vols. (Oxford, 1989), 3:941–1075. Cf. also, Elliott R. Wolfson, "Mystical-Theurgical Dimensions of Prayer in *Sefer ha-Rimmon*," *Approaches to Judaism in Medieval Times* 3 (1988): 41–79.

119. The verse is mentioned several times in the *Zohar*: Behar (Ra'aya' mehemna' [= R.M.]) 3:109a; Shelaḥ (R.M.) 3:169b, 175b, 176a; Ḥuqqat 3:183b; cf. also *Tiqqunei ha-Zohar* 21.

120. See especially *Mishnat ha-Zohar*, 1:134–135 (*Wisdom*, 1:272–73). The *sefirot* are described as openings or gates through which mortals can enter into the divine mysteries. The first gate is the lowest *sefirah* or *malkhut*. The description quoted by Arama is also devoid of sexual allusions which predominate in the *Zohar* (*Mishnat ha-Zohar*, 2:262, 272–80; *Wisdom*, 3:957, 966–74), although this is not the case in the *Ra'aya' mehemna'* and *Tiqqunei ha-Zohar* (ibid., 2:263). Arama may be quoting a later source.

121. See, for example, the recent study of the fourteenth-century homilist and kabbalist Joshua Ibn Shuaib by Carmi Horowitz, *The Jewish Sermon in 14th Century Spain: The Derashot of R. Joshua ibn Shu'eib*, Harvard Judaic Monographs, 6 (Cambridge, Mass., 1989), 14–16, 90–100, 130–132, 159–170.

122. Others were Ḥasdai Crescas and David Messer Leon. See Zeev Harvey, "Yesodot qabbaliyyim be-*Sefer 'Or ha-Shem* le-R. Ḥasdai Qresqas," *Meḥqerei Yerushalayim be-maḥashevet Yisra'el* 2:1 (September 1982): 75–110; Hava Tirosh-Rothschild, "Sefirot as the Essence of God in the Writings of David Messer Leon," *AJS Review* 7/8 (1982–83): 409–25.

123. Concerning this school, see Gershom Scholem, "Li-yedi'at ha-qabbalah bi-Sefarad 'erev ha-geirush," *Tarbiẓ* 24 (1954–55): 167–206.

124. See Joseph Sambari, *Divrei Yosef* (Jerusalem, 1981), 143.

125. E.g., 6:1 and 7:10. See B.T. Megillah 15b concerning 6:1.

126. Cf. *Zohar* Qedoshim (R.M.) 3:82b (to Est 3:3); *Tiqqunei ha-Zohar*, 21 to Est 1:19. In actual fact, most of the Esther quotations used by the *Zohar* are taken totally out of context. *Tiqqunei ha-Zohar* 21 seems to address itself to the text more directly and interprets several verses in context (5:1, 3:9, 2:14).

127. See above, n. 119.

128. For Esther as the *shekhinah*, see Moses De Leon, *Sheqel ha-qodesh*, ed. A. W. Greenup (London, 1911; repr. Jerusalem, 1969), 91.

129. My thanks to Elliott Wolfson for this insight. Concerning the quality of justice and its relation to the *siṭra' 'aḥra'* or force of evil in the world, see *Mishnat ha-Zohar*, 1:224–25 (*Wisdom*, 1:376–79). The sins of Israel increase the power of the *siṭra' 'aḥra'*, as was the case in the Book of Esther, where the sins of the Israelites caused them to be put in grave danger.

130. *EKE*, 38.

131. B.T. Megillah 13a.

132. B.T. Sanhedrin 74b.

133. B.T. Sanhedrin 74b.

134. That is, the *sefirah malkhut* or *shekhinah*.

135. *EKE*, 41–42. *Keneset Yisra'el, 'olam, shekhinah,* and *qarqa' 'olam* all represent the *sefirah malkhut* in the kabbalistic system. See Moses Cordovero, *Pardes rimmonim* (Munkacz, 1905–06; repr. Jerusalem, 1961–62) Sha'ar 'erkhei ha-kinnuyim 2:23a, 33b, 39a, 41a.

136. There are other kabbalistic sources that identify Esther with the *shekhinah* using the passage in B.T. Megillah: "Esther was greenish." See, for example, *Ma'arekhet ha-'elohut* (Mantua, 1557–58; repr. Jerusalem, 1963), 74b, and Azriel of Gerona, *Peirush ha-'aggadot*, ed. Isaiah Tishby (Jerusalem, 1944–45; repr. Jerusalem, 1982), 52.

137. Perhaps from *marei dakhya'* ("pure myrrh") which was one interpretation given to his name.

138. Cf. Ps 22:21.

139. See examples in E. Ben Yehudah, *Millon ha-lashon ha-'ivrit* (Jerusalem, 1910–59), s.v. "*MRQ*."

140. Cf. *Wisdom of the Zohar*, 2:848 (Zohar 3:127a). Of course, allegories of the soul were very common in Christian exegetical literature. Cf. Dante Alighieri's letter to Can Grande della Scala, *Epistolae: Letters of Dante*, trans. Paget Toynbee (Oxford, 1920), 199. Dante offers a fourfold interpretation of the Exodus from Egypt, the anagogical being "the passing of the sanctified soul from the bondage of corruption of this world to the liberty of everlasting glory." The moral sense refers to the conversion of the soul from a state of sin to one of grace. The parallel to Saba is quite clear.

141. In actual fact, Saba is rather less daring than he could be and chooses his words carefully so as not to reveal too much of the secret doctrines.

142. B.T. Megillah 15a.

143. The phrase first appears in the Talmud, B.T. Berakhot 34b and Sanhedrin 99a, where it refers metaphorically to the reward of the righteous in the world to come—a return to the pristine state of Eden, free of cares and woe. A similar phrase appears in Targum Pseudo-Jonathan (seventh-eighth century), to Gn 27:25, where the author claims that Jacob gave Isaac to drink from "the wine stored in its grapes from the days of the creation of the world" (*min ḥamra' de-'iṣṭena' be-'invoyei min yomei sheirui 'alma'*). The phrase here

would seem to mean wine that was made at the time of creation and then stored away so that it is in the most pristine state possible, without any contamination. In kabbalistic terms, the significance of this wine is in that it is in one of the highest *sefirot* (*binah*) and is not contaminated with *din* which is harsh and severe. See Cordovero, *Pardes rimmonim*, 2:20b–21a.

144. Cf. *Zohar* 3:12b: "Sometimes wine is good and sometimes it is for punishment, i.e., for justice (*dina'*)."

145. Concerning Saba's views on redemption, see below, pp. 91–94.

146. It has recently appeared in a critical edition, *Sefer Yosippon*, ed. David Flusser, 2 vols. (Jerusalem, 1978–80) (henceforth referred to as *SY*). Volume 1 contains the text, and volume 2, the introduction and textual variants.

147. Ibid., 2:62–69.

148. Ibid., 1:48–54.

149. See Tobias ben Eliezer, "Midrash Leqaḥ ṭov ʿal 'Ester" in Buber, *Sifrei de-'aggadeta'*, 52r [= 103]; Gersonides, 42r, 46v (cf. *SY*, 53); Kaspi, in Last, *Millu'im*, 21 (cf. *SY*, 49); Ḥayyun, fol. 79v (cf. *SY*, 53). Zechariah, 10r, refers to book 2 of Ben-Guryon with reference to Vashti's refusal to come before Ahasuerus, but this source does not appear in Flusser's edition. Cf. also Saba, *EKE*, 80.

150. *SY*, 49, lines 11–14.

151. *SY*, 50, lines 37–42.

152. *SY*, 48–49, lines 1–10.

153. *SY*, 53, lines 93–107.

Chapter 2. Non-Jewish Sources for Exegesis

1. A few years earlier, in 1240, Hermann the German translated Averroës' Middle Commentary on Aristotle's *Ethics* into Latin. See L. V. Berman, "Ibn Rushd's Middle Commentary on the *Nicomachean Ethics* in Medieval Hebrew Literature," in *Multiple Averroès: Actes du Colloque International organisé à l'occasion du 850ᵉ anniversaire de la naissance d'Averroès, Paris, 20-23 septembre 1976* (Paris, 1978), 293.

2. It was completed on February 9, 1321, at Beaucaire in Provence and first revised in September of that year. The second revision was completed on July 16, 1322. See L. V. Berman, "Greek into Hebrew: Samuel ben Judah of

Marseilles, Fourteenth Century Philosopher and Translator," in *Jewish Medieval and Renaissance Studies*, ed. Alexander Altmann (Cambridge, Mass.), 295. A third much expanded revision was produced by a member of the philosophical school centered in Marseilles in the fourteenth century, called the *me'ayyenim*. This version seems to have been the "official" version of the school of *me'ayyenim*. See L.V. Berman, "Ketav-yad ha-mekhunneh 'Shoshan limmudim' ve-yaḥaso li-'qehal ha-me'ayyenim' ha-provansali," *Kiryat Sefer* 53 (1978): 368, 372. According to Berman, the translator was either Judah ben Isaac Kohen, a student of Samuel ben Judah, or another member of the school.

3. Berman, "Greek into Hebrew," 297; id., "Ibn Rushd's Middle Commentary," 297–98.

4. See above, n. 1.

5. Alguadez was critical of Samuel b. Judah's translation because it followed the Arabic very closely and was very difficult to understand. See Berman, "Greek into Hebrew," 296.

6. Much of the story of the influence of this commentary on late medieval Jewish literature and intellectual life has yet to be told. See Berman, "Ibn Rushd's Middle Commentary," 300–301.

7. Called *Terumat kesef*. It is extant only in manuscript: MSS. BP (Parma) 2630, (De Rossi 424), BA (Vatican) ebr. 296, BL (Oxford) Poc. 17 (Uri 397) (Neubauer 1427), fols. 121–210, and ÖN (Vienna) 161, fols. 1–46r. The latter two are the best copies.

8. See *Terumat kesef*, ma'amar 3, MS. BL (Oxford) Poc. 17 (Uri 397), fol. 132v.

9. Cf. 1 Chr 29:30, "the circumstances that came upon him" העתים אשר עברו עליו.

10. השמיעה אל הזקנים בעלי הנסיונות באורך ימיהם אינו למטה מאד מן השמיעה אל המופתים (*Millu'im, 22*).

11. See Artistotle, *Nicomachean Ethics*, 1123a34–1125a18, and Kaspi's *Terumat kesef*, MS. BL (Oxford) Poc. 17 (Uri 397), fol. 152.

12. Indeed, when one looks at Aristotle's description of the magnanimous man, one can without much difficulty find several attributes that suit the figure of Mordecai in the Book of Esther. For instance, according to Aristotle, "The magnanimous man does not take petty risks, nor does he court danger, because there are few things that he values highly; but he takes great risks and when he faces danger he is unsparing of his life, because to him there are some circumstances in which it is not worth living" (Aristotle, *Nicomachean Ethics*,

1124b7–9). It does not require much stretching of the imagination to see how this description could be applied to Mordecai.

13. See *Terumat kesef*, MS. ÖN (Vienna) 161, fol. 19v, *ha-dibbur be-shivvui* = *Nicomacheam Ethics*, 1137a32–1138a3. It would seem that the term *shivvui* corresponds to "equity" in English. From this it would seem that Kaspi assumed his readers would be familiar with the *Ethics*. It should be mentioned that Kaspi wrote his *Epitome* for his elder son as a moral guide for him on which he was to "meditate day and night." See Berman, "Ibn Rushd's Middle Commentary," 297.

14. It will be recalled that Kaspi applied the same term to Mordecai. See above.

15. MS. BP (Parma) 2211 (De Rossi 177), fol. 41r–v. Cf. Averroës, *Ha-Nusaḥim ha-'Ivriyyim shel ha-ma'amar ha-revi'i shel ha-bei'ur ha-'emṣa'i shel 'Ibn Rushd le-"Sefer ha-middot 'al-shem Niqomakhos" le-'Aristo*, ed. L. V. Berman (Jerusalem, 1981), p. 53, lines 2–4, and p. 57, lines 22–24. Ḥadidah's text corresponds most closely to the third revised version of Samuel's translation.

16. MS. BP (Parma) 2211, fol. 43r–v; cf. *Nicomachean Ethics* 1:4, 1095a14–1096a10. The late Professor L. V. Berman who was engaged in editing Samuel's translation of Averroës' Middle Commentary on the *Ethics* informed me that this quotation as well corresponds most closely to the third revised version of the translation.

17. Most recent edition: *Sefer ha-middot* (Lemberg, 1867).

18. See A. R. D. Pagden, "The Diffusion of Aristotle's Moral Philosophy in Spain, ca. 1400–ca. 1600," *Traditio* 31 (1975): 291–99.

19. See Wilensky, *R. Yiṣḥaq 'Aramah*, 183–221. I shall deal in another context with the influence of the *Ethics* on his views on Vashti's trial.

20. *Arama*, fols. 163v–164r.

21. See Aristotle, *Ethics* 8:10, 1160a31–1161a7.

22. See *Encyclopaedia Judaica* (Jerusalem), s.v. "Translations and Translators."

23. See Amable Jourdain, *Recherches critiques sur l'âge et l'origine des traductions latines d'Aristote*, revised and expanded edition by Charles Jourdain (Paris, 1843), 70.

24. See, e.g., Frank Talmage, *David Kimhi: The Man and the Commentaries* (Cambridge, Mass., 1975), 70–72; id., "David Kimhi and the Rationalist Tradition," *Hebrew Union College Annual* 39 (1968): 177–218. Abraham Ḥadidah

is probably the first to apply this method to Aristotle's *Ethics*, although we cannot be certain of this since we cannot date him with any certainty. The fact that he used the third revised version of Samuel's commentary is not very helpful for dating him, since it was completed about the middle of the fourteenth century (See Berman, "'Shoshan limmudim,'" 372) and, as Professor Berman informed me in a personal communication, was being quoted and copied in the late fifteenth century, at least in Italy.

25. In his *Malmad ha-talmidim*, Sefarim ha-yoṣe'im la-'or 'al yedei Ḥevrat Meqisei nirdamim (Lyck, 1866; repr. Jerusalem, 1967–68).

26. See A. S. Halkin, "Why was Levi ben Abraham Hounded?" *Proceedings of the American Academy for Jewish Research* 34 (1966): 65–67.

27. Toward the end of his introduction, Zechariah launches into a lengthy tirade against the philosophers, "those who are accustomed to interpret figuratively the stories of the Torah (*la'asot ṣurah* [i.e., "allegorize"] *be-sippurei ha-Torah*)." Zechariah specifically mentions Rabbi David Bilia, the author of the book *Me'or 'einayim*, who he claims "interpreted the story of Rebecca figuratively," and who it seems is to be identified with R. David ben Yom Tov Ibn Bilia, the fourteenth-century Portuguese rabbi and scholar. The fact that he is mentioned in *Meqor ḥayyim* of Samuel Zarza (Mantua, 1559), who also wrote a philosophical commentary on the Torah, gives weight to this assumption. See *Encyclopaedia Judaica* (Jerusalem), s.v. "Ibn Bilia." This is confirmed by N. Allony, "David 'Ibn Bilyah vi-yeṣirotav," in *'Areshet* (Jerusalem, 1943), 377, n. 2 who mentions our commentary. See also Israel Zinberg, *A History of Jewish Literature*, trans. and ed. Bernard Martin, 12 vols. (Cleveland, 1972–78), 3:157–58. On the allegorical interpretation of Scripture among the Jews, see ibid., 3:59–62 and Frank Talmage, "Apples of Gold: The Inner Meaning of Sacred Texts in Medieval Judaism," In *Jewish Spirituality: From the Bible Through the Middle Ages*, ed. Arthur Green, World Spirituality, 13 (New York, 1986), 313–355. Zechariah (p. 6a) says that David Bilia gives the following interpretation of the name Ahasuerus in his book: "He was called Ahasuerus because he was a brother (*'aḥ*) to Israel in their troubles and poison (*rosh*) to Haman since he hanged him and his sons." Now this interpretation is in the same style of the interpretations given by the sages in the Talmud and Midrash (see, e.g., B.T. Megillah 11a; *Midrash Esther Rabbah* 1:1–3), and Zechariah says as much (although it should be noted that the author of this *derash* is much more favorably disposed to Ahasuerus than were the sages). But apparently for Zechariah, the fact that it was given by David Bilia is enough to discredit it, and he declares his intention to clarify that this story tells of the "miracles that the Holy One blessed be He performed for our forefathers at that time" (ibid.). Zechariah's reference to David Bilia is the only indication we have (except for the case of Judah Gibbor) that there may have been attempts to interpret the

book of Esther allegorically. The comment that he quotes is not allegorical, and we have no evidence that there were other comments or a separate commentary by Bilia to Esther. But, if Zechariah's agitation over this point is any indication, then the possibility of the existence of such commentaries cannot be entirely ruled out. Allony, "David 'Ibn Bilyah," 380, attributes an Esther commentary to Ibn Bilia, doubtlessly on the basis of the reference in Zechariah. But I believe that this attribution is based on a misreading of the text. The line in question reads as follows:

וכבר התחיל הכופר הנז׳ לומר בספרו הנקרא אחשורוש לפי שהיה אח לישראל בצרותיהם ורוש להמן שתלה אותו ואת בניו.

The key word is הנקרא. The phrase בספרו הנקרא אחשורוש (in his book called Ahasuerus) makes sense out of context but not in context. If one emends this word to read שנקרא, then the text makes sense and translates as follows: "This aforementioned heretic already began to say in his book [*Me'or 'einayim*?] *that he was called Ahasuerus* because he was a brother to Israel in their troubles and poison to Haman since he hanged him and his sons" [emphasis added].

28. Zechariah's caution does not prevent him from ascribing to Haman knowledge of Aristotle (p. 14b), a curious but understandable anachronism.

29. Gibbor's exposition is found at the end of his *Sefer Mo'adim*, MS. HUC-JIR 839 (formerly Schwager 1), fols. 105v–106r. My thanks to Philip Miller, Librarian of the Hebrew Union College–Jewish Institute of Religion, New York, for bringing this passage to my attention. Cf. his doctoral dissertation entitled "At the Twilight of Byzantine Karaism: The Anachronism of Judah Gibbor" (New York University, 1985).

30. See Arthur Hyman, "The Liberal Arts and Jewish Philosophy," in *Arts libéraux et philosophie au moyen âge: actes du quatrième Congrès International de Philosophie Médiévale, Université de Montréal, Montréal, Canada, 27 août–2 septembre, 1967* (Montreal, 1969), 110; also cf. Wolfson, "Classification of Sciences," 263–315.

31. Cf. Maimonides, *Guide of the Perplexed*, introd. (Shlomo Pines trans.), 3; and Joseph ibn Kaspi's *Sefer ha-musar*, in *Hebrew Ethical Wills* ed. Israel Abrahams, 2 vols. (Philadephia, 1926; repr. Philadelphia, 1976), 1:144.

32. We have noted the stress laid by Kaspi and Shemariah b. Elijah on the need for the mastery of these two disciplines for the proper understanding of Scripture. See above, pp. 13, 239.

33. Shalom Rosenberg's dissertation on Jewish logical treatises in the fourteenth century, "Logiqah ve-'onṭologyah ba-filosofyah ha-yehudit ba-me'ah ha-14," provides ample evidence of activity in this area. For a convenient survey of grammatical literature, see Hirschfeld, *Literary History*.

34. See the useful survey by Arthur M. Lesley, "A Survey of Medieval Hebrew Rhetoric," *Approaches to Judaism in Medieval Times* 1 (1984): 107–33, esp. 119–23, which deals with the twelfth to fifteenth centuries in Spain, Provence, and Italy, and the bibliography published by Isaac Rabinowitz, "Pre-Modern Jewish Study of Rhetoric: An Introductory Bibliography," *Rhetorica* 3 (1985):137–44.

35. This work has never been published and exists in two manuscripts: MS. BN (Paris) héb. 325, fols. 89–144 and MS. BL (Oxford) Mich. 350 (Neubauer 2052), fols. 97–203. A section of it has been translated by Marc Saperstein, in *Jewish Preaching 1200–1800: An Anthology* (New Haven, Conn., 1989), 387–92.

36. This work, first published in Mantua before 1480 has recently been reprinted with an introduction by Roberto Bonfil (Jerusalem, 1981). It has now also been critically edited and translated by Isaac Rabinowitz under the title *The Book of the Honeycomb's Flow* (Ithaca, N.Y., 1983); cf. also Abraham Melammed, "Reṭoriqah u-filosofyah be-*Sefer Nofet ṣufim* la-Rav Yehudah Meser Le'on," *Italia* 1 (1978): 7–39 (Hebrew section); Alexander Altmann, "*Ars Rhetorica* as Reflected in Some Jewish Figures of the Italian Renaissance," in his *Essays in Jewish Intellectual History* (Hanover, N.H., 1981), 97–118.

37. See edition and Hebrew translation by A. S. Halkin entitled *Sefer ha-ʿiyyunim ve-ha-diyyunim* (Jerusalem, 1975), 12–21.

38. Averroës, *Bei'ur 'Ibn Rushd le-"Sefer ha-halaṣah" le-'Arisṭo*, trans. Todros Todrosi, ed. Jacob Goldenthal (Leipzig, 1842).

39. My thanks to Arthur Lesley for this insight.

40. By this time the influence of Christian works cannot be ruled out.

41. Gersonides seems to have been the first to pay attention to this matter. See below, p. 170.

42. Arama, 158r. The printed version lists only four.

43. Arama's Esther commentary is not the only work in which he deals with the conditions that need to be met by a petitioner making a request. He elaborates on this subject in his major work, *'Aqeidat Yiṣḥaq*, ed. H. Y. Pollak, 5 vols. (Pressburg, Czechoslovakia, 1849), 2:98b-99a (Sermon No. 44), where he discusses it in the context of the theophany at Sinai. According to Arama, God took pains to fulfill all the requirements for a proper petition when he set the scene for the giving of the Torah to Israel. Here Arama lists six conditions: (1) timing, (2) place, (3) means (*'emṣa'i*), (4) the proper phrasing of the request, (5) the ability of the one being petitioned to grant the request (it should not be

too difficult for him), and (6) its suitability to the person being asked (a request could be in theory quite easy for someone to grant, but there might be some other factor involved which made it difficult or impossible for him to do so). Arama illustrates these six conditions with biblical examples and then demonstrates how God saw to it that all were met when he gave the Torah to Israel.

44. I:xxvi.38–xxvii.41.

45. Cicero's *De inventione*, along with the anonymous *Rhetorica ad Herennium* were two of the most popular classical works of rhetoric in the Middle Ages. See Harry Caplan, "A Medieval Commentary on the *Rhetorica ad Herennium*," in his *Of Eloquence: Studies in Ancient and Medieval Rhetoric*, ed. Anne King and Helen North (Ithaca, N.Y., 1970), 248.

46. Boethius in his *De differentiis topicis* IV, *Patrologia Latina* 64, 1212C-D (English trans. by Eleonore Stump [Ithaca, N.Y., 1978], 89), is the first Latin author to use the term "circumstances" in describing Cicero's attributes of actions and also one of the earliest to list them in terms of questions. Cf. Michael C. Leff, "'Boethius' *De differentiis topicis*, Book IV," in *Medieval Eloquence: Studies in the Theory and Practice of Medieval Rhetoric*, ed. James J. Murphy (Berkeley and Los Angeles, 1978), 11–12. On the history of classification of circumstances, see Odon Lottin, *Psychologie et morale aux XIIe et XIIIe siècles*, 6 vols. (Gembloux, Belgium, 1942–60), 4:505–8. My thanks to Professor Leonard Boyle for this last reference.

47. Here, the influence of the science of dialectic on rhetoric is evident. The main sources for this influence were Boethius, Marius Victorinus, and Aristotle (especially his *Organon*), who were studied avidly in the cathedral schools in the twelfth century. See Caplan, "A Medieval Commentary," 256–57.

48. See A. de Poorter, "Un manuel de prédication médiévale," *Revue néo-scolastique de philosophie* 25 (1923): 196–97.

49. *Nicomachean Ethics* 3:1, 1109b30 ff.

50. Now modern scholars are also taking note. See, e.g., David J. A. Clines, *The Esther Scroll: The Story of the Story*, Journal for the Study of the Old Testament supplement series, 30 (Sheffield, 1984), 101–3.

51. Zechariah at this point quotes Aristotle's *Politics* with regard to four things that someone making a request of another should have in mind. Curiously, these four things bear a strong resemblance to the words of the Book of Esther making Zechariah's quotation of his source (which I could not trace) suspect.

52. See, e.g., Charles B. Faulhaber, "The *Summa Dictaminis* of Guido Faba," in *Medieval Eloquence*, 88, 92; Anonymous of Bologna, "The Principles of Letter Writing (*Rationes dictandi*)," trans. James J. Murphy, in *Three Medieval Rhetorical Arts*, ed. James J. Murphy (Berkeley and Los Angeles, 1971), 16–18.

53. See, e.g., Alan of Lille, *The Art of Preaching*, trans. Gillian R. Evans, Cistercian Studies Series, 23 (Kalamazoo, Mich., 1981), 20-21.

54. Cf. Robert Chazan, ed. *Church, State and Jew in the Middle Ages* (New York, 1980), 14, who remarks on the importance for Jewish survival in the Middle Ages of the marshaling of proper arguments for the proper audience. The study of medieval Hebrew rhetoric is still in its infancy. Over sixty years ago, Harry Caplan in "The Four Senses of Scriptural Interpretation and the Medieval Theory of Preaching," *Speculum* 4 (1929): 290 (repr. in his *Of Eloquence*, 103), commented on the paucity of information available on medieval Jewish rhetoric, both sacred and secular. Work has begun in this field in the past decade (see nn. 34, 36 above), but much remains to be done.

55. Some prominent homilists were Jacob Anatoli, Joshua and Joel Ibn Shuaib, Isaac Aboab, Isaac Arama, and Abraham Saba.

56. See, e.g., Baer, *Jews in Christian Spain*, 2:166.

57. See Charles Faulhaber, *Latin Rhetorical Theory in Thirteenth and Fourteenth Century Castile*, University of California Publications in Modern Philology, vol. 103 (Berkeley and Los Angeles, 1971), 9. See also, Ottavio Di Camillo, *El humanismo castellano del siglo XV* (Valencia, 1976), 41–66. I would reiterate Harry Caplan's suggestion that a comparative study of Jewish and Christian preaching in that period would prove fruitful, (See Caplan, "Four Senses," 290) and would suggest that the works of Isaac Arama and his contemporaries would be suitable material for such a study. An important beginning has been made by Marc Saperstein in his anthology, *Jewish Preaching 1200–1800*. Israel Bettan's *Studies in Jewish Preaching* (Cincinnati, 1939), which devotes a chapter to Arama (pp. 130–191) does not address the question of external influences.

58. *"Kol 'otan ha-devarim 'einan divrei ḥokhmah kelal ve-ṭipshut hem."* See Maimonides' letter on astrology in Alexander Marx, "The Correspondence Between the Rabbis of Southern France and Maimonides about Astrology," *Hebrew Union College Annual* 3 (1926): 351.

59. On astrology among the Jews in the Middle Ages, see Senior Sachs, in *Ha-Yonah* 1 (1851): 59–93; David Rosin, "Die Religionsphilosophie der Abraham Ibn Ezra," *Monatsschrift für die Geschichte und Wissenschaft des Judentums* 42 (1898): 247–52, 305–15, 345–82, 394–402; Marx, "Correspondence," 311–25; *Encyclopedia Judaica* (Jerusalem), s.v. "Astrology." Don Isaac Abravanel was also a firm believer in astrology. See Netanyahu, *Abravanel*, 118–25.

60. E.g., Ibn Ezra, Gersonides, Isaac b. Joseph ha-Kohen, "Ramah."

61. To further demonstrate the truth and authenticity of astrological beliefs, R. Isaac devotes a lengthy excursus to the explanation of the first chapter of Jonah. According to him, the sailors on the ship sailing for Tarshish were well-versed in astrology and astronomy and could tell from their calculations that the storm that befell them was of an extraordinary nature. For this reason they sought extraordinary means to save themselves from death.

62. See Yitzhak Baer, "*Sefer Minḥat qena'ot* shel 'Avner mi-Burgos, ve-hashpa'ato 'al Ḥasdai Qresqas," *Tarbiẓ* 11 (1939–40): 188–206.

63. Isaac Pulgar, *'Ezer ha-dat* (London, 1906), 49–84, XVII–XXIV. Pulgar presents his case in the form of a disputation between a scholar (*ḥaver*) and an astrologer (*hover*).

64. Arama, *Ḥazut qashah*, ed. H. Y. Pollak (Pressburg, Czechoslovakia, 1849), 33 (Issued with Arama's *'Aqeidat Yiṣḥaq*, vol. 5); quoted in Baer, *Jews in Christian Spain*, 2:256.

65. On the problem of Averroism in later medieval Spanish Jewry, see Baer, *Jews in Christian Spain*, 2:253–59; Daniel J. Lasker, "Averroistic Trends in Jewish-Christian Polemics in the Late Middle Ages," *Speculum* 55 (1980): 294–304; and Solomon Alami, *'Iggeret musar*, 46: "for there are now many people who deny providence in their stupidity, and there are only a handful who believe in reward and punishment and when they speak to each other they fail to mention the next world and do not long for it."

66. *Kitvei Rabbeinu Baḥya*, 338–41.

67. On the colors of the planets in ancient and medieval astrology, see Auguste Bouché-Leclercq, *L'Astrologie grecque* (Paris, 1899), 313–18, and al-Biruni, *Kitāb al-tafhīm*, trans. R. Ramsay Wright (London, 1934), 240. All sources agree on the blackness of Saturn and the redness of Mars. Venus, according to al-Biruni is pure white according to some and greenish according to others. Some mention blue as a color associated with Jupiter. We must assume that Baḥya had another astrological source for this identification.

68. *Kitvei Rabbeinu Baḥya*, 338. Ahasuerus is associated with black on the basis of the midrash that says that in his days the faces of Israel were blackened like the rims of a pot (*hushḥeru peneihem shel Yisra'el ke-shulei qederah*; B.T. Megillah 11a); the name אחשורוש in Hebrew contains the four letters of the Hebrew word for black שחור, albeit in a different order. Haman is associated with red, on the basis of his descent from Esau = Edom = red; Mordecai with blue since he went out from before the king wearing royal *blue* and white robes (*levush malkhut tekhelet va-ḥur*); and Esther with green on the basis of the midrashic statement that "Esther was greenish" (B.T. Megillah 13a). There is

probably some significance to the association of her Hebrew name *Hadassah* ("myrtle") as well.

69. *Kitvei Rabbeinu Baḥya*, 340.

70. B.T. Megillah 15a, to Est 5:1.

71. *Kitvei Rabbeinu Baḥya*, 339.

72. Commentary A, to 3:5.

73. Zechariah, p. 16a. Cf. Saba, *EKE*, 79: "I also think that Esther saw that Haman's constellation (*ma'arekhet*) was steadily growing and she thought that perhaps it still was destined to rise according to its fate (*mazzal*). Therefore, Esther wished to invite him on the third day and to raise him up to an even higher position, equal to that of the king . . . so that he could not possibly in a thousand years rise up any higher except on the 'gallows that he prepared for him' (Est 6:4). Therefore, she wanted him to be in this position for a day or two and then she would bring him down."

74. See B.T. Shabbat 151b and *Exodus Rabbah* 31:14. The rabbinic opinion is based on Dt 15:10, "Because for (*bi-gelal*) this thing," and Prv 20:26, "A wise king winnows out the wicked and turns the wheel (*'ofan*) upon them."

75. See Pierre Courcelle, *"La Consolation de Philosophie" dans la tradition littéraire: Antécedents et postérité de Boèce* (Paris, 1967), 113–52; Alfred Doren, "Fortuna im Mittelalter und in der Renaissance," *Vorträge der Bibliothek Warburg* 2 (1922–23): 71–144.

Chapter 3. Literary Concerns

1. Kara, 3:93–94. Cf. *Midrash Rabbah* to Song 6:12 (English trans., p. 273) where 4:1 and 8:15 are juxtaposed.

2. *'Oṣar ṭov* (1878): 31.

3. See his comment to Est 1:20, 3:89.

4. Kara, 3:93 (to 8:10). According to Kara, those sent by Mordecai were sent on swift horses in order to catch up to the first group of couriers.

5. See Kara, 3:95 (to 10:1).

6. See Paton, *Esther*, 186–87.

7. The same or similar idea is found in "A"'s commentary and in that of Immanuel of Rome.

8. Cf. Tobias ben Eliezer who suggests that the verse refers to clothing or money to accompany her.

9. See comment to 9:23, ibid. אחינו בית ישראל אשר בכל מדינות המלך אחשורוש ידע לכם שכבר החלו לעשות יום טוב במקומנו. ("Our brethren, the House of Israel, let it be known to you that a holiday has already begun to be observed in our locale.")

10. Of course, additions such as these to the Esther story were made already by Hellenistic Jews and incorporated in the targumim and later midrashic compilations. See Carey Moore, ed., *Daniel, Esther and Jeremiah: The Additions*, Anchor Bible, 44 (Garden City, N.Y., 1977), 153–252. The major additions included Mordecai's dream and Esther's prayer before appearing before Ahasuerus.

11. Arama, fol. 150v.

12. See Chapter 8 below, for other attempts to protect Ahasuerus's reputation.

13. I have not seen any evidence that other commentators who preceded Arama did not take the book seriously. Perhaps, he means that they did not seriously confront the problems in the text that seem so obvious to him and which he tries to deal with in his commentary.

14. Arama, fols. 160v–61r.

Chapter 4. Theological Issues

1. The most recent attempt to grapple with the issue is Michael V. Fox, "The Religion of the Book of Esther," *Judaism* 39 (1990): 135–47. See also Eliezer Segal, "Human Anger and Divine Intervention in Esther," *Prooftexts* 9 (1989): 247–56, which deals with certain midrashic interpretations of the story focusing on the theme of anger.

2. Cf. Martin Luther's complaint that the book of Esther "judaizes too much" in his *Tischreden*, 6 vols., D. Martin Luthers Werke, (Weimar, 1912–21), 1:208 (no. 475).

3. For a survey of Christian exegesis of the book, see Gillis Gerleman, *Esther*, Biblischer Kommentar Altes Testament, 21 (Neukirchen-Vluyn, 1970–73), 1–7; Paton, *Esther*, 101–18. The figures of Vashti and Esther, for example, were taken to symbolize the Synagogue and the Church; see Marie-Louise Thérel, "L'origine du thème de la synagogue répudiée," *Scriptorium* 25 (1971): 285–90. My thanks to Richard Menkis for bringing this article to my attention.

4. See, for example, Bernhard Anderson, "The Place of the Book of Esther in the Christian Bible," *Journal of Religion* 30 (1950): 32–43; and on the

Jewish side, Shalom Ben-Chorin, *Kritik des Estherbuches: Eine theologische Streitschrift* (Jerusalem, 1938); Albert S. Goldstein, "Megillath Esther: The Original Purim Shpiel Stage Script," *Journal of Reform Judaism* 26:2 (Spring, 1979): 89–104.

5. Ratzaby, "Mi-peirush," 759–60. Cf. B.T. Megillah 7a, which seems to be the source for this comment. This section of the commentary is fragmentary, so it is difficult to follow Saadiah's line of argumentation.

6. Ibid., 763.

7. See David Rosin, "Die Religionsphilosophie Abraham Ibn Ezra's," *Monatsschrift für die Geschichte und Wissenschaft des Judentums* 43 (1899): 231.

8. Ibid., 86.

9. Ibid., 239.

10. See 4:14, p. 26; see also above.

11. It should be pointed out that in the extant fragments of Saadiah's commentary published by Ratzaby, Mordecai is not mentioned as author of the scroll.

12. Which begins *Bereshit bara' 'Ashima*. Ashima here actually stands for the Tetragrammaton, which was pronounced *Shemah* by the Samaritans. This confusion, based on the reference to a god Ashima in the Bible (2 Kgs 17:30) led to the mistaken belief in the Middle Ages that the Samaritans worshipped the god Ashima. See S. Lowy, *The Principles of Samaritan Biblical Exegesis*, Studia Post-Biblica, vol. 28 (Leiden, 1977), 139, 244; J. A. Montgomery, *The Samaritans, the Earliest Jewish Sect: Their History, Theology and Literature* (Philadelphia, 1907), 213 (n. 28), 321.

13. Ibn Ezra rejects on linguistic grounds the argument that the term *mi-maqom 'aḥer* (4:14) refers to God, since the word *maqom* or place never refers to God in biblical texts. This meaning is found only in rabbinic literature, and hence, its usage in Esther would be anachronistic. Saadiah also rejects this verse as referring directly to God. He mentions the rabbinic source which refers to God as *maqom* but argues that this is not a name referring to God's essence. (See Ratzaby, "Mi-peirush," 764). It should be noted that in version B Ibn Ezra deals with the problem of the absence of God's name from the book in the body of his commentary, at 4:14 (*VA*, 26). This seems to be another reflection of the different approaches he takes in the two commentaries. In B he does not raise any theological or philosophical issues, as he does in A, and his language is less technical, devoid of difficult philological as well as grammatical terminology. See Walfish, "Two Commentaries," 323–43 for a detailed comparison of the two commentaries.

14. Immanuel also quotes an argument that is essentially identical with Ibn Ezra's.

15. See his commentary, p. 13b. The phrase whose initial letters spell out the divine name is *Yavo' Ha-melekh Ve-Haman Ha-yom* (5:4). This is found in *Sha'arei binah*, the commentary of Eleazar ben Judah of Worms, p. 39. The phrase whose final letters spell out the divine name is *kI khaletaH 'elaV ha-ra'aH* (7:7). This is found in one of the Ashkenazic commentaries, MS. BL (Oxford) Opp. 27 (Ol. 256) (Neubauer 268), fol. 263v. See Lehmann's note, in *Sha'arei binah* to 7:7, p. 54. Lehmann ascribes both commentaries to the school of Eleazar of Worms, i.e., the German Pietists of the twelfth and thirteenth centuries.

16. Cf. B.T. Ḥullin 139b. Cf. also the *Zohar* (Ra'aya' mehemna'), 3:276a, which speaks of the *Shekhinah* hiding Esther from Ahasuerus. But the *Zohar* uses Ps 32:7 *'attah seter li*, "you are a hiding place for me." Cf. also Abraham Saba (*EKE*, 83) who attributes the following to the sages: "she was called Esther because in her days the Lord hid his face from Israel." His midrashic source may no longer be extant.

17. See the introduction to his commentary, fol. 142v. His view on miracles is discussed more fully below.

18. See *'Aggadat 'Ester*, 38; *Panim 'aḥerim A*, 47; *Yalquṭ Shim'oni* 1056, p. 1059, col. 1; *'Abba' Guryon*, 35.

19. *'Abba' Guryon*, 32–34; *Esther Rabbah* 7:13.

20. B.T. Megillah 13b.

21. *'Abba' Guryon*, 38.

22. B.T. Megillah 15b–16a.

23. Ibid., 15b. *Esther Rabbah* 10:1.

24. For other examples of Rashi's attempts to highlight God's intervention in the Esther story, see Kamin-Rozik, "Sibbatiyyut kefulah," 553–58.

25. E.g., Zechariah, 15a:

ראו ועיינו ההשגחה העצומה של האל יתברך שנתחברו כמה מקרים לימשך מהם
תכלית אחר והוא הצלת האומה הזאת.

26. Gersonides, Lesson 9, p. 44b.

27. Ibid., Lesson 10. Cf. B.T. Megillah 11b.

28. Ibid., Lesson 16, p. 45a.

29. Ibid., Lesson 22.

30. Ibid., Lesson 25, p. 45b.

31. Ibid., Lesson 26.

32. Ibid., Lesson 38, p. 47b.

33. Ibid., Lesson 43, pp. 47b–48a. Cf. *Esther Rabbah* 10:9.

34. Ibid.

35. Ibid.

36. Ibid., Lesson 50, pp. 48b–49a.

37. Ibid., Lesson 28, p. 45b.

38. Ibid., Lesson 30, p. 46a.

39. Ibid., Lesson 34, p. 46b.

40. Referring to his argument concerning the two sets of letters discussed below, pp. 129–32.

41. B.T. Pesaḥim 64b. Cf. the words of Rabbi Jannai: "A man should never stand in a place of danger assuming that a miracle would be wrought for him, for perhaps it will not be wrought" (B.T. Shabbat 32a).

42. Kara, 3:95 (to 10:3).

43. See, for example, the following story in the Talmud: "R. Simeon the Sidonite expounded: When the wicked Nebuchadnezzar cast Hananiah, Mishael, and Azariah into the fiery furnace, Yurqamu, the Prince of Hail, stood before the Holy One, blessed be He, and said to Him: 'Sovereign of the universe, let me go down and cool the furnace and deliver those righteous men from the fiery furnace.' Said Gabriel to him: 'The might of the Holy One, blessed be He, will not be [revealed] thereby, for you are the Prince of Hail and all know that water extinguishes fire. But let me, the Prince of Fire, go down and cool it from within and heat it from without and thus perform a miracle within a miracle.' The Holy One, blessed be He, then said: 'Go down.' At that moment, Gabriel began [to praise God] and said: 'and the truth of the Lord endureth forever' (B.T. Pesaḥim 118a–b)." Cf. E. E. Urbach, *The Sages: Their Concepts and Beliefs*, trans. Israel Abrahams, 2 vols. (Jerusalem, 1975), 1:104.

44. See *Genesis Rabbah* 5:9. Mishnah 'Avot 5:6; Urbach, *Sages*, 1:113–15.

45. See Alexander Guttmann, "The Significance of Miracles for Talmudic Judaism," *Hebrew Union College Annual* 20 (1947): 363–97.

46. The connotation for *le-ṭayyel* of amusing oneself and for *divrei ṭiyyulim* of amusement, has not been recorded by Hebrew lexicographers. In rabbinic literature, *le-ṭayyel* has the connotation of walking for pleasure or amusement. See Nathan b. Jehiel, *'Arukh ha-shalem*, s.v. "*ṭiyyel.*" The use of the word to signify amusement without walking seems to have been a medieval development.

47. See n. 44 above.

48. See Howard Kreisel, "Miracles in Medieval Jewish Philosophy," *Jewish Quarterly Review* 75 (1984–85): 99–133.

49. See Maimonides, *Eight Chapters of Maimonides on Ethics*, ed. and trans. Joseph I. Gorfinkle (New York, 1912; repr. New York, 1956), 90–91, and bibliography cited there; id., *Guide of the Perplexed*, 2.29.

50. See Maimonides' *Ma'amar teḥiyyat ha-metim* in his *'Iggerot*, ed. and trans. Joseph Kafiḥ (Jerusalem, 1971), 98–99; also ed. and trans. Joshua Finkel, *Proceedings of the American Academy for Jewish Research* 9 (1939): 34 (col. 49).

51. Kreisel, "Miracles," 115.

52. Ibid., 122–33.

53. This opinion seems to have originated in al-Ghazzālī's *Tahāfut al-falāsifah*, who argues that it should be possible, even according to the view of the philosophers, for matter to take on different forms and divest itself of them in a very short space of time. See Kreisel, "Miracles," 105. This view influenced many medieval Jewish philosophers. See, e.g., Gersonides, *Milḥamot ha-Shem* (Riva da Trento, 1560), 75a, and Kreisel, "Miracles," 126. Cf. Isaac Arama, *'Aqeidat Yiṣḥaq*, 2:19b.

54. This should be Gabriel. See B.T. Pesaḥim 118a–b, quoted above, n. 43. Also Reuben Margaliot, *Mal'akhei 'elyon*, 2nd ed. (Jerusalem, 1964), 24, 68.

55. Or to Judah Halevi's category of "things transformed from one form to another." See Harry A. Wolfson, "Judah Halevi on Causality and Miracles," in *Sefer ha-yovel—Me'ir Vaksman* (= *Meyer Waxman Jubilee Volume*), English section (Chicago, 1966), 149.

56. See Naḥmanides, "The Law of the Eternal is Perfect," in his *Writings and Discourses*, trans. Charles B. Chavel, 2 vols. (New York, 1978), 1:68–69. Also his *Commentary on the Torah*, 5 vols. (New York, 1971–76), 2:174 (to Ex 13:16). Cf. Eliezer Schweid, "Ha-Petiḥut la-mufla' ki-yesod ha-'emunah (ha-nes ba-filosofyah ha-yehudit shel yemei-ha-beinayyim me-R. Se'adyah Ga'on 'ad R. Ḥasdai Qresqas," in his *Ṭa'am ve-haqashah* (Ramat-Gan, 1970), 195–97.

57. Simeon ben Ẓemaḥ Duran, *Magen 'avot* (Livorno, Italy, 1785; repr. Jerusalem, 1969), 99a.

58. See Arama, *'Aqeidat Yiṣḥaq*, 1:110a (Sermon 15). Arama uses the same prooftext—*Genesis Rabbah* 5:5—that Maimonides did, in order to explain his theory of two natures. Cf. Wilensky, *R. Yiṣḥaq 'Aramah*, 123.

59. Arama, introduction to Esther commentary, fol. 142v.

60. Commentary to 1:22, fols. 146r–v.

61. Commentary to 2:5, 2:15, fols. 147r, 148v.

62. Cf. Ben-Sasson, "Galut u-ge'ullah," 225–27.

63. Zechariah, 19a.

64. It is not unusual for midrashic motifs to appear in medieval illuminated manuscripts, both Jewish and Christian. This fact is copiously illustrated throughout Gabrielle Sed-Rajna, *The Hebrew Bible in Medieval Illuminated Manuscripts* (New York, 1987). See also the bibliography cited there, pp. 165–67.

65. Cf. *Esther Rabbah*, petiḥta 5; 7:2.

66. Saba, *EKE*, 20 quoting Ps 104:35. Cf. Saba, *Ṣeror ha-mor*, 4:125.

67. See Ex 17:16. Saba reads the verse as follows: Since the hand of Amalek is upon the throne of the Lord, therefore, the Lord will wage war upon Amalek until his memory is wiped out, and this will occur in the days of the Messiah. See *EKE*, 4–5. Cf. Rashi to Ex 17:16.

68. Intimations that the faith of the Israelites was still far from pure a generation after Sinai can be detected in Joshua 24:14–19. Saba bases his remarks on these verses. See *EKE*, 4.

69. See B.T. Shabbat 88a.

70. See also *EKE*, 93, for a more detailed comparison of Sinai and Purim.

71. EKE, 93. Cf. Avraham Gross, "Hishtaqfut geirushei Sefarad u-Portugal be-feirush 'al Megillat 'Ester," in *Proceedings of the Ninth World Congress of Jewish Studies, Jerusalem, August 4–12, 1985, Division B, History of the Jewish People, vol. 1: From the Second Temple Until the Middle Ages* (Jerusalem, 1986), 158, who points out that Saba's idealizing of the characters and events in the book may very well be a symptom of his dissatisfaction with the state of the Jewish people in his own times. It was also possible to see Israel's trial at the hands of Haman in a more positive light as an attempt by God to cause Israel to

repent and thereby bring them closer to redemption. See the comment of Tobias ben Eliezer at the end of the introduction to *Midrash Leqaḥ ṭov*, p. 88: "Just as God set up Haman in order to bring Israel back to virtue, so may He set up a king whose decrees are as severe as Haman's who will cause them to repent before the advent of the Messiah son of David. These are the pangs of the Messiah when the nations will stand over Israel." This statement should be understood in the context of the messianic fervor generated by the Crusades at the end of the eleventh century.

Part II. The World of the Exegete

1. For art, see, for example, Sed-Rajna, *The Hebrew Bible*, 27, 37, 40, 56, 121 (Goliath dressed as a medieval knight), 140–41 (Job's latter days) and many others.

2. For literature, see, for example, Lawrence L. Besserman, *The Legend of Job in the Middle Ages* (Cambridge, Mass., 1979), 75, who refers to the portrayal of Job as a lamenting medieval nobleman in fourteenth- and fifteenth-century English and French poetry, or Charles A. Huttar, "Frail Grass and Firm Tree: David as a Model of Repentance in the Middle Ages and Early Renaissance," in *The David Myth in Western Literature*, ed. Raymond-Jean Frontain and Jan Wojcik (West Lafayette, Ind., 1980), 49, who shows how David's behavior as a penitent was refashioned by medieval and early Renaissance authors such as William Caxton in terms of the ascetic piety of their own age.

Chapter 5. Persia through European Eyes

1. Cf. RSV: "I was in Susa the capital which is in the province of Elam, or NJV: "I was in the fortress of Shushan, in the province of Elam."

2. *VA*, 18.

3. This distinction gained few adherents in the Middle Ages. The opinion of Immanuel of Rome is discussed in Appendix II. According to Isaac ben Joseph ha-Kohen: "a *medinah* is an area, part of a larger area consisting of small towns and large, recognized and differentiated from other areas by their form of writing, although the language in all of them is the same (to 1:22, IbJ, fol. 57r). Cf. also Gersonides: "*medinah* means a region with many towns (to 1:1, p. 39b).

4. This verse was rearranged to conform with Ibn Ezra's comment.

5. The question that immediately comes to mind after following this argument is: If Esther were living in the king's palace, how could she conceal her origins? Ibn Ezra had thought of this problem and was careful to specify that Esther was living with the king's servants, apparently under Mordecai's

watchful but discreet eye and so her background or relation to Mordecai did not become known. See below, p. 124.

6. See 3:15A/B, 4:6B, 4:8A/B, 4:17B, 6:9B, 8:14B, 8:15A/B, 9:6B, 9:12A/B, 9:14B, 9:18B.

7. See John D. Hoag, *Western Islamic Architecture* (London, New York, 1963), 23, and for greater detail, Évariste Lévi-Provençal, *Histoire de l'Espagne musulmane*, 2nd ed., 3 vols. (Paris, 1950–53), 2:130–37.

8. See J. L. Fleischer, "Maddua' yaṣa'," 334–35.

9. See Eliyahu Ashtor, *The History of the Jews in Moslem Spain*, trans. Aaron Klein and Jenny Machlowitz Klein, 3 vols. (Philadelphia, 1973–84), 1:308–9; S. W. Baron, "The Jewish Factor in Medieval Civilization," *Proceedings of the American Academy for Jewish Research* 12 (1942): 4–5 (repr. in his *Ancient and Medieval Jewish History*, ed. L. A. Feldman [New Brunswick, N.J., 1972], 241–42). Other cities in Andalusia also had Jewish majorities or sizable Jewish populations. Cf. Baron, "Jewish Factor," 4–6; Ashtor, *Jews of Moslem Spain*, 1:291–354.

10. So Immanuel of Rome (fol. 184r), Isaiah of Trani (3:297), Gersonides (41b), and Joseph Naḥmias (4a). For instance, Isaiah comments on "in Susa the capital" (1:2)—"the capital is the palace, and Susa is the city, and the city is called *Shushan ha-birah*, that is, the city in which the palace of the king is located."

11. It should be noted that this plan corresponds more closely to city plans in later medieval Christian Spain, while Ibn Ezra's corresponds closely to the situation in Islamic Spain.

12. See above, p. 19.

13. See Appendix II below.

14. See Appendix I below, p. 218.

15. It is corrupt according to some modern scholars. See Moore, *Esther*, 7.

16. See U. T. Holmes, *Daily Life in the Twelfth Century* (Madison, Wisc., 1952), 194; Alwin Schultz, *Das Hofische Leben zur Zeit der Minnesinger*, 2nd rev. ed., 2 vols. (Leipzig, 1889), 1:76–78, 365, 630. On p. 76, Schultz cites sources that use the word *cortines* for hangings.

17. It should be noted that none of the medievals were aware of the Persian word *karpas*, which means "fine linen" but which most modern exegetes translate as "cotton cloth" (See Francis Brown, S. R. Driver, and Charles A. Briggs, *A Hebrew and English Lexicon of the Old Testament* [Oxford,

1907], s.v. *karpas*; Paton, *Esther*, 144), as in the Sanskrit, *karpasa*. Those that did comment on the word *karpas*, explained it as meaning green, obviously having in mind the vegetable *karpas* or celery, whose color is green.

18. Immanuel, fol. 184v–185r; Schultz, *Leben*, 365, mentions an outdoor banquet for which hangings were used in order to provide shade.

19. Gersonides, 39b, applies the grammatical rule of *moshekhet ʿaṣmah ve-ʾaḥeret ʿimmah* ("governs itself and another word") to the *beit* of *ba-ḥaṣar* which he sees as governing both *ḥur* and *ʾargaman*. He reads the verse as follows: The courtyard was decorated with (*be-*) white, green, and blue garments suspended from linen cords and with (*be-*) purple curtains suspended from silver rods and marble columns. This text differs from the printed editions and follows that of MS. BN (Paris) héb. 248, fol. 153v. For the term *moshekhet ʿaṣmah ve-ʾaḥeret ʿimmah*, see Leo Prijs, *Die grammatikalische Terminologie Abraham ibn Ezra's* (Basel, 1950), 77; Chaim Heller, *Untersuchungen über die Peschitta* (Berlin, 1916), 17.

20. Cf. the following story which appears in *ʾAbba' Guryon*, 11, *Panim ʾaḥerim B*, 30, *Yalquṭ Shimʿoni* 1048, p. 1054, col. 1, and Targum Sheni, ad loc., with slight variations: "R. Levi said: 'The following was the custom of the Persians: They had a large cup which held four *shimṣiyyot* [a measure?; so *Yalquṭ*; Buber emends to *sheminiyyot*, or "eighths," *ʾAbba' Guryon*, 6, n. 163] which was called *pusqa'* [or *patqa'*, *ʾAbba' Guryon*, *Panim ʾaḥerim*; or *pitqa'*, Targum Sheni] which they would give to every [guest] to drink from and which he had to empty even if he died or went mad. And the Persian nobles would grease the cup-bearer's palm so that they would not be offered this cup. But Ahasuerus did not introduce this cup into his banquet, saying "whoever wishes to drink may do so."'" The foregoing was the version in the *Yalquṭ*.

21. *Niṭei naʿamanim*, 10a:

אין אונס. אין נחל הימנו; שלא תאמר כוס אחד היו מביאים לפני כל אחד ואחד ושותה פעם אחת ואחר כך נחלו הימנו ואין שותה הימנו יותר, כמנהג כמה המדינות. לכך נאמר, אין אונס, שלא היו נחלים הימנו, כי לשון אונס שבמקרא אינו כלשון אונס שבמשנה. את של מקרא לשון גזילה, כמו כל רז לא אנס לך (דנ' ד:ו), וזאת של משנה מחמת האונס והמפתה את הבתולה.

Although the words *ʿones* and *mefateh* do not appear in rabbinic sources in conjunction with a *betulah*, they do appear together in several places. See, e.g., M. Ketubbot 3:4, Sheviʿit 10:2, Yevamot 7:5, 11:1, and Sanhedrin 1:1. This text is also found in MS. UB (Erlangen, Germany) 1263, fol. 150v.

22. Cf. Crescas du Caylar, "Piyyuṭ le-Yom Purim," MS. BL (London) Add. 19,663, fol. 21r:

חמר חדת ועתיק לבן אדמדם / על כל רב ביתו מצותו קדם/ כי אינך ידע רוח האדם/ מי יכשר הזה או זה.

("Wine new and old, white and red / he commanded every palace steward [to bring] / for one cannot know which will suit / the taste of each individual.")

23. The best white wines came from Rhineland, Alsace, and Saint Emilion; the best reds, from Orleans. See Robert Delort, *Life in the Middle Ages*, trans. Robert Allen (New York, 1973), 39.

24. See Alfred Franklin, *La vie privée d'autrefois: Les repas* (Paris, 1889), 106.

25. He is possibly alluding to tournaments. The translation is a free one: בעשותו לפניהם מיני הגבורות והתענונות שהם מטכסיסי המלכות.

26. Baldus, another fourteenth-century Post-Glossator (commentator on the Roman civil law code after the composition of the *Glossa magna* of Accursius) also makes a similar distinction. See Walter Ullmann, *The Medieval Idea of Law as Represented by Lucas de Penna: A Study in Fourteenth-Century Legal Scholarship* (London, 1946), 175–80, esp. 178–79.

27. "La cabeza del reino;" see Bonifacio Palacios Martín, *La Coronación de los Reyes de Aragón*, 1204–1410 (Valencia, 1975), 105–12, esp. 107.

28. See J. N. Hillgarth, *The Spanish Kingdoms, 1250–1516*, 2 vols. (Oxford, 1976–78), 1:369.

29. Pere III, *Chronicle*, trans. Mary Hillgarth, introduction and notes by J. N. Hillgarth, 2 vols., Medieval Sources in Translation, 23 (Toronto, 1980), 11.

30. Ibid., 2:3, pp. 190–91.

31. Hillgarth, introduction to Pere III, *Chronicle*, 14.

32. Pere III, *Chronicle*, 2:15, pp. 198–99.

33. Ibid., 199, n. 16.

34. One interesting deviation from his contemporary setting is his assertion that the nobles crowned the king. Pere III and his father Alfons III had crowned themselves.

35. See Hillgarth, introduction to Pere III, *Chronicle*, 14–15. Also Joseph N. Strayer, *On the Medieval Origins of the Modern State* (Princeton, N.J., 1970), 74: "Policy was made by the king and his Council," referring to England and France.

36. Hillgarth, *Kingdoms*, 1:391.

37. Joseph F. O'Callaghan, *A History of Medieval Spain* (Ithaca, N.Y., 1975), 452.

38. Astruc, 216. See below pp. 181–82 for futher discussion of this passage.

39. My thanks to Dr. Jaume Riera i Sans of Barcelona for pointing this out to me and for sharing with me the results of his research on the *le'azim* in Astruc's commentary.

40. This account is based mainly on Hillgarth, *Kingdoms*, 1:369–71. See also Pere III, *Chronicle*, chap. 4, 391–453, and *Aragón en su historia* (Saragossa, 1980), 134–59.

41. See *Midrash 'Abba' Guryon*, 16: *'Amar R. Simon: "zeh shivṭo shel Yissakhar."* ("R. Simon said: 'This is the tribe of Issachar' "). Cf. B.T. Megillah 12b: *Man ḥakhamim? Rabbanan yod'ei ha-'ittim she-yode'in le-'abber shanim ve-liqboa' ḥodashim* ("Who are the wise men? The Rabbis who know the times, who know how to proclaim leap years and fix the months"). The tribe of Issachar was traditionally associated with learning and scholarship. See Rashi's comment to Gn 49:15.

42. *'Oṣar ṭov* (1878):26.

43. *Niṭ'ei na'amanim*, 10a.

44. Or *statuti* in Italian.

45. Isaiah of Trani, *Peirush*, 3:298. Perhaps he associated *'ittim* with *dat va-din* in the latter half of the verse. Also cf. Eccl 8:5 where *'et* and *mishpaṭ* are juxtaposed.

46. In his second commentary, however, he explains the phrase simply as advisors, "those that are able to make known what it is proper to do at all times taking into consideration the changing circumstances." See below. However, he does offer the following interpretation as another opinion: "There are those who say that 'those who know the times' are astrologers and the meaning of law (*dat*) is the laws of the heavens (*ḥuqqot shamayim*); 'and judgment,' those that know the judgments of the constellations (*ba'alei dinei ha-mazzalot*) who are called in the Book of Daniel astrologers (*gazrin*) (Dn 2:27, 5:11)." The text for this comment is based on MS. BP (Parma) 2062, which contains several readings that are better than those in MS. BN (Paris) héb. 334. Cf. section on "Astrology in the Commentaries" above, p. 55.

47. "Ramah" also offers this interpretation as one of several; he refers to *ḥakhmei ha-zemanim she-'averu* ("the scholars of times past," i.e., historians).

48. This reading is based on the text of MS. BN (Paris) héb. 248, fol. 154r.

49. Gersonides, 40a. Other exegetes that interpret "those that know the times" as astrologers are Moses b. Isaac Ḥalayo, Isaac ben Joseph ha-Kohen, Abraham Ḥadidah and "Ramah." For Ḥalayo and "Ramah," this is only one of several interpretations that they offer.

50. Ḥalayo, fol. 7v: *yode'ei ha-'ittim hem ha-yode'im ha-dinin ve-ha-mishpaṭim ha-re'uyim la'asot be-khol 'et u-ve-khol zeman ke-fi hishtannut ha-sibbot.* Cf. Ibn Ezra B: *Yo'aṣim le-hodi'a ha-ra'ui la'asot be-khol 'et ke-fi hishtannut ha-sibbot.* (MS. Bibliothèque Nationale (Paris) héb. 334, fol. 76v). The influence is obvious.

51. Naḥmias, 6a: *Yode'ei minhag ha-'ittim she-'averu 'al ha-melakhim ha-qadmonim.* This closely resembles Ibn Ezra A: *ḥakhmei ha-mazzalot, 'o ha-'ittim she-'averu 'al ha-melakhim ha-qadmonim.*

52. The phrase appears eight times in the Talmud. See, for example, B. T. Kiddushin 74a, Ketubbot 85b, 94a–b, and would seem to be a contraction of the word שודא, meaning "gift" or "discretion" of the judges. See J. T. Ket. 10:4 (p. 33d–34a); Jastrow, *Dictionary*, s.v. שודא; Nathan b. Jehiel, *'Arukh ha-shalem*, s.v. שד. The possibility also exists that the word derives from the root שדא, "to throw." But see *Babylonian Talmud*, trans. under editorship of I. Epstein, 35 vols. (London, 1935–52), Ketubbot 85b, p. 54, n. 12.

53. B.T. Sanhedrin 46a.

54. Ibid. 45b.

55. In the passage from which R. Zechariah quotes, the Talmud makes this explicit: "It has been taught: R. Eliezer ben Jacob said: I have heard that the court may, [when necessary,] impose flagellation and pronounce [capital] sentences even where not warranted by the Torah; yet not with the intention of disregarding the Torah but [on the contrary] in order to safeguard it. It once happened that a man rode a horse on the Sabbath in the Greek period and he was brought before the Court and stoned, not because he was liable thereto but because it was [practically] required by the times. Again it happened that a man once had intercourse with his wife under a fig tree. He was brought before the *Beth din* [court] and flogged, not because he merited it, but because the times required it." See B.T. Sanhedrin 46a. (Epstein ed., p. 303) The phrase in the Talmud for "the times required it" is *ha-sha'ah ṣerikhah le-khakh*. Perhaps R. Zechariah chose not to quote this passage because the word used is *sha'ah*, not *'et*. While the phrase *ha-kol le-fi ha-'et ve-ha-zeman* which R. Zechariah includes in his quotation is not to be found in the talmudic passage he refers to, it can, however, be found in a relevant context in the sermons of the fourteenth-century rabbi Nissim b. Reuben Gerondi (although it may not be original to him). Sermon eleven, which is based on Dt 16:18–20, the portion dealing with the appointment of judges and the administration of justice in the Israelite community, discusses the different jurisdictions of the judge and the king. According to R. Nissim, the duty of the judge is to judge righteously according to the letter of the Torah. However, if this were the only recourse, it would

result in certain crimes going unpunished, and this would be detrimental to the political order. In order to correct this imbalance, for the sake of the general welfare of society (*yishuvo shel ʿolam*), God commanded that kings be appointed. It is to the king that the task of assuring the maintenance of order in society is relegated. R. Nissim refers to the passage from the B.T. Sanhedrin quoted above, warning his reader not to challenge his theory on the basis of that passage from which it would seem that the court is appointed in order to judge "according to what the season and time require (*ke-fi tiqqun ha-ʿet ve-ha-zeman*)." This would only be the case if there were no king or if the court were given this jurisdiction by the king. R. Nissim's use of the phrase *ke-fi tiqqun ha-ʿet ve-ha-zeman* with reference to the same passage from the Talmud that R. Zechariah quotes is noteworthy and suggests that R. Zechariah may have been familiar with R. Nissim's sermons, or some common source, or at the very least, suggests the possibility of the existence of a Spanish tradition of interpretation of this passage of the Talmud. See Nissim ben Reuben Gerondi, *Sheneim ʿasar derashot le-ha-Ran*, ed. L. A. Feldman (Jerusalem, 1973–74), 189–92. It should also be pointed out that R. Zechariah's use of the term *shuda' de-dayyanei* (see n. 54 above), or "the discretion of the judges," does not correspond to its usage in the Talmud. In the Talmud, it is used to refer to a case in which two parties have equal claims on a piece of goods or property and there is no objective way of determining whose claim is stronger. See, e.g., B.T. Ketubbot 85b, Kiddushin 74a, and Rashi ad loc.; also Menachem Elon, *Ha-Mishpaṭ ha-ʿivri: toledotav, meqorotav, ʿeqronotav*, 3rd ed., 3 vols. (Jerusalem, 1988), 2:999–1000; Z. H. Chajes, *The Student's Guide to the Talmud*, trans. Jacob Shachter, 2nd rev. ed. (New York, 1960), 126. Such a case is left to the discretion of the judges. R. Zechariah uses the term to apply to the discretion a judge may use in deciding how severe a penalty to assign for a criminal act, taking into consideration the circumstances under which the act was committed. The extension of the field of usage of the term may reflect a medieval development, or it may be R. Zechariah's own innovation based on the talmudic passage he was quoting.

56. Concerning the imposition of extraordinary sanctions not authorized by Jewish law and the making of adjustments in the law in the talmudic and medieval periods, see Aaron M. Schreiber, *Jewish Law and Decision-Making: A Study Through Time* (Philadelphia, 1979), 375–424; Elon, *Mishpaṭ ha-ʿivri*, 1:391–712, esp. 413–39.

57. This term is also found in Joseph Albo, *Sefer ha-ʿiqqarim*, ed. and trans. Isaac Husik, 4 vols. in 5 (Philadelphia, 1929–30), 1:78–79, who distinguishes between three kinds of law—natural, positive or conventional, and divine. His definition of *dat nimusit*, (positive or conventional law,) is as follows: "a law ordered by a wise man or men to suit the place and the time and the nature of the persons who are to be controlled by it, like the laws and

statutes enacted in certain countries among the ancient idolaters, or those who worship God as human reason dictates without any divine revelation." This corresponds to the *lex humana* of Thomas Aquinas. See ibid., pp. 2–3, n. 1, and p. 79, n. 1. Cf. also, Maimonides, *Guide of the Perplexed* 2.40, trans. S. Pines, 383–84, who discusses the character of *nomos* or man-made law. The term in Arabic is *sharīʿa nāmūsiyya* of which *dat nimusit* is a literal translation.

58. Cf. the definition given by Albo, *'Iqqarim*, 1:78. The term "law" (*dat*) applies to every rule or custom in vogue among a large group of people. It may be a body of rules embracing a great many commands, as in the expression "all that knew law (*dat*) and judgment (*din*) (Est 1:13) or it may be applied to a single command, as in the expression "And a decree (*dat*) was given out in Shushan" (Est 9:14). It is applied to a divine law, as in the expression, "At his right hand was a fiery law (*dat*) unto them" (Dt 33:2), as well as to a positive human law, like the laws of the Medes and the Persians. Saba's definition centers more around the time-bound or temporal nature of the *datot*, while Albo's definition is more formalistic, stressing its application to a large group of people. Their understanding of Dt 33:2 is quite different. For Albo, it simply refers to divine law, whereas for Saba it specifically alludes to the special enactments of human law, which receive their divine sanction from this verse. Cf. also Zechariah ben Saruḳ, discussed above, whose understanding of the verse is similar to that of Saba, although based on different words.

59. This became available to Jewish scholars in the fourteenth century. See discussion on the *Ethics* and the commentaries in Chapter 2.

60. "Ramah," fol. 2r: *yodeʿei ha-filosofyah ha-medinit li-shpoṭ ke-fi ha-ʿet ve-ṣorekh ha-shaʿah*. Cf. Gersonides, who also mentions *filosofyah medinit*.

61. Chapter 13 in the translation of Meir Alguadez.

62. *Ḥasid* is the term used by Alguadez for the "equitable man," *ḥasidut*, for "equity".

63. *Ethics of Aristotle*, trans. J. A. K. Thomson, rev. with notes and appendices by Hugh Tredennick, introduction and bibliography by Jonathan Barnes (Harmondsworth, England, 1976), 199.

64. It is also possible that Arama was influenced here by the same sermon of R. Nissim Gerondi mentioned above in which he differentiates between judges who are required to judge according to a true and righteous justice (*mishpaṭ ṣodeq 'amitti*) and kings who are necessary for the purpose of maintaining the political order (*tiqqun seder medini*) and attending to the need of the hour (*ṣorekh ha-shaʿah*). See n. 55 above. The classic case of Jewish law requiring amendment in order to bring it in line with the needs of society is to be found in B.T. Sanhedrin 40b, which discusses all the conditions that someone accused

of murder or idolatry must fulfill before he or she can be convicted. For example, a murderer, before committing the act, had to have been warned of the consequences of his action and had to have acknowledged the warning verbally; he had to express his awareness of the consequences of his actions—i.e., that he was liable to the death penalty; and furthermore, he had to commit the act immediately upon hearing the warning, or else it could be argued that he had forgotten it. Concerning all this R. Nissim comments: "There is no doubt that all this is proper from the viewpoint of just law (*mishpaṭ ṣedeq*), for why should a man be killed without knowing that he had put himself in a position where he would be liable to death if he transgressed? For this reason it was necessary that he receive a warning and all the other things mentioned in that *baraita*. This is the true just law in itself which is given over to the judges. But if criminals were punished only in this way, the political order would be totally destroyed (*yippased ha-siddur ha-medini le-gamrei*), for murderers would multiply and they would have no fear of punishment. Therefore, the Lord, may He be blessed, ordained the establishment of the institution of kingship for the sake of the general welfare of society (*yishuvo shel ʿolam*). . . . The king may pass judgment in cases in which a proper warning was not given according to his view of the need of the political collective. We find then that the [purpose of] appointing a king is the same in Israel and the nations, for it is necessary for maintaining the political order. But the appointing of judges is peculiar to and more necessary for Israel, as it is written, "and they shall judge the people with righteous judgment" (Dt 16:18), i.e., by the appointing of judges, and their mandate is to judge the people with true and righteous judgments." See *Sheneim ʿasar derashot le-ha-Ran*, 190. An opinion very similar to that of R. Nissim is attributed to R. Solomon ibn Adret (1235–1310). See Schreiber, *Jewish Law*, 378. We see then that R. Nissim differentiates clearly between the roles of the judge and the king, the latter being required to step in to deal with cases in which the general welfare of society would be threatened if only the just law were applied. It would seem that the roles that Arama assigns to the two types of judges—those dealing with more theoretical and idealized legal [or conventional] justice and those dealing with applied situational justice—may have been influenced by his reading of R. Nissim, who, although not distinguishing between two types of justice and judges, does assign the judges and the king jurisdictions quite similar to those that Arama assigns to his two types of judges. It may well be, then, that Arama's theory is based on elements borrowed from both Aristotle and R. Nissim. Leon Feldman, in his introduction to *Sheneim ʿasar derashot le-ha-Ran*, 44, refers to R. Nissim's influence on later scholars, including Isaac Arama.

65. Saba, *EKE*, 34–35, expresses similar ideas. Cf. Ullmann, *Medieval Idea*, 152–53.

66. See Brian Tierney, "Public Expediency and Natural Law: A

Fourteenth-Century Discussion on the Origins of Government and Property," in *Authority and Power: Studies on Medieval Law and Government Presented to Walter Ullmann on his Seventieth Birthday*, ed. Brian Tierney and Peter Linehan (Cambridge, 1980), 167–82.

67. Ibid., 170.

68. Ibid., 171.

Chapter 6. Jewish-Gentile Relations

1. Several scholars have pointed out the definite Diaspora orientation of the book, which stresses adaptation to conditions in the Diaspora rather than an overriding concern with the return to Zion. See W. Lee Humphreys, "A Life-style for Diaspora: A Study of the Tales of Esther and Daniel," *Journal of Biblical Literature* 92 (1973): 211–17, 222–23; Jon D. Levenson, "The Scroll of Esther in Ecumenical Perspective," *Journal of Ecumenical Studies* 13 (1976): 446–51; Sidnie Ann White, "Esther: A Feminine Model for Jewish Diaspora," in *Gender and Difference in Ancient Israel*, ed. Peggy L. Day (Minneapolis, 1989), 165, 167, 173.

2. For a description of some special Purims, see Philip Goodman, ed., *The Purim Anthology* (Philadelphia, 1964), 14–37. Cf. also Yosef H. Yerushalmi, *Zakhor: Jewish History and Jewish Memory* (Seattle, 1979), 46–48.

3. See B.T. Sanhedrin 74b: "Abbaye said: 'Esther was like the ground [i.e., totally passive]. Rabba said: 'When they [the Gentiles] do it [force a Jew to transgress] for their own pleasure [and not for the purpose of denying the tenets of Judaism] it is different."

4. *Zohar* (Ra'aya' mehemna), Ki teṣe', 3:276a. The *Zohar*'s comment is based on the root *STR* which means "to hide" and is contained in the name Esther. The sages, of course, as Ginzberg, *Legends*, 6:460 points out, never went this far and even maintained that the last Darius was the offspring of Ahasuerus's marriage with Esther.

5. *Perushei ha-Torah le-R. Yehudah he-Ḥasid*, 133.

6. The issue of martyrdom and the failure of most Spanish Jews to give their lives for their faith were questions of great concern for the exiles from Spain. Saba deals with this topic again in *Ṣeror ha-mor* (Warsaw, 1879), 5:15–16. See also Azriel Shohat, "Qiddush ha-shem be-hagutam shel megorshei Sefarad u-mequbbelei Ṣefat," in *Milḥemet qodesh u-marṭirologyah be-toledot Yisra'el u-ve-toledot ha-'ammim* (Jerusalem, 1967–68), 131–34, and sources quoted there.

7. Saba, *EKE*, 40. Saba also suggests that Esther should have tried to

kill Ahasuerus, as the daughter of Rabbi Johanan had done to the Greek governor. Saba gives the Jerusalem Talmud as his source for this story. A similar story is quoted by Nissim ben Reuben in his "novellae" to the code of Isaac Alfasi, Shabbat 23a. He quotes his source as "the midrash." For the connection between this legend and the story of Judith and Holofernes and for a compilation and analysis of other midrashic parallels, see A. M. Dubarle, *Judith: Formes et sens des diverses traditions*, 2 vols. (Rome, 1966), 1:80–110, 2:98–177. Concerning R. Nissim's text in particular, see ibid., 1:106–7. The Johanan mentioned by Saba is Johanan the high priest of the Hasmonean family. Saba seems to be the only source to confuse him with the sage, Rabbi Johanan.

8. See Gross, "Rabbi 'Avraham Saba'," 222.

9. Eleazer ben Judah, *Sha'arei binah*, 17 (to 2:10).

10. *Perushei ha-Torah le-R. Yehudah he-Ḥasid*, 133. The threat of being held for ransom was constantly hanging over the heads of Jewish communities in Christian Europe. Jews were often imprisoned as a result of blood libels or host desecration libels or for the purpose of extorting money from them. A statement ascribed to R. Judah the Pious, praises the person who ransoms captives because he saves men from torture and women from dishonor. (The source of this statement has eluded me.) On the whole question of ransoming captives see Eliezer Bashan, *Shivyah u-fedut ba-ḥevrah ha-yehudit be-'arṣot ha-Yam ha-tikhon (1391–1830)* (Ramat-Gan, 1980).

11. *'Oṣar ṭov* (1878): 27. Note that already among the northern French, there seems to be a tendency to shy away from ascribing to the king himself malicious intent against the Jews. Both Kara and "A" see the officers as not letting the king take a Jewish woman as queen and do not attribute such discriminatory views to the king himself. But see below, p. 184.

12. Ibn Ezra is the only exegete to raise the issue of religious observance in the Gentile court. As for other violations of Jewish law by Mordecai and Esther, only Rashi mentions that Mordecai transgressed Jewish law by fasting on the first day of Passover. See his comment on 4:17, which is based on the comment of Rav, B.T. Megillah 15a. See also *Pirqei de-Rabbi 'Eli'ezer* 50.

13. Ibn Ezra's comment should be seen against the background of the Almohade persecutions which were visited upon the Jewish communities in Spain and North Africa in the 1140s. See A. S. Halkin, "Le-toledot ha-shemad bi-yemei ha-'Almuvaḥidin," in *The Joshua Starr Memorial Volume: Studies in History and Philology*, Jewish Social Studies Publications, no. 5 (New York, 1953), 101–10. Ibn Ezra himself wrote a dirge about the persecutions called "*'Ahah yarad 'alei Sefarad*" ("Alas, there has descended upon Spain"). In the second stanza he mentions "daughters and precious ones delivered to a foreign religion." See Abraham Ibn Ezra, *Qoveṣ ḥokhmat ha-Raba'*, ed. David Kahana,

2 vols. (Warsaw, 1894; repr. Jerusalem, 1970–71), 140–43. Hava Lazarus-Yafeh, "'Ester ha-malkah—min ha-'anusim? Peirusho shel Raba' le-'Ester 2:10," *Tarbiẓ* 57 (1987–88): 121–2, suggests that it is possible to see here the influence of the Moslem concept of *taqīyya*, the principle of dissimulation of one's religious beliefs in order to avoid persecution, or *kithmān*, meaning concealing of one's true identity. The fact that crypto-judaism is almost exclusively a Spanish phenomenon suggests to her that the influence of Islam was crucial in allowing this practice to spread among the Jews in Spain, while it was much less widespread in Christian countries where martyrdom was the norm. While this suggestion is tantalizing, it is not without its problems. First, the phenomenon of crypto-Judaism can be traced back to the Visigothic period in Spain, long before the Moslem conquest. See Solomon Katz, *The Jews in the Visigothic and Frankish Kingdoms of Spain and Gaul* (Cambridge, Mass., 1937). Second, *taqīyya* is more characteristic of Shiite than of Sunni Islam, and the latter version was the one that Ibn Ezra would have been exposed to.

14. See Cecil Roth, *History of the Marranos*, 4th ed. (New York, 1974), 186. To this very day, the Conversos of Belmonte, Portugal, venerate "Holy Queen Esther" and observe the "Fast of Queen Esther" with great devotion. See Anita Novinsky and Amilcar Paulo, "The Last Marranos," *Commentary* 43 (May, 1967): 77, 81.

15. Roth, *Marranos*, 188. Some Karaite scholars discuss the possibility of fasting three days, or even seventy days (the time lapsed between the sending of Haman's letters and Mordecai's) but reject both possibilities and conclude that only the Purim celebration is binding on future generations, not the Fast of Esther. See Judah Hadassi, *'Eshkol ha-kofer* (Eupatoria, Crimea, 1836), 93a–94b; Elijah Bashyazi, *Sefer ha-miṣvot shel ha-Yehudim ha-Qara'im* (Israel, 1966), 79a.

16. The sages identified the Kish mentioned in Mordecai's genealogy with Kish, the father of Saul, and so Esther is also a descendant of the first king of Israel. See B.T. Meg. 13b.

17. "Ramah," fol. 5r, may also credit this tradition. He wonders why, if Mordecai wanted Esther to be queen, he did not say from whom she was descended. After all, better someone with royal blood than a foundling (*'asufit*).

18. Joseph Ḥayyun, fol. 71v, expresses similar sentiments. Cf. also Tobias ben Eliezer, *Midrash Leqaḥ ṭov* to 2:10.

19. The romantic idea crops up again in Isaac Arama's commentary (fol. 147r), according to which Mordecai forbade Esther to reveal her people and kindred in order that the king might think that she was a descendant of the House of David. It will be recalled that according to Arama, the fact of Esther's

Jewishness was known to all. Apparently, the possibility of Esther being descended from King Saul was not significant for him.

20. E.g., Rashi, Joseph Kara, Joseph Naḥmias, Moses Ḥalayo, Ibn Ezra, Isaac ben Joseph, Abraham Saba.

21. See the discussion of this question, above, pp. 97–100.

22. See above, p. 24.

23. *GK*, 37. Kaspi seems to be recalling the situation at the time of the Exodus when God hardened the hearts of Pharaoh and the Egyptians. According to Maimonides, this was not meant to deprive them of their free will in this situation but to punish them for their wicked deeds in the past. See his *Eight Chapters*, 94–98.

24. Kaspi also points out Mordecai's wisdom in forbidding the Jews from touching the booty, although they were given permission to do so in the second set of letters. He says that this was a very wise move, although he declines to specify why he thinks so. Then, he adds, with what seems to be no small measure of pride: "If they took less money than was allowed in the letters, they made up for it in bodies, for they killed many, and many did not begin to rise up against them as long as they were taunting them, saying, 'So, you think you're going to kill us?' And so on, as is the custom of our people when they have power" (*GK*, 40). Perhaps here we have an expression of the frustration of the medieval Jews at the powerlessness of the Jewish community, and a hint at the role the Book of Esther played in fostering pride in the successes of Jewish communities that did have power in the past and hope in the restoration of such power in the future.

25. *Esther Rabbah* 10:13. The text actually reads "bear" (*dov*), but the midrash identifies the words *dov* and *ze'ev* ("wolf") which was identified with Media. See *Midrash Rabbah: Esther*, trans. by Maurice Simon (London, 1939), 6, n. 5; 123, n. 1.

26. Cf. 1 Targum to Est 9 where Amalek is also mentioned several times.

27. Gersonides, 43a to 9:1, 13.

28. Ibid., to 9:13.

29. IbJ, fols. 64r, 72v.

30. *EKE*, 90. See also Saba, *Ṣeror ha-mor*, 5:65.

31. Re Saba's view of Amalek, see also above, pp. 91–94.

32. Ḥayyun, 89r.

33. On the declining situation of the Jewish community in Portugal in the mid–fifteenth century, see Baron, *History*, 10:213–15. In 1449, an anti-Jewish riot in Lisbon was quelled with great difficulty, and in the succeeding decades, the Cortes passed numerous restrictions against the Jews. Still the situation for the Jews was far better in Portugal than in Spain. This passage provides additional evidence that the commentary was written well before the expulsion from Portugal and even before the expulsion from Spain. See Hacker, "R. Yosef Ḥayyun," 279–80, who has gathered evidence that demonstrates that Ḥayyun was active in the third quarter of the fifteenth century and died well before the expulsion from Spain.

34. Understanding *ṣarim* (9:2) to mean their enemies rather than those who were besieging them.

35. Kaspi's reaction noted above is a notable exception.

36. The same applies to the statement he makes about the expulsion near the end of his commentary (p. 19a) which was quoted above, p. 89. Cf. Ben-Sasson, "Dor golei Sefarad," 53–59, who shows that many contemporary Jewish scholars sympathized with the aims of the Catholic monarchs and therefore saw their expulsion as a logical, correct, and not unjust result of royal policy.

37. *EKE*, 65.

38. Compare Maimonides' characterization of Edom and Ishmael in his *Epistle to Yemen*, ed. A. S. Halkin, trans. Boaz Cohen (New York, 1952), iii. He distinguishes between two classes of opponents to the Jews, the first who try to destroy the law of Israel by means of violence and brute force. Among this group are Amalek, Titus, and Hadrian, i.e., Edomites. The other group consists of the most intelligent and educated among the nations, such as the Syrians, Persians, and Greeks. They try to demolish Israel's law through arguments and controversies. Elsewhere (p. xviii) referring to the Arabs, Maimonides, who, it will be recalled, endured the Almohade persecutions, says: "Never did a nation molest, degrade, debase, and hate us as much as they." His view of the Arabs is far more negative than Saba's, and he certainly does not class the Persians with them, as does Saba, and nowhere does he express as high an opinion of the intellectual attainments of the Christians as Saba does. For him, the Persians are among the intelligent and educated and fight the Jews with speech. Evidently, these scholars' different experiences affected their opinions regarding the character of these different groups of Gentiles.

39. Elsewhere (*EKE*, 92) Saba praises the simple believers who are pure

in their faith and well-intentioned and seems to express a preference for such simple souls over the more learned and more sophisticated scholars, well-versed in rabbinic lore, who put their knowledge to ill use. This would seem to be part of a recurrent anti-intellectual tendency in his writings. See above, p. 35.

40. NJV notes meaning of Hebrew uncertain; RSV translates "a nation tall and smooth."

41. Cf. the statement in *Zohar* 2:17a: "'A slave-girl who supplants her mistress' (Prv 30:23): This is Hagar who gave birth to Ishmael who performed many evils against Israel, and ruled over them and afflicted them with many afflictions and decreed against them many forced conversions (*shemadot*) and who rule over them to this very day and do not allow them to maintain their religion. There is no exile more difficult for Israel than that of Ishmael." As Ronald Kiener, "The Image of Islam in the Zohar," *Jerusalem Studies in Jewish Thought* 8 (1989): 153, points out, this statement was written in the wake of the Almohade persecutions, whose memory must have still been fresh in the minds of the Spanish Jewish intellectuals in the late thirteenth century. Saba was probably aware of this statement which may have influenced his views on Moslems. It is not clear whether he concurred with its conclusion.

42. Concerning the whole question of medieval Jewish attitudes to Christians and Moslems, see the article by Bernard Septimus, "'Taḥat 'Edom ve-lo' taḥat Yishma"el'—gilgulo shel ma'amar," *Zion* 47 (1981–82): 103–11. Cf. also Moshe Hallamish, "'Aspeqṭim 'aḥadim bi-she'elat yaḥasam shel ha-mequbbalim le-'ummot ha-'olam," in *Filosofyah Yisre'elit*, ed. Asa Kasher, Moshe Hallamish (Tel Aviv, 1983), 49–71. It would seem that during most of the Middle Ages, there was a definite preference among Spanish Jews for life under Christian rule over that under Moslem rule. Only in the late fourteenth and fifteenth centuries in the face of Christian persecutions and expulsions did a shift in attitude take place, and even then it was not universal. Saba's attitude is relatively balanced. Consider the words that Solomon Ibn Verga puts in the mouth of one of his kings: "Why do the Christians hate the Jews so much? If it is because they killed our Savior—*why the Arabs hate the Jews more* [emphasis added], and they [i.e., the Jews] did not kill their prophets, for I have heard that they do not allow them to walk by the side of the road, but only in the middle, like horses." *Sheveṭ Yehudah*, 154. See Septimus, "Taḥat 'Edom," 109.

43. On Amalek in Saba's view of history, see above, pp. 97–100. According to some kabbalists, Jews' souls originated from the divine while Gentile souls from the forces of the *siṭra' 'aḥra'* or the demonic. See Hallamish, "'Aspeqṭim," 50–51.

44. This is based on *Zohar* 2:32a; see also Kiener, "Image of Islam," 49–51.

45. The imperfection being that Muslims only perform *milah* (cutting the foreskin) and not *peri'ah* (pulling down the membrane to fully expose the corona). See Elliott Wolfson, "Circumcision and the Divine Name," *Jewish Quarterly Review* 78 (1987–88): 98–99, esp. nn. 61, 63. A further defect in Islamic circumcision is the fact that that it takes place long after the eighth day. Cf. also Kiener, "Image of Islam," 54–61.

46. See Saba, *Ṣeror ha-mor*, 1:37a. For other positive statements concerning Ishmael, see Yosef Shapira, *Bi-shevilei ha-ge'ullah*, 2 vols. (Jerusalem, 1946–47), 1:155. In the medieval messianic midrash, *Nisterot R. Shim'on ben Yoḥai*, published in *Beit ha-Midrash*, ed. A. Jellinek, 6 vols. (Vienna, 1853–77; repr. Jerusalem, 1967), 3:78–82, Ishmael is given a positive role in the salvation of Israel, and his dominion over Israel is seen as ultimately beneficial. Cf. C. M. Horowitz, ed. *Beit 'eqed ha-'aggadot* (Frankfurt am Main, 1881; repr. Jerusalem, 1966–67), 51–55. As early a source as the Talmud (B.T. Shabbat 11a) has the statement: "Better under Ishmael, than under a stranger" (*taḥat Yishma''el ve-lo' taḥat nokhri*). Marcus Jastrow, *Dictionary of the Targumim, the Talmud Babli and Yerushalmi* (London, 1903), s.v. *Yishma''el*, suggests better Arabic dominion than Byzantine. Cf. Rashi ad loc.: "stranger—Edomites, who are more cruel." So, Rashi and Maimonides could easily correspond to the two Jews in Saba's parable. To each, the exile under which he suffered, seemed the worst imaginable. Of course, the use of Esau and Edom as a symbol for Roman and then Christian domination goes back to the Talmud and Midrash. See the study by Irit Aminoff, "The Figures of Esau and the Kingdom of Edom in Palestinian Midrashic-Talmudic Literature in the Tannaic and Amoraic Periods" (Ph.D. diss., Melbourne University, 1981); and Gerson D. Cohen, "Esau as a Symbol in Early Medieval Thought," in *Jewish Medieval and Renaissance Studies*, ed. Alexander Altmann (Cambridge, Mass., 1967), 19–48.

47. Ben-Sasson, "Dor golei Sefarad," 47–52.

48. *Neveh Shalom*, 169a. The seething waters refer to the waters of baptism. The translation here, which is my own, puts the verbs in the perfect tense, although NJV and RSV use the conditional "would have," since this fits in better with the author's intent.

49. Isaac Abravanel, *Commentary to Joshua* (Jerusalem, 1954–55), 53a.

50. *Ma'amar ha-'aḥdut*, chapter 3. Quoted in Ben-Sasson, "Dor golei Sefarad," 49.

51. Ben-Sasson, "Dor golei Sefarad," 47–52.

52. The other is discussed below, p. 161.

Chapter 7. The State of the Jewish People in the Diaspora

1. Cf. the comment of another northern French exegete that when Mordecai told the king's servants that he was Jewish, he became an object of scorn to them (*nitbazzeh be-'eineihem*), *Nit'ei na'amanim*, 10b, to 3:4.

2. Kara, 3:90 (to 3:6). Cf. Joseph Ḥayyun ad loc., fol. 76v.

3. Kara, 3:89 (to 2:10).

4. See below, pp. 166–68, 181–82.

5. IbJ., fol. 63v. Rather than understand *'ein shoveh* as an impersonal phrase meaning "it does not profit," as do most exegetes, R. Isaac takes the phrase to mean "there is no one to argue for their abandonment." He understands *le-hanniḥam* as "to abandon them" rather than "to let them be," as do most other exegetes. See above, Chapter 1, pp. 24–25.

6. On Jewish serfdom, see Salo W. Baron, "'Plenitude of Apostolic Powers' and Medieval 'Jewish Serfdom,'" in his *Ancient and Medieval Jewish History*, ed. L. A. Feldman (New Brunswick, N.J., 1972), 284–307; id., "Medieval Nationalism and Jewish Serfdom," in *Studies and Essays in Honor of Abraham A. Neuman*, ed. Meir Ben-Horin, Bernard D. Weinryb, and Solomon Zeitlin (Leiden, 1962), 17–48 (rev. version in his *Ancient and Medieval Jewish History*, 308–22).

7. On the legal status of the Jews and their protection by the royal powers, see Baron, *History*, 11:3–76, esp. 4–13 on Jewish serfdom, 22–33 on protection for persons and property, and 39–55 on religious safeguards. The *Siete Partidas*, a law code established by Alfonso X (1252–1284) in Castile and which went into effect in the fourteenth century, provided that "no force nor pressure must in any manner be applied to any Jew so that he turn Christian" (ibid., 40). In effect, this guaranteed the Jews their freedom of religion. This may be significant with regard to Astruc's statement that "it is a law for them from the king that they should not be forced to do anything that violates their faith" (Astruc, p. 216). For more information concerning the Jews' legal status in the Middle Ages, see Guido Kisch, *The Jews in Medieval Germany: A Study of their Legal and Social Status* (Chicago, 1949), 129–70, 179–84, 331–33.

8. Moore, *Esther*, 42.

9. See, e.g., Peretz Bernstein, *Jew-Hate as a Sociological Problem*, trans. David Saraph (New York, 1951), 232–80.

10. B.T. Megillah 13b. Cf. Samuel b. Meir who mentions besides the Jews' refusal to intermarry with Gentiles their refusal to join the king's army when he is gathering his forces on the Sabbath.

11. See p. 164.

12. Similarly, Joseph ibn Yaḥya, writing in Italy in the sixteenth century, points out that it was the Jews' dispersion among the nations which facilitated their expulsion since they existed nowhere in sufficient numbers to put up effective resistance against their attackers. See his commentary to Esther, chapter 3 (Bologna, 1534–35), 37a, quoted in Ben-Sasson, "Galut u-ge'ullah," 223.

13. One need search no further back in history than this century for sufficient corroboration of this statement. Sadly enough, many local inhabitants of France, Poland, Ukraine, and other countries were only too glad to lend a hand to the Germans in their bloody task of murdering the Jews of Europe.

14. The dating of this work is problematic, and estimates range from the fourth to the eleventh centuries. The date given here is that preferred by Yehuda Komlos (see *EJ* (1971), s.v. "Targum Sheni." See also Joshua Berman, "Aggadah and Antisemitism: the Midrashim to Esther 3:8," *Judaism* 38 (1989): 186, n. 1.

15. Jewish law requires four species to be used on the festival of *Sukkot* (Tabernacles)—the fruit of the citron and branches of willow, palm, and myrtle. The Talmud (B.T. Sukkah 31–34) refers to the latter three, bound together, as *hosha'not*. This is also the name given to the special prayers recited while making a circuit of the synagogue holding the four species. These prayers took their name from the recurring refrain—*hosha'na'* ("please save us")—which distinguishes them. The word is also used for the five twigs of willow tied together with a palm leaf and smitten in the synagogue on the seventh day of *Sukkot* (*Hosha'na' rabbah*) to symbolize the casting away of one's sins.

16. Or "perform the *hosha'na'* service." See previous note.

17. See Bernard Grossfeld, ed., *The Targum to the Five Megilloth* (New York, 1973), 134–39.

18. Berman, "Aggadah," 188, speculates that this is an example of eighth-century Purim Torah. If it is, it is the earliest specimen we have of this genre of literature. This kind of accusation is found in earlier midrashic sources and was quite common in the ancient world. Cf. J. N. Sevenster, *The Roots of Pagan Antisemitism in the Ancient World*, Supplements to Novum Testementum 41 (Leiden, 1975), 89–144; see also M. D. Herr, "Sin'at Yisra'el ba-'Imperyah ha-Romit le-'or sifrut Ḥazal," in *Sefer zikkaron le-Vinyamin deh-Fris* (Jerusalem, 1968–69), 149–59; reprinted in *Yehudim ve-Yahadut be-'einei ha-'olam ha-helenisṭi* (Jerusalem, 1973–74), 33–43.

19. See Vamberto Morais, *A Short History of Antisemitism* (New York, 1976), 48, 52–53.

20. Ibid., 49–50.

21. The meaning of Aramaic ארניא is uncertain.

22. See Buber, *Sifrei de-'aggadeta'*, 68.

23. See Berman, "Aggadah and Antisemitism," 192–94.

24. The dating of *Midrash Panim 'aḥerim* is uncertain. It seems to be another version of *Midrash 'Abba' Guryon*, which probably dates from the early eighth century. See Chanoch Albeck in Yomtov Lipmann Zunz, *Ha-Derashot be-Yisra'el* (Jerusalem, 1946), 424–25. But the polemic would seem to contain early elements of the Jewish-Christian debate and should be dated to the patristic period. It is not necessary, as Berman, "Aggadah and Antisemitism," 194, seems to suggest, to postulate a medieval setting for these remarks. It is curious that the passage seems to imply that the prayer of eighteen benedictions which contains the *birkat ha-minim* and the following blessing is recited on the Sabbath. It is actually recited during the daily prayers and not on the Sabbath.

25. *Neveh Shalom*, 69b.

26. Ibid.

27. See Ben-Sasson, "Dor golei Sefarad," 53–59.

28. Ben-Sasson, "Dor golei Sefarad," 59.

29. Ibid., 55–59.

30. Grossfeld, *Targum*, 139.

31. MS. SUB (Hamburg) Cod. Heb., 235, fol. 131v. This passage is also quoted in H. J. Zimmels, "Ketav-yad Hamburg," 252.

32. See James Parkes, *The Jew in the Medieval Community*, 2nd ed. (New York, 1976), 334, 360–71; Guido Kisch, "The Jews in Medieval Law," in *Essays on Antisemitism*, ed. Koppel Pinson (New York, 1946), 110.

33. See Baron, *History*, 12:143. In medieval England, Jews were permitted by law to sell pawned objects after a year and a day. See H. G. Richardson, *English Jewry Under the Angevin Kings* (London, 1960), 109. German law also allowed Jewish lenders to dispose of unredeemed pledges. See Kisch, *Jews in Medieval Germany*, 220–21.

34. It should be pointed out that German law also provided that Jews did not have to return pledges on their Sabbath. See Kisch, *Jews in Medieval Germany*, 184–85. Therefore, the case mentioned by R. Avigdor accurately reflects the reality of the times.

35. See Parkes, *Jew*, 351–55. This case demonstrates well the need for caution in the use of nondocumentary material as a source for historical studies. Although, the presence of a certain topic or theme in the material being analyzed can be helpful, one cannot draw any conclusions from its absence. The recent study of Jewish moneylending in the Middle Ages by Joseph Shatzmiller, *Shylock Reconsidered: Jews, Moneylending and Medieval Society* (Berkeley and Los Angeles, 1990), presents a much more balanced view of moneylending and of the image of the Jew as moneylender than has been commonly held until recently. In many communities, Jews were honored and respected for the important role they played in the economy and were not scorned at all. Of course, the view that usury was a sin was fostered by the Church and this came to the fore at various times. But the prevailing attitude was not at all as one-sided and hostile as one would have expected.

36. It is absent from midrashic sources.

37. Arama, fol. 153r. Moses Ḥalayo also mentions that the Jews do not pay their poll taxes because they are poor. On the other hand, in Astruc's commentary, Haman's offer of 10,000 talents of silver is made to offset the losses in tax revenue the king would suffer when the Jews were disposed of.

38. Baron, *History*, 12:198–238.

39. Cf. Richardson, *English Jewry*, 227; Baron, *History*, 12:281. Similarly, it has been suggested that the expulsion of the Jews from France in 1306 was for purely fiscal reasons. Once Philip had confiscated the Jews' goods and filled his coffers, he had no more use for them and so expelled them. See Simon Schwarzfuchs, "The Expulsion of the Jews from France (1306)," in *The Seventy-fifth Anniversary Volume of the Jewish Quarterly Review*, ed. Abraham A. Neuman and Solomon Zeitlin (Philadelphia, 1967), 487–88.

40. See Parkes, *Jew*, 149–54; Robert Chazan, *Medieval Jewry in Northern France* (Baltimore, 1973), 65.

41. See Jean Regné, *History of the Jews in Aragon: Regesta and Documents, 1213–1327* (Jerusalem, 1978), Index, s.v. "Taxation, Punishment for Non-Payment of," 652. It should be noted that some Jewish authorities permitted evading paying customs duties if the customs agent was a non-Jew. The principle of "The law of the kingdom is law" applied only to direct levies by the king. See Shilo, *Dina' de-malkhuta' dina'*, 293–95.

42. See, e.g., Regné, *Jews in Aragon*, nos. 3009, 3040.

43. Cf. Baer, *Jews in Christian Spain*, 2:250.

44. On the economic decline of Spanish Jewry in the fifteenth century and its increasing marginality, see Stephen Haliczer, "The Expulsion of the

Jews and the Economic Development of Castile," in *Hispania Judaica: Studies on the History, Language, and Literature of the Jews in the Hispanic World*, ed. J. M. Solà-Solé, S. G. Armistead, J. H. Silverman, Biblioteca Universitaria Puvill, I. Estudios, 3 vols. to date (Barcelona, 1980—), 1:43–47; Henry Kamen, *The Spanish Inquisition* (London, 1965), 18–25. But cf. Baer, *Jews in Christian Spain*, 2:315–19, who shows that some prominent Jews were heavily involved in tax-farming for the sovereigns right up to the expulsion.

45. See above, Chapter 5, pp. 112–13.

46. Literally, *be-shihi pihi*, which was understood in the Middle Ages to be an acronym for *Shabbat ha-yom, Pesaḥ ha-yom*, meaning "today is the Sabbath, today is Passover." Gentiles have always been amazed at the number of holidays in the Jewish calendar. The suggestion by Cassel and Bernstein that *shihi pihi* means something akin to "shilly-shally" in English or *Larifari* in German is not convincing. See Grossfeld, ed., *Targum*, 137–38.

47. On the role of the Jews in the overthrow of the Visigoths, see Ashtor, *Jews of Moslem Spain*, 1:10–24, 407–8. On Alonso de Espina, see Baer, *Jews in Christian Spain*, 2:287–89. Cf. also the attack on the Jews in 1007 during the time of Robert, King of France, which was based on the charge that the Jews were "one people spread throughout all the provinces which does not obey us." The terminology is taken from Est 3:8. See A. M. Habermann, ed., *Sefer Gezeirot 'Ashkenaz ve-Ṣarefat: divrei zikhronot mi-benei ha-dorot she-bi-tequfat Mas'ei ha-ṣelav u-mivḥar piyyuṭeihem* (Jerusalem, 1945), 19, quoted in Chazan, *Church, State, and Jews*, 293–94.

48. Abraham Shalom, *Neveh Shalom*, 69b. Cf. Ben-Sasson, "Dor golei Sefarad," 53–54.

Chapter 8. The Royal Court

1. See Évariste Lévi-Provençal, *L'Espagne musulmane au Xème siècle: Institutions et vie sociale* (Paris, 1932), 44: "Le principe de l'autorité absolue du monarque, qui caractérise toute l'histoire musulmane, ne semble avoir subi aucune atteinte en Espagne: à toutes les époques, l'émir d'abord, puis le calife, et même après eux, les petits dynastes provinciaux du XIe siècle, ont joui, au moins en théorie, d'un pouvoir illimité sur toute l'étendue de leurs États, en pleine indépendance de la communauté musulmane établie hors d'Espagne."

2. Ibid., 113–14.

3. MS. BN (Paris) héb. 334, fol. 76r.

4. Lévi-Provençal, *Espagne musulmane*, 99.

5. Ibid., 53.

6. Ibid., 88.

7. Ibid., 89. It may be relevant to note that Ibn Ezra's relative Moses Ibn Ezra (ca. 1055–after 1135) held the title *ṣāḥib al-shurṭa*, or "chief of police," in Granada before he was forced to leave in 1090 when the Jewish community there was destroyed. It is not certain whether he actually held this position in court. See *Encyclopaedia Judaica* (Jerusalem), s.v. "Ibn Ezra, Moses ben Jacob."

8. MS. BN (Paris) héb. 334, fol. 76v.

9. Lévi-Provençal, *Espagne musulmane*, 56.

10. The text is that of the anonymous exegete, published in *'Oṣar ṭov* but the reading followed here is that of MS. BML (Florence) Plut. III.8, fol. 471v. The text of the last line is uncertain. MSS. BML (Florence) Plut. III.8, fol. 472r, BL (London) Add. 26,924, fol. 261r, BL (Oxford) Opp. Add., fol. 24, fol. 165v and SBB (Berlin) Or.Qu. 514, p. 446, all read *ki-reṣono shel melekh*, according to the desire of the king. MS. BP (Parma) 2203 (i.e., the text printed in *'Oṣar ṭov* (1878), p. 27, reads *ve-'amar ka-'asher hayah reṣono la-melekh* or *li-melokh*, which could mean "he spoke to the king according to his desire," or "as it was his desire to become king." The last possibility is the most tantalizing, but the manuscript evidence is too confusing to decide which reading is correct.

11. Such imaginative comments, which depart radically from the conventional understanding of the text's plain meaning and whose exegetical justification is weak at best, were typical of some later thirteenth-century Ashkenazic commentaries, such as those of R. Moses Zaltman, son of Judah the Pietist. See Lange, ed. *Perushei ha-Torah le-R. Yehudah he-Ḥasid*. In the case of "A," it is uncharacteristic.

12. See Chapter 6 above, pp. 122–23.

13. Literally, "both he and she." Esther would make Ahasuerus jealous by her advances to Haman and he would have them both killed.

14. B.T. Megillah 15b.

15. R. Shemariah was very much aware of the pagan nature of Persian society and religion. Cf. his comment to 3:1, quoted below.

16. See Chapter 3 above, pp. 68–72.

17. *Le-hishtaddel be-hishtaddelut hekhraḥi me'od. Hishtaddelut* here seems to be used with the connotation of intercession much like the term *shetadlanut*, an

equivalent from the same root *ShDL* which appears in later East European Jewish sources. See E. Ben-Yehuda, *Millon*, s.v. "*hishtaddelut*," "*shetadlanut*."

18. Cf. the words of R. Eliezer of Modi'im, quoted above: "She made the king jealous of him, and she made the princes jealous of him."

19. See *Sefer Yosippon* (ed. Flusser), 1:53.

20. Gersonides, Lesson 35, p. 46b. Cf. B.T. Megillah 15b, *Panim 'aḥerim A*, 48, Tobias ben Eliezer, *Leqaḥ ṭov*, 106.

21. *'Oṣar ṭov* (1878): 29.

22. See Baer, *Jews in Christian Spain*, index, s.v. "informers." Also David Kaufmann, "Jewish Informers in the Middle Ages," *Jewish Quarterly Review*, o.s. 8 (1895–96): 217–38, 527–28; Francisco de Asis de Bofarull y Sans, "Los judíos malsines," *Boletin de la Real Academia de Buenas Letras de Barcelona* 6 (1911–12): 207–16; Francisco Cantera-Burgos, "Etimologia de la palabra 'malsin,'" *Anales de la Universidad de Madrid: Letras* 4 (1935): 202–3. My thanks to Professor Joseph Shatzmiller for the last reference.

23. According to the rabbinic opinion that Haman and Memucan were one and the same person. See B.T. Megillah 12b. Several other exegetes, e.g., Isaac ben Joseph ha-Kohen, Moses b. Isaac Ḥalayo, Abraham Shalom, Abraham Saba, and Zechariah Saruḳ, also share this opinion. See above, Chapter 1, p. 33.

24. The manuscript reads: "and they will rejoice yet be silent," but this does not make sense in this context, and the words, "they will rejoice" may have been added by association, since they are part of the verse in Ps 107:30.

25. Astruc's use of the Catalan word *juredicció* for authority is another example of his use of vernacular words to clarify his comments.

26. Isaac Arama portrays Haman in much the same way. See above, pp. 70–72.

27. See Americo Castro, *The Structure of Spanish History*, trans. Edmund L. King (Princeton, N.J., 1954), 533, n. 142. Castro's summary is based on the "Cronica del Rey Don Juan, primero de Castilla e de Leon" in *Biblioteca de Autores Españoles*, vol. 68 (Madrid, 1877), 66, which was also consulted.

28. See Baer, *Jews in Christian Spain*, 1:376.

29. See David Knowles, *The Evolution of Medieval Thought* (London, 1962), 192.

30. This is not to suggest that Gersonides' *to'alot* show direct influence of

Aristotle's *Ethics*. Most of them are plain common sense. Rather, what he is doing here and in his other commentaries is in keeping with similar enterprises carried out by his Christian contemporaries and predecessors. Manuals for proper behavior in court were quite common in this period. See, for example, the large number of works written for the guidance of rulers and princes beginning with the *Policraticus* of John of Salisbury (twelfth century). Many other works of a similar nature are cited in Lester K. Born, "The Perfect Prince: A Study in Thirteenth- and Fourteenth-Century Ideals," *Speculum* 3 (1928): 470–504. In the Renaissance such works were even more common. Cf. Baldesar Castiglione, *The Book of the Courtier*, trans. Charles S. Singleton (Garden City, N.Y., 1959). The early Middle Ages has recently been treated by C. Stephen Jaeger, *The Origins of Courtliness: Civilizing Trends and the Formation of Courtly Ideals, 939–1210* (Philadelphia, 1985).

31. Gersonides, Lesson 7, p. 44a.

32. Ibid., Lesson 8, p. 44a–b.

33. Ibid., Lesson 30, p. 46a.

34. Ibid., Lesson 39, p. 47a.

35. Ibid., Lesson 19, p. 45a.

36. Ibid., Lesson 21, p. 45a.

37. Ibid., Lesson 36, p. 47a.

38. Ibid., Lesson 37, p. 47a.

39. Ibid., Lesson 37, p. 47a.

40. Cf. section on court intrigues above, pp. 164–65.

41. Ibid., Lesson 47, p. 48a–b.

42. Ibid., Lesson 45, p. 48a.

43. Ibid., Lesson 46, p. 48a.

44. Ibid., Lesson 27, p. 45b.

45. Joseph Shatzmiller, "Ha-Ralbag u-qehillat 'Oranzh," 123, 126. Shatzmiller also cites examples of advice to courtiers from other biblical commentaries of Gersonides.

46. Gersonides, Lesson 1, p. 44a.

47. Ibid., Lesson 2, p. 44a.

48. Ibid., Lesson 3, p. 44a.

49. Ibid., Lesson 4, p. 44a. The comment of "Ramah," fol. 1v to this verse makes explicit what Gersonides implies: "On the basis of this passage we should question present-day custom whereby men eat at the same table with women."

50. Gersonides, Lesson 5, p. 44a. In general, when not dealing with the figure of Esther, our exegetes reflect the prevailing medieval attitudes to women. Isaac ben Joseph ha-Kohen (fol. 56r), reflecting the rabbinic view, states that woman was created to serve man. Among the attributes that Ibn Ezra associates with women are impulsiveness (*VA*, 27), and timidity (*VA*, 29, reading *mitpaḥedet*, rather than *'einah mitpaḥedet*). Solomon Astruc (p. 216), however, again probably reading the Aragonese situation into his commentary, considers that Vashti shared power with Ahasuerus on an equal footing and that he made a similar offer to Esther.

51. See Haim Beinart, "Demutah shel ha-haṣranut ha-yehudit bi-Sefarad ha-noṣrit," in *Qevuṣot 'illit u-shekhavot manhigot be-toledot Yisra'el u-ve-toledot ha-'ammim: qoveṣ harṣa'ot she-hushme'u ba-kenes ha-'asiri le-'iyyun be-hisṭoryah (Ḥanukkah, 5725)* (Jerusalem, 1966), 55–71.

52. See p. 174 below.

53. See Ben-Sasson, "Dor golei Sefarad," 34. But see Saperstein, *Decoding the Rabbis*, 159–60, in which Isaac ben Yedaiah's serious misgivings about courtiership are expressed.

54. See n. 56 below for court Jews in Moslem Spain; for Christian Spain, see Baer, *Jews in Christian Spain*, 1:282 (re Solomon ibn Adret) 2:91, 114, 126–30 (re Ḥasdai Crescas), and Benzion Netanyahu, *Don Isaac Abravanel*, 3rd ed. (Philadelphia, 1972), 53–56 (re Isaac Abravanel). See also Ben-Sasson, "Dor golei Sefarad," 30–31 (re Joseph ibn Shushan).

55. Halakhic scholars were quite considerate of the special situation that Jewish courtiers found themselves in and went out of their way to lighten their burden of religious observance. An example is the *Ṣeidah la-derekh* (Warsaw, 1879–80) of Menahem ben Aaron ibn Zeraḥ (ca. 1310–85) which is a book of laws, precepts, and homilies written with the Jewish courtier in mind. It was dedicated to Don Samuel Abravanel who had helped R. Menahem escape the persecution in Alcala de Henares in 1368. Cf. also Ben-Sasson, "Dor golei Sefarad," 34, who quotes Joseph Karo's justification for allowing courtiers to follow Gentile practices: "One can say [in justification of this permission] that when it is a question of saving Jews, they have the power to be lenient. For when there are Jews close to the throne they stand in the breach to nullify decrees."

56. For their careers, see Ashtor, *Jews of Moslem Spain*, 1:155–227 (for Ḥasdai), 2:41–189 (for Samuel and his son Joseph).

57. See Abraham Ibn Daud, *The Book of Tradition*, ed. and trans. Gerson D. Cohen (London, 1967), 97–98.

58. Lévi-Provençal, *Espagne musulmane*, 69.

59. Astruc, 223; see p. 186 below.

60. Gersonides, Lesson 27, p. 45b.

61. Ibid., Lesson 18, p. 45a, reading *bi-shelom he-melekh* as in MS. BN (Paris), héb. 248, fol. 163v rather than *be-sibbat ha-melekh*, which is the reading in the printed version.

62. Gersonides, Lesson 17, p. 45a.

63. Ibid., Lesson 15, p. 44b.

64. Ibid., Lesson 15, pp. 44b–45a.

65. Lesson 23, p. 45b.

66. Ibid., Lesson 24.

67. Ibid., Lesson 29, pp. 45b–46a.

68. Ibid., Lesson 12, p. 44b.

69. Ibid., Lesson 44, p. 45a.

70. Alami, *'Iggeret musar*, ed. A. M. Habermann (Jerusalem, 1945–46), 40–51.

71. Ibid., 46. Ben-Sasson, "Dor golei Sefarad," 29, stresses that Alami's tract was an exception to the prevailing mood of unbridled adulation and reverence for the courtier class which prevailed throughout the Middle Ages and beyond.

72. As Ben-Sasson points out, the courtier class was equally revered by kabbalists and rationalists.

73. Cf. the encomium to Isaac ben Yedaiah's ideal courtier, Astrueget, of Carcassonne which bears many similarities (Saperstein, *Decoding the Rabbis*, 161–67).

74. *EKE*, 38; cf. n. 55 above.

75. This is how he explains Gn 39:6, ibid.

76. *Va-yehi 'ish yehudi.*

77. *'Ish yehudi hayah.*

78. Ibid.

79. Ibid., 97.

80. Cf. *Pirqei de-Rabbi 'Eli'ezer* 50, "because he [Mordecai] was a righteous Jew, a direct descendant of the patriarchs, and also of the royal seed and he was engaged [in the study of] the Torah all his days, and not a morsel of unclean food ever entered his mouth, for all these reasons he was called *yehudi* (a Jew).

81. A most glaring case in point might be that of Don Abraham Senior, the most influential Jewish courtier in the final decades before the expulsion, who ended up converting to Christianity rather than give up his position of power and influence. See Baer, *Jews in Christian Spain*, 2:436.

82. *EKE*, 97.

83. It is conceivable that as a model for his portrayal of Mordecai as courtier, Saba may have had his contemporary Don Isaac Abravanel in mind. See also, in this context, pp. 48–49 above for Isaac Arama's portrayal of Mordecai as the ideal leader, in Aristotelian terms.

84. See B.T. Megillah 13b; Targum Rishon to 2:21; *'Abba' Guryon*, 20, *Pirqei de-Rabbi 'Eli'ezer* 50; *Panim 'aḥerim B*, 65–66.

85. *Panim 'aḥerim B*, 65; *'Abba' Guryon*, 20.

86. Arama, fol. 151v; Zechariah, p. 11b.

87. See also Netanyahu, *Don Isaac Abravanel*, 34, 274.

88. See Saperstein, *Decoding the Rabbis*, 159–60.

89. See pp. 158–59 above, where this passage is quoted and discussed.

90. *Neveh Shalom*, 69a.

91. Cf. Gersonides, p. 41a, according to whom Ahasuerus had made a God out of Haman. Were it not for this, "it would not have been proper for him to transgress the king's command in order to deny honor to one of his officers."

92. Cf. Shmuel Shilo, *Dina' de-malkhuta' dina'* (Jerusalem, 1974) for a detailed historical survey of this principle. In the Middle Ages, this principle was considered by all scholars to apply to taxes and duties imposed by the king

and to his direct decrees and by most to matters governing interpersonal relations as well. Ibid., 131–42.

93. Saba, *EKE*, 60, *Yalquṭ Shim'oni* 1054 (p. 1057, col. 1); *Pirqei de-Rabbi 'Eli'ezer* 50; *Panim 'aḥerim A*, 46. Cf. Targum Rishon to 3:2 which mentions a monument set up for Haman.

94. See *'Abba' Guryon*, 22, *sam 'aṣmo 'avodah zarah*; *Esther Rabbah* 7:8: *ve-rasha' zeh 'oseh 'aṣmo 'avodah zarah*.

95. Cf. B.T. Sanhedrin 61b.

96. Based on a statement in the Talmud (B.T. Berakhot 7b) that "it is permissible to initiate quarrels with wicked people," Shalom's homily tries to explain Mordecai's motives for refusing to bow down to Haman. For a summary, see Davidson, *Abraham Shalom*, 6–7.

97. *EKE*, 60; cf. *Panim 'aḥerim B*, 66, *Yalquṭ Shim'oni* 1054.

98. The attitude in the Talmud is no less respectful. Cf. the blessing one is to say upon seeing a Gentile king, B.T. Berakhot 58a.

99. E.g., Joseph Kara, Ibn Ezra, Abraham Shalom, Joseph Naḥmias, and others.

100. *Neveh Shalom*, 69a.

101. For other reflexes of Pere's reign in Astruc's commentary, see Chapter 5 above, pp. 112–13.

102. Baer, *Jews in Christian Spain*, 2:32.

Chapter 9. The Jews and the Monarchy

1. For modern exegetes, who consider the work a historical novella, this is less of a problem, since the transformations in Ahasuerus's character can be explained on literary grounds.

2. Comment to 1:1. Cf. B.T. Megillah 11a.

3. Rashi to 7:3: *Let my life be spared.* that I not be slain on the thirteenth of Adar, the day on which *you* decreed a decree of death against my people and my kindred [emphasis added].

4. Ibid.

5. Kara, 3:88. His anger caused him to act too quickly against Vashti (to 1:12).

6. Ibid., "It is not becoming even for a commoner to show his wife's beauty in public, even more so for a king" (1:11).

7. Kara, 3:91 (to 3:11, 4:8).

8. Ibid., 3:92 (to 4:14).

9. Comment to 4:14, see *'Oṣar ṭov* (1878): 26–27.

10. Zechariah, 12a, in Hebrew: *ʿalah be-libbo she-hu' maspiq be-ʿaṣmo.*

11. Ibid. "Then he said that Haman achieved greatness when the king commanded that all of his servants who were standing at the king's gate should bow down and prostrate themselves before Haman, and Mordecai refused to bow down and prostrate himself. This caused Haman to become angry with him and for this reason he desired to destroy, to slay, and to annihilate all of the Jews, and our sages said "to destroy" [refers to] their law [= religion], "to slay" their body, "to annihilate" their money, for this is the whole man, i.e., the soul, the body, and money which holds the two together (*ha-maʿamid ḥibburam*), as I explained with regard to the word *yequm* ["as the sages said, 'and every living thing (*yequm*) that followed them' [literally, "that was at their feet"] (Dt 11:6)—this refers to man's wealth. And why is it called *yequm*? Because it stands him up on his feet; ibid., 3a]. Now note that at first Haman only sought to destroy, i.e., to destroy their law as it says, Haman sought to destroy all the Jews' (3:6)." Zechariah is not being altogether accurate here because 3:6 only says that Haman's aim was to destroy (*le-hashmid*) the Jews. When he spoke to the king in 3:9, he used the word *le-'abbedam*, which according to Zechariah [and others, see below] refers to the Jews' money. I was unable to locate the rabbinic sources Zechariah refers to here. His may be the only witness to these sources.

12. It should be noted that although Zechariah also understands *le-'abbedam* as referring to the wealth of the Jews, he, unlike several of his compatriots, does not use this point in order to defend Ahasuerus's reputation. Similarly, he understands the phrase "and the people to do with as you please" as giving Haman permission to do whatever he wished. Again this contrasts with the interpretations of several other Spanish exegetes who used this phrase to defend the king. See below.

13. Cf. Zechariah, 12a. Zechariah attributes this interpretation to the sages. I was unable to trace his source. See note 11 above. This is a good example of the medieval appropriation and elaboration of a rabbinic source. The rabbinic comment must have referred to the words in 3:13, based on the general principle that, if the text uses a series of synonyms, each one must have a different connotation. The medievals picked up on this and applied the rabbinic interpretation of *le-'abbed* in 3:13 to *le-'abbedam* in 3:9 and then used it for their own purposes.

14. NJV translates: "for the adversary is not worthy of the king's trouble."

15. See, e.g., MS. BL (London) Add. 26,924 (i.e., one of the second group of manuscripts of "A'"s commentary).

16. Ibid., 217; cf. Baron, *History*, 11:279, for an interesting medieval parallel in which the Emperor Maximilian of Austria allowed the Jews to be expelled from Styria, Carinthia, and Carniola in exchange for a 16,000 pound indemnity for the loss of Jewish taxation. See also Solomon Ibn Verga, *Shevet Yehudah*, ed. Azriel Shohat (Jerusalem, 1946–47), 54, where Gonzalo Martinez makes a similar offer to King Alfonso XI. This passage is discussed in greater detail below, pp. 192–93.

17. On the practice of bribery by Jews in the Middle Ages, see Parkes, *Jew*, 149–54, esp. 151–54.

18. For a summary of expulsions of Jewish communities in the later Middle Ages, see Baron, *History*, 11:209–11 (England), 214–25 (France), 236–43 (Spain), 246–49 (Portugal), 271–80 (Holy Roman Empire).

19. See Baron, *History*, 11:193–201. Cf. Schwarzfuchs, "Expulsion of the Jews from France," 482–89, who attributes the expulsion from France in 1306 to Philip the Fair's financial policies.

20. So RSV; NJV reads: "The money and the people are yours to do with as you see fit."

21. B.T. Sanhedrin 105b.

22. As is mentioned in Ezra chap. 1 and 6, apparently referring to Cyrus and Darius.

23. B.T. ʿAvodah Zarah 10b.

24. B.T. Megillah 11a.

25. See B.T. Megillah 12a; also Ginzberg, *Legends*, 4:370, 6:454, and sources quoted there.

26. For a fuller discussion of this passage, see above, pp. 136–39.

27. See Yosef H. Yerushalmi, *The Lisbon Massacre of 1506 and the Royal Image in the Shebet Yehudah*, Hebrew Union College Annual Supplements, no. 1 (Cincinnati, 1976), 35–66.

28. Ibn Verga, *Sheveṭ Yehudah*, 70.

29. Yerushalmi, *Lisbon Massacre*, 38–39.

30. Ibid., 42.

31. Pp. 53–54.

32. See Hillgarth, *Spanish Kingdoms*, 1:339–42; Baer, *Jews in Christian Spain*, 1:356–59.

33. Cf. Targum Sheni, to Esther 3:8.

34. Cf. *Esther Rabbah* 7:13.

35. This is Ibn Verga's censored version. He fails to mention that Alfonso ordered that the Jews be imprisoned and arrests were actually carried out in some cities. See Baer, *Jews in Christian Spain*, 1:357.

36. Yerushalmi, *Lisbon Massacre*, 35–36.

37. It will be recalled that two contemporaries, Joseph Ḥayyun and Zechariah ben Saruḳ did not hesitate to do so.

38. *Mishnah*, trans. Herbert Danby (Oxford, 1933), 447.

39. See, e.g., Isaac Abravanel, *Naḥalat 'Avot* (New York, 1953), 71, who warns against the sins of court life. The comment of Isaac b. Yedaiah is of special interest because it is given from the point of view of the courtier rather than the preacher or moralist and warns of the dangers that court life entails. See Saperstein, *Decoding the Rabbis*, 159–60. See also the discussion on courtiers, above, pp. 172–77.

40. Joseph Naḥmias, *Peirush Pirqei 'Avot*, ed. Moshe Aryeh Bamberger (Paks, Romania, 1906–7; repr. in *Peirushei Rabbi Yosef ben Naḥmias* [Jerusalem, 1983?]), 5b; quoted in Benzion Dinur, ed., *Yisra'el ba-golah*, 2nd ed., 2 vols. in 10 (Tel-Aviv, 1958–72), vol. 2, bk. 1, pp. 279–80.

41. *Mishnah* (Danby), 448.

42. See *Peirushei Rabbeinu Yonah mi-Geirondi ʿal massekhet 'Avot*, ed. Mosheh Shelomoh Kasher and Yaʿaqov Yehoshuaʿ Blekharovits (Jerusalem, 1968–69), 22; quoted in Bernard Septimus, "Piety and Power in Thirteenth-Century Catalonia," in *Studies in Medieval Jewish History and Literature*, ed. Isadore Twersky (Cambridge, Mass., 1979), 213.

43. On the almost universal good opinion that the Spanish Jews had of the courtier class and the beneficial functions it fulfilled for the community, see Ben-Sasson, "Dor golei Sefarad," 28–34. See also pp. 172–77 above.

44. As does Septimus, "Piety and Power," 212.

45. Ibid., 213.

46. See pp. 116–19.

47. See pp. 117–20 above.

48. B.T. Megillah 16b.

Concluding Remarks

1. *Peshaṭ* (plain or contextual meaning), *Remez* (philosophical or allegorical interpretation), *Derash* (midrashic interpretation) and *Sod* (mystical interpretation).

2. On the whole question of PaRDeS and the fourfold interpretation of Scripture among the Jews, see Peretz Sandler, "Li-ve'ayat Pardes ve-ha-shiṭah ha-merubba'at," in *Sefer 'Averbakh* [Auerbach] ed. A. Biram, Pirsumei ha-Ḥevrah le-ḥeqer ha-Miqra' be-Yisra'el, 1, (Jerusalem, 1955), 222–35. Sandler demonstrates that even the *Zohar* is not consistent in its terminology so that there was certainly no fully formed system prior to the *Zohar*. He also argues (p. 229) contra Wilhelm Bacher, "L'exégèse biblique dans le Zohar," *Revue des études juives* 22 (1891): 33–46, that one should not try to see this phenomenon as totally Christian-influenced since the Christians themselves were not entirely consistent with regard to the number of senses of interpretation they postulated or with regard to their terminology. Gershom Scholem, "The Meaning of the Torah in Jewish Mysticism," in his *On the Kabbalah and its Symbolism*, trans. Ralph Manheim (New York, 1965), 61–62, tends to agree with Bacher, arguing that the simultaneous appearance of the idea in three kabbalistic authors, all living in Christian Spain strongly suggests that they were working with the Christian idea of the fourfold interpretation of Scripture which they had adopted. Cf. also Amos Funkenstein, "Naḥmanides' Symbolical Reading of History," in *Studies in Jewish Mysticism*, ed. Joseph Dan and Frank Talmage (Cambridge, Mass., 1982), 133–42, who discusses Naḥmanides' levels of interpretation. In the most recent contribution to this topic, A. van der Heide comes to the same conclusion as Sandler, although following a different line of reasoning. Heide argues that several threefold systems of interpretation were already current in philosophical circles and subsequently, with the rise of the kabbalistic movement, the need was felt among the kabbalists for a fourth mystical sense. He sees the Christian influence as marginal, providing the form of the theory but not its contents. See his "PARDES," 147–59, esp. 155–56. It is puzzling to note that despite the efforts of Bacher, Sandler, Scholem, and Heide, the term *PaRDeS* is still used, even in scholarly circles to give a comprehensive definition of the concerns of traditional Jewish exegesis (ibid., 148, 153–54), the claim even being made that the four terms were already in use in rabbinic literature. For a case in point, see Aryeh Grabois, "L'Exégèse rabbinique," in *Le Moyen Âge et la Bible*, ed. Pierre Riché and Guy Lobrichon

(Paris, 1984), 234, and the article by Grabois on the Bible in the *Dictionary of the Middle Ages*, ed. Joseph R. Strayer, 13 vols. (New York, 1982–1989), s.v. "Bible," 2:212.

3. This is in contrast to some modern exegetes who subordinate Esther to Mordecai or even place her in a completely negative light. See White, "Esther," 165–66. Much of the discussion about Esther focuses on her being a Jew in a Gentile environment and the problems this raises. It is her Jewishness rather than her sex which is the issue. Even Vashti does not fare badly with our exegetes. Were it not for considerations of state and the need for the king to save face before the populace, most would have said that she did not deserve to be punished for her defiant action.

4. Uriel Simon, *Four Approaches*, has analyzed four distinct medieval approaches to the Psalms. His study should be extended into the later Middle Ages and his approach applied to other biblical books.

5. While some prominent exegetes of the late Middle Ages have received monographic treatment, by and large these works have used their biblical commentaries as sources from which to glean information concerning their philosophy or views on various subjects. Their exegesis has not been studied per se. See, for example, the works by Charles Touati on Gersonides, Sarah Heller-Wilensky on Isaac Arama, and Benzion Netanyahu on Isaac Abravanel. But this state of affairs is also changing. See the recent article by Elliot Wolfson on Naḥmanides' kabbalistic hermeneutic, "By Way of Truth," and Herring's translation and study of Joseph ibn Kaspi's *Gevia' kesef*, an example of philosophical biblical commentary.

6. A case in point is Beattie, *Ruth*. In Simon's work, which is exemplary, the primary focus is on Abraham Ibn Ezra. Talmage's *David Kimhi* provides a model for future studies of individual exegetes.

7. Jeremy Cohen, "*Be Fertile and Increase*" is a most recent attempt to do just that. There are a few others, but as I said in the introduction, the territory is largely uncharted.

Appendix I

1. Ahrend, *Commentaire*, 184, concurs, although he gives no indication of having studied the question anew.

2. See David Rosin, *Rabbi Samuel ben Meir als Schrifterklärer* (Breslau, 1880), 73–74; Abraham Berliner, *Peleiṭat Soferim* (Breslau, 1872): 21; Samuel Poznanski, "Mavo," xxx; Salomon Buber, ed., *Peirush R. Yosef Qara' 'al Megillat 'Eikhah* (Breslau, 1900), 12–13, n. 7; Eppenstein, *Peirushei R. Yosef*

Qara', 10; Littmann, *Kara*, 8. Of these scholars, Rosin, Buber, Littmann, and Berliner identify these commentaries as definitely being Kara's. Poznanski seems to agree as well. Eppenstein refuses to commit himself and does not admit to the existence of an identified commentary to Esther by Joseph Kara.

3. Of course, it is also possible that the attribution in the Hamburg MS. is mistaken or that another R. Joseph we are not familiar with is the author.

4. Therefore, Ahrend's assertion, *Commentaire*, 184, apparently based on those of previous scholars, that the material published by Geiger is all attributed to Rashbam needs to be revised.

5. Dr. Malachi Beit-Arie, of the Jewish National and University Library in Jerusalem offered his opinion that the Warsaw (now Jerusalem) manuscript may be of Byzantine provenance and that this might have some relation to the author's origin. But there is no other evidence on which to base this assumption.

6. Once in the Esther commentary itself (see above p. 5) and twice in the two versions of his autobibliography, *Qevuṣat kesef* (See Mesch, *Studies*, 37). For the Hebrew version of the Parma recension, see Kaspi, *'Asarah kelei kesef*, 1:xxiv; for the Munich recension see Ernest Renan, *Les écrivains juifs français du XIVe siècle* (Paris, 1893; repr. Westmead, Farnborough, Hants., 1969), 543.

7. Touati, *Pensée*, 43–44; Feldman, introd. to *Wars*, 4. See also Joseph Shatzmiller, "Ha-Ralbag u-qehillat 'Oranzh bi-yemei ḥayyav," *Meḥqarim be-toledot 'am Yisra'el ve-'Ereṣ-Yisra'el* 2 (1972): 111–26.

8. Shatzmiller, "Ha-Ralbag u-qehillat 'Oranzh," 122.

9. See J. Shatzmiller, "'Od 'al ha-Ralbag u-qehillat 'Oranzh bi-yemei ḥayyav," *Meḥqarim be-toledot 'am Yisra'el ve-'Ereṣ-Yisra'el* 3 (1974): 141–42.

10. The Torah, Early Prophets, Isaiah (not extant), Proverbs, Job, Song of Songs, Ruth, Ecclesiastes, Esther, Daniel, Ezra-Nehemiah, and Chronicles.

11. For a list and discussion of Gersonides works, see Touati, *Pensée*, 49–82; Feldman, introduction to *Wars*, 8–30.

12. I would like to thank Professor Joseph Hacker of the Hebrew University of Jerusalem for the references to the works of Isaac ben Ḥayyim.

13. The name Ḥadidah appears several times in the collection of documents on Spanish Jewry edited by Fritz (Yitzhak) Baer, *Die Juden im Christlichen Spanien*, 2 vols. (Berlin, 1929–36; repr. Westmead, Farnborough, Hants., 1970): 1:1005, 2:447, 474–75. Also ibid., 2:425, Moses and Isaac Hadida, two brothers of Toledo. Ḥadidah also mentions his teacher Shem Ṭov. There were several famous people by that name in Spain in the late fourteenth and early fifteenth century, and the name was quite common in general in Spain.

14. In commenting on 9:26 he says that one of the ways of finding out about terrible events is through a person who lived through them and then he quotes "non vaias a pariente si non a sabiente," or "do not go to a relative but to one who knows." The possibility that this is a scribal addition cannot be ruled out but seems unlikely.

15. One possible candidate for authorship is Rabbi Mattityah Ha-Yitzhari, a scholar who lived in Spain in the late fourteenth and early fifteenth centuries and participated in the Tortosa disputation. Concerning him, see Adolf Neubauer, "R. Mattitya Ha-Yiṣhari," *Revue des études juives* 9 (1884): 116–19, and the introduction by Dov Rappel to his edition of Mattityah's *Peirush 'Alef-Beit (Ps 119)* (Tel Aviv, 1978), 9–11. He is known to have written commentaries on Mishnah 'Avot and Psalm 119, a book of sermons for Sabbaths and festivals and a supercommentary on Ibn Ezra's Torah commentary. However, there is no firm evidence to link him to this commentary and we shall continue to refer to the author as "Ramah."

16. E.g., he uses the term *ḥaluqqah* ("category") at 2:10 and *to'elet be-middot* ("a lesson in ethics") at 2:11, a term which he probably borrowed from Gersonides.

17. Sources for Arama's biography are listed in Sarah H. Wilensky, *R. Yiṣḥaq 'Aramah u-mishnato* (Jerusalem, 1956), 26, n. 30.

18. See the colophon at the end of *Ṣeror ha-mor* to Be-midbar, Manor, "Le-toldotav," 230, and Gross, "Rabbi 'Avraham Saba', 211, n. 30; apparently, he wrote most of his commentary on Be-midbar in Alcazarquivir and completed it in Fez.

19. *Ṣeror ha-mor* has been published several times, the last complete edition being Warsaw, 1879; repr. Tel Aviv, 1974–75. The first volume of a new edition by Yosef 'Alnaqavah has recently appeared (Moshav Gedid, 1985–).

20. *'Eshkol ha-kofer 'al Megillat Rut*, ed. Eliezer Segal (Bartfeld, 1907); *'Eshkol ha-kofer 'al Megillat 'Ester*, ed. Eliezer Segal (Drohobycz, 1903); both recently reprinted (Jerusalem, 1980–81). The commentary on Lamentations is no longer extant.

21. The introduction to which is found in MS. Sassoon 919, pp. 85–89.

22. On which, see Avraham Gross, "Peirush ha-tefilot 'al derekh ha-sod ha-meyuḥas le-Rabbi 'Avraham Saba'," *'Asuppot* 1 (1986–87): 189–97.

23. See Elijah Mizraḥi, *Mayim 'amuqqim* (Berlin, 1778; repr. Jerusalem, 1969–70), responsa no. 25, 26, pp. 14b–15a, where two letters by one Abraham Saba are addressed to Mizraḥi. Manor, "Le-toldotav," 221–24 supports this

identification, and Gross, "R. 'Avraham Saba'," 213–14, concurs, and even brings additional proof to support the hypothesis that Saba lived in Adrianople toward the end of his life.

24. See Joseph Sambari, *Divrei Yosef*, Qunṭresim, meqorot u-meḥqarim, 54 (Jerusalem, 1981), 143; Manor, "Le-toldatav," 224–26; Gross, "R. 'Avraham Saba'," 214–15.

25. Abraham Ibn Ezra does refer to the Karaites in one place in his commentary (at 9:31): "they have assumed for themselves and for their descendants the obligation of the fasts. According to most this refers to the Fast of Esther. And the *deniers* [i.e., the Karaites] said that the text is referring to the three days that they fasted in Nisan and all of Israel should always fast on these days." But see above, chapter 6, n. 15.

Appendix II

1. Ibn Ezra understood the word to mean city, following the Arabic *madina*. On the problems created for Ibn Ezra by this comment and reaction to it from other medieval exegetes, see Chapter 5 above.

2. Immanuel, Commentary on Esther, MS. BP (Parma) 2843 (De Rossi 615), fol. 182r. Immanuel here distinguishes between *mikhtav* ("alphabet") and *ketav* ("script") the latter having developed under local influence. (It should be noted that at one place in this passage Immanuel uses *ketav* to mean "alphabet." This may have been a scribal error or an inconsistency on the part of the author.) This terminology may have been unique to Immanuel. Professor Chaim Rabin of the Hebrew University, Jerusalem, has informed me that there exists no lexicon of Hebrew linguistic terms for the Middle Ages and that very little was written by Jews on such linguistic matters.

3. Perhaps one should read *'arim* ("cities") instead of *'araṣot*, although it is difficult to imagine how the words might have been interchanged.

4. Dante Alighieri, *De vulgari eloquentia*, ed. Aristide Marigo, vol. 6 of *Opere di Dante*, ed. Michele Barbi, (Florence, 1938), 1.8.6, pp. 52–56.

5. E.g., Alfred Ewert, "Dante's Theory of Language," *Modern Language Review* 35 (1940): 358: "I can find no source for the account of the diversification of tongues in Europe here given by Dante." See also J. Cremona, "Dante's Views on Language," in *The Mind of Dante*, ed. U. Limentani (Cambridge, 1965), 154; Gustav Gröber, *Grundriß der Romanischen Philologie*, 2nd ed., 2 vols. (Strassburg, 1904–6), 1:5–6; B. Terracini, "Natura ed origine del linguaggio umano nel 'De Vulgari Eloquentia,'" in his *Pagine e appunti di linguistica storica* (Florence, 1957), 237–46; Bruno Nardi, *Dante e la cultura medievale*, 2nd ed.

(Bari, 1949), 217–47. The most comprehensive work on theories of language development throughout history is Arno Borst, *Der Turmbau von Babel: Geschichte der Meinungen über Ursprung und Vielfalt der Sprachen und Völker*, 4 vols. in 6 (Stuttgart, 1957–63). On Dante, see ibid., 869–77.

6. For a well-reasoned appraisal of the relationship between the two poets, see Umberto Cassuto, *Dante e Manoello* (Florence, 1921); Hebrew version: *Danṭeh ve-ʿImmanuʾel ha-Romi* (Jerusalem, 1965). Cassuto argues convincingly that the two never knew each other, but that Immanuel borrowed directly from Dante and other Italian poets.

7. Immanuel, *Commento . . . al capitolo I della Genesi*, 22, 27, 38, 39–40.

BIBLIOGRAPHY

MEDIEVAL COMMENTARIES ON THE BOOK OF ESTHER IN PRINT AND IN MANUSCRIPT*

This is the first of a projected series of bibliographies of medieval Jewish biblical exegesis. An attempt has been made to be as complete as possible in this listing, except for the commentaries of Rashi, Abraham Ibn Ezra, and Gersonides. Because of the large number of manuscripts for each of these commentaries, (over 100 for Rashi, over thirty each for the other two) listing them would have swollen the bibliography considerably. I have listed for these three exegetes first editions and manuscripts consulted for research on this book. I consider this listing to be preliminary and would welcome additions and corrections from interested scholars.

In this bibliography and elsewhere in this book, a slight deviation from common manuscript citation practice has been made. The manuscripts are listed by depository library (usually abbreviated) followed by city. This form of citation is more accurate and facilitates locating and ordering the manuscripts by any interested party. I hope that this innovation will be well-received in scholarly circles.

The numbers at the end of the manuscript entries refer to the

* The author gratefully acknowledges the financial support of the Social Sciences and Humanities Research Council of Canada which enabled him to carry out the research for this bibliography. He would also like to express his thanks to Binyamin Richler and the staff of the Institute of Microfilmed Hebrew Manuscripts at the Jewish National and University Library, Jerusalem, for their assistance.

accession numbers of the Institute of Microfilmed Hebrew Manuscripts at the Jewish National and University Library, Jerusalem. Manuscript catalogue numbers or page numbers are supplied when available to direct the reader to additional information. The characterizations of the anonymous manuscripts are impressionistic and not meant to be definitive. Similarly, the information concerning dates and provenance are taken from the catalogue of the Institute and are not based on an independent paleographical study of the manuscripts. Unless otherwise indicated, all items were examined and verified by the author.

MANUSCRIPT CATALOGUES

BA (Milan) = Bernheimer, Carlo. *Codices hebraici Bybliothecae Ambrosianae*. Florence, 1933.

BA (Vatican) = Cassuto, Umberto. *Codices Vaticani Hebraici: Codices 1–115*. Vatican City, 1956.

BC (Verona) = Tamani, G. "Manoscritti Ebraici nella Biblioteca Comunale di Verona." *Rivista degli Studi Orientali* 45 (1970):217–43.

BL (London) = Margoliouth, G. *Catalogue of the Hebrew and Samaritan Manuscripts in the British Museum*. 4 vols. London, 1899–1935.

BL (Oxford) = Neubauer, Adolph, and A. E. Cowley. *Catalogue of the Hebrew Manuscripts in the Bodleian Library and in the College Libraries of Oxford*. 2 vols. Oxford, 1886–1906.

BR (Leiden) = Steinschneider, Moritz. *Catalogus Codicum Hebraeorum Bibliothecae Academiae Lugduno-Batavae*. Leiden, 1858.

BS (Munich) = Steinschneider, Moritz. *Die Hebräischen Handschriften der K. Hof- und Staatsbibliothek in München*. Munich, 1875.

CUL (Cambridge) = (1) Schiller-Szinessy, S.M. *Catalogue of the Hebrew Manuscripts Preserved in the University Library Cambridge*. Vol. 1. Cambridge, 1876. No more published.
(2) Loewe, Herbert. *Handlist of Hebrew and Samaritan Manuscripts in*

the Library of the University of Cambridge. Revised and completed by D. Pearson and Raphael Loewe. Cambridge, 1927 (unpublished typescript).

IK (Vienna) = Schwarz, Arthur Zacharias. *Die hebräischen Handschriften in Österreich [ausserhalb der Nationalbibliothek in Wien]*. Part 1. Leipzig, 1931.

JC (London) = Neubauer, Adolph. *Catalogue of the Hebrew Manuscripts in the Jews' College, London*. Oxford, 1886. Repr. Westmead, Farnborough, Hants., 1969.

JTS (Breslau) = Loewinger, D. S., and B. D. Weinryb. *Catalogue of the Hebrew Manuscripts in the Library of the Juedisch-Theologisches Seminar in Breslau*. Publication of the Leo Baeck Institute. New York, 1965.

Montefiore = Hirschfeld, Hartwig. *Descriptive Catalogue of the Hebrew MSS. of the Montefiore Library*. London, 1904. Repr. Westmead, Farnborough, Hants., 1969.

ÖN (Vienna) = Schwarz, Arthur Zacharias. *Die hebräischen Handschriften der Nationalbibliothek in Wien*. Vienna, 1925.

SBB (Berlin) = Steinschneider, Moritz. *Die Handschriften Verzeichnisse der Königlichen Bibliothek zu Berlin: Verzeichniss der hebraeischen Handschriften*. 2 vols. Berlin, 1878.

SUB (Frankfurt a.M.) = Roth, Ernst, and Leo Prijs. *Hebräische Handschriften [der Staats- und Universitätsbibliothek Frankfurt am Main]*. Verzeichnis der orientalischen Handschriften in Deutschland, vol. 6, Hebräische Handschriften, Part 1a. Wiesbaden, 1982.

SUB (Hamburg) = (1) Steinschneider, Moritz. *Catalog der hebraïschen Handschriften in der Stadtbibliothek zu Hamburg und der sich anschliessenden in anderen Sprachen*. Hamburg, 1878.
(2) Roth, Ernst, and Hans Striedl. *Die Handschriften der Sammlung H. B. Levy an der Staats- und Universitätsbibliothek Hamburg*. Verzeichnis der orientalischen Handschriften in Deutschland, vol. 6 Hebräische Handschriften, Part 3. Wiesbaden, 1984.

Sassoon = Sassoon, David Solomon. *Ohel Dawid: Descriptive Catalogue of the Hebrew and Samaritan Manuscripts in the Sassoon Library*. 2 vols. London, 1932.

TC (Cambridge) = Loewe, Herbert. *Catalogue of the Manuscripts in the Hebrew Character Collected and Bequeathed to Trinity College Library by the Late William Aldis Wright*. Cambridge, 1926.

UB (Erlangen) = Striedl, Hans and Ernst Roth. *Hebräische Handschriften*. Verzeichnis der Orientalischen Handschriften in Deutschland, vol. 6, Part 2. Wiesbaden, 1965.

THE COMMENTARIES

Anonymous. MS. BA (Milan) G.7 sup., fols. 37r–38r (Bernheimer 41/2) (no. 12272)
fourteenth century; quotes Ibn Ezra; includes *gemaṭria*.

Anonymous (Ashkenazic). MS. BA (Vatican) Ebr. 48, fols. 117v–119v (Cassuto, p. 70) (no. 165)
fourteenth century.

Anonymous. MS. BA (Vatican) Ebr. 72, fol. 126v (Cassuto, p. 108) (no. 189)
fifteenth century; only until 1:10; ascribed to Solomon ibn Parḥon.

Anonymous (Florilegium). In *Binyamin Ze'ev yiṭraf: Notes from Various Authors on Psalms, Job, the Megilloth (except Ruth) and Ezra*, edited by H. J. Mathews, 42–43. Amsterdam, 1878 (originally published in *Israelietische Letterbode* 4 (1878–79): 40–41); transcription of MS. BL (London) Add. 24,896, fols. 418r–v (Margoliouth 237/24) (no. 5428)
fourteenth century, clear Spanish cursive.

Anonymous (Karaite). MS. BL (London) Or. 2520, fols. 175r–v (Margoliouth 328a, 26) (no. 6295)
fifteenth century; fragment in Judeo-Arabic on 2:9.

Anonymous. MS. BL (London) Or. 3661, fols. 3r–10v (Margoliouth 4:154 (supplementary list)) (no. 6413)
from 5:13 to end; quotes Ibn Ezra.

Anonymous (Persian). MS. BL (London) Or. 10577, fols. 136r–v (Gaster 1082) (no. 7400)
Hebrew-Persian glossary; fifteenth to sixteenth century; only to 1:13.

Anonymous (Arabic). MS. BL (Oxford) Heb.c.19, fols. 123r–v (Neubauer 2628/32) (no. 21621; photo no. 3316)
Arabic glossary covering 1:3–9:29; possibly eleventh century or may be late, i.e., post-medieval (Yemenite?).

Anonymous (Arabic). MS. BL (Oxford) Heb.f.56, fol. 103r (Neubauer 2821/31 (photo no. 3389)
fragment; glossary in Arabic on 5:2–10:3; square script; very legible.

Anonymous (Ashkenazic). MS. BL (Oxford) Opp. 27 (Ol. 256), fols. 259r–262r (Neubauer 268/4e) (no. 16736)

Anonymous (Ashkenazic). MS. BL (Oxford) Opp. 27 (Ol. 256), fols. 262r–263v (Neubauer 268/4e) (no. 16736)

Anonymous (Ashkenazic). MS. BL (Oxford) Opp. 31 (Ol. 260), fols. 79v–81r (Neubauer 271/3a) (no. 16739)
fourteenth to fifteenth centuries.

Anonymous (Ashkenazic). MS. BL (Oxford) Opp. 31 (Ol. 260), fols. 118r–v (Neubauer 271/7) (no. 16739)
fourteenth to fifteenth century; scattered comments; quotes *ḥasid.*

Anonymous (Ashkenazic). MS. BL (Oxford) Opp. 720 (Ol. 83), fols. 89r–90r (Neubauer 1576) (no. 16944)
fifteenth century; scattered comments; see Eleazar ben Judah, supposed author.

Anonymous. MS. BN (Paris) héb. 152, fols. 320r–332r (Zotenberg, p. 16) (no. 4139)
dated 1533, Saffrou; difficult to read; may be late (i.e., post-medieval).

Anonymous. MS. BN (Paris) héb. 249, fols. 184v–208r (Zotenberg, p. 32) (no. 4274) dated 1345; *peshaṭ* commentary; quotes Rashi, Ibn Ezra; 191r–192v missing; cut off near end.

Anonymous (Glossary). MS. BN (Paris) héb. 301, fols. 124r–126r (Zotenberg, p. 39–40) (no. 4319)
thirteenth century; French glossary on the Bible in Hebrew script.

Anonymous (Glossary). In Meyer Lambert and Louis Brandin, *Glossaire hébreu-français du XIIIe siècle: recueil de mots hébreux bibliques avec traduction française* (Paris, 1905), 55–56.
transcription of MS. BN (Paris) héb. 302, fols. 31v–32r (Zotenberg, p. 40) (no. 4320)
dated 1240; French glossary on the Bible in Hebrew script; possible author: Joseph ben Samson?

Anonymous. MS. BN (Paris) héb. 334, fols. 198v–204r (Zotenberg, p. 45; not mentioned in the catalogue) (no. 2937)
lengthy glosses on the chapter on Esther in *Pirqei de-Rabbi Eliezer*; begins with 1:19; quotes Joseph Kara, Eleazar ha-Qalir (יקר ימיני בדת ימין רוכץ; 199r); includes comments attributed to Judah he-Ḥasid.

Anonymous (Midrashic). MS. BN (Paris) héb. 831, fols. 418–432v (Zotenberg, p. 141) (no. 30737)
fifteenth to sixteenth century, Spanish; possibly post-medieval.

Anonymous (Midrashic). MS. BNU (Strasbourg) 101/10 (no. 4375; photo no. 957.10)
fourteenth to fifteenth century; Genizah fragments on 1:13–2:14.

Anonymous (Midrashic). "Peirush 'Ester le-fi peirush raboteinu za"l." MS. BP (Parma) 1888, fols. 20r–25r (De Rossi 1150/2) (no. 13050)
fifteenth century, Italian; ends in the middle of chapter 8.

Anonymous (Midrashic). MS. BP (Parma) 1895, fol. [1]r–[52]v (De Rossi 520/1) (no. 13052)
sixteenth century (possibly post-medieval); until 8:16.

Anonymous (Glossary). MS. BP (Parma) 2391, fols. 8v–9v (De Rossi 1047/1) (no. 13256)
fifteenth to sixteenth century, Italian; meanings of difficult words

Anonymous (Glossary). MS. BP (Parma) 2780 (De Rossi 637), fols. 40r–41r (no. 13629)
fourteenth century; *le'azim* in Old French with philological notes.

Anonymous (Midrashic). "Midrash Megillah." MS. BP (Parma) 2868, fols. 163r–165v (De Rossi 390) (no. 13762).

Anonymous. MS. BP (Parma) 2921, fols. 76v–78r (De Rossi 389/4) (no. 13689)
fifteenth century; Masoretic notes.

Anonymous (Glossary). MS. BP (Parma) 2924, fols. 42v–44r (De Rossi 60) (no. 13692)
dated 1279, Taillebourg; *le'azim* in Old French.

Anonymous (Midrashic). MS. BP (Parma) 3136, fols. 39v–47r (De Rossi 405) (no. 13878)
fourteenth century, Ashkenazic.

Anonymous (Midrashic, Judeo-German). "Peirush 'Ester." MS. BP (Parma) 2510, fols. 226r–245r (De Rossi, Jud. Germ. 1) (no. 14079)
fifteenth century, Ashkenazic.

Anonymous. MS. BS (Munich) Cod. Hebr. 5, fols. 129v–132v (vol. 2) (Steinschneider, p. 2) (no. 2526)
dated 1233; Northern French; interpolations (mainly midrashic) in Rashi's commentary not mentioned in the catalogue.

Anonymous (Midrashic). MS. BS (Munich) Cod. Hebr. 5, fols. 149v (= 150v)–152v (= 153v) (vol. 2) (no. 2526)
dated 1233; Northern French.

Anonymous. MS. CUL (Cambridge) T-S F I(2)/24 (no. 18912; photo no. 2329)
Genizah fragment; no complete comments.

Anonymous (Midrashic). MS. CUL (Cambridge) T-S F I(2)/67 (photo no. 2329)
Genizah fragment from chapters 1 and 2.

Anonymous. MS. JC (London) 6, fols. 58r–62v (no. 4675)
fourteenth to fifteenth century; marginal notes to another anonymous commentary ("A"); see below.

Anonymous. MS. JTSA (New York) L1052 (Mic. 1183), fol. 130r–v (no. 24255)
fifteenth century, Spanish; a few scattered comments; see Appendix I (pp. 222–23) for discussion.

Anonymous. MS. JTSA (New York) L1065, fols. 209r–233r (no. 24267)
seventeenth century; definitely late, but quotes among others Shemariah ben Elijah; very difficult cursive script.

Anonymous (Judeo-Arabic). In *Ḥamesh Megillot ʿim peirushim ʿatiqim*, ed. Joseph Kafiḥ, 323–25 (Jerusalem, 1961–62); see also pp. 299–300.
dated 1482; Yemenite; transcription of MS. Kafiḥ 50, fols. 52r–55v (no. 33542).

Anonymous (Midrashic). MS. Montefiore 9, fols. 251r–255r (Hirschfeld, 2) (no. 4533)
fourteenth to fifteenth century; "Ramsgate Yalquṭ"; quotations from the Talmud arranged in order of the biblical verses.

Anonymous. MS. Oriental Institute (St. Petersburg) B 396, fols. 3r–v (no. 46933)
1277–85; Italian; short commentary on selected verses.

Anonymous (Midrashic). MS. RSL (Moscow) Günzburg 349, fols. 120r–125r (no. 47697)

Anonymous (Northern French). MS. Russian National Library (St. Petersburg) Evr. I. 21, fols. 27r–35r
available on microfilm at the Bodleian Library, Oxford, under call no. Or. Film 295/4; (not seen).

Anonymous (Judeo-Arabic). "Sharḥ Megillat 'Ester." MS. SBB (Berlin) Or. Qu. 943, fols. 28r–29v (no. 1861; 2192; photo no. 11/10)
only part of the introduction (4 pp.).

Anonymous (Judeo-German). MS. SBB (Berlin) Or. Qu. 701, fols. 94r–95v (Steinschneider 146) (no. 1749)
fifteenth to sixteenth century; glosses; not as Steinschneider surmises "ein Auszug aus RSHY mit Zusätzen."

Anonymous (Kabbalistic). MS. Sassoon 560, pp. 105–16 (*Ohel Dawid*, p. 84) (no. 8861)
fifteenth century; sold at a public auction, November, 1978; mentions Samael, *sefirot* (p. 113).

Anonymous (Northern French). MS. SUB (Hamburg) Cod. Hebr. 32, fols. 95v–100v (Steinschneider no. 37) (no. 885)
Published by Jellinek as *Peirushim* [etc.] (see under Kara, Joseph).

Anonymous. MS. TC (Cambridge) F.12.135, fol. 8v (Loewe, 94) (no. 12194)
fourteenth century; supercommentary on Rashi; *le'azim* in German.

Anonymous (Northern French). MS. UB (Erlangen 1263), fols. 151r–153v (Striedl-Roth, 62) (no. 35862)
Northern French; 13th century?; 1:10 to end; includes comments of Rashbam.

Anonymous (Glossary). MS. UB (Leipzig) 1099, fols. 231r–232v (no. 19507)
Le'azim with a short commentary; ends at 8:14.

Anonymous ("A"). "Peirush Megillat *'Ester.*" *'Oṣar ṭov* (1878):26–32 (transcription of MS. BP (Parma) 2203).

— MS. BA (Vatican) Urb. Ebr. 20, fols. 37r–40v (no. 659)
fourteenth century.
— MS. BL (London) Add. 26,924, fols. 260v–263v (Margoliouth 175/II.1) (no. 5451)
fourteenth century.
— MS. BL (Oxford) Opp. Add. 4° 52, fols. 133r–136v (Neubauer 322/8) (no. 17241)
fourteenth century.
— MS. BL (Oxford) Opp. Add. fol. 24, fols. 165r–167v (Neubauer 364) (no. 17283)
fifteenth century.

— MS. BML (Florence) Plut. III.8, fols. 471v–473v (no. 17281)
fourteenth century, Italian.
— MS. BN (Paris) héb. 162, fols. 271r–273r (Zotenberg, p. 17) (no. 4149)
Italy, before 1342.
— MS. BP (Parma) 2203, fols. 29v–33v (De Rossi 456) (no. 13379)
fifteenth century, Italian.
— MS. CUL (Cambridge) Add. 378.2, fols. 48r–50v (Schiller-Szinessy, 71) (no. 15908)
— MS. IŻH (Warsaw) 260, fols. 30r–35v (no. 10125)
dated 1425/6, Italian; ascribed to Rashi; partly damaged.
— MS. JC (London) 6, fols. 58r–62v (Neubauer, *Catalogue*, 2) (no. 4675)
fourteenth to fifteenth century.
— MS. JTS (Breslau) 104, fols. 125v–128r (Loewinger-Weinryb, 26/6)
missing since World War II; attributed to Joseph Kara.
— MS. RSL (Moscow) Günzburg 122, fols. 41r–44r (no. 6802)
dated 1390/1, Italian; ascribed to Rashi.
— MS. SBB (Berlin) Or. Qu. 514, fols. 445–51 (Steinschneider, no. 65) (no. 1699)
dated 1289; ascribed to Rashi.

Abraham ben Judah (Karaite). MS. BR (Leiden) Or. 4739 (Warn. 1), fols. 234r–235v (Steinschneider, pp. 1–5) (no. 28054)
philological, *peshaṭ*; 16th century?

Arama, Isaac. *Megillat 'Ester u-feirushah.* Constantinople, 1518.
— "Peirush Megillat 'Ester le-ha-R. Yiṣḥaq 'Aramah z.ṣ.v.l. 'im peirush ha-R. Yosef ha-Kohen z.l. u-fei' ha-R. 'Avraham Saba' z.ṣ.v.l." MS. BL (Oxford) Opp. Add. 4° 106, fols. 141r–184v (Neubauer 2334/3) (no. 21026)
Dated Marrakesh 1587.
— MS. JTSA (New York) L463, fols. 142v–164r. (no. 23739)
sixteenth century, Spanish cursive.
— MS. JTSA (New York) L1065 (Mic. 1195), fols. 209r–233r (no. 24267)
seventeenth century, Italian cursive; excerpts only.

— MS. SUB (Frankfurt am Main) hebr. 8° 185, fols. 29r–v, 32r–v (no. 22031)
only fragments—the first containing the end of the introduction and the beginning of the commentary, the second the middle of the introduction.
— MS. TC (Cambridge) F.12.5, fols. 29r–44v. (Loewe, 47) (no. 12149)

Astruc, Solomon. In *Midreshei ha-Torah*. Ed. Simon Eppenstein, 215–24. Berlin, 1899.
— MS. BA (Milan) N.149 sup., fols. 104v–109v (Bernheimer 32/4) (no. 12909)
fourteenth century.
— MS. Montefiore (London) 279, fols. 20r–23r (Hirschfeld, *Catalogue*, p. 89) (no. 5242)

Avigdor ben Elijah. MS. SUB (Hamburg) Cod. Hebr. 235, fols. 130r–132v (Steinschneider, no. 45, p. 16) (no. 1041)

Baḥya ben Asher. "Kad ha-qemaḥ" In *Kitvei Rabbeinu Baḥya*, ed. C. B. Chavel, 329–41. Jerusalem, 1969. s.v. "Purim."
— *Kad ha-qemaḥ*. Constantinople, 1515, pp. 64a–66b (1st ed.)
———. Venice, 1546, pp. 59b–62a (2nd ed.)

Baḥya ben Asher. "Kad ha-qemaḥ." (English). In his *Encyclopedia of Torah Thoughts*, ed. Charles B. Chavel, 521–28. New York, 1980. only a partial translation.

Dernegra, Astruc.
no longer extant; quoted in commentary of Solomon Astruc to 6:13, p. 221; cf. Moritz Steinschneider in *Hebraïsche Bibliographie* 16 (1876): 92–93.

Eleazar ben Judah, of Worms. *Sha'arei binah: Peirush Megillat 'Ester*, ed. Manfred R. Lehmann. New York, 1980.
Based on a manuscript from the Lehmann collection, copied in Damascus in 1634.
— *Peirush Rabbeinu 'El'azar mi-Germaiza zal 'al ha-Torah ve-'al Megillat 'Ester*, ed. Joseph Gad, 61–72. London, 1948–49. Comments collected from various sources; it should be noted that

most of the comments in Gad's collection appear in the Lehmann edition but not in that of Konyevsky (next entry)
— "Peirush Megillat 'Ester me-ḥakhmei 'Ashkenaz." MS. BL (London) Or. 10855 (Gaster, 748), fols. 136r–45v. (no. 8170) Damascus, 1668–69
— MS. JTSA (New York) L1065 (Mic. 1195), fols. 209r–233r (no. 24267)
seventeenth century, Italian cursive; scattered comments in an anthologized commentary.

Eleazar ben Judah, of Worms, supposed author. "Peirush 'Ester." In *Peirush ha-Roqeaḥ 'al ha-Megillot*, ed. Chaim Konyevsky. 2 vols. Benei Beraq, 1984–85, 1:11–98.
edition of MS. BL (Oxford) Opp. 720 (see above s.v. Anonymous [Ashkenazic]); the author is Ashkenazic but not Eleazar ben Judah; see Lehmann's introd. to his edition.
———. "Nimmuqei 'Ester." In *Qiryat sefer: nimmuqei Ḥamesh Megillot ve-hafṭarot meyussad 'a.p. masorah ḥaserot vi-yeterot ve-gimaṭri'ot* [etc.], ed. Ben Zion Gasenbauer, 6a–8a. Lemberg, 1907–8.

Eleazar ben Moses ha-Darshan. MS. BA (Vatican) Ebr. 460, fols. 11r–13v (no. 525)
fifteenth to sixteenth century, Ashkenazic; includes *gemaṭriot, ḥaser ve-yater.*
Gersonides. "Bei'ur 'Aḥashverosh." In *Peirush Ḥamesh Megillot*, 40a–50a. Riva da Trento, 1559–60 (1st ed.)
———. In *Qehillot Mosheh*, 4 vols. Amsterdam, 1724–27. 4:326a–339b (2nd ed.)
— "Peirush 'Ester." in *Peirush Ralbag 'al Ḥamesh Megillot*, 39b–49b. Königsberg, 1860. Repr. Jerusalem, 1970–71 (3rd ed.)
———. MS. BN (Paris) héb. 248, fols. 153r–171r (no. 4273)

Gibbor, Judah (Karaite). "Sefer Mo'adim." MS. HUC-JIR (Cincinnati) 839 (formerly Schwager 1), fols. 78r–106r. (no. 11327)
discussion of halakhic matters pertaining to Purim and Megillat Ester; includes comments (some allegorical) on selected verses.

Ḥadidah, Abraham ben Judah. "Peirush Megillat 'Ester." MS. BP (Parma) 2211, fols. 41r–49v (De Rossi 177) (no. 13367)
fifteenth to sixteenth century.

Ḥalayo, Moses ben Isaac. MS. ÖN (Vienna) Hebr. 178, fols. 1v–36r (Schwarz 34/1) (no. 1445)
sixteenth century, cursive
— MS. JNUL (Jerusalem) Heb. 8° 3427, fols. 24v–63r (no. 10128) fourteenth to fifteenth century, Italian; formerly MS. IŻH (Warsaw) 286 and before that IK (Vienna) II.9 (cf. Schwarz, *Hebräischen Handschriften in Oesterreich*, 47).

Ḥayyun, Joseph ben Abraham. MS. RSL (Moscow) Günzburg 168, fols. 60r–97v. (no. 6848)
sixteenth century, Spanish cursive.
— MS. JTSA (New York) L496, fols. 11r–35v (no. 23773) from 2:8 till the end.

Ibn Balaam, Judah ben Samuel. MS. BL (Oxford) Heb.d.68, fol. 31v (Neubauer 2836/11) (photo no. 3212)
fragment in Judeo-Arabic; from beginning until 1:8.

Ibn Ezra, Abraham ben Meir [Version A]. In *Peirush 'al Ḥamesh Megillot*. Constantinople, 1505. (1st ed.)
— In standard editions of the Rabbinic Bible. (*Miqra'ot gedolot*); see *Sarei ha-'elef*, 167.
— MS. BL (London) Add. 24,896, fols. 384v–402r (Margoliouth 237) no. 5428)
— MS. BC (Verona) 204 (82.4), fols. 105r–111v (Tamani, no. 23, p. 240) (no. 32678)
fifteenth century.
[Version B]. *Va-yosef 'Avraham*, ed. Joseph Zedner.
London, 1850. Repr. *Kitvei R. 'Avraham 'Ibn 'Ezra'*, vol. 5. Jerusalem, 1971–72.
— MS. BL (London) Harley 269 (Margoliouth 235), fols. 210r–218v (no. 4833)
This is the MS. used by Zedner; part of chapter 1 missing; supplied by Leopold Dukes from the Paris MS. and published in *Literaturblatt des Orients* 11(1850): 341.
— MS. BN (Paris) héb. 334, fols. 75v–86r (Zotenberg, p. 45) (no. 2937)
— MS. BL (Oxford) Poc. 184, fols. 32v–39v (Neubauer 2243) (no. 20526)

— MS. BP (Parma) 2062 fols. 105v–113v (De Rossi 584) (no. 13139)
dated 1383/4.
— MS. BA (Vatican) Ebr. 78, fol. 124r–134v (Cassuto, pp. 115–17) (no. 198)

Ibn Janaḥ, Jonah. In *Peirush le-khitvei ha-qodesh*, 2nd ed., ed. A. Z. Rabinowitz, 285. Tel Aviv, 1935/6.
florilegium.
—. In Wilhelm Bacher, *Aus der Schrifterklärung des Abulwalîd Merwân ibn Ganâh (R. Jona)*, Jahresbericht der Landes-Rabbinerschule in Budapest, 1888/89, 110. Budapest, 1889.

Ibn Shuaib, Joshua. [Sermon on Parashat Zakhor]. In his [*Derashot 'al ha-Torah*], 36a–37b. Constantinople, 1523.
no title page, colophon, or page numbers
—. In his [*Derashot ha-Torah*], 31a–32b. Kraków, 1573.
in the sermon for parashat Teṣaveh.
— MS. BA (Vatican) Ebr. 42, fols. 88v–92r (Cassuto, p. 57) (no. 158)
dated 1463.
— MS. BL (London) Or. 9974, fols. 56r–58v (no. 7022)
— MS. BL (Oxford) Hunt. 232, fols. 14r–16v (Neubauer 983) (no. 22459)
before 1420/21, Spanish
— MS. BL (Oxford) Mich. 149, fols. 103r–107v (Neubauer 982) (no. 22458)
fifteenth to sixteenth century, Spanish
— MS. BN (Paris) héb. 237, fols. 73v–76v (Zotenberg, p. 30) (no. 4264)
dated 1437.
— MS. BN (Paris) héb. 238, fols. 65r–68r (Zotenberg, p. 30) (no. 4265)
dated 1461.
— MS. BN (Paris) héb. 239, fols. 65r–68r (Zotenberg, p. 30) (no. 4266)
dated 1469, oriental.
— MS. BS (Munich) Cod. Hebr. 9, fols. 112r–17r (Steinschenider, p. 3) (no. 25954)
Venice, 1550/1.

— In "Sefer Shemot, ʿim hafṭarot, targum, targum ʿarvi, Midrash Tanḥuma' u-derashot Yehoshuʿa 'n Shuʿaib." MS. JTSA (New York) ENA 1790.
not seen.
— MS. MK (Jerusalem) 39, fols. 62r–64r (no. 20031)
dated 1477; Bijar, Iran.
— MS. Montefiore (London) 60, fols. 109v–15v (Hirschfeld, *Catalogue*, p. 12) (no. 4579)
fifteenth century.
— "Derashah le-farashat Zakhor." In *Derashot ʿal ha-Torah.* MS. RSL (Moscow) Günzburg 64, fols. 57v–60v (no. 6744)
sixteenth century, Italian.

Immanuel ben Solomon, of Rome. *Commento sopra il libro di Ester (P. Megillat 'Ester).* Transcribed by Pietro Perreau. Parma, 1880, handwritten transcription of the Parma MS; only 60 copies made.
— MS. BP (Parma) 2844 (De Rossi 615), fols. 184r–217v (no. 12296)
fifteenth century, Italian.
— MS. BL (Oxford) Mich. 455, fols. 45v–46r (Neubauer 146/1) (no. 16210)
fifteenth century, Italian;
fragment only, covering 1:1–1:3.

Isaac ben Joseph, ha-Kohen. "Peirush Megillat 'Aḥashverosh." MS. BL (Oxford) Opp. Add. 8° 36, fols. 70r–73v (Neubauer 2425/9) (no. 21704)
sixteenth century Spanish (oriental); incomplete; from middle of 1:15–3:7.
— MS. BL (Oxford) Opp. Add. 4° 106 (Neubauer 2334), fols. 132r–184r (no. 21026) (See above s.v. Arama)
— MS. JTSA (New York) L1052, fols. 51v–76v. (no. 24255)
— MS. JTSA (New York) L1065 (Mic. 1195), fols. 209r–233r (no. 24267)
seventeenth century, Italian cursive;
scattered comments only.
— MS. RSL (Moscow) Günzburg 158, fols. 182r–205r (no. 6838)
fifteenth to sixteenth century, oriental.
— MS. SUB (Frankfurt a.M.) heb. 8° 124, fols. 2r–33r (Roth-

Prijs, no. 132, p. 180) (no. 26469)
very difficult to read.

Isaiah ben Mali, di-Trani. In *Peirush Nevi'im u-Khetuvim le-Rabbeinu Yesha'yah ha-rishon mi-Ṭrani*, 3 vols. Jerusalem, 1977–78, 3:297–304
based on the Rome MS.
— MS. BA (Rome) Or. 72, fols. 230v–236r (no. 11715)
dated 1327.
— MS. BM (Rouen) Or. 11 (1485), fols. 127r–129v (no. 6653)

Israel (student of Asher ben Yeḥiel)
no longer extant; quoted in commentary of Joseph Ibn Naḥmias, p. 6 (to 1:1).

Jacob ben Asher. *Parpera'ot le-ḥokhmah.*
no longer extant; quoted in commentary of Joseph Naḥmias to 5:4, p. 26.

Jacob ben Reuben (Karaite). In *Sefer ha-'osher*, 17a–17b.
Eupatoria, 1836.
— MS. BN (Paris) héb. 191, fols. 309r–311v (Zotenberg, p. 24) (no. 4175)
— MS. BR (Leiden) Or. 4746 (Warn. 8), fols. 324v–327r (Steinschneider, pp. 24–26) (no. 28060)
— MS. BR (Leiden) Or. 4769 (Warn. 31), fols. 287v–291r (Steinschneider, pp. 134–35) (no. 28069)
— MS. JRL (Manchester) 2020, fols. 197r–198v (no. 16063)
dated 1538/9.

Japheth ben Eli, ha-Levi (Karaite). MS. BN (Paris) héb. 295, fols. 123r–172v (Zotenberg, p. 39) (no. 4313)
in Judeo-Arabic; dated 1662/3, oriental.
— MS. Lichaa 10, fols. 1v–45v

Joseph Bekhor Shor
no longer extant; quoted in commentary of Avigdor ben Elijah, fol. 130r.

Judah ben Samuel, he-Ḥasid, supposed author. In *Perushei ha-Torah le-R. Yehudah he-Ḥasid*, ed. I. S. Lange, 133–34. Jerusalem, 1974.

Kara, Joseph ben Simeon. In *Ḥamesh Megillot ʿim targum suri ha-mekhuneh Peshiṭa ve-ʿim peirush ʿal ha-Megillot*, ed. Adolf Hübsch (Yoffen), 58b–76b. Prague, 1866.
— transcription of MS. Národni Knihovna v Praze (Prague) XVIII F6, fols. 305v–309r (no. 23100)
fifteenth century.
— In *Peirushim ʿal ʾEster, Rut ve-ʾEikhah le-R. Menaḥem bar Ḥelbo* [et al.], ed. Adolph Jellinek, 1–22. Leipzig, 1855. Repr. Jerusalem, 1966.
— transcription of MS. SUB (Hamburg) Cod. Hebr. 32 (see above under Anonymous, p. 315)
— In Joseph Bekhor Shor. *Peirush ʿal ha-Torah*, ed. Joseph Gad. 3 vols. Jerusalem, 1959, 3:88–97.
— MS. UB (Erlangen) 1263, fols. 150r–151r (Striedl-Roth, *Hebräische Handschriften*, 2:62) (no. 35862)
only until 1:9; from 1:10 to end another anonymous commentary
— MS. IŻH (Warsaw) 848 (no. 30970)
only on Esther 1; nineteenth century.

Kaspi, Joseph ibn. "Gelilei kesef: Peirush li-megillat ʾEster."
In *ʿAsarah kelei kesef*, ed. Isaac Last, vol. 2, pp. 29–39. Pressburg, Czechoslovakia, 1902–3. Repr. Jerusalem, 1969–70. Transcription of MS. BN (Paris) with variants from MS. BS (Munich).
— [Additions to his Esther commentary]. In *Milluʾim: Recensionen, Varianten und Ergänzungen zu der ed. ʿAsarah kelei kesef*, ed. Isaac Last, 20–22. Pressburg, Czechoslovakia, 1904.
Transcription of MS. BL (Oxford); incomplete; first two paragraphs from MS wanting.
— MS. BL (Oxford) Opp. 211 (Ol. 272), fols. 26r–28r. (Neubauer 362/a) (no. 17281)
fourteenth century.
— "Gelilei kesef." MS. BN (Paris) héb. 1092, fols. 83r–88v (Zotenberg, p. 201) (no. 15732)
fifteenth to sixteenth century, Italian.
— "Gelilei kesef." MS. SUB (Hamburg) Levy 144, fols. 172v–176v. (Striedl-Roth, 157) (no. 1584)
— MS. Montefiore 297, fols. 49v–55r (Hirschfeld, p. 92) (no. 5249)
— MS. BS (Munich) Cod. Hebr. 265, fols. 79r–83v. (Steinschneider, pp. 129–30) (no. 1660)
fourteenth century.

— "Gelilei kesef." MS. BP (Parma) 2478 (De Rossi 755), fols. 145r–148r (no. 13482)
dated 1474.

Levi ben Gershom, see Gersonides.

Maimon. MS. JTSA (New York) Mic. 1735, fols. 126v–129v (no. 10833)
fifteenth century, Sephardic cursive; midrashic; fragment only—from 1:13–2:10.

Maimonides, Moses. In *Torat ha-Rambam 'al ha-Tanakh*, vol. [6]: *Nakh*, ed. Meir David Ben-Shem, 187–189. Jerusalem, 1977–78
florilegium.

Maimonides, Moses, supposed author. *Peirush Megillat 'Ester be-'Arvit meyuḥas le-ha-Rambam*. Livorno, 1759–60.
— Hebrew translation by Y. Y. Rivlin. Jerusalem, 1951–52.
Cf. Hartwig Hirschfeld, "Notiz über einen dem Maimuni untergeschobenen arabischen Commentar zu Esther," in *Semitic Studies in Memory of George Alexander Kohut* (Berlin, 1897), 248–53 who demonstrates that this commentary dates from the early seventeenth century.

Menaḥem ben Solomon, supposed author. MS. SBB (Berlin) Or. Fol. 707 (Steinschneider, 34 B6f) (no. 2028)
Cf. *Hebraeische Bibliographie* 17 (1877): 41; thirteenth to fourteenth century; fragment—1:5–13, 8:9–26.

Moses ben Maimon, see Maimonides

Moses ben Naḥman, see Naḥmanides

Naḥmanides. In *Peirushei ha-Ramban 'al Nevi'im u-Khetuvim*, compiled by Charles B. Chavel, 215–19. Jerusalem, 1963–64. Repr. Jerusalem, 1985–86
florilegium.

Naḥmias, Joseph ben Joseph. *Peirush Megillat 'Ester*, ed. M. L. Bamberger. Frankfurt am Main, 1891.

— 2nd ed. Podgorze, 1899.
— Repr. *Peirushei Rabi Yosef Naḥmi'as 'al Mishlei, Megillat 'Ester, Yirmeyahu, Pirqei 'Avot ve-Seder 'Avodat Yom ha-kippurim.* Israel, [198–?]
— transcription of MS. BS (Munich) Cod. Hebr. 264, fols. 84r–96r. (Steinschneider, p. 128) (no. 1681)

Naḥmias, Joseph ben Joseph (German). *Commentar zum Buche Ester.* Frankfurt a.M., 1893.

Nethanel ben Isaiah. In Menasheh Refa'el Lihman [Manfred Lehmann], "Peirush li-Megillat 'Ester le-Rabbeinu Netan'el ben Yesha'yah meḥabber Midrash Me'or ha-'afelah, in *Sefer zikkaron le-ha-Rav Yiṣḥaq Nisim,* ed. Meir Benayahu, seder 3, *Rishonim va-'aḥaronim,* 341–58 (Jerusalem, 1984–85)
14th century, Yemenite.

Ralbag, see Gersonides.

"RaMaH." "Megillat 'Aḥashverosh le-ha-RaMaH." MS. BN (Paris) héb. 261, fols. 1r–15v. (Zotenberg, p. 34) (no. 27840)

Rashbam, see Samuel b. Meir.

Rashi. In *Peirush Ḥamesh Megillot.* [Bologna?], 1477.
1st ed.; other editions listed in *Sarei ha-'elef,* 1:139 and Julius Fürst, *Bibliotheca Judaica,* 3 vols. in 2 (Leipzig, 1849; repr. Hildesheim, 1960), 2:78–81.
— *Miqra'ot gedolot* (Rabbinic Bible) (many eds.)
— MS. BL (Oxford) Opp. 34 (Ol. 63), fols. 225r–226r (Neubauer 186) (no. 16250)
— MS. BN (Paris) héb. 164, fols. 4v–6v (Zotenberg, p. 17) (no. 4151)
— MS. BA (Vatican) EBr. 94, fol. 108r–109r (Cassuto, pp. 136–38) (no. 253)
thirteenth century.
— In *Musaf Rashi,* compiled by M. D. Ben-Shem, 2 vols. Jerusalem, 1983/4–84/5, 2:209–11
florilegium.
— In *Rashi la-Miqra' be-feirusho la-Talmud,* compiled by Yoel

Florsheim, 3 vols. Jerusalem, 1981–89, 3:241–45
florilegium from Rashi's Talmud commentary.

Rashi (English). In *The Megilloth and Rashi's Commentary with Linear Translation: Esther, Song of Songs, Ruth.* Trans. Avraham Schwartz and Yisroel Schwartz, 1–56. New York, 1983.

Rashi (Latin). *'Ester 'im p' Rashi = Scholia Rabi Salomonis Jarchi in librum Esther.* Trans. Louis Henri d'Aquin. Paris, 1622.
— In *R. Salomonis Jarchi . . . Commentarius hebraicus in librr. Joshuae, Judicum, Ruth . . . Estherae . . . Latin versus.* Trans. Johann Friedrich Breithaupt. Gotha, Germany, 1714.

Saadiah ben Joseph. In Yehuda Ratzaby, "Mi-peirush R. Se'adyah li-Megillat 'Ester," in *Sefer yovel li-khevod . . . Yosef Dov ha-Levi Soloveiṣ'iq [Soloveitchik],* ed. Sha'ul Yisre'eli, Naḥum Lam [Norman Lamm] and Yiṣḥaq Refa'el [Yitzhak Raphael], 1153–78. Jerusalem, 1983–84.
six Genizah fragments; rest of commentary no longer extant.

Saadiah Figo (Picho?)
no longer extant; quoted in commentary of Joseph Ibn Naḥmias, p. 13 (to 1:18).

Saba, Abraham. *'Eshkol ha-kofer 'al Megillat 'Ester,* ed. Eliezer Segal. Drohobycz, 1903. Repr. Jerusalem, 1980–81.
— with source references, corrections, and notes by S. Reiss [Shene'ur Zusha Raiz] Flushing, N.Y. 1965–66.
— MS. BL (Oxford) Opp. Add. 4° 106 (Neubauer 2334), fol. 133r–184r (abridged) (no. 21026)
see above s.v. Arama, p. 316.
— MS. IŻH (Warsaw) 89, fols. 1r–55r (entire MS) (no. 10092)
dated 1556/7, Sephardic.
— MS. JTSA (New York) Mic. 5572, fols. 1r–60r (entire MS) (no. 37336)
sixteenth century, Sephardic.
— MS. RSL (Moscow) Günzburg 935, fols. 21r–96r (no. 48279)
dated 1560
— MS. SUB (Frankfurt am Main) hebr. 8° 40, fols. 120r–199v (= 2r–80v) (Roth-Prijs, pp. 60–61) (no. 25898)

fifteenth to sixteenth century, Sephardic; first part very difficult to read; seems quite different from the printed version; fols. 134–39 missing in film.
— MS. SUB (Frankfurt am Main) hebr. 8° 163, fols. 123r–211v (no. 10606)
— MS. TC (Cambridge) F.12.15, fols. 1r–22r (2nd group) (Loewe, 59) (no. 12161)
dated 1538; begins with 4:7.

Salmon ben Jeroham (Karaite)
no longer extant; see Pinsker, *Liqquṭei qadmoniyyot* (Vienna, 1860; repr. Jerusalem, 1967–68), 2:133.

Samuel ben Meir, Rashbam. In *Peirushim 'al 'Ester* [etc.]
— In Abraham Geiger, "Liqquṭim mi-peirushei R. Yosef ben Shim'on Qara' u-venei doro." In *Niṭei na'amanim*, ed. S. Z. Heilberg, 9b–11a. Breslau, 1847.
— MS. Hamburg Cod. Hebr. 32; see under Joseph Kara and Anonymous (Northern French) for full details.
— MS. BN (Paris) 50, fols. 346v–359v (Zotenberg, p. 6) (no. 3104)
fifteenth century; ascribed in catalogue to Rashi; first section corresponds to R. Samuel sections in Hamburg MS.
— MS. UB (Erlangen) 1263, fols. 151r–153v (no. 35862) see above under Anonymous.

Samuel de Vidas.
no longer extant; quoted in commentary of Zechariah ben Saruḳ, p. 6b.

Shalom, Abraham, "[Sermon for Parashat Zakhor]." In his *Neveh Shalom*, 68b–72b. Venice, 1575. Repr. 2 vols. Jerusalem, 1966–67; Westmead, Farnborough, Hants., 1969.

Shemariah b. Elijah, of Crete. MS. CUL (Cambridge) Mm. 6.26.2, fols. 1r–8r (Schiller-Szinessy, Catalogue, 33/1) (no. 15870)
dated 1410; on 6:3 to end.
— "'Elef ha-magen." [Commentary on the *'Aggadot* of B.T. Megillah, chap. 1]. MS. CUL (Cambridge) Mm. 6.26.2, fols. 8v–111v.

— MS. JTSA (New York) L1065 (Mic. 1195), fols. 209r–33r (no. 24267)
scattered comments; see above s.v. "Arama."

Solomon ben Isaac, see Rashi

Tamakh, Abraham ben Isaac, ha-Levi, supposed author. In L. A. Feldman, "R. 'Avraham ben Yiṣḥaq ha-Levi Tamakh, ḥakham Girondi mi-sof ha-'elef ha-ḥamishi; qeṭa'im mi-peirusho li-Megillat 'Ester," *Ha-Darom* 24/25 (1967): 186–94
attribution doubtful; see discussion in Appendix I above, pp. 222–23.

Tanḥum ben Joseph, ha-Yerushalmi. In "Kitāb al-bayān." MS. BL (Oxford) Poc. 320, fols. 216r–227r (Neubauer 363) (no. 17282)
fourteenth century, oriental; in Judeo-Arabic.

Tobias ben Eliezer. "Midrash Leqaḥ ṭov 'al 'Ester." In *Sifrei de-'aggadeta' 'al Megillat 'Ester*, ed. Salomon Buber, 83–112. Vilna, 1886.
based on MS. IŻH (Warsaw) with variants from MS. BS (Munich).
— MS. BL (Oxford) Laud. Or. 101, fols. 252v–264r (Neubauer, 240/8) (no. 16376)
dated 1462/3, Italian.
— "Peirush Megillat 'Ester." In MS. BP (Parma) 2879, fols. 26r–37v (De Rossi 206) (no. 13372)
fourteenth to fifteenth century.
— MS. BS (Munich) Cod. Hebr. 77, fols. 27v–40r (Steinscheider, pp. 49–50) (no. 1167)
dated 1397.
— "Pei' Megillat 'Ester." In MS. CUL (Cambridge) Add. 378(9), pt. 1, fols. 32v–47r (Loewe, Handlist, 123) (no. 16297)
dated 1361, Bologna.
— MS. IŻH (Warsaw) 30, fols. 41v–52v (no. 11601)
formerly IK (Vienna) IV, 4 (Schwarz 35)
dated 1480/1, Oriental.
— MS. JTSA (New York) L825, fols. 1r–26v (ENA 1205) (no. 24059)
difficult to read; signs of water damage; contains marginal notes.

Yefet ben Eli, see Japheth ben Eli

Zechariah ben Saruḳ. *Peirush Megillat 'Aḥashverosh.* Venice, 1565.
— MS. BL (Oxford) Opp. Add. 4° 106, fol. 140r–v (Neubauer 2334)
Introduction only; for title and other information, see above s.v. "Arama."
— MS. BL (Oxford) Opp. 593 (Ol. 1179), fols. 142r–169v (Neubauer 2180) (no. 20643)
sixteenth century; end missing; ends at top of p. 18a in printed edition.
— MS. Montefiore 43, fols. 1r–16r (Hirschfeld, *Catalogue*, p. 8) (no. 4565)
dated 1585.

OTHER PRIMARY SOURCES

Abrahams, Israel, ed. *Hebrew Ethical Wills.* 2 vols. Philadelphia, 1926. Reprint (2 vols. in 1). Philadelphia, 1976.

Abravanel, Isaac. *Naḥalat 'Avot.* New York, 1953.

———. *Peirush 'al Nevi'im rishonim.* Jerusalem, 1954–55.

'Aggadat 'Ester. See under Buber, Salomon.

al-Biruni. *Kitāb al-tafhīm.* Trans. Robert Ramsay Wright. London, 1934.

Alami, Solomon. *'Iggeret musar.* Ed. A. M. Habermann. Sifriyyat meqorot, 8. Jerusalem, 1945–46.

Alan of Lille. *The Art of Preaching.* Trans. Gillian R. Evans. Cistercian Studies Series, 23. Kalamazoo, Mich., 1981.

Anatoli, Jacob. *Malmad ha-talmidim.* Sefarim ha-yoṣe'im la-'or 'al-yedei Ḥevrat Meqiṣei nirdamim. Lyck, 1866. Reprint. Jerusalem, 1967–68.

Anonymous of Bologna. "The Principles of Letter Writing (*Rationes dictandi*)." Trans. James J. Murphy. In *Three Medieval Rhetorical Arts*, ed. James J. Murphy, 5–25. Berkeley and Los Angeles, 1971.

Albo, Joseph. *Sefer ha-'iqqarim*. Ed. and trans. Isaac Husik. 4 vols. in 5. Philadelphia, 1929–30.

Alkabez, Solomon. *Sefer Menot ha-Levi: Midrash Megillat 'Ester*. Lwow, 1911. Reprint. Brooklyn, N.Y., 1976.

Arama, Isaac. *'Aqeidat Yiṣḥaq*. Ed. Ḥ. Y. Pollak. 5 vols. Pressburg, Czechoslovakia, 1849.

———. *Ḥazut qashah*. Ed. Ḥ. Y. Pollak. Pressburg, Czechoslovakia, 1849 (issued with *'Aqeidat Yiṣḥaq*, vol. 5).

Aristotle. *Ethics of Aristotle*. Trans. J. A. K. Thomson; revised with notes and appendices by Hugh Tredennick; introduction and bibliography by Jonathan Barnes. Harmondsworth, Middlesex, 1976.

———. *Historia animalium*. Trans. D. W. Thompson. Oxford, 1910.

———. *Sefer ha-middot*. [= *Nicomachean Ethics*]. Trans. Meir Alguadez; ed. Isaac Satanow. Lemberg, 1867.

Astruc, Solomon. *Midreshei ha-Torah*. Ed. Simon Eppenstein. Berlin, 1899.

Averroës. *Bei'ur 'Ibn Rushd le-"Sefer ha-halaṣah" le-'Aristo*. Trans. Todros Todrosi; ed. Jacob Goldenthal. Leipzig, 1842.

———. *Ha-Nusaḥim ha-'ivriyyim shel ha-ma'amar ha-revi'i shel ha-bei'ur ha-'emsa'i shel 'Ibn Rushd le- "Sefer ha-middot 'al-shem Niqomakhos" le-'Aristo*. Ed. L. V. Berman. Jerusalem, 1981.

Azriel of Gerona. *Peirush ha-'aggadot*. Ed. Isaiah Tishby. Jerusalem, 1944–45. Repr. Jerusalem, 1982.

Baḥya ben Asher. *Bei'ur 'al ha-Torah*. Ed. C. B. Chavel. 3 vols. Jerusalem, 1966.

———. *Kitvei Rabbeinu Baḥya.* Ed. C. B. Chavel. Jerusalem, 1969.

Bashyazi, Elijah. *Sefer ha-miṣvot shel ha-Yehudim ha-Qara'im: 'Adderet 'Eliyahu.* Israel, 1966.

Boethius. *Boethius's "De topicis differentiis."* Trans. Eleonore Stump. Ithaca, N.Y., 1978.

———. *De differentiis topicis.* In *Patrologia Latina,* ed. J. P. Migne. vol. 64, cols. 1173–1218. Paris, 1891.

Buber, Salomon, ed. *Sifrei de-'aggadeta 'al Megillat 'Ester.* Vilna, 1886.

———, ed. *'Aggadat 'Ester.* Lwow, 1897.

Cordovero, Moses. *Pardes rimmonim.* Munkacz, 1905–06. Reprint. Jerusalem, 1961–62.

Crescas du Caylar, "Piyyuṭ le-Yom Purim." MS. BL (London) Add. 19,663, fols. 21r–32v (Margoliouth 700)

Dante, Alighieri. *De vulgari eloquentia.* Ed. Aristide Marigo. Opere di Dante, ed. Michele Barbi, vol. 6. Florence, 1938.

———. *Epistolae: Letters of Dante.* Trans. Paget Toynbee. Oxford, 1920. 2nd ed. Oxford, 1966.

David ben Judah, he-Ḥasid. *The Book of Mirrors.* Ed. D. C. Matt. Brown Judaic Studies, no. 30. Chico, Calif., 1982.

De Leon, Moses. *Sheqel ha-qodesh.* Ed. A. W. Greenup. London, 1911. Reprint. Jerusalem, 1969.

Duran, Solomon ben Zemah. *Magen 'avot.* Livorno, Italy, 1785. Reprint. Jerusalem, 1969.

Epstein, Isidore, ed. *Babylonian Talmud.* 35 vols. London, 1935–52.

Falaquera, Shem Tob. *Reshit ḥokhmah.* Ed. Moritz David. Berlin, 1902. Reprint. Jerusalem, 1969–70.

Flusser, David, ed. *Sefer Yosippon.* 2 vols. Jerusalem, 1978–80.

Gersonides (Levi ben Gershom, Ralbag). *Milḥamot ha-Shem.* Livorno, Italy, 1560.

———. *Perush 'al ha-Torah.* Venice, 1547.

Grossfeld, Bernard, ed. *The Targum to the Five Megilloth.* New York, 1973.

Hadassi, Judah. *'Eshkol ha-kofer.* Eupatoria, 1836.

Hillel ben Samuel, of Verona. *Sefer Tagmulei ha-nefesh.* Ed. Giuseppe Sermoneta. Jerusalem, 1981.

Horowitz, C. M., ed. *Beit 'eqed ha-'aggadot.* Frankfurt am Main, 1881. Repr. Jerusalem, 1966–67.

Ibn Daud, Abraham. *The Book of Tradition.* Ed. and trans. Gerson D. Cohen. London, 1967.

Ibn Ezra, Abraham ben Meir. "Ha-Perush ha-qaṣar le-sefer Daniel." Ed. Aharon Mondshine. Master's thesis, Bar-Ilan University, 1977.

———. *Qoveṣ ḥokhmat ha-Raba.* Ed. David Kahana. 2 vols. Warsaw, 1894. Repr. Jerusalem, 1970–71.

———. *Sefer 'Ibn 'Ezra' le-sefer Shemot.* Ed. J. L. Fleischer. Vienna, 1926.

———. *Sefer Ṣaḥot.* Ed. Gabriel Lippmann. Fürth, 1827.

Ibn Ezra, Moses ben Jacob. *Sefer ha-'iyyunim ve-ha-diyyunim.* Ed. A. S. Halkin. Jerusalem, 1975.

Ibn Janaḥ, Jonah. *Kitāb al-Mustalhīk.* In his *Opuscules et traités*, trans. and ed. Joseph and Hartwig Derenbourg. Paris, 1880.

———. *Sefer ha-riqmah.* Ed. Michael Wilensky. 2nd ed. 2 vols. Jerusalem, 1964.

———. *Sefer ha-shorashim.* Ed. Wilhelm Bacher. Berlin, 1896.

Ibn Shem Tov, Joseph ben Shem Tov. "'Ein ha-qore'." MS. BN (Paris) héb. 325, fols. 89–144 and MS. BL (Oxford) Mich. 350 (Neubauer 2052), fols. 97–203.

Ibn Verga, Solomon. *Shevet Yehudah.* Ed. Azriel Shohat. Jerusalem, 1946–47.

Ibn Yaḥya, Joseph. *Perush Ḥamesh Megillot, Tehillim, Mishlei, 'Iyyov, Divrei ha-yamim.* Bologna, 1538.

Immanuel ben Solomon. *Il commento di Emanuele Romano al capitolo I della Genesi.* Ed. Franco M. Tocci. Rome, 1963.

———. *Der Kommentar des Immanuel ben Salomon zum Hohenliede.* Ed. S. B. Eschwege. Frankfurt am Main, 1908.

———. *Perush Mishlei.* Naples, 1487. Repr. with introduction by David Goldstein. Jerusalem, 1981.

———. *Maḥberot 'Immanu'el ha-Romi.* Ed. Dov Jarden. 2 vols. Jerusalem, 1957.

Isaac ben Ḥayyim, ha-Kohen. [Commentary on the Song of Songs]. MS. BL (London) Add. 26,960 (Margoliouth 230), fols. 5r–46v.

———. "Ma'ayan ganim ve-'Eṣ ḥayyim." MS. BL (Oxford) Heb. f. 16 (Neubauer 2770).

Isaiah ben Mali, di-Trani. *Perush Nevi'im u-Khetuvim le-Rabbeinu Yesha'yah ha-rishon mi-Ṭrani.* 3 vols. Jerusalem, 1977–78.

Jacob ben Asher. *Perush Ba'al ha-Ṭurim 'al ha-Torah.* Ed. Ya'aqov Rainis. Benei-Beraq, 1971.

Jacob ben Reuben. *Sefer ha-'osher.* Eupatoria, 1836.

John I, of Castile and Leon. *Cronica del Rey Don Juan, primero de Castilla e de Leon.* In *Biblioteca de Autores Españoles,* vol. 68. Madrid, 1877.

Joseph Bekhor Shor, *Perush 'al ha-Torah*. Ed. Joseph Gad. 3 vols. Jerusalem, 1959.

Judah ben Jehiel Messer Leon. *The Book of the Honeycomb's Flow*. Ed. and trans. Isaac Rabinowitz. Ithaca, N.Y., 1983.

———. *Sefer Nofet ṣufim*. Mantua, before 1480. Repr. with introduction by Roberto Bonfil. Jerusalem, 1981.

Kalonymos ben Kalonymos. *Sendschreiben an Joseph Kaspi*. Ed. Joseph Perles. Munich, 1879.

Kara, Joseph. *Peirush R. Yosef Qara' 'al Megillat 'Eikhah*. Ed. Salomon Buber. Breslau, 1900.

———. *Peirush Rabbi Yosef Qara' le-Sefer 'Iyyov*. Ed. Moshe Ahrend. Jerusalem, 1988.

———. *Peirushei Rabbi Yosef Qara' li-Nevi'im Rishonim*. Ed. Simon Eppenstein. Jerusalem, 1972.

Kaspi, Joseph ibn. *Mishneh kesef*. Ed. Isaac Last. 2 vols. Pressburg, Czechoslovakia, 1905.

———. *Sefer ha-musar*. In *Hebrew Ethical Wills*, ed. Israel Abrahams. Philadelphia, 1926. Repr. Philadelphia, 1976.

———. "Terumat kesef." MS. BL (Oxford) 17 (Uri 397), fols. 121–210.

———. "———." MS. BP (Parma) 2630 (De Rossi 424), fols. 1r–39v.

———. "———." MS. BA (Vatican) ebr. 296, fols. 1r–79v.

———. "———." MS. ÖN (Vienna) 161, fols. 1–46r.

Kimḥi, David. *Perush RaDaQ 'al Tehillim, Sefer ḥamishi, 107–50*. Ed. Jacob Bosniak. New York, 1954.

———. *Sefer ha-shorashim*. Ed. J. H. R. Biesenthal and F. Lebrecht. Berlin, 1847. Repr. Jerusalem, 1966–67.

Kimḥi, Joseph. *Sefer ha-galui*. Ed. H. J. Mathews. Berlin, 1887. Repr. Jerusalem, 1966–67.

Lachower, Fischel, and Isaiah Tishby, eds. *Mishnat ha-Zohar*. 2 vols. Jerusalem, 1948/9–1961.

Lachower, Fischel, and Isaiah Tishby, eds. *The Wisdom of the Zohar*. Trans. David Goldstein. 3 vols. Oxford, 1989.

Levi ben Gershom, see Gersonides.

Luther, Martin. *Tischreden*. 6 vols. D. Martin Luthers Werke. Weimar, 1912–21.

Maʿarekhet ha-ʾelohut. Mantua, 1557–58. Repr. Jerusalem, 1963.

Maimonides (Moses ben Maimon, Rambam). *Epistle to Yemen*. Ed. A. S. Halkin. Trans. Boaz Cohen. New York, 1952.

———. *The Eight Chapters of Maimonides on Ethics*. Trans. Joseph I. Gorfinkle. New York, 1912. Repr. New York, 1966.

———. *Guide of the Perplexed*. Trans. Shlomo Pines. Chicago, 1963.

———. *ʾIggerot*. Ed. and trans. Joseph Kafiḥ. Jerusalem, 1971.

———. *Maimonides' Treatise on Resurrection*. Ed. and trans. Joshua Finkel. *Proceedings of the American Academy of Jewish Research* 9 (1939):1–130.

Mattityah ha-Yiṣhari. *Peirush ʾAlef-Beit (Ps 119)*. Ed. Dov Rappel. Tel Aviv, 1978.

Menaḥem ben Aaron ben Zeraḥ. *Ṣeidah la-derekh*. Warsaw, 1879–80.

Messer Leon, Judah ben Jehiel, see Judah ben Jehiel Messer Leon.

"Midrash *ʾAbbaʾ Guryon* ʿal ʾEster." In *Sifrei de-ʾaggadeta ʿal Megillat ʾEster*, ed. Salomon Buber, 1–42. Vilna, 1886.

"Midrash Megillat 'Ester." In *'Aguddat 'aggadot*, ed. Chaim M. Horowitz. Berlin, 1881. Repr. Jerusalem, 1966–67.

Midrash on Psalms. Trans. William Braude. 2 vols. Yale Judaica Series, vol. 13. New Haven, 1959.

"Midrash Panim 'aḥerim, VSS. A and B." In *Sifrei de-'aggadeta 'al Megillat 'Ester*, ed. Salomon Buber, 43–82. Vilna, 1886.

Midrash rabbah. 2 vols. Warsaw, 1878.

Midrash Rabbah: Esther. Trans. Maurice Simon. London, 1939.

Midrash Tehillim. Ed. Salomon Buber. Vilna, 1891.

The Mishnah. Trans. Herbert Danby. Oxford, 1933.

Mizraḥi, Elijah. *Mayim 'amuqqim*. Berlin, 1778. Repr. Jerusalem, 1969–70.

Moore, Carey, ed. *Daniel, Esther and Jeremiah: The Additions*. Anchor Bible, 44. Garden City, N.Y., 1977.

Moses ben Maimon, see Maimonides.

Naḥmanides (Moses ben Naḥman, Ramban). *Commentary on the Torah*. Trans. Charles B. Chavel. 5 vols. New York, 1971–76.

———. *Writings and Discourses*. Trans. Charles B. Chavel. 2 vols. New York, 1978.

Naḥmias, Joseph ben Joseph. *Peirush 'al sefer Mishlei*. Ed. M. L. Bamberger. Berlin, 1911.

———. *Peirush 'al sefer Yirmiyah*. Ed. M. L. Bamberger. Frankfurt am Main, 1913.

———. *Perush Pirqei 'Avot*. Ed. M. L. Bamberger. Paks, Romania, 1907.

———. Bamberger, M. L. "Peirush seder ʿavodah le-R. Yosef ben Naḥmias." *Jahrbuch der Jüdisch-Literarischen Gesellschaft* 6 (1908): 1–17 (Hebrew section).

Nissim ben Reuben Gerondi. *Sheneim ʿasar derashot le-ha-Ran.* Ed. L. A. Feldman. Jerusalem, 1973–74.

"Nisterot R. Shimʿon ben Yoḥai." In *Beit ha-midrash*, ed. Adolph Jellinek, 3:78–82. Vienna, 1855. Repr. Jerusalem, 1967.

Pedro IV, of Aragon, see Pere III, of Catalonia.

Pere III, of Catalonia (Pedro IV, of Aragon). *Chronicle.* Trans. Mary Hillgarth, with introduction and notes by J. N. Hillgarth. 2 vols. Medieval Sources in Translation, 23. Toronto, 1980.

Pirke de Rabbi Eliezer (*The Chapters of Rabbi Eliezer the Great*). Trans. Gerald Friedlander. 2nd ed. New York, 1965.

Pirqei de-Rabbi ʾEliʿezer. Jerusalem, 1972–73.

Pulgar, Isaac. *ʿEzer ha-dat.* Ed. George S. Belasco. London, 1906.

Rabinowitz, Z. M., ed. *Ginzei Midrash.* Tel Aviv, 1977.

Ralbag, see Gersonides.

Rambam, see Maimonides.

Rashbam, see Samuel b. Meir.

Regné, Jean. *History of the Jews in Aragon: Regesta and Documents, 1213–1327.* Ed. Yom Tov Assis. Hispania Judaica, 1. Jerusalem, 1978.

Saadiah Gaon. *The Book of Doctrines and Beliefs.* Abridged edition, trans. Alexander Altmann. Philosophia Judaica. Oxford, 1946. Repr. in *Three Jewish Philosophers.* New York, 1960.

———. *ʾEgron.* Ed. Nehemiah Allony. Jerusalem, 1969.

Saba, Abraham. *'Eshkol ha-kofer 'al Megillat Rut*. Ed. Eliezer Segal. Bartfeld, 1907. Repr. Jerusalem, 1980–81.

———. [Introduction to his commentary on the Ten Sefirot]. In MS. Sassoon 919, pp. 85–89.

———. *Ṣeror ha-mor*. 5 vols. in 1. Warsaw, 1879. Repr. Tel Aviv, 1974–75.

———. "Ṣeror ha-mor." MS. BL (Oxford) Opp. Add. 4° 11 (Neubauer 250).

Sambari, Joseph. *Divrei Yosef*. Qunṭresim, meqorot u-meḥqarim, 54. Jerusalem, 1981.

Samuel ben Meir (Rashbam). *The Commentary of Samuel ben Meir Rashbam on Qoheleth*. Ed. and trans. Sara Japhet and Robert B. Salters. Jerusalem, Leiden, 1985.

———. *Peirush ha-Torah*. Ed. David Rosin. Breslau, 1881. Repr. Jerusalem, 1969–70.

———. *Rabbi Samuel ben Meir's Commentary on Genesis*. Trans. Martin I. Lockshin. Lewiston, N.Y., 1989.

Sefer Yosippon. See under Flusser, David.

Tiqqunei ha-Zohar. Livorno, Italy, 1853.

Yalquṭ Shim'oni. 2 vols. Jerusalem, 1959–60.

Zarza, Samuel. *Meqor ḥayyim*. Mantua, 1559.

Zohar. 3 vols. Vilna, 1882.

SECONDARY SOURCES

Aescoly, A. Z., ed. *Ha-Tenu'ot ha-meshiḥiyyot be-Yisra'el*. Jerusalem, 1956.

Ahrend, Moshe M. "Peirush Rashbam le-'Iyyov?" *Alei sefer* 5 (1977–78):25–48.

———. *Le commentaire sur Job de Rabbi Yoséph Qara*. Hildesheim, 1978.

Alcover Sureda, Antonio Maria, ed. *Diccionari Català-Valencià-Balear*. 10 vols. Palma de Mallorca, 1951–62.

Allony, Nehemiah. "David 'Ibn Bilyah vi-yeṣirotav." In *'Areshet: Sefer shanah shel 'Iggud Soferim Datiyyim*, ed. Yiṣḥaq Werfel, 377–86. Jerusalem, 1943.

Altmann, Alexander. "*Ars Rhetorica* as Reflected in Some Jewish Figures of the Italian Renaissance." In his *Essays in Jewish Intellectual History*, 97–118. Hanover, N.H., 1981.

———. "Moses Narboni's 'Epistle on Shi'ur Qoma': A Critical Edition of the Hebrew Text with an Introduction and an Annotated English Translation." In *Jewish Medieval and Renaissance Studies*, ed. Alexander Altmann, 225–88. Cambridge, Mass., 1967.

———. *Studies in Religious Philosophy and Mysticism*. Ithaca, N.Y., 1969.

American Academy for Jewish Research. *Rashi Anniversary Volume*. New York, 1941.

Aminoff, Irit. "The Figures of Esau and the Kingdom of Edom in Palestinian Midrashic-Talmudic Literature in the Tannaic and Amoraic Periods." Ph.D. diss., Melbourne University, 1981.

Anderson, Bernhard. "The Place of the Book of Esther in the Christian Bible." *Journal of Religion* 30 (1950): 32–43.

Ankori, Zvi. *Karaites in Byzantium: The Formative Years, 970–1100*. New York, 1959.

Aragón en su historia. Saragossa, 1980.

Ashtor, Eliyahu. *The History of the Jews in Moslem Spain*. Trans. Aaron Klein and Jenny Machlowitz Klein. 3 vols. Philadelphia, 1973–84.

Avineri, Yitzhak. *Millon peirushei Rashi la-Miqra' ve-la-Talmud Bavli.* Tel Aviv, 1949. Repr. in his *Heikhal Rashi,* vol. 2. Jerusalem, 1985.

Bacher, Wilhelm. "L'exégèse biblique dans le Zohar." *Revue des études juives* 22 (1891): 33–46.

Baer, Fritz (= Yitzhak), ed. *Die Juden im Christlichen Spanien.* 2 vols. Berlin, 1929–36. Repr. Westmead, Farnborough, Hants., 1970.

———. "Sefer Minḥat qena'ot shel 'Avner mi-Burgos ve-hashpa'ato 'al Ḥasdai Qresqas." *Tarbiẓ* 11 (1939–40): 188–206.

———. *A History of the Jews in Christian Spain.* 2 vols. Philadelphia, 1961–66.

Banitt, Menahem. *Rashi, Interpreter of the Biblical Letter.* Tel Aviv, 1985.

Baron, Salo W. "'Plenitude of Apostolic Powers' and Medieval Jewish Serfdom." In his *Ancient and Medieval Jewish History,* ed. L. A. Feldman, 284–307. New Brunswick, N.J., 1972.

———. "Medieval Nationalism and Jewish Serfdom." In *Studies in Honor of Abraham A. Neuman,* ed. Meir Ben-Horin, Bernard D. Weinryb, and Solomon Zeitlin, 17–48. Leiden, 1962. (Revised version in his *Ancient and Medieval Jewish History,* 308–22).

———. "The Jewish Factor in Medieval Civilization." *Proceedings of the American Academy for Jewish Research* 12 (1942): 1–48. (Repr. in his *Ancient and Medieval Jewish History,* 239–67).

———. *A Social and Religious History of the Jews.* 2nd ed. 18 vols. New York, 1952–83.

Bashan, Eliezer. *Shivyah u-fedut ba-ḥevrah ha-yehudit be-'arṣot ha-Yam ha-tikhon (1391–1830).* Ramat-Gan, 1980.

Beattie, D. R. G. *Jewish Exegesis of the Book of Ruth.* Journal for the Study of the Old Testament, Supplement Series, 2. Sheffield, 1977.

Beinart, Haim. "Demutah shel ha-ḥaṣranut ha-yehudit bi-Sefarad hanoṣerit." In *Qevuṣot ʿillit u-shekhavot manhigot be-toledot Yisra'el u-ve-toledot ha-ʿammim: qoveṣ harṣa'ot she-hushmeʿu ba-kenes ha-ʿasiri le-ʿiyyun be-hisṭoryah (Ḥanukkah, 5725)*, 55–71. Jerusalem, 1966.

Ben-Chorin, Shalom. *Kritik des Estherbuches: eine theologische Streitschrift.* Jerusalem, 1938.

Ben-Sasson, H. H. "Dor golei Sefarad ʿal ʿaṣmo." *Zion* 26 (1961): 23–64.

———. "Galut u-ge'ullah be-ʿeinav shel dor golei Sefarad." In *Sefer Yovel le-Yiṣḥaq Ber*, ed. S. Ettinger [et al.], 216–27. Jerusalem, 1960.

Ben-Yehuda, Eliezer. *Millon ha-lashon ha-ʿivrit.* 16 vols. Jerusalem, 1910–59.

Benayahu Meir. "Vikkuaḥ ha-qabbalah ʿim ha-halakhah." *Daʿat* no. 5 (Summer, 1980):61–115.

Berliner, Abraham. *Peleiṭat soferim.* Breslau, 1872.

Berman, Joshua. "Aggadah and Antisemitism: The Midrashim to Esther 3:8." *Judaism* 38 (1989): 185–96.

Berman, L. V. "Greek into Hebrew: Samuel ben Judah of Marseilles, Fourteenth Century Philosopher and Translator." In *Jewish Medieval and Renaissance Studies*, ed. Alexander Altmann, 289–320. Cambridge, Mass., 1967.

———. "Ibn Rushd's Middle Commentary on the *Nicomachean Ethics* in Medieval Hebrew Literature." In *Multiple Averroès: Actes du Colloque International organisé à l'occasion du 850e anniversaire de la naissance d'Averroès, Paris, 20–23 septembre, 1976*, 287–321. Paris, 1978.

———. "Ketav-yad ha-mekhunneh 'Shoshan limmudim' ve-yaḥaso li-ʿqehal ha-meʿayyenim' ha-provansali." *Kiryat Sefer* 53 (1978): 368–72.

Bernstein, Béla. *Die Schrifterklärung des Bachja b. Asher ibn Chalawa und ihre Quellen*. Berlin, 1891. (Also published in *Magazin für die Wissenschaft des Judenthums* 18 (1891): 27–47, 85–118, 165–96.)

Bernstein, Peretz. *Jew-Hate as a Sociological Problem*. Trans. David Saraph. New York, 1951.

Besserman, Lawrence L. *The Legend of Job in the Middle Ages*. Cambridge, Mass., 1979.

Bettan, Israel. "Isaac Arama: The Preacher's Preacher." *Hebrew Union College Annual* 12–13 (1937–38): 583–634. Repr. in his *Studies in Jewish Preaching*, 130–91. Cincinnati, 1939.

Blumenfeld, I., ed. *'Oṣar neḥmad*. 4 vols. Vienna, 1856–63. Repr. Jerusalem, 1966–67.

Bofarull y Sans, Francisco de Asis de. "Los judíos malsines." *Boletin de la Real Academia de Buenas Letras de Barcelona* 6 (1911–12): 207–16.

Born, Lester K. "The Perfect Prince: A Study in Thirteenth- and Fourteenth-Century Ideals." *Speculum* 3 (1928): 470–504.

Borst, Arno. *Der Turmbau von Babel: Geschichte der Meinungen über Ursprung und Vielfalt der Sprachen und Völker*. 4 vols. in 6. Stuttgart, 1957–63.

Bouché-Leclercq, Auguste. *L'Astrologie grecque*. Paris, 1899.

Bowers, R. H. *The Legend of Jonah*. The Hague, 1971.

Brin, Gershon. "Qavvim le-feirush ha-Torah shel R. Yehudah he-Ḥasid." In *Meḥqarim be-sifrut ha-Talmud, bi-leshon Ḥazal u-ve-farshanut ha-Miqra'*, ed. M. A. Friedman, Avraham Tal, and Gershon Brin, 215–26. Tel Aviv, 1983.

———. "R. Judah he-Hasid: Early Bible Exegete Rediscovered." *Immanuel*, no. 12 (Spring, 1981): 21–31.

———. *Meḥqarim be-feirusho shel R. Yosef Qara'*. Tel Aviv, 1990.

Brown, Francis, S. R. Driver, and Charles A. Briggs. *A Hebrew and English Lexicon of the Old Testament.* Oxford, 1907.

Burckhardt, Titus. *Die Maurische Kultur in Spanien.* Munich, 1970.

Cantera-Burgos, Francisco. "Etimologia de la palabra 'malsin'." *Anales de la Universidad de Madrid: Letras* 4 (1935): 202–3.

Caplan, Harry. "A Medieval Commentary on the *Rhetorica ad Herennium.*" In his *Of Eloquence: Studies in Ancient and Medieval Rhetoric*, ed. Anne King and Helen North, 247–70. Ithaca, N.Y., 1970.

———. "The Four Senses of Scriptural Interpretation and the Medieval Theory of Preaching." *Speculum* 4 (1929): 282–90. (Repr. in his *Of Eloquence: Studies in Ancient and Medieval Rhetoric*, ed. Anne King and Helen North, 93–104. Ithaca, N.Y., 1970).

Cassuto, Umberto. *Dante e Manoello.* Florence, 1921.

———. *Danṭeh ve-ʿImmanuʾel ha-Romi.* Trans. Menahem Dorman. Jerusalem, 1965.

Castro, Americo. *The Structure of Spanish History.* Trans. Edmund L. King. Princeton, N.J., 1954.

Catane, Moche. *ʾOṣar ha-leʿazim: ha-milim ha-Ṣarefatiyyot she-be-feirushei Rashi ʿal ha-Tanakh.* Jerusalem, 1990.

Chajes, Z. H. *The Student's Guide to the Talmud.* Trans. Jacob Shachter. 2nd rev. ed. New York, 1960.

Chazan, Robert. *Medieval Jewry in Northern France.* Baltimore, 1973.

———, ed. *Church, State and Jew in the Middle Ages.* New York, 1980.

Clines, David J. A. *The Esther Scroll: The Story of the Story.* Journal for the Study of the Old Testament supplement series, 30. Sheffield, 1984.

Cohen, Gerson D. "Esau as Symbol in Early Medieval Thought." In *Jewish Medieval and Renaissance Studies*, ed. Alexander Altmann, 19–48. Cambridge, Mass., 1967.

Cohen, Jeremy. *"Be Fertile and Increase, Fill the Earth and Master It": The Ancient and Medieval Career of a Biblical Text*. Ithaca, N.Y., 1989.

———. *The Friars and the Jews*: the Evolution of *Medieval Anti-Judaism*. Ithaca, N.Y., 1982.

Courcelle, Pierre. *"La Consolation de Philosophie" dans la tradition littéraire: antécedents et postérité de Boèce*. Paris, 1967.

Cremona, J. "Dante's Views on Language." In *The Mind of Dante*, ed. U. Limentani, 138–62. Cambridge, 1965.

Daniélou, Jean. *From Shadows to Reality: Studies in the Biblical Typology of the Fathers*. Trans. Walstan Hibberd. London, 1960.

Darmesteter, Arsène. "Les gloses françaises de Raschi dans la Bible." *Revue des études juives* 53 (1907): 161–93; 54 (1907): 1–34, 205–35; 55 (1908): 72–83; 56 (1908): 70–98.

Davidovitz, Tmima. "Peirushei ha-Raba' le-'Ester." *Sinai* 101 (1987–88): 113–25.

Davidson, Herbert. *The Philosophy of Abraham Shalom: A Fifteenth Century Exposition and Defense of Maimonides*. University of California Publications, Near Eastern Studies, vol. 5. Berkeley and Los Angeles, 1964.

Delort, Robert. *Life in the Middle Ages*. Trans. Robert Allen. New York, 1973.

Di Camillo, Ottavio. *El humanismo castellano del siglo XV*. Valencia, 1976.

Dictionary of the Middle Ages. Ed. Joseph R. Strayer. 13 vols. New York, 1982–89.

Dinur, Benzion, ed. *Yisra'el ba-golah*. 2nd ed. 2 vols. in 10. Tel Aviv, 1958–72.

Doren, Alfred. "Fortuna im Mittelalter und in der Renaissance." *Vorträge der Bibliothek Warburg* 2 (1922–23): 71–144.

Dreksler, Mordekhai. *Meqonen 'evlenu*. Seini, Romania, 1932.

Dubarle, A. M. *Judith: Formes et sens des diverses traditions*. 2 vols. Rome, 1966.

Duval, Yves-Marie. *Le Livre de Jonas dans la littérature chrétienne grecque et latine: Sources et influence du commentaire sur Jonas de saint Jérôme*. 2 vols. Paris, 1973.

Eilberg-Schwartz, Howard. "Who's Kidding Whom?: A Serious Reading of Rabbinic Word-Plays." *Journal of the American Academy of Religion* 55 (1987): 765–88.

Einstein, Berthold. *R. Josef Kara und sein Kommentar zu Kohelet*. Berlin, 1886. Reprint. Tel Aviv, 1970.

Elon, Menachem. *Ha-Mishpaṭ ha-'ivri: toledotav, meqorotav, 'eqronotav*. 3rd ed. 3 vols. Jerusalem, 1988.

Encyclopaedia Judaica. 10 vols. Berlin, 1928–34. (A-Lyra).

Encyclopaedia Judaica. 16 vols. Jerusalem, 1971–72.

Enṣiqlopedyah ha-'ivrit. 32 vols. Jerusalem, 1949–80/81.

Enṣiqlopedyah miqra'it. 8 vols. Jerusalem, 1950–82.

Eppenstein, Simon. "Studien über Joseph ben Simon Kara als Exeget." *Jahrbuch der Jüdisch-Literarischen Gesellschaft* 4 (1906): 238–68.

Epstein, Abraham. "R. Yosef Qara' ve-ha-peirush li-Bereshit Rabba' ha-meyuḥas le-Rashi." *Ha-Ḥoqer* 1 (1891): 29–35. (Repr. in his *Mi-qadmoniyyot ha-Yehudim*, 328–36. Jerusalem, 1956–57.)

Even-Shoshan, Avraham. *Qonqordanṣyah ḥadashah le-Torah Nevi'im u-Khetuvim.* 3 vols. in 4. Jerusalem, 1977.

Ewart, Alfred. "Dante's Theory of Language." *Modern Language Review* 35 (1940): 355–66.

Faulhaber, Charles. *Latin Rhetorical Theory in Thirteenth and Fourteenth Century Castile.* University of California Publications in Modern Philology, vol. 103. Berkeley and Los Angeles, 1971.

———. "The *Summa dictaminis* of Guido Faba." In *Medieval Eloquence: Studies in the Theory and Practice of Medieval Rhetoric,* ed. James J. Murphy, 85–111. Berkeley and Los Angeles, 1978.

Federbush, Simon, ed. *Rashi: His Teachings and Personality: Essays on the 850th Anniversary of his Death.* New York, 1958.

Feliks, Jehuda. *'Olam ha-ṣomeaḥ ha-miqra'i.* 2nd ed. rev. Ramat-Gan, 1968.

Fleischer, J. L. "Maddua' yaṣa' Rabbeinu 'Avraham 'Ibn 'Ezra' mi-Sefarad?" *Mizraḥ u-ma'arav* 3 (1929): 325–35.

———. "Matai ve-'eifoh ḥibber 'Ibn 'Ezra' *Sefer Safah berurah* shello?" *Ha-Ṣofeh le-ḥokhmat Yisra'el* 13 (1929): 82–88.

———. "Rabbeinu 'Avraham 'Ibn 'Ezra' be-Ṣarefat: Hitgoreruto va-'avodato ha-sifrutit sham." *Mizraḥ u-ma'arav* 4 (1930): 352–60; 5 (1930–32): 38–46, 217–24, 289–300.

———. "Rabbeinu 'Avraham 'Ibn 'Ezra' va-'avodato ha-sifrutit ba-'ir Roma'." *'Oṣar ha-ḥayyim* 9 (1933): 18–22, 85–86, 96–99, 134–36, 152–55.

Fox, Michael V. "The Religion of the Book of Esther." *Judaism* 39 (1990): 135–47.

Franklin, Alfred. *La vie privée d'autrefois: Les repas.* Paris, 1889.

Friedländer, Michael. *Essays on the Writings of Abraham Ibn Ezra.* Ibn Ezra Literature, vol. 4. London, 1877.

Funkenstein, Amos. "Basic Types of Christian Anti-Jewish Polemics in the Later Middle Ages." *Viator* 2 (1971): 373–82.

———. "Ha-Temurot be-vikkuaḥ ha-dat she-bein Yehudim le-Noṣerim ba-me'ah ha-12." *Zion* 33 (1968): 125–44.

———. "Naḥmanides' Symbolical Reading of History." In *Studies in Jewish Mysticism*, ed. Joseph Dan and Frank Talmage, 129–50. Cambridge, Mass., 1982.

———. "Parshanut ṭippologit 'eṣel ha-Ramban." *Zion* 45 (1979–80): 35–49.

Galliner, Julius. *Abraham Ibn Esra's Hiobkommentar auf seine Quellen untersucht*. Berlin, 1901.

Gaster, Moses, ed. "The Oldest Version of Midrash Megillah." In his *Studies and Texts in Folklore, Magic, Medieval Romance, Hebrew Apocrypha and Samaritan Archaeology*. 3 vols. London, 1925–28. 3:44–49.

Geiger, Abraham. "Nosafot 'al devar R. Shemaryah ha-'Iqriṭi." *He-Ḥalus* 10 (1853): 158–60.

Gelles, Benjamin J. *Peshat and Derash in the Exegesis of Rashi*. Leiden, 1981.

Gerleman, Gillis. *Esther*. Biblischer Kommentar Altes Testament, 21. Neukirchen-Vluyn, 1970–73.

Ginzberg, Louis. *Legends of the Jews*. 7 vols. Philadelphia, 1913–38.

Golb, Norman. *Toledot ha-Yehudim ba-'ir Ru'an bi-yemei ha-beinayim*. Tel Aviv, 1976.

Goldstein, Albert S. "Megillath Esther: The Original Purim Shpiel Stage Script." *Journal of Reform Judaism* 26:2 (Spring, 1979): 89–104.

Goodman, Philip, ed. *The Purim Anthology*. Philadelphia, 1964.

Gottlieb, Ephraim. *Ha-Qabbalah be-khitvei Baḥya ben 'Asher*. Jerusalem, 1970.

Grabois, Aryeh. "L'exégèse rabbinique." In *Le Moyen Âge et la Bible*, ed. Pierre Riché and Guy Lobrichon. Bible de tous les temps, 4. Paris, 1984.

———. "The *Hebraica Veritas* and Jewish-Christian Intellectual Relations in the Twelfth Century." *Speculum* 50 (1975): 613–34.

Greenberg, Moshe, ed. *Parshanut ha-Miqra' ha-Yehudit: Pirqei Mavo'*. Jerusalem, 1983.

Grober, Gustav. *Grundriß der Romanischen Philologie*. 2nd ed. 2 vols. Strassburg, 1904–6.

Gross, Abraham. "The World of Abraham Saba." Ph.D. diss., Harvard University, 1982.

———. "Hishtaqfut geirushei Sefarad u-Portugal be-feirush 'al Megillat 'Ester." In *Proceedings of the Ninth World Congress of Jewish Studies, Jerusalem, August 4–12, 1985*: Division B, *History of the Jewish People*, vol. 1, *From the Second Temple Until the Middle Ages*, 153–58. Jerusalem, 1986.

———. "Rabbi 'Avraham Saba' ha-megorash bi-shenei geirushim." In *Sefer ha-zikkaron le-ha-Rav Yiṣḥaq Nissim*, vol. 4, *Qabbalat ha-Ari, te'udot 'al qehilot ve-'ishim*, 205–24. Jerusalem, 1984–85.

Gross, Heinrich. *Gallia Judaica*. Paris, 1897. Repr. with suppl. Amsterdam, 1969.

Grossman, Abraham. "Ha-Peirush li-Megillat Qohelet ha-meyuḥas la-Rashbam." *Tarbiẓ* 45 (1975–76): 336–40.

———. "'Od 'al peirush ha-Rashbam le-Qohelet." *Tarbiẓ* 48 (1978–79): 172.

———. "Ha-Polmos ha-Yehudi-ha-Noṣri ve-ha-parshanut ha-Yehudit la-Miqra' be-Ṣarefat ba-me'ah ha-12 (le-farashat ziqato shel R.Y. Qara' 'el ha-polmos," *Zion* 51 (1985–86): 29–60.

Güdemann, Moritz. *Geschichte des Erziehungswesens und der Cultur der abendländischen Juden während des Mittelalters und des neueren Zeit.* 3 vols. Vienna, 1880–88. Repr. Amsterdam, 1966.

Guttmann, Alexander. "The Significance of Miracles for Talmudic Judaism." *Hebrew Union College Annual* 20 (1947): 363–406.

Hacker, Joseph. "Defusei Qushta' ba-me'ah ha-16." *'Areshet* 5 (1972): 457–93.

Haliczer, Stephen. "The Expulsion of the Jews and the Economic Development of Castile." In *Hispania Judaica: Studies on the History, Language and Literature of the Jews in the Hispanic World*, ed. J. M. Solà-Solé, S. G. Armistead, J. H. Silverman. Biblioteca Universal Puvill, I. Estudios. 3 vols. to date, 1:39–47. Barcelona, 1980–84.

Halkin, A. S. "Le-toledot ha-shemad bi-yemei ha-'Almuvaḥidin." *In The Joshua Starr Memorial Volume: Studies in History and Philology*, 101–10. Jewish Social Studies Publications, no. 5. New York, 1953.

———. "Why was Levi ben Abraham Hounded?" *Proceedings of the American Academy for Jewish Research* 34 (1966): 65–76.

Hallamish, Moshe. "'Aspeqṭim 'aḥadim bi-she'elat yaḥasam shel ha-mequbbalim le-'ummot ha-'olam." In *Filosofyah Yisre'elit*, ed. Asa Kasher and Moshe Hallamish, 49–71. Tel Aviv, 1983.

Hamburger, J. *'Avigdor Kohen Ṣedeq*. Mainz, 1900.

Harvey, Zeev. "Yesodot qabbaliyyim be-*Sefer 'Or ha-Shem* le-Rabbi Ḥasdai Qresqas." *Meḥqerei Yerushalayim be-maḥashevet Yisra'el* 2, no. 1 (September, 1982): 75–110.

Heide, Albert van der. "Rashi's Biblical Exegesis: Recent Research and Developments." *Bibliotheca Orientalis* 41 (1984): 292–318.

———. "PARDES: Methodological Reflections on the Theory of the Four Senses." *Journal of Jewish Studies* 34 (1983): 147–59.

Heinemann, Isaak. *Darkhei ha-'aggadah*. 2nd ed. Jerusalem, 1954.

Heller, Chaim. *Untersuchungen über die Peschitta*. Berlin, 1916.

Herr, M. D. "Sin'at Yisra'el ba-'Imperyah ha-Romit le-'or sifrut Ḥazal." In *Sefer zikkaron le-Vinyamin deh-Fris*, 149–59. Jerusalem, 1968–69. Repr. in *Yehudim ve-Yahadut be-'einei ha-'olam ha-helenisṭi*, 33–43. Jerusalem, 1973–74.

Herring, Basil. *Joseph Ibn Kaspi's "Gevia Kesef": A Study in Medieval Jewish Philosophic Bible Commentary*. New York, 1982.

Hillgarth, J. N. *The Spanish Kingdoms, 1250–1516*. 2 vols. Oxford, 1976–78.

Hirschfeld, Hartwig. "The Arabic Portion of the Cairo Genizah at Cambridge (Tenth Article)." *Jewish Quarterly Review*, o.s. 17 (1904–05): 712–25.

———. *Literary History of Hebrew Grammarians and Lexicographers*. London, 1926.

Hoag, John D. *Western Islamic Architecture*. London, 1963.

Holmes, U. T. *Daily Life in the Twelfth Century*. Madison, Wis., 1952.

Horowitz, Carmi. *The Jewish Sermon in 14th Century Spain: the Derashot of R. Joshua ibn Shu'eib*. Harvard Judaic Monographs, 6. Cambridge, Mass., 1989.

Humphreys, W. Lee. "A Life-style for Diaspora: A Study of the Tales of Esther and Daniel." *Journal of Biblical Literature* 92 (1973): 211–23.

Huttar, Charles A. "Frail Grass and Firm Tree: David as a Model of Repentance in the Middle Ages and Early Renaissance." In *The David Myth in Western Literature*, ed. Raymond-Jean Frontain and Jan Wojcik, 38–55. West Lafayette, Ind., 1980.

Hyman, Arthur. "The Liberal Arts and Jewish Philosophy." In *Arts libéraux et philosophie au moyen âge: actes du quatrième Congrès International de Philosophie Médiévale, Université de Montréal,*

Montréal Canada, 27 août–2 septembre, 1967, 99–110. Montreal, 1969.

Jaeger, C. Stephen. *The Origins of Courtliness: Civilizing Trends and the Formation of Courtly Ideals, 939–1210*. Philadelphia, 1985.

Japhet, Sara. "Kivvunei meḥqar ve-hilkhei ruaḥ be-ḥeqer parshanut yemei ha-beinayim bi-Ṣefon Ṣarefat," in *Yedi'on ha-'Iggud ha-'olami le-mada'ei ha-Yahadut (Newsletter of the World Union of Jewish Studies)* 25 (1984–85): 3–18; also published in *Meḥqarim ba-Miqra' u-va-Talmud*, ed. Sara Japhet, 17–39. Jerusalem, 1987.

———. "Peirush ha-Rashbam 'al Megillat Qohelet." *Tarbiẓ* 44 (1974–75): 72–94.

———. "Peirush ha-Rashbam 'al Megillat Qohelet." *Tarbiẓ* 47 (1977–78): 243–46.

Jastrow, Marcus. *Dictionary of the Targumim, Talmud Babli and Yerushalmi and Midrashic Literature*. London, 1903.

Jourdain, Amable. *Recherches critiques sur l'âge et l'origine des traductions latines d'Aristote*. Revised and expanded edition by Charles Jourdain. Paris, 1843.

Kadushin, Max. *Organic Thinking*. New York, 1938. Repr. New York, 1976.

Kamen, Henry. *The Spanish Inquisition*. London, 1965.

Kamin, Sarah. "Rashi's Exegetical Categorization with respect to the Distinction Between Peshat and Derash; According to his Commentary to the Book of Genesis and Selected Passages from his Commentaries to other Books of the Bible." *Immanuel* 11 (1980): 16–32.

———. *Rashi: peshuṭo shel Miqra' u-midrasho shel Miqra'*. Jerusalem, 1986.

Kamin-Rozik, Sarah. "'Sibbatiyyut kefulah' be-feirush Rashi li-

Megillat 'Ester: ʿiyyun be-shiqqulav shel Rashi bi-veḥirat peirushei Ḥazal." In *Sefer Yiṣḥaq 'Aryeh Zeligman: ma'amarim ba-Miqra' u-va-ʿolam ha-ʿatiq*, ed. Yair Zakovitch and Alexander Rofé. 3 vols. Jerusalem, 1982, 2:547–58 (Hebrew section).

Kasher, Hannah. "Pitronot balshaniyyim li-veʿayot te'ologiyyot mi-mishnato shel Yosef 'ibn Kaspi." In *Dat ve-safah: ma'amarim be-filosofyah kelalit vi-yehudit*, ed. Moshe Hallamish and Asa Kasher, 91–96. Tel Aviv, 1981.

Katz, Jacob. *Exclusiveness and Tolerance*. New York, 1961.

———. *Halakhah ve-qabbalah*. Jerusalem, 1984.

Katz, Solomon. *The Jews in the Visigothic and Frankish Kingdoms of Spain and Gaul*. Cambridge, Mass., 1937.

Kaufmann, David. "Jewish Informers in the Middle Ages." *Jewish Quarterly Review*, o.s. 8 (1895–96): 217–38, 527–28.

Kellner, Menachem M. "R. Levi ben Gerson: A Bibliographical Essay." *Studies in Bibliography and Booklore* 12 (1979): 13–23.

Kiener, Ronald. "The Image of Islam in the Zohar." *Jerusalem Studies in Jewish Thought* 8 (1989): 43*–65*.

Kisch, Guido. "The Jews in Medieval Law." In *Essays in Antisemitism*, ed. Koppel Pinson. New York, 1946.

———. *The Jews in Medieval Germany: A Study of their Legal and Social Status*. Chicago, 1949.

Knowles, David. *The Evolution of Medieval Thought*. London, 1962.

Kohen, Yosef. "Megillat 'Ester ba-'aspaqlaryah shel ḥakhmei Ṣefat ba-me'ah ha-16." *She'arim*, 4 March, 6 March, 1966.

Kreisel, Howard. "Miracles in Medieval Jewish Philosophy." *Jewish Quarterly Review* 75 (1984–85): 99–133.

Lasker, Daniel J. "Averroistic Trends in Jewish-Christian Polemics in the Late Middle Ages." *Speculum* 55 (1980): 294–304.

Last, Isaac. "*Sharshoth Kesef*: The Hebrew Dictionary of Roots by Joseph ibn Kaspi." *Jewish Quarterly Review*, o.s. 19 (1907): 651–87. Repr. with Kaspi, Joseph. *Tam ha-Kesef*, ed. I. Last. London, 1913.

Lazarus-Yafeh, Hava. "'Ester ha-malkah—min ha-'anusim? Peirusho shel Raba' le-'Ester 2:10." *Tarbiẓ* 57 (1987–88): 121–22.

Leff, Michael C. "Boethius' *De differentiis topicis, Book IV*." In *Medieval Eloquence: Studies in the Theory and Practice of Medieval Rhetoric*, ed. James J. Murphy, 3–24. Berkeley and Los Angeles, 1978.

Leibowitz, Nechama. "Darko shel Rashi be-hava'at midrashim be-feirusho la-Torah." In her *'Iyyunim ḥadashim be-sefer Shemot be-'iqvot parshaneinu ha-rishonim ve-ha-'aḥaronim*. 2nd ed., 495–524. Jerusalem, 1970.

———, and Moshe Ahrend. *Peirush Rashi la-Torah: 'iyyunim be-shiṭṭato*. Tel Aviv, 1990.

Lerner, M. B. "Tashlum peirush R. Yiṣḥaq 'Aramah li-Megillat Rut. In *Sefer zikkaron li-Shemu'el Qalman Mirsqi* [*Mirsky*], ed. Gersion Appel, 105–23. New York, 1971.

Lesley, Arthur M. "A Survey of Medieval Hebrew Rhetoric." *Approaches to Judaism in Medieval Times* 1 (1984): 107–33.

Levenson, Jon D. "The Scroll of Esther in Ecumenical Perspective." *Journal of Ecumenical Studies* 13 (1976): 440–52.

Lévi-Provençal, Évariste. *Histoire de l'Espagne musulmane*. 2nd ed. 3 vols. Paris, 1950–53.

———. *L'Espagne musulmane au Xème siècle; Institutions et vie sociale*. Paris, 1932.

Levin, Israel. *Rabbeinu 'Avraham 'Ibn 'Ezra': Ḥayyav ve-shirato*. Tel Aviv, 1969.

Lewis, Jack P. *A Study of the Interpretation of Noah and the Flood in Jewish and Christian Literature.* Leiden, 1968.

Libowitz, N. S. *Rabbi 'Avraham Saba' u-sefarav.* Brooklyn, 1936.

Liebes, Yehuda. "Keiṣad nitḥabber Sefer ha-Zohar." *Meḥqerei Yerushalayim be-maḥashevet Yisra'el* 8 (1989): 1–72.

Lipschuetz, E. M. *Rashi.* In his *Ketavim,* 1:9–196. Jerusalem, 1947. Repr. Jerusalem, 1976.

Littmann, Martin. *Josef ben Simeon Kara als Schrifterklärer.* Breslau, 1887.

Loewinger, D. S., and B. D. Weinryb. *Catalogue of the Hebrew Manuscripts in the Library of the Juedisch-Theologisches Seminar in Breslau.* Wiesbaden, 1965.

Lottin, Odon. *Psychologie et morale aux XIIe et XIIIe siècles.* 6 vols. Gembloux, Belgium, 1942–60.

Lowy, S. *The Principles of Samaritan Biblical Exegesis.* Studia post-biblica, vol. 28. Leiden, 1977.

Luzzatto, S. D. [article in] *Kerem ḥemed* 7 (1843): 68.

Maimon, Y. L., ed. *Sefer Rashi.* Jerusalem, 1955.

Malter, Henry. *Saadia Gaon: His Life and Works.* Philadelphia, 1921.

Manor, Dan. "Galut u-ge'ullah be-khitvei R. 'Avraham Saba' ʿal reqaʿ goralo ha-'ishi ve-goral sefarav." M.A. thesis, Hebrew University, Jerusalem, 1974.

———. "Kitvei R. 'Avraham Saba'." *Sefunot* 18 (n.s. 3) (1984–85): 336–37.

———. "Le-toldotav shel R. 'Avraham Saba'." *Meḥqerei Yerushalayim be-maḥashevet Yisra'el* 2 (1982–83): 208–31.

Marcus, Ivan. "Exegesis for the Few and for the Many: Judah he-

Ḥasid's Biblical Commentaries." *Jerusalem Studies in Jewish Thought* 8 (1989): 1★–24★

Margaliot, Reuben. *Mal'akhei ʿelyon*. 2nd ed. Jerusalem, 1964.

Marx, Alexander. "The Correspondence Between the Rabbis of Southern France and Maimonides about Astrology." *Hebrew Union College Annual* 3 (1926): 311–58.

Mehlman, Israel. "Peraqim be-toledot ha-defus be-Saloniqi." In his *Genuzot sefarim*, 43–102. Jerusalem, 1976.

Melamed, E. Z. "Le-feirush Nakh shel R. Yeshaʿyah mi-Ṭrani." In *Meḥqarim ba-Miqra' u-va-Mizraḥ ha-qadmon muggashim li-Shemu'el A. Livenshṭam [Loewenstamm] bi-melot lo shivʿim shanah*, 279–302. Jerusalem, 1978.

Melammed, Abraham. "Reṭoriqah u-filosofyah be-*Sefer Nofet ṣufim* la-Rav Yehudah Meser Le'on." *Italia* 1 (1978): 7–39 (Hebrew section).

Mesch, Barry. *Studies in Joseph ibn Kaspi*. Études sur le Judaïsme médiéval, vol. 8. Leiden, Netherlands, 1975.

Miller, Philip. "At the Twilight of Byzantine Karaism: The Anachronism of Judah Gibbor." Ph.D. diss., New York University, 1985.

Moldenke, Harold N., and Alma L. Moldenke. *Plants of the Bible*. Waltham, Mass., 1952.

Montgomery, J. A. *The Samaritans, the Earliest Jewish Sect: Their History, Theology and Literature*. Philadelphia, 1907.

Moore, Carey A., trans. *Esther*. The Anchor Bible, 7B. Garden City, N.Y., 1971.

Morais, Vamberto. *A Short History of Antisemitism*. New York, 1976.

Nardi, Bruno. *Dante e la cultura medievale*. 2nd ed. Bari, 1949.

Nathan ben Jehiel. *'Arukh ha-shalem*, ed. Alexander Kohut. 8 vols. Vienna, 1878–92.

Netanyahu, Benzion. *Don Isaac Abravanel*. 3rd ed. Philadelphia, 1972.

Neubauer, Adolf. "Literary Gleanings, VIII. Joseph ben Joseph Nahmias." *Jewish Quarterly Review*, o.s. 5 (1893): 709–13.

———. "R. Mattitya Ha-Yiṣhari." *Revue des études juives* 9 (1884): 116–19.

Nigal, Gedaliah. "Pereq be-haguto shel dor geirush Sefarad." *Sinai* 74 (1973–74): 67–80.

Novinsky, Anita, and Amilcar Paulo. "The Last Marranos." *Commentary* 43 (May, 1967): 76–81.

O'Callaghan, Joseph F. *A History of Medieval Spain*. Ithaca, N.Y., 1975.

'Oṣar neḥmad, see Blumenfeld, I., ed. *'Oṣar neḥmad*.

Pagden, A. R. D. "The Diffusion of Aristotle's Moral Philosophy in Spain, ca. 1400–ca. 1600." *Traditio* 31 (1975): 287–313.

Pakhter, Mordekhai. "Sifrut ha-derush ve-ha-musar shel ḥakhmei Ṣefat ba-me'ah ha-16 u-ma'arekhet ra'ayonoteha ha-'iqqariyyim." Ph.D. diss., Hebrew University, Jerusalem, 1976.

Palacios Martín, Bonifacio. *La Coronación de los Reyes de Aragón, 1204–1410*. Valencia, 1975.

Parkes, James. *The Jew in the Medieval Community*. 2nd ed. New York, 1976.

Paton, L. B. *A Critical and Exegetical Commentary on the Book of Esther*. The International Critical Commentary. New York, 1908.

Pfeiffer, R. H. *Introduction to the Old Testament*. New York, 1941.

Pines, Shlomo. "Histabberut ha-tequmah me-ḥadash shel medinah yehudit le-fi Yosef 'ibn Kaspi u-le-fi Shpinozah," *'Iyyun* 14 (1963):289–317. Repr. in his *Bein maḥashevet Yisra'el le-maḥashevet ha-'ammim*, 277–305. Jerusalem, 1977.

Poorter, A. de. "Un manuel de prédication médiévale: le MS. 97 de Bruges." *Revue néo-scolastique de philosophie* 25 (1923): 192–209.

Poznanski, Samuel. "Mitteilungen aus handschriftlichen Bibel-Commentaren. II. Die in Josef b. Josef Ibn Nachmias' Mišlê-Commentar citirten Autoren." *Zeitschrift fur Hebräische Bibliographie* 1 (1896): 118–21.

———. Introduction to *Peirush 'al Yeḥezkel u-Terei 'asar*, by Eliezer of Beaugency. Sefarim ha-yoṣe'im la-'or 'al-yedei Ḥevrat Meqiṣei nirdamim. Warsaw, 1913.

Preus, James S. "Theological Legitimation for Innovation in the Middle Ages." *Viator* 3 (1972): 1–26.

Prijs, Leo. *Die grammatikalische Terminologie Abraham ibn Ezra's*. Basel, 1950.

Rabinowitz, Isaac. "Pre-Modern Jewish Study of Rhetoric: An Introductory Bibliography." *Rhetorica* 3 (1985): 137–44.

Raḥaman, Yosefah. "'Ibbud midrashim be-feirusho shel Rashi la-Torah." In *Meḥqarim be-sifrut ha-Talmud, bi-leshon Ḥazal u-ve-farshanut ha-Miqra'*, ed. Mordechai Akiva Friedman, Avraham Tal, Gershon Brin. Te'udah, 3, 261–68. Tel Aviv, 1983.

———. "Bei'ur derekh ha-limmud shel ha-midrash be-feirush Rashi la-Torah." In *'Iyyunim ba-Miqra': sefer zikkaron li-Yehoshu'a Me'ir Grinṣ [Y. M. Grintz]*, ed. Benjamin Uffenheimer. Te'udah, 2, 111–27. Tel Aviv, 1982.

Reifmann, Jakob. "Toledot Rabbeinu Baḥya." *'Alummah* 1 (1936): 69–101.

Renan, Ernest. *Les écrivains juifs français du XIVe siècle*. Paris, 1893. Repr. Westmead, Farnborough, Hants., 1969.

Richardson, H. G. *English Jewry Under the Angevin Kings*. London, 1960.

Rosenberg, Shalom. "Higgayon, safah u-farshanut ha-Miqra' bi-khetavav shel R. Yosef 'ibn Kaspi." In *Dat ve-safah: ma'amarim be-filosofyah kelalit vi-yehudit*, ed. Moshe Hallamish and Asa Kasher, 105–13. Tel Aviv, 1981.

———. "Logiqah ve-'onṭologyah ba-filosofyah ha-yehudit ba-me'ah ha-14." 2 vols. Ph.D. diss., Hebrew University, Jerusalem, 1974.

Rosin, David. "Die Religionsphilosophie der Abraham Ibn Ezra's." *Monatsschrift für die Geschichte und Wissenschaft des Judentums* 42 (1898): 17–23, 58–73, 108–15, 154–61, 200–214, 241–52, 305–15, 345–62, 394–407, 444–57, 481–505; 43 (1899): 22–31, 75–91, 125–33, 168–84, 231–40.

———. *Rabbi Samuel ben Meir als Schrifterklärer*. Breslau, 1880.

Roth, Cecil. *History of the Marranos*. 4th ed. New York, 1974.

Sachs, Senior. [article in] *Ha-Yonah* 1 (1851): 59–93.

Salfeld, Siegmund. *Das Hohelied Salomos bei den jüdischen Erklärern des Mittelalters*. Berlin, 1879 (originally published in *Magazin für die Wissenschaft des Judenthums* 5 (1878): 110–78; 6 (1879): 20–48, 129–169, 189–209).

Salters, Robert B. "Observations on the Commentary on Qohelet by R. Samuel ben Meir." *Hermathena* 127 (1979): 51–62.

Sandler, Peretz. "Li-ve'ayat Pardes ve-ha-shiṭah ha-merubba'at." In *Sefer 'Averbakh* [*Auerbach*], ed. A. Biram, 222–35. Pirsumei ha-Ḥevrah le-ḥeqer ha-Miqra' be-Yisra'el, 1. Jerusalem, 1955.

Saperstein, Marc. *Decoding the Rabbis: A Thirteenth Century Commentary on the Aggadah*. Harvard Judaic Monographs, 3. Cambridge, Mass., 1980.

———. ed. *Jewish Preaching 1200–1800: An Anthology*. New Haven, Conn., 1989.

Scholem, Gershom. "Li-yedi'at ha-qabbalah bi-Sefarad 'erev ha-geirush." *Tarbiẓ* 24 (1954–55): 167–206.

———. "The Meaning of the Torah in Jewish Mysticism." Chap. 2 in *On the Kabbalah and its Symbolism*. Trans. Ralph Manheim. New York, 1965.

Scholem, Gershom. *Kabbalah*. Jerusalem, 1974.

———. *Major Trends in Jewish Mysticism*. New York, 1938.

Schreiber, Aaron M. *Jewish Law and Decision-Making: A Study Through Time*. Philadelphia, 1979.

Schultz, Alwin. *Das Hofische Leben zur Zeit der Minnesinger*. 2nd rev. ed. 2 vols. Leipzig, 1889.

Schwarzfuchs, Simon. "The Expulsion of the Jews from France (1306)." In *The Seventy-fifth Anniversary Volume of the Jewish Quarterly Review*, ed. Abraham A. Neuman and Solomon Zeitlin, 482–89. Philadelphia, 1967.

Schweid, Eliezer. "Ha-Petiḥut la-mufla' ki-yesod ha-'emunah (ha-nes ba-filosofyah ha-yehudit shel yemei-ha-beinayyim me-R. Se'adyah Ga'on 'ad R. Ḥasdai Qresqas." In his *Ṭa'am ve-haqashah*, 172–206. Ramat-Gan, 1970.

Sed-Rajna, Gabrielle. *The Hebrew Bible in Medieval Illuminated Manuscripts*. New York, 1987.

Segal, Eliezer. "Human Anger and Divine Intervention in Esther." *Prooftexts* 9 (1989): 247–56.

Segal, M.H. *Parshanut ha-Miqra'*. 2nd ed. Jerusalem, 1971.

Septimus, Bernard. "'Taḥat 'Edom ve-lo' taḥat Yishma''el'—gilgulo shel ma'amar." *Zion* 47 (1982): 103–11.

———. "Piety and Power in Thirteenth-Century Catalonia." In *Studies in Medieval Jewish History and Literature*, ed. Isadore Twersky, 197–230. Cambridge, Mass., 1979.

Sermoneta, Giuseppe. "Jehudah ben Mošeh ben Dani'el Romano, traducteur de Saint Thomas." In *Hommage à Georges Vajda: Études d'histoire et de pensée juives*, ed. Gérard Nahon and Charles Touati, 231–62. Louvain, 1980.

Sevenster, J. N. *The Roots of Pagan Antisemitism*. Supplement to Novum Testamentum, 41. Leiden, 1975.

Shapira, Yosef. *Bi-shevilei ha-ge'ullah*. 2 vols. Jerusalem, 1946–47.

Shatzmiller, Joseph. "Ha-Ralbag u-qehillat 'Oranzh bi-yemei ḥayyav." *Meḥqarim be-toledot 'am Yisra'el ve-'Ereṣ Yisra'el* 2 (1972): 111–26.

———. "'Od 'al ha-Ralbag u-qehillat 'Oranzh bi-yemei ḥayyav." *Meḥqarim be-toledot 'am Yisra'el ve-'Ereṣ Yisra'el* 3 (1974): 139–43.

———. *Shylock Reconsidered: Jews, Moneylending and Medieval Society*. Berkeley and Los Angeles, 1990.

———. "Terminologie politique en hébreu médiéval: jalons pour un glossaire." *Revue des études juives* 142 (1983): 133–140.

Shereshevsky, Esra. "The Significance of Rashi's Commentary on the Pentateuch." *Jewish Quarterly Review* 54 (1963–64): 58–79.

———. *Rashi: The Man and his World*. New York, 1982.

Shilo, Shmuel. *Dina' de-malkhuta' dina'*. Jerusalem, 1974.

Shohat, Azriel. "Qiddush ha-Shem be-hagutam shel megorshei Sefarad u-mequbbelei Ṣefat." In *Milḥemet qodesh u-marṭirologyah be-toledot Yisra'el u-ve-toledot ha-'ammim*, 131–46. Jerusalem, 1967–68.

Signer, Michael A. "Exégèse et enseignement: Les commentaires de Joseph ben Simeon Kara." *Archives juives* 18 (1982): 60–63.

Simon, Uriel. "R. 'Avraham 'Ibn 'Ezra'—Bein ha-mefaresh le-qor'av." In *Proceedings of the Ninth World Congress of Jewish Studies, Panel Sessions: Bible Studies and Ancient Near East*, 1:23–42. Jerusalem, 1988.

———. *'Arba' gishot le-sefer Tehillim.* Ramat-Gan, 1982.

———. *Four Approaches to the Book of Psalms: From Saadiah Gaon to Abraham Ibn Ezra.* Trans. Lenn J. Schramm. Albany, N.Y., 1991.

Sirat, Colette. "Mikhtav 'al ḥiddush ha-'olam me'et Shemaryah ben 'Elya 'Iqriṭi." *'Eshel Be'er Sheva'* 2 (1980): 199–227.

Smalley, Beryl. *The Study of the Bible in the Middle Ages.* 2nd ed. Notre Dame, Ind., 1964.

Sonne, Isaiah. "Tokh kedei qeri'ah, III: Geneivah sifrutit, 'o, ṭa'ut ha-madpis?" *Kiryat Sefer* 7 (1930–31): 279–81.

Sperber, Manes, ed. *Rachi: Ouvrage collectif.* Paris, 1974.

Spiro, Abraham. "The Ascension of Phinehas." *Proceedings of the American Academy for Jewish Research* 22 (1953): 91–114.

Steinschneider, Moritz. "Miscellen." [on Astruc Dernegrah] *Hebräische Bibliographie* 16 (1876): 92–93.

———. *Die hebräischen Übersetzungen des Mittelalters und die Juden als Dolmetscher.* Berlin, 1893. Repr. Graz, Austria 1956.

Strayer, Joseph N. *On the Medieval Origins of the Modern State.* Princeton, N.J., 1970.

Talmage, Frank E. "Apples of Gold: The Inner Meaning of Sacred Texts in Medieval Judaism. In *Jewish Spirituality: From the Bible Through the Middle Ages,* ed. Arthur Green, 313–356. Jewish Spirituality, 13. New York, 1986.

———. "David Kimhi and the Rationalist Tradition." *Hebrew Union College Annual* 39 (1968): 177–218.

———. *David Kimhi: The Man and the Commentaries.* Harvard Judaic Monographs, 1. Cambridge, Mass., 1975.

———. "Keep Your Sons From Scripture: The Bible in Medieval

Jewish Scholarship and Spirituality." In *Understanding Scripture*, ed. Clemens Thoma and Michael Wyschogrod, 81–101. New York, 1987.

Terracini, Benvenuto. "Natura ed origine del linguaggio umano nel 'De Vulgari Eloquentia.'" In his *Pagine e appunti di linguistica storica*, 237–46. Florence, 1957.

Thérel, Marie-Louise. "L'origine du thème de la synagogue répudiée." *Scriptorium* 25 (1971): 285–90.

Tierney, Brian. "Public Expediency and Natural Law: A Fourteenth-Century Discussion on the Origins of Government and Property." In *Authority and Power: Studies on Medieval Law and Government Presented to Walter Ullmann on his Seventieth Birthday*, ed. Brian Tierney and Peter Linehan, 167–82. Cambridge, 1980.

Tirosh-Rothschild, Hava. "*Sefirot* as the Essence of God in the Writings of David Messer Leon." *AJS Review* 7/8 (1982–83): 409–25.

Touati, Charles. *La pensée théologique et philosophique de Gersonide*. Paris, 1973.

Touitou, Elazar. "Peshaṭ ve-'apologeṭiqah be-feirush ha-Rashbam le-sippurei Mosheh she-ba-Torah." *Tarbiẓ* 51 (1981–82): 227–39.

———. "Shiṭato ha-parshanit shel Rashbam 'al reqa' ha-meṣi'ut ha-hisṭorit shel zemanno." In *'Iyyunim be-sifrut Ḥazal, ba-Miqra' u-ve-toledot Yisra'el muqdash le-Prof. 'Ezra' Ṣiyyon Melammed*, ed. Y. D. Gilat, C. Levine, and Z. M. Rabinowitz, 48–74. Ramat-Gan, 1982.

———. "'Al shiṭato shel Rashbam be-feirusho la-Torah." *Tarbiẓ* 48 (1978–79): 248–73.

———. "'Al gilgulei ha-nusaḥ shel peirush Rashi la-Torah." *Tarbiẓ* 56 (1986–87): 211–42.

Twersky, Isadore. "Joseph ibn Kaspi: Portrait of a Medieval Jewish Intellectual." In *Studies in Medieval Jewish History and Literature*, ed.

Isadore Twersky, 231–57. Harvard Judaic Monographs, 2. Cambridge, Mass., 1979.

———. "Joseph ibn Kaspi: Portrait d'un intellectuel juif médiéval." In *Juifs et Judaisme de Languedoc*, ed. M. Vicaire and B. Blumenkranz, 185–204. Toulouse, 1977.

Ullmann, Walter. *The Medieval Idea of Law as Represented by Lucas de Penna: A Study in Fourteenth-Century Legal Scholarship*. London, 1946.

Urbach, E. E. *The Sages: Their Concepts and Beliefs*. Trans. Israel Abrahams. 2 vols. Jerusalem, 1975.

Vogelstein, Hermann, and Paul Rieger. *Geschichte der Juden in Rom*. 2 vols. Berlin, 1895–96.

Walfish, Barry. "The Two Commentaries of Abraham Ibn Ezra on the Book of Esther." *Jewish Quarterly Review* 79 (1988–89): 323–43.

Weil, Gérard E. "Sur une bibliothèque systématiquement pillée par les Nazis: Le catalogue des manuscrits et incunables retrouvés de la Bibliothek des Jüdisch-theologischen Seminars in Breslau." In *Hommage à Georges Vajda: Études d'histoire et de pensée juives*, ed. Gérard Nahon and Charles Touati, 579–604. Louvain, 1980.

Weiser, Asher. "Raba'—toledotav u-sefarav." *Sinai* 75 (1973–74): 197–209.

White, Sidnie Ann. "Esther: A Feminine Model for Jewish Diaspora." In *Gender and Difference in Ancient Israel*, ed. Peggy L. Day, 161–77. Minneapolis, 1989.

Wiener, Aharon. *The Prophet Elijah in the Development of Judaism*. London, 1978.

Wilensky, Sarah Heller. *R. Yiṣḥaq 'Aramah u-mishnato*. Jerusalem, 1956.

Williams, A. L. *Adversus Judaeos: A Bird's-eye View of Christian 'Apologiae' Until the Renaissance*. Cambridge, 1935.

Wolfson, Elliot R. "Mystical-Theurgical Dimensions of Prayer in *Sefer ha-Rimmon.*" *Approaches to Judaism in Medieval Times* 3 (1988): 41–79.

———. "By Way of Truth: Aspects of Naḥmanides' Kabbalistic Hermeneutics." *AJS Review* 14 (1989): 103–78

———. "Circumcision and the Divine Name." *Jewish Quarterly Review* 78 (1987–88): 77–112.

Wolfson, Harry A. "Judah Halevi on Causality and Miracles." In *Sefer ha-yovel—Me'ir Vaqsman (= Meyer Waxman Jubilee Volume).* English section, 137–53. Chicago, 1966.

———. "The Classification of Sciences in Medieval Jewish Philosophy." In *Hebrew Union College Jubilee Volume*, 263–315. Cincinnati, 1925. (Repr. in his *Studies in the History of Philosophy and Religion.* 2 vols. Cambridge, Mass., 1973–77, 1:493–545).

———. *Philo.* 2 vols. Cambridge, Mass., 1947.

Yerushalmi, Yosef H. *The Lisbon Massacre of 1506 and the Royal Image in the Shebet Yehudah.* Hebrew Union College Annual Supplements, no. 1. Cincinnati, 1976.

———. *Zakhor: Jewish History and Jewish Memory.* Seattle, Wash., 1979.

Zimmels, Hirsch Jakob. "Ketav-yad Hamburg Cod. hebr. 45 ve-yiḥuso le-Rav 'Avigdor Kohen-Ṣedeq." In *Ma'amarim le-zikhron R. Ṣevi Pereṣ Ḥayot [Chajes]*, 248–61. Vienna, 1933. (Hebrew section).

———. "Le-toledot R. 'Avigdor be-R. 'Eliyahu Kohen Ṣedeq mi-Vinah." *Ha-Ṣofeh le-ḥokhmat Yisra'el* 15 (1931): 110–26.

Zinberg, Israel. *A History of Jewish Literature.* Trans. and ed. Bernard Martin. 12 vols. Cleveland, 1972–78.

Zohari, Ḥayyim. *Midreshei 'aggadah ve-halakhah be-feirush Rashi la-Torah (be-hashva'ah la-meqorot).* 2 vols. Jerusalem, 1978.

Zohary, Michael. *Plants of the Bible.* Cambridge, 1982.

ADDENDUM

Fürst, Julius. *Bibliotheca Judaica*. 3 vols. in 2. Leipzig, 1849. Repr. Hildesheim, 1960.

Kasher, M. M. and J. B. Mandelbaum. *Sarei ha-'elef*. 2nd ed. 2 vols. Jerusalem, 1978.

INDEXES

The following abbreviations are used in the indexes:

A = Ahasuerus
E = Esther
H = Haman
M = Mordecai
V = Vashti

Author and Title Index

"A" (anonymous northern French exegete), 3, 208–209, 211–212; and midrash, 26; as grammarian, 17; literary awareness, 64; on 1:3, 240,n6; on 2:3, 240,n7; on 4:4, 240,n9; on A, 184; on A's reaction to Jews' victory, 196–197; on court intrigues, 161–162; on decoration of courtyard, 103–105; on drinking customs, 107, 108; on E concealing her Jewishness, 124, 126; on E's plea for her people, 165; on king's advisors, 114; on M's encounter with other courtiers, 180

Abner of Burgos, 57

Abraham ben Judah, 229

Abravanel, Isaac, 178, 238,n23; on Christians, 139–140

Alami, Solomon (*'Iggeret musar*), 174

Albo, Joseph, on three kinds of law, 275,n57

Alguadez, Meir, 46, 47

Alonso de Espina (*Fortalitium fidei*), 154

Anatoli, Jacob, 50

Arama, Isaac, 3, 8, 225–226, 237,n13, n16; and kabbalah, 36–37; literary awareness, 68–74; on 7:4, 21; on 9:25, 23; on absence of God's name, 78; on Averroists, 58; on Bigthan and Teresh, 177; on court procedure, 160–161; on decoration of courtyard, 107; on drinking customs, 107; on E's ancestry, 280, n19; on E's Jewishness, 164; on E's plea for her people, 165–166; on expelling Jews, 187; on government and leadership, 48–

Subject Index

Joseph, 175
Judaism, threat to majority religion, 146
Judges, discretion of, 275,n55; duties, 274,n55, 276,n64
Jupiter, force of good, 58
Justice, administration of, 276–277, n64

Kabbalah, 36–43
Kabbalists, vs. rationalists, 36
Karaites, 32, 280,n15
King's palace, architecture of, 102
King's servants, M's enemies, 180; M's friends, 181
Kings, duties of, 274,n55, 276,n64
Kish, 280,n16
Kithmān, 280,n13
Korah's assembly, 86

Languages, differentiation of, 231–233
Law, different kinds of, 275,n57, 276,n58
Laws, desirable qualities of, 48
Leader, desirable qualities of, 48
*Le'*azim. *See* vernacular words
Lexicography, 13–25
Logic, 13
Lottery, see Haman, lottery
Lucena, Jewish city, 100

Mordecai, 1, 29, 31; adoption of E, 173; as active intellect, 50; as leader, 48–49; as legislator, 48–49; as tax collector, 173; as Venus, 58; as vizier, 173; at palace gate, 158–159; author of book, 77; bravery, 38; compared with Joseph, 175–176; criticised for confronting H, 178; criticised for not protecting E, 122; discovers plot vs. A, 80; dream, 31, 80; efforts to undo evil decree, 81; fasted on first day of Passover, 279,n12; father from tribe of Benjamin, 32; force of good, 59; had legal grounds for not bowing down, 181–182; helped king raise taxes, 186; ideal Jewish courtier, 172–177; Jewishness maintained in exile, 175; letter, 67; magnanimous person, 47; merit of, 82; mother from tribe of Judah; omitted God's name from book intentionally, 77; only Jew in palace compound, 98; position at court, 158–159; power over H, 38; prayer of, 43; refusal to bow down to H, 28, 44, 47, 57, 69–70, 173, 178–180, 181; relation to other courtiers, 180–182; rise to power, 175–176, 202; royal lineage, 38; success in public life, 174; symbol of redemption, 41; watched over E in court, 269,n3; well-informed of court affairs, 171
Madīnat al-Zahrā', 100
Manuel of Portugal, 193
Mars, force of evil, 58
Martinez de Oviedo, Gonzalo, 192–193
Martyrdom, 278,n6
Memucan 116, 118, 162; = H, 33, 168, 291,n23; force of evil, 51
Messiah, 89
Midrashic literature, 25–36
Miracles, 82, 83–89; hidden, 79, 87–89
Moneylending, 150
Moses' rod, 86
Moses' signs, 86
Moslems, 32, 135–138

Nebuchadnezzar, 30, 184
Nepotism, seen as virtue, 170

Index of Scriptural Citations

Hebrew Bible

9:19, 17, 35, 246,n74
9:23, 262,n9
9:24, 67
9:25, 23, 83
9:26, 27, 28, 303,n14
9:27, 27, 93
9:29, 29
9:31, 89, 248,n92, 304,n25
10:1, 64, 173, 262,n5
10:2, 85, 175, 190
10:3, 47, 175, 194, 211
Daniel
2:27, 273,n46
5:11, 273,n46
5:13, 125
7:5, 133
8:2, 98
Ezra
1:6, 298,n22
1 Chronicles
12:33, 17, 113–114
29:1, 98
29:30, 254,n9
2 Chronicles
17:6, 47
17:12, 98
27:4, 98

Septuagint

Est 2:21, 177
Est 7:8, 244, n56

Targumim

Targum Pseudo-Jonathan
Gn 27:25, 252,n143
Targum Rishon to Esther
2:21, 295,n84
3:2, 296,n93
4:1, 30
9, 281,n26
Targum Sheni to Esther
1:8, 271,n20
3:8, 145, 150, 299,n33

New Testament

Mt 13:15, 147

Mishnah

'Avot
5:6, 266, n44
1:10, 194
2:3, 194
Ketubbot
3:4, 271, n21
Sanhedrin
1:1, 271, n21
Shabbat
9:7, 16
Shevi'it
10:2, 271, n21
Yevamot
7:5, 271, n21
11:1, 271, n21

Babylonian Talmud

'Avodah zarah
10b, 298,n23
Berakhot
7b, 296,n96
10b, 247,n82
34b, 252,n143
58a, 296,n98
Ḥullin
139b, 265,n16
Ketubbot
85b, 274,n52, 275,n55
94a-b, 274,n52
Kiddushin
74a, 274,n52, 275,n55

Index of Manuscripts by Depository Libraries

This index lists manuscripts in the Esther bibliography as well as those cited in the notes.

Berlin, Staatsbibliothek zu Berlin—Preussischer Kulturbesitz
- Or. Fol. 707, 324
- Or. Qu. 514, 290,n10, 316
- Or. Qu. 701, 315
- Or. Qu. 943, 314

Breslau, Jüdisch-Theologisches Seminar
- 104, 211, 316

Budapest, Bibliotheca Academiae Scientiarum Hungaricae
- Kaufmann Collection A29, 229

Cambridge, Trinity College
- F.12.5., 317
- F.12.15, 327
- F.12.135, 315

Cambridge, University Library
- Add. 378.1, 328
- Add. 378.2, 316
- Mm. 6.26.2, 249,n101, 327
- T-S F I(2)/24, 313
- T-S F I(2)/67, 313

Cincinnati, Hebrew Union College-Jewish Institute of Religion
- 839, 318

Erlangen, Universitätsbibliothek, 1263, 237,n11, 271,n21, 315, 323, 327

Florence, Biblioteca Medicea Laurenziana
- Plut. III.8, 290,n10, 316

Frankfurt a.M., Staats- und Universitätsbibliothek
- hebr. 8° 40, 326–327
- hebr. 8° 124, 224, 321–322
- hebr. 8° 163, 327
- hebr. 8° 185, 317

Hamburg, Staats- und Universitätsbibliothek
- Cod. Hebr. 32, 208, 210, 211, 246,n72, 315, 323, 327
- Cod. Hebr. 235, 212, 287,n31, 317
- Levy 144, 323

Jerusalem, Jewish National and University Library
- Heb. 8° 3427, 319

Jerusalem, Mosad ha-Rav Kuk
- 39, 321

Jerusalem, Kafiḥ
- 50, 314

Lausanne, Lichaa
- 10, 322

70375242R00224

Made in the USA
Lexington, KY
12 November 2017